The Informational City

The Informational City

Information Technology, Economic Restructuring, and the Urban–Regional Process

Manuel Castells

Basil Blackwell

First published 1989
First published in paperback 1991

Basil Blackwell Ltd
108 Cowley Road, Oxford OX4 1JF, UK

Basil Blackwell Inc.
3 Cambridge Center
Cambridge, Massachusetts 02142, USA

British Library Cataloguing in Publication Data

A CIP catalogue record for this book is available from the British Library.

Library of Congress Cataloging in Publication Data

Castells, Manuel.
    The informational city: information technology, economic
restructuring, and the urban-regional process/Manuel Castells.
        p. cm.
    Bibliography: p.
    Includes index.
    ISBN 0–631–15988–6 ISBN 0–631–17937–2 (pbk.)
    1. Information technology.   2. Technology—Social aspects.
  3. High technology industries—Location.   4. Space in economics.
  I. Title.
HC79.I55C37   1989
330.9173′2—dc20

Typeset in 10/12 pt Plantin by Times Graphics
Printed in Great Britain by TJ Press, Padstow

Contents

Acknowledgements

This book has benefited greatly from the support of a number of institutions and people who deserve full credit for it without having to share the author's responsibility for the analyses presented here.

The project of the book was conceived during my year as a Guggenheim Fellow in 1982–3, taking advantage of the intellectual leisure I was able to enjoy thanks to the support of the John H. Simon Guggenheim Memorial Foundation. Throughout the period of research and writing, between 1983 and 1988, I relied on institutional and staff support from the Institute of Urban and Regional Development, from the Berkeley Roundtable on the International Economy, and from the Institute of International Studies, University of California at Berkeley.

A number of colleagues had the patience to read and comment on the various drafts of this work, and they were decisive in influencing the final form of the book. For that my deepest gratitude goes to Norman Glickman, Bennett Harrison, Peter Hall, Allen Scott, Amy Glasmeier, Vicente Navarro, Steve Cohen, Michael Teitz, and the late Philippe Aydalot. Other scholars were extremely helpful in providing ideas and information that are important elements of this book. Among these are Michael Smith, John Mollenkopf, Ed Soja, Saskia Sassen, Martin Carnoy, Derek Shearer, Michael Storper, Anna Lee Saxenian, Peter Schulze, Richard Gordon, Alejandro Portes, Ed Blakely, Susan Fainstein, Norman Fainstein, Richard Sennett, Ira Katznelson, Claude Fischer, and, as always, Alain Touraine.

Finally, this book is, to a great extent, the product of an intellectual milieu generated around my seminar on "The Political Economy of High Technology" in the Department of City and Regional Planning at Berkeley. I want to thank publicly the graduate students who have helped me, over the years, in developing and correcting my own analyses, particularly Jay Stowsky, François Bar, Lionel Nicol, Barbara Baran, Rebecca Skinner, Pei-Hsiung Chin, Lee Goh, Lisa Bornstein, Roberto Laserna, Katharyne Mitchell, Raymond Wu, and Penny Gurstein.

The expression of my gratitude to all the people and institutions who have contributed to the research and thinking formalized in this book amounts to a public recognition of the fact that all intellectual products are, to a large extent, collective enterprises ultimately synthesized in the solitude of authoring.

Berkeley, California
June 1988

To Françoise

Introduction

A technological revolution of historic proportions is transforming the fundamental dimensions of human life: time and space. New scientific discoveries and industrial innovations are extending the productive capacity of working hours while superseding spatial distance in all realms of social activity. The unfolding promise of information technology opens up unlimited horizons of creativity and communication, inviting us to the exploration of new domains of experience, from our inner selves to the outer universe, challenging our societies to engage in a process of structural change.

Yet, as in previous historical instances of major technological transformation, prophecies tend to take the place of analysis in efforts to comprehend the emerging social and spatial forms and processes. Futurologists predict the evolution of society on the basis of linear extrapolation of characteristics of new technologies, without taking into account the historical mediation exercised by social organization between the potential of new technologies and their effects in actuality. We are told, for example, that telecommunications allows work at home in "electronic cottages," while firms become entirely footloose in their location, freed in their operations by the flexibility of information systems and by the density and speed of the transportation network. Or that people can stay at home, and yet be both open to an entire world of images, sounds, and communication flows, and potentially interactive, thus superseding the need for cities as we have known them until the coming of the information age. Historical optimism and moralistic pessimism both convey in different tones an equally simplistic message of technological determinism, be it the liberation of the individual from the constraints of the locale, or the alienation of social life disintegrating in the anonymity of suburban sprawl.

In fact, none of these prophecies stands up to the most elementary confrontation with actual observation of social trends. Telecommunications is reinforcing the commanding role of major business concentrations around the world. Salaried work at home in effect means mainly sweated labor in the garment industry while "telecommuting" is practiced by a negligible fraction of workers in the US. Intensely urban Paris is the success story for the use of home-based telematic systems, while the American equivalent of the French Minitel completely failed to attract customers in the Los Angeles area, the ultimate suburban frontier. High-technology industries are key ingredients of new economic growth in some regions, but are unable to generate a developmental dynamic in other contexts. Societies and economies stubbornly resist being molded by the application of new technologies: in fact, they mold the technologies, selecting their patterns of diffusion, modifying their uses, orienting their functions. New information technologies do have a fundamental impact on societies, and therefore on cities and regions, but their effects vary according to their interaction with the economic, social, political, and cultural processes that shape the production and use of the new technological medium.

This book aims at analyzing the relationship between new information technologies and the urban and regional processes in the broader context of historical transformation in which these technologies emerge and evolve. Our hypothesis is that this context is characterized simultaneously by the emergence of a new mode of socio-technical organization (which we call the *informational mode of development*) and by the restructuring of capitalism, as the fundamental matrix of institutional and economic organization in our societies.

Technological revolutions are always part of a broader process of change in the techno-economic paradigm which forms the basis of the processes of production, consumption, and management. Scientific discovery and technological innovation are both an integral part and a consequential effect of such change. Accordingly, in order to assess the urban and regional impacts of new technologies, we must address the overall transformation of the relationships between production, society, and space, of which new technologies are a fundamental instrument.

Furthermore, in the particular historical period under examination, that is, the emergence and diffusion of new information technologies in the last quarter of the twentieth century, the effects of these technologies on society and space have also been fundamentally conditioned by a substantial modification of the social system that constitutes the structural basis of most of the world – capitalism. The restructuring of capitalism in the late 1970s and 1980s, as a response to the structural crisis of the 1970s, has been accomplished by extensive use of the potential offered by the new technologies, whose maturation reached a crucial point during just that decade: the microprocessor was invented in 1971; gene-splicing techniques were discovered in 1973; the microcomputer was introduced in 1975; and so on. The application of new technologies, and their effects on social organization, were largely conditioned by the characteristics and development of the restructuring process.

It could probably be argued that there are some causal links between the emergence of the informational mode of development, the blossoming of information technologies, and the process of the restructuring of capitalism. However, such an argument pertains to the study of the social sources of technological innovation, and is outside the scope of this book. My approach here is more simple, and is focused on a specific research question. I argue that there is a historically articulated complex of transformations which concerns, simultaneously, capitalism as a social system, informationalism as a mode of development, and information technology as a powerful working instrument. It is this complex socio-economic-technical matrix that is transforming societies, and thus cities and regions. I will analyze the current transformations of spatial forms and processes as a specific manifestation of the interaction between the informational mode of development (in its two dimensions: technological and organizational) and the restructuring of capitalism.

A major methodological issue arises with the attempt to develop this analytical perspective into empirical research. The process of restructuring is not a pure mechanism of adjustment. It is a politically determined process, enacted by governments and organizations. Therefore, by adopting a comprehensive research perspective that embraces both structural transformation and socio-economic restructuring, certain social effects could be attributed to new technologies, or to the informational mode of development, which are in fact linked to the historical circumstances of a given regime, for example the Reagan administration in the US or the Thatcher government in the UK. While it is impossible to discuss fully here the epistemological implications of articulating the analyses of structure and process in explaining social change, it is important to consider the question for the sake of clarity in the presentation of the research findings contained in this book.

While restructuring processes are implemented by social actors, they differ from other policies or decisions in their reference to the overall dynamics of the social system: they are responses to the structural challenges to the expansionary logic of a given system at a particular historical juncture. Crises determine social conflicts and political debates, resulting, sometimes, in restructuring processes which, on the basis of political coalitions and political strategies, modify the rules of the social system while preserving its fundamental logic. Restructuring does not necessarily come about; other outcomes of crises are revolution, or a long period of "muddling through" social inertia. Furthermore, although restructuring cannot happen independently of the political process, when it finally does occur its significance goes beyond the political orientation or the personal interests of the political actors, notwithstanding the importance of those actors for the implementation and final results of the restructuring process. In the 1980s, restructuring clearly took place in the US under Reagan and in the UK under Thatcher; but it also took place in France under a socialist government, with communist participation, the traditional socialist policies to deal with the crisis within the parameters of capitalism having failed in 1981–3. Restructuring took place in most of western Europe: in the Pacific Rim, given impetus by the internationalization of the economy; and in the Third World, as a result of austerity policies often dictated by international financial institutions. Each restructuring process followed a specific path, depending upon the economic, social, and political conditions of the various countries; but in all cases it had to deal with similar policy questions and went through similar political debates, converging on a restricted set of economic policies.

The orientations and outcomes of the restructuring process were not ineluctable, nor had they to develop exactly along the lines they in fact did. However, once they had taken place, they shaped societies, technologies, and space in a particular direction which is now full of historical meaning. Regardless of what could have happened with new information technologies in a different historical context, the fact that they blossomed in their potential applications at the moment when capitalism was transforming itself to enter a new stage of development is of fundamental significance. Capitalist restructuring has been a key force in reshaping cities and regions in the late 1970s and 1980s, in framing the production and use of new information technologies, and in forging the relationships between new technologies and new spatial forms and processes. In turn, technological innovation and territorial restructuring have also deeply modified the emerging socio-economic system. It is this complex generation of a new urban–regional process that I will try to unveil in this book.

The focus of empirical research in this analysis will be on the United States. This is a necessary limit imposed on the study in order to be able to understand the whole set of interactions between restructuring, technology, and space within a relatively homogeneous geographic, cultural, and institutional context. Furthermore, the US is the most advanced society, or at least has been until now, in the production and use of new information technologies, and is the country that has embarked on the boldest process of capitalist restructuring during the 1980s. Given its size and its widespread connections with the international economy, it offers greater potential for in-depth examination of the new spatial processes associated with the informational mode of development than any other country could. The US is of course exceptional on many counts, and the empirical results it provides should not be extrapolated to other contexts without the necessary interpretation and adaptation to the specific conditions of other economies and societies. Nevertheless, I would claim wider validity for this analytical perspective than mere empirical observation of the spatial structure of the US alone. It is actually an inquiry into the socio-spatial effects of two macro-processes (restructuring and informationalism) that are fundamental to all advanced capitalist societies. So, while the analysis in this book utilizes almost exclusively American data, the research questions investigated and the relationships propounded are intended to aid understanding of the techno-economic transformation of the urban–regional process in a broad range of social contexts.

A second deliberate limit imposed on this study is the focus on the relationship between information technologies and the spatial dimension of the processes of production and management, leaving aside the study of social life and residential patterns. There is an obvious reason for this, namely, the impossibility of addressing all questions in a book that is already too dense and sufficiently complex. However, there are also methodological and theoretical reasons for this choice. On the former count, very little reliable empirical research has been done on the interaction between communication techno-logies and urban social life, in a field particularly biased by ideology, and it is therefore difficult to make any serious assessment of the current transform-ations as they relate to technological change. On the latter, it is my hypothesis that the fundamental impacts of information technologies are taking place in the organization of production and management, and in the sphere of the exercise of power by state institutions. Accordingly, it is necessary first to understand the transformation of the fundamental parameters of the new urban–regional system, before being able to investigate the changes occurring in the private sphere.

The research presented in this book relies on a significant quantity of documents and secondary sources that I have collected over several years in order to examine specific research questions determined at the onset of the inquiry. In a very fundamental way, the studies cited in this text constitute its database. I make no claim to present the arguments of their authors or to dis-cuss alternative interpretations, except when the analytical purpose requires it. I do not undertake a review of the literature on the different subjects exa-mined in the book. My analysis of data and observations is geared toward test-ing a series of specific hypotheses, in the process of building an argument. The reader interested by the various research perspectives referred to in this book should consult these studies directly rather than relying on the interpretation given here. While being extremely careful never to distort the empirical findings reported in this book, their use and their presentation have been selected according to a specific research perspective, without engaging in any major debate, in order to maintain the focus on my particular analytical propositions.

The organization of the book is straightforward. The first chapter presents the theoretical framework, defines what is understood by the "informational mode of development" and by the "restructuring of capitalism," summarizes the characteristics of the current technological revolution, and attempts to formalize the links between captialism, informationalism, and technological change. This theoretical framework is not developed and used in all its dimensions, given the specific purpose of this book, which is to arrive at an understanding of the new urban–regional process. The usefulness of this theoretical construction is in providing a conceptual basis for the specific analyses that are presented, and empirically tested, in the subsequent and substantive chapters of the book.

These substantive chapters examine sequentially the urban–regional transformations determined first by the informational mode of development, and then by the process of capitalist restructuring. Chapter 2 examines the relationship between the production of new information technologies and spatial patterns, while chapter 3 analyzes the territorial effects of the use of information technologies in services and office activities. Chapters 4, 5, and 6 study the impact of the interaction between socio-economic restructuring and information technologies on cities and regions, in the three dimensions proposed as characteristic of the restructuring process: the new relationships between capital and labor; the transformation of the state, with the transition from the "welfare state" to the "warfare state"; and the internationalization of the economy. Throughout these analyses runs, in different forms, a major theme: the emergence of a *space of flows* which dominates the historically constructed space of places, as the logic of dominant organizations detaches itself from the social constraints of cultural identities and local societies through the powerful medium of information technologies. The conclusion examines alternative spatial projects that may be pursued in counteraction of the domination of flows.

Behind the pages of this book lies the unifying intellectual objective: to understand how the interaction between technology, society, and space generates a new urban–regional process as the material basis of our lives at the dawn of the information age. This book is an investigation into the historical rise of the Informational City.

1

The Informational Mode of Development and the Restructuring of Capitalism

Introduction: Modes of Production, Modes of Development, and Social Structure

Technological change can only be understood in the context of the social structure within which it takes place. Yet such an understanding requires something more than historically specific description of a given society. We must be able to locate technology in the level and process of the social structure underlying the dynamics of any society. On the basis of a theoretical characterization of this kind we may then go on to investigate the actual manifestations of the interaction between technology and the other elements of social structure in a process that shapes society and, therefore, space. To proceed along these lines it is necessary to introduce some theoretical propositions and to advance a few hypotheses that attempt to place the analysis of technological change and economic restructuring, as presented in this chapter, within the framework of a broader social theory that informs the overall investigation undertaken in this book.

The analytical focus here is on the emergence of a new mode of development, which I will call the "informational mode," in historical interaction with the process of restructuring of the capitalist mode of production. Therefore, definitions are needed of the concepts of mode of production, mode of development, and restructuring. Such definitions, if they are to be theoretical and not simply taxonomic, require succinct presentation of the broader social theory that lends analytical meaning to such concepts as tools of understanding social structures and social change. For the purposes of this book, the presentation of the overall theoretical framework must be reduced to the few elements indispensable for communicating my hypothesis that the interaction between modes of production and modes of development is at the source of the generation of new social and spatial forms and processes.

This theoretical perspective postulates that societies are organized around human processes structured by historically determined relationships of production, experience, and power.[1] Production is the action of humankind on matter to appropriate and transform it for its benefit by obtaining a product, consuming part of it (in an unevenly distributed manner), and accumulating the surplus for investment in accordance with socially determined goals. Experience is the action of human subjects on themselves within the various dimensions of their biological and cultural entity in the endless search for fulfillment of their needs and desires. Power is that relationship between human subjects which, on the basis of production and experience, imposes the will of some subjects upon others by the potential or actual use of violence.

Production is organized in class relationships that define the process by which the non-producers appropriate the surplus from the producers. Experience is structured around gender/sexual relationships, historically organized around the family, and characterized hitherto by the domination of men over women. Sexuality, in the broad, psychoanalytic sense, and family relationships, structure personality and frame symbolic interaction.

Power is founded upon the state, since the institutionalized monopoly of violence in the state apparatus ensures the domination of power holders over their subjects. The symbolic communication between subjects on the basis of production, experience, and power, crystallizes throughout history on specific territories and thus generates cultures.

All these instances of society interact with one another in framing social phenomena; however, given the particular research interest of this work in the relationship between technological change and economic restructuring, the effort of theoretical definition will here be focused on the structure and logic of the production process.

Production has been defined above as the purposive action of humankind to appropriate and transform matter, thus obtaining a product. It is a complex process because each one of its elements is itself made up of relationships between other elements. Humankind, as a collective actor, is differentiated in the production process between labor and the organizers of production; labor is internally differentiated and stratified according to the role of the producers in the production process. Matter includes nature, human-modified nature, and human-produced matter,[2] the labors of history forcing us to move away from the classic distinction between humankind and nature which has been largely superseded by the reconstruction of our environment through millenia of human action.

The relationship between labor and matter in the process of work is also complex: it includes the use of means of production to act upon matter, on the basis of energy and knowledge. Technology refers to the type of relationship established between labor and matter in the production process through the intermediation of a given set of means of production enacted by energy and knowledge.[3]

The product is itself divided into two main categories, according to its utilization in the overall process of production and reproduction: reproduction and surplus. Reproduction includes three sub-categories: reproduction of labor, reproduction of social institutions (ultimately enforcing relationships of production), and reproduction of means of production and their technological support basis. The surplus is the share of the product that exceeds the historically determined needs for the reproduction of the elements of the production process. It is divided again into two major categories, according to its destination: consumption and investment. Consumption is stratified according to societal rules. Investment is geared toward the quantitative and qualitative expansion of the production process according to the objectives determined by the controllers of the surplus.

Social structures interact with production processes by determining the rules for the appropriation and distribution of the surplus. These rules constitute modes of production, and these modes define social classes on the basis of social relationships of production. The structural principle by which the surplus is appropriated, thus designating the structural beneficiary of such appropriation, namely the dominant class, characterizes a mode of production. In contemporary societies there are two fundamental modes of production: capitalism and statism. Under capitalism, the separation between producers and their means of production, the commodification of labor, and the private ownership of the means of production on the basis of control of commodified surplus (capital), determine the basic principle of appropriation and distribution of surplus by the capitalist class, not necessarily for its exclusive benefit, but for the processes of investment and consumption decided by that class in the specific context of each unit of production under its control. Under statism, the control of the surplus is external to the economic sphere: it lies in the hands of the power-holders in the state, that is, in the apparatus benefiting from the institutional monopoly of violence. In both cases there is expropriation of the producers from their control over the surplus, although criteria for the distribution of consumption and allocation of investment vary according to the respective structural principles of each mode of production. Capitalism is oriented toward profit-maximizing, that is, toward increasing the amount and proportion of surplus appropriated on the basis of the control over means of production. Statism is oriented toward power-maximizing, that is, toward increasing the military and ideological capacity of the political apparatus for imposing its goals on a greater number of subjects and at deeper levels of their consciousness.

Modes of production do not appear as a result of historical necessity. They are the result of historical processes in which a rising social class becomes dominant by politically, and often militarily, defeating its historical adversaries, building social alliances and obtaining support to construct its hegemony. By hegemony I understand, in the Gramscian tradition, the historical ability of a given class to legitimate its claim to establish political institutions and cultural values able to mobilize the majority of the society, while fulfilling its specific interests as the new dominant class.

The social relationships of production, and thus the mode of production, determine the appropriation and distribution of the surplus. A separate, yet fundamental question is the *level* of such surplus, determined by the productivity of a particular process of production, that is, by the ratio of the value of each unit of output to the value of each unit of input. Productivity levels are themselves dependent on the relationship between labor and matter as a function of the use of means of production by the application of energy and knowledge. This process is characterized by technical relationships of production, defining a *mode of development*. Thus, modes of development are the technological arrangements through which labor acts upon matter to generate the product, ultimately determining the level of surplus. Each mode of development is defined by the element that is fundamental in determining the productivity of the production process. In the agrarian mode of development, increases in the surplus result from quantitative increases in labor and means of production, including land. In the industrial mode of development, the source of increasing surplus lies in the introduction of new energy sources and in the quality of the use of such energy. In the informational mode of development, the emergence of which is hypothesized here, the source of productivity lies in the quality of knowledge, the other intermediary element in the relationship between labor and the means of production. It should be understood that knowledge intervenes in all modes of development, since the process of production is always based on some level of knowledge. This is in fact what technology is all about, since technology is "the use of scientific knowledge to specify ways of doing things in a reproducible manner."[4] However, what is specific to the informational mode of development is that here knowledge intervenes upon knowledge itself in order to generate higher productivity. In other words, while in the pre-industrial modes of development knowledge is used to organize the mobilization of greater quantities of labor and means of production, and in the industrial mode of development knowledge is called upon to provide new sources of energy and to reorganize production accordingly, in the informational mode of development knowledge mobilizes the generation of new knowledge as the key source of productivity through its impact on the other elements of the production process and on their relationships. Each mode of development has also a structurally determined goal, or performance principle, around which technological processes are organized: industrialism is oriented toward economic growth, that is, toward maximizing output; informationalism is oriented toward technological development, that is, toward the accumulation of knowledge. While higher levels of knowledge will result in higher levels of output, it is the pursuit and accumulation of knowledge itself that determines the technological function under informationalism.

Social relationships of production, defining modes of production, and technical relationships of production (or productive forces), defining modes of development, do not overlap, although they do interact in contemporary societies. In this sense, it is misleading to pretend that the informational mode of development (or post-industrial society) replaces capitalism, since, as Alain Touraine, Radovan Richta, and Daniel Bell indicated years ago,[5] these are different analytical planes, one referring to the principle of social organization, the other to the technological infrastructure of society. However, there are between the two structural processes complex and significant interactions which constitute a fundamental element in the dynamics of our societies.

Societies are made up of a complex web of historically specific relationships that combine modes of production, modes of development, experience, power, and cultures. Under capitalism, because of its historical reliance on the economic sphere as the source of power and legitimacy, the mode of production tends to organize society around its logic, without ever being able to exhaust the sources of social reproduction and social change within the dynamics of capital and labor. However, given the structural preponderance of capitalist social relationships in the class structure, and the influence they exercise on culture and politics, any major transformation in the processes by which capital reproduces itself and expands its interests affects the entire social organization. Modes of production – and capitalism is no exception – evolve with the process of historical change. In some instances, this leads to their abrupt supersession; more often, they transform themselves by responding to social conflicts, economic crises, and political challenges, through a reorganization that includes, as a fundamental element, the utilization of new technical relationships of production that may encompass the introduction of a new mode of development. By *restructuring* is understood the process by which modes of production transform their organizational means to achieve their *unchanged* structural principles of performance. Restructuring processes can be social and technological, as well as cultural and political, but they are all geared toward the fulfillment of the principles embodied in the basic structure of the mode of production. In the case of capitalism, private capital's drive to maximize profit is the engine of growth, investment, and consumption.

Modes of development evolve according to their own logic; they do not respond mechanically to the demands of modes of production or of other instances of society. However, since technical relationships are historically subordinated to social relationships of production, experience, and power, they tend to be molded in their structure and orientation by restructuring processes. On the other hand, they do have a specific logic that dominant social interests ignore only at the risk of spoiling their technological potential – as, for example, a narrow orientation toward secretive, applied military technology can frustrate scientific advancement. Modes of development emerge from the interaction between scientific and technological discovery and the organizational integration of such discoveries in the processes of production and management. Since these processes are dependent upon the overall social organization, and particularly upon the dynamics of the mode of production, there is indeed a close interaction between modes of development and modes of production. This interaction occurs in different forms according to the pace of historical change. There is a continuous, gradual adaptation of new technologies to the evolving social relationships of production; there are also periods of major historical change, either in technology or in social organization. When historical circumstances create a convergence between social change and technological change, we witness the rise of a new technological paradigm, heralding a new mode of development. This, I contend, is what has brought the rise of the informational mode of development in the last quarter of the twentieth century.

The New Technological Revolution and the Informational Mode of Development

The New Technological Paradigm

During the two decades from the late 1960s to the late 1980s a series of scientific and technological innovations have converged to constitute a new technological paradigm.[6] The scientific and technical core of this paradigm lies in microelectronics, building on the sequential discoveries of the transistor (1947), the integrated circuit (1957), the planar process (1959), and the microprocessor (1971).[7] Computers, spurred on by exponential increases in power and dramatic decreases in cost per unit of memory, were able to revolutionize information processing, in both hardware and software. Telecommunications became the key vector for the diffusion and full utilization of the new technologies by enabling connections between processing units, to form information systems. Applications of these microelectronics-based information systems to work processes in factories and offices created the basis for CAD/CAM (computer aided design/computer aided manufacturing) and Flexible Integrated Manufacturing, as well as for advanced office automation, paving the way for the general application of flexible integrated production and management systems. Around this nucleus of information technologies, a number of other fundamental innovations took place, particularly in new materials (ceramics, alloys, optical fiber), and more recently, in superconductors, in laser, and in renewable energy sources. In a parallel process, which benefited from the enhanced capacity to store and analyze information, genetic engineering extended the technological revolution to the realm of living matter. This laid the foundations for biotechnology, itself an information technology with its scientific basis in the ability to decode and reprogram the information embodied in living organisms.[8]

Although the scientific foundations of these discoveries had already come into existence, over timescales varying from field to field, the relatively simultaneous emergence of these various technologies, and the synergy created by their interaction, contributed to their rapid diffusion and application, and this in turn expanded the potential of each technology and induced a broader and faster development of the new technological paradigm.[9] A key factor in this synergistic process relates to the specific nature of this process of innovation: because it is based on enhanced ability to store, retrieve, and analyze information, every single discovery, as well as every application, can be related to developments in other fields and in other applications, by continuous interactions through the common medium of information systems, and communicating by means of the common language of science, in spite of the persistence of specialization in different scientific fields.

Social, economic, and institutional factors have, as I will argue, been decisive in the coming together of these different scientific innovations under the form of a new technological paradigm.[10] However, the specificity of the new technologies plays a major role in the structure and evolution of this paradigm, and imposes the materiality of their internal logic on the articulation between the process of innovation and the process of social organization. The new technological paradigm is characterized by two fundamental features.[11] First, the core new technologies are *focused on information processing*. This is the primary distinguishing feature of the emerging technological paradigm. To be sure, information and knowledge have been crucial elements in all technological revolutions, since technology ultimately boils down to the ability to perform new operations, or to perform established practices better, on the basis of the application of new knowledge. All major technological changes are in fact based on new knowledge. However, what differentiates the current process of technological change is that *its raw material itself is information, and so is its outcome*. What an integrated circuit does is to speed up the processing of information while increasing the complexity and the accuracy of the process. What computers do is to organize the sets of instructions required for the handling of information, and, increasingly, for the generation of new information, on the basis of the combination and interaction of stored information. What telecommunications does is to transmit information, making possible flows of information exchange and treatment of information, regardless of distance, at lower cost and with shorter transmission times. What genetic engineering does is to decipher and, eventually, program the code of the living matter, dramatically expanding the realm of controllable information processing.

The output of the new technologies is also information. Their embodiment in goods and services, in decisions, in procedures, is the result of the application of their informational output, not the output itself. In this sense, the new technologies differ from former technological revolutions, and justify calling the new paradigm the "informational technological paradigm," in spite of the fact that some of the fundamental technologies involved in it (for example, superconductivity) are not information technologies. But the paradigm itself exists and articulates a convergent set of scientific discoveries by focusing on information processing and by using the newly found informational capacity to enable articulation and communication throughout the whole spectrum of technological innovations. Furthermore, with the progress of the new technological revolution, the machines themselves take second place to the creative synergy made possible by their use as sources of productivity. This trend is often referred to in the literature as the growing importance of software over hardware, a theme stimulated but the promise of research in such fields as artificial intelligence. However, this is still an open debate in scientific terms. Better design of integrated circuits, ever larger-scale integration, enhanced telecommunications capability, and the use of new material in the manufacturing of information-processing devices, are in the medium-term perspective probably more important than artificial intelligence as a basis for information-handling and information-generation capacity. The fundamental trend overall seems to depend not so much on the somewhat obsolete idea of the growing dominance of software over hardware, as on the ability of new information technologies to generate new information, thus emphasizing the specific nature of their output *vis-à-vis* former technological paradigms.

The second major characteristic of the new technologies is in fact common to all major technological revolutions.[12] The main effects of their innovations are on *processes*, rather than on *products*.[13] There are, of course, major innovations in products, and the surge of new products is a fundamental factor in spurring new economic growth. However, the deepest impact of innovation is associated with the transformation of processes.[14] This was also the case with the two industrial revolutions associated with technical paradigms organized respectively around the steam engine and around electricity.[15] In both cases, energy was the pivotal element which, by gradually penetrating all processes of production, distribution, transportation, and management, revolutionized the entire economy and the whole society, not so much because of the new goods and services being produced and distributed, but because of the new ways of performing the processes of production and distribution, on the basis of a new source of energy that could be decentralized and distributed in a flexible manner. The new energy-based industrial and organizational processes gave birth to goods and services, hence products, that could not even have been imagined before the diffusion of energy-processing devices. But it was the revolution in energy, with its influence on all kinds of processes, that created the opportunity for the surge in new products. Process commands products, although functional, economic, and social feedback effects are crucial to an understanding of the historical process.

Similarly, in the current informational revolution, what new information technologies are about in the first place is process. A chip has value only as a means of improving the performance of a machine for an end-use function. A computer is a tool for information handling, whose usefulness for the organization or individual using it depends on the purpose of the information-processing activity. A genetically modified cell will take on its actual significance in its interaction with the whole body. While all social and biological activities are in fact processes, some elements of these processes crystallize in material forms that constitute goods and services, the usual content of economic products. Technological revolutions are made up of innovations whose products are in fact processes.

These two major characteristics of the informational technological paradigm [16] have fundamental effects on its impact on society. (Society itself, as stated above, frames and influences technological innovation in a dialectical relationship of which, at this point, we are only examining one factor, namely, the influence of new technologies on social organization.)

A fundamental consequence is derived from the essential process-orientation of technological innovation. Because processes, unlike products, enter into all spheres of human activity, their transformation by such technologies, focusing on omnipresent flows of information, leads to modification in the material basis of the entire social organization. Thus, new information technologies are transforming the way we produce, consume, manage, live, and die; not by themselves, certainly, but as powerful mediators of the broader set of factors that determines human behavior and social organization.

The fact that new technologies are focused on information processing has far-reaching consequences for the relationship between the sphere of socio-cultural symbols and the productive basis of society. Information is based upon culture, and information processing is, in fact, symbol manipulation on the basis of existing knowledge; that is, codified information verified by science and/or social experience. Thus, the predominant role of new information technologies in the process of innovation is to establish ever more intimate relationships among the culture of society, scientific knowledge, and the development of productive forces. If information processing becomes the key component of the new productive forces, the symbolic capacity of society itself, collectively as well as individually, is tightly linked to its developmental process. In other words, the structurally determined capacity of labor to process information and generate knowledge is, more than ever, the material source of productivity, and therefore of economic growth and social well-being. Yet this symbolic capacity of labor is not an individual attribute. Labor has to be formed, educated, trained, and retrained, in flexible manipulation of symbols, determining its ability constantly to reprogram itself. In addition, productive organizations, social institutions, and the overall structure of society, including its ideology, will be key elements in fostering or stalling the new information-based productive forces. The more a society facilitates the exchange of information flows, and the decentralized generation and distribution of information, the greater will be its collective symbolic capacity. It is this capacity which underlies the enhancement and diffusion of information technologies, and thus the development of productive forces.

In this sense, the new informational technological paradigm emphasizes the historical importance of the Marxian proposition on the close interaction between productive forces and social systems.[17] Perhaps it is only in the current historical period, because of the close connection between information and culture through the human mind, and thus between productivity and social organization, that such inspired anticipation bears its full meaning. However, if this perspective is to be intellectually fruitful it must be purified both from any ideological assumption of historical directionality and from any value judgement. The development of productive forces by the liberation of information flows does not require that capitalism be superseded. In fact, state-planned societies have proved more resistant to the new technological revolution than market-based economies, in contradiction of Marx's prophecy that socialism possessed a superior ability to develop productive forces. Equally unfounded is the opposite ideological position which states that market forces are innately superior in steering development in information technologies. Japan's leadership in the field has been built on strong, systematic state intervention in support of national companies, to raise their technological level in pursuit of the national goal of establishing Japan as a world power on non-military grounds.

The key mechanism for the development of productive forces in the new informational technological paradigm seems to be the ability of a given social organization to educate and motivate its labor force while at the same time setting up an institutional framework that maximizes information flows and connects them to the developmental tasks. The social and political means of achieving such goals vary historically, as do the societal outcomes of the development processes. However, not all these processes are undetermined, and relationships can certainly be found between social structures, techno-economic development, and institutional goals. Nevertheless, the present purpose is more limited and more focused. It is sufficient here to pinpoint the fact that because the new productive forces are information based, their development is more closely related than ever to the characteristics of symbolic production and manipulation in every society, actually fulfilling the hypothesis proposed by Marx on the relationship between social structure and techno-economic development.

From the characteristics of the process-orientation of information-based technological derives a third fundamental effect of the new technological paradigm on social organization: namely, increased *flexibility* of organizations in production, consumption, and management. Flexibility, in fact, emerges as a key characteristic of the new system taking shape;[18] yet it takes place within a context of large-scale production, consumption, and management, generally associated with large organizations and/or extended organizational networks. What happens is that new technologies build on the organizational capacity resulting from the industrial form of production and consumption, particularly during its mature stage (generally associated with what has been labeled in the literature as "Fordism," a very misleading term[19]); but they contribute both to transforming this system and enhancing that organizational capacity by preserving the economies of scale and the depth of organizational power, while overcoming rigidity and facilitating constant adaptation to a rapidly changing context. In this way, the historical oppositions between craft production and large-scale manufacture, between mass consumption and customized markets, between powerful bureaucracies and innovative enterprises, are dialectically superseded by the new technological medium, which ushers in an era of adaptive organizations in direct relationship with their social environments.[20] By increasing the flexibility of all processes, new information technologies contribute to minimizing the distance between economy and society.

The Organizational Transition from Industrialism to Informationalism

The new technological paradigm has fundamental social consequences linked to the specific logic of its basic characteristics. Yet, the new technologies are themselves articulated into a broader system of production and organization, whose ultimate roots are social, but to whose development new technologies powerfully contribute.[21] It is this complex, interacting system of technology and organizational processes, underlying economic growth and social change, that we call a *mode of development*. It is not the product of new technologies, nor are the new technologies a mechanical response to the demands of the new organizational system. It is the convergence between the two processes that changes the technical relationships of production, giving rise to a new mode of development. The previous section presented in summary form the relatively autonomous evolution of technological innovation which has led to the emergence of the informational technological paradigm. This section will examine, even more succinctly, the main organizational and structural trends that characterize the transition from the industrial to the informational mode of development.

The main process in this transition is not the shift from goods to services but, as the two main theorists of the "post-industrial society"[22] proposed many years ago, Alain Touraine in 1969 and Daniel Bell in 1973, the emergence of information processing as the core, fundamental activity conditioning the effectiveness and productivity of all processes of production, distribution, consumption, and management. The new centrality of information processing results from evolution in all the fundamental spheres of the industrial mode of development, under the influence of economic and social factors and structured largely by the mode of production. Specifically, the secular trend toward the increasing role of information results from a series of developments in the spheres of production, of consumption, and of state intervention.

In the sphere of *production*, two major factors have fostered information-processing activities within the industrial mode of development. The first is the emergence of the large corporation as the predominant organizational form of production and management.[23] An economy based on large-scale production and centralized management generated the growing number of information flows that were needed for efficient articulation of the system. The second resides within the production process itself (considering production in the broad sense, that is including production of both goods and services), and is the shift of the productivity sources from capital and labor to "other factors" (often associated with science, technology, and management), as shown by the series of econometric analyses in the tradition best represented by Robert Solow.[24] The hard core of these information-processing activities is composed of knowledge, which structures and provides adequate meaning to the mass of information required to manage organizations and to increase productivity.

In the sphere of *consumption,* two parallel processes have emphasized the role of information. On the one hand, the constitution of mass markets, and the increasing distance between buyers and sellers, have created the need for specific marketing and effective distribution by firms, thus triggering a flurry of information-gathering systems and information-distributing flows, to establish the connection between the two ends of the market.[25] On the other hand, under the pressure of new social demands, often expressed in social movements, a growing share of the consumption process has been taken over by collective consumption, that is, goods and services directly or indirectly produced and/or managed by the state,[26] as a right rather than as a commodity, giving rise to the welfare state. The formation of the welfare state has produced a gigantic system of information flows affecting most people and most activities, spurring the growth of bureaucracies, the formation of service delivery agencies, and consequently the creation of millions of jobs in information handling.[27]

In the sphere of *state intervention*, the past half-century has seen a huge expansion of government regulation of economic and social activities that has generated a whole new administration, entirely made up of information flows and information-based decision processes.[28] Although variations in the mode of production lead to a bureaucratic cycle, with upswings and downturns in the trend toward regulation, state intervention is in more subtle ways a structural feature of the new mode of development, in a process that Alain Touraine has characterized as "la société programmée."[29] This is the process by which the state sets up a framework within which large-scale organizations, both private and public, define strategic goals, which may be geared toward international economic competitiveness or military supremacy, that permeate the entire realm of social activities without necessarily institutionalizing or formalizing the strategic guidance of these activities. To be able to steer a complex society without suffocating it, the modern state relies on a system of "neo-corporatist" pacts, in Philippe Schmitter's terms, [30] which mobilize and control society through a system of incentives and disincentives made up of storage of information, emission of signals, and management of instructions. The state of the informational mode of development, be it under capitalism or under statism, exercises more intervention than ever, but it does so by controlling and manipulating the network of information flows that penetrate all activities. It does not follow that society is doomed to the Orwellian vision, since the intervention of the state will be informed by the political values emerging from the dynamics of the civil society, and thus its enhanced power could be used to counteract the built-in bureaucratic tendencies of state apparatuses. [31] As Nicos Poulantzas wrote ten years ago: "This statism does not refer to the univocal reinforcement of the State, but it is rather the effect of one tendency, whose two poles develop unevenly, toward the simultaneous reinforcing–weakening of the State." [32] The attempt by the state to override the contradiction between its increasing role and its decreasing legitimacy by diffusing its power through immaterial information flows greatly contributes to the dramatic explosion of information-processing activities and organizations. This is because the state sets up a series of information systems that control activities and citizens' lives through the codes and rules determined by those systems.

These structural trends, emerging and converging in a society largely dominated by the industrial mode of development, pave the way for the transformation of that mode, as information processing, with its core in knowledge generation, detracts from the importance of energy in material production, as well as from the importance of goods-producing in the overall social fabric. However, this transformation of the mode of development could not be accomplished without the surge of innovation in information technologies which, by creating the material basis from which information processing can expand its role, contributes to the change both in the structure of the production process and in the organization of society. It is in this sense that I hypothesize the formation of a new, informational mode of development: on the basis of the convergence through interaction of information technologies and information-processing activities into an articulated techno-organizational system.

The Interaction between Technological Innovation and Organizational Change in the Constitution of the Informational Mode of Development

The convergence between the revolution in information technology and the predominant role of information-processing activities in production, consumption, and state regulation, leads to the rise of the new, informational mode of development. This process triggers a series of new structural contradictions which highlight the relative autonomy of technological change in the process of social transformation. In fact, the diffusion of new technologies under the new mode of development calls into question the very processes and organizational forms that were at the basis of the demand for information technologies. This is because these organizational forms were born within the industrial mode of development, under the influence of the capitalist mode of production, and generally reflect the old state of technology. As the new technologies, and the realm of the possibilities they offer, expand, those same organizational forms that were responsible for the demand for new technologies are being rendered obsolete by their development. For instance, the large corporation was critical in fostering the demand for computers. But as microcomputers increase in power and become able to constitute information systems in harness with advanced telecommunications, it is no longer the large, vertical conglomerate but the network which is the most flexible, efficient form of management.

In another crucial development, the old form of the welfare state loses relevance. Previously, its operation had called for the expansion of information-processing activities: but as information itself becomes a productive force, so the social characteristics of labor reproduction (and thus of collective consumption: education, health, housing, etc.) become key elements in the development of productive forces, embodied in the cultural capacity of labor to process information. Thus, the old, redistributive welfare state becomes obsolete, not so much because it is too expensive (this is the capitalist critique, not the informational challenge), as because it has to be restructured to connect its redistributional goals with its new role as a source of productivity by means of the investment in human capital.

A third manifestation of the process of institutional change set in motion by the new technologies concerns the role of the state. The expansion of state regulatory intervention underlay the explosion of government-led information activities, enhancing its dominant role, within the limits of its legitimacy. However, rapid innovation in information technologies has created the facility for two-way information flows, making it possible for civil society to control the state on democratic principles, without paralyzing its effectiveness as a public interest agency. In this situation, the persistence of bureaucratic aloofness, once deprived of its former technical justification, emphasizes authoritarian tendencies within the state, delegitimizes its power, and prompts calls for institutional reform toward more flexible and more responsive government agencies.

The organizational transformation of the mode of development, then, leads to the expansion of information technologies, whose effect triggers pressure for further organizational change. The informational mode of development is not a rigid structure, but a constant process of change based on the interaction between technology and organization. Yet the logic of this process of change does not depend primarily on the interaction between these two planes, for modes of development are conditioned in their historical evolution by the dynamics of specific societies, themselves largely conditioned by the contradictions and transformations of the modes of production that characterize them. More specifically, the evolution of the informational mode of development, with its changing interaction between technology and organizational structures, depends, in our societies, on the restructuring of the capitalist mode of production that has taken place in the past decade. The transition between modes of development is not independent of the historical context in which it takes place; it relies heavily on the social matrix initially framing the transition, as well as on the social conflicts and interests that shape the transformation of that matrix. Therefore, the newly emerging forms of the informational mode of development, including its spatial forms, will not be determined by the structural requirements of new technologies seeking to fulfil their developmental potential, but will emerge from the interaction between its technological and organizational components, and the historically determined process of the restructuring of capitalism.

The Restructuring of Capitalism in the 1980s

When social systems experience a structural crisis, as a result of historical events acting on their specific contradictions, they are compelled either to change their goals, or to change their means in order to overcome the crisis. When the system changes its goals (or structural principles of performance), actually becoming a different system, there is a process of social transformation. When the system changes the institutionalized means by which it aims to achieve its systemic goals, there is a process of social restructuring. Each restructuring process leads to a new manifestation of the system, with specific institutional rules which induce historically specific sets of contradictions and conflicts, developing into new crises that potentially trigger new restructuring processes. This sequence goes on until the social equation underlying both structures and processes makes possible historical change to replace the old system by a new one.

The transformation of the capitalist mode of production on a global scale follows, in general terms, this social logic. The Great Depression of the 1930s, followed by the dislocation of World War II, triggered a restructuring process that led to the emergence of a new form of capitalism very different from the laisser-faire model of the pre-Depression era.[33] This new capitalist model, often characterized by the misleading term "Keynesianism,"[34] relied on three major structural modifications:[35]

(1) A social pact between capital and labor which, in exchange for the stability of capitalist social relationships of production and the adaptation of the labor process to the requirements of productivity, recognized the rights of organized labor, assured steadily rising wages for the unionized labor force, and extended the realm of entitlements to social benefits, creating an ever-expanding welfare state.

(2) Regulation and intervention by the state in the economic sphere: key initiatives in the accumulation process, stimulation of demand through public expenditures, and absorption of surplus labor by increasing public employment.

(3) Control of the international economic order by intervention in the sphere of circulation via a set of new international institutions, organized around the International Monetary Fund and under the hegemony of the United States, with the imposition of the dollar (and to some extent the pound) as the standard international currency. The ordering of world economic processes included the control by the center of the supply and prices of key raw materials and energy sources, most of these being produced by a still largely colonized Third World.

This state-regulated capitalism assured unprecedented economic growth, gains in productivity, and prosperity in the core countries for about a quarter of a century. In retrospect, history will probably consider these years as the golden age of western capitalism.

As I have shown elsewhere,[36] these same structural elements that accounted for the dynamism of this model were the very factors that led to its crisis in the 1970s, under the stress of its contradictions, expressed through rampant inflation that disrupted the circulation process, and under the pressure of social movements and labor struggles whose successful social and wage demands lowered the rate of profit. The oil shocks of 1974 and 1979 were precipitant events which, acting on structurally determined inflation, drove the circulation of capital out of control, prompting the need for austerity policies and fiscal restraint, and thus undermining the economic basis for state intervention. Although in strictly economic terms the increase in oil prices was not the cause of the structural crisis, its impact was crucial in calling into question the post-World War II model of capitalism, because of the pervasive effects of energy cost and supply in an economic system relying on an industrial mode of development based upon energy.

The crisis of the system in the 1970s revealed the declining effectiveness of the mechanisms established in the 1930s and 1940s in ensuring the fulfillment of the basic goals of the capitalist economy.[37] Labor was steadily increasing its share of the product. Social movements outside the workplace were imposing growing constraints on the ability of capital and bureaucracies to organize production and society free from social control. The state entered a fiscal crisis brought on by the contradiction between growing expenditures (determined by social demands) and comparatively decreasing revenues (limited by the need to preserve corporate profits).[38] The international order was disrupted by the surge of Third World nationalism (simultaneously opposed, supported, and manipulated by the strategies of the superpowers), and by the entry into the international economy of new competitive actors. The structural difficulty of making hard choices led companies to pass costs on into prices, the state to finance its intervention through debt and money supply, and the international economy to prosper through financial specu-lation and irresponsible lending in the global markets. After a series of unsuccessful stop-and-go policies, the second oil shock of 1979 revealed the depth of the crisis and necessitated a restructuring process that was undertaken simultaneously by both governments and firms, while interna-tional institutions such as the IMF imposed the new economic discipline throughout the world economy.

A new model of socio-economic organization had to be established which would be able to achieve the basic aims of a capitalist system, namely: to enhance the rate of profit for private capital, the engine of investment, and thus of growth; to find new markets, both through deepening the existing ones and by incorporating new regions of the world into an integrated capitalist economy; to control the circulation process, curbing structural inflation; and to assure the social reproduction and the economic regulation of the system through mechanisms that would not contradict those estab-lished to achieve the preceding goals of higher profit rates, expanding demand, and inflation control.

On the basis of these premises, a new model of capitalism emerged which, with national variations and diverse fortunes, actually characterizes most of the international system in the late 1980s. Reducing the new model to its essentials, we can summarize it in three major features which simultaneously address the four goals stated above as the fundamental requirements for the restructuring of capitalism to operate successfully.

(1) *The appropriation by capital of a significantly higher share of surplus from the production process*. This is a reversal of the historical power relationship between capital and labor, and a negation of the social pact achieved in the 1930s and 1940s. This fundamental goal is achieved by combining increases in productivity and increases in exploitation, by means of a fundamental restructuring of the work process and of the labor market which includes the following aspects:

(a) Higher productivity derived from technological innovation, combined with the uneven distribution of the productivity gains in favor of capital.
(b) Lower wages, reduced social benefits, and less protective working conditions.
(c) Decentralization of production to regions or countries characterized by lower wages and more relaxed regulation of business activities.
(d) Dramatic expansion of the informal economy, at both the core and the periphery of the system. By the informal economy is meant income-generating activities that are unregulated by the institutional system, in a context where similar activities are regulated. Much of the develop-ment of the informal economy has to do with the dismantling in practice of many provisions of the welfare state, for example, avoiding

payment of social benefits and contravening the legislation protecting workers.[39]

(e) A restructuring of labor markets to take in growing proportions of women, ethnic minorities, and immigrants, namely, those social groups which, because of institutionalized discrimination and social stigma, are most vulnerable in society and thus in the marketplace.[40] However, it is important to observe that such vulnerability is socially determined. Should the social context change, this supposedly docile labor would not be incorporated into the new labor markets. For example, while immigration has boomed during the restructuring process in the US, it has been practically halted in western Europe. Although part of the difference has to lie in the ability of the US to create millions of new unskilled jobs, a substantial factor is the unionization and rising consciousness of immigrant workers in Europe during the 1970s, to the point where, in countries such as Switzerland and Germany, they have become the militant vanguard among factory workers.[41] It makes little sense for European management to continue to import labor which, despite its social vulnerability, could turn into a focus for militancy while not being responsive to the same mechanisms of integration that are operative with respect to native workers.

(f) The weakening of trade unions – a fundamental, explicit goal of the restructuring process in most countries, and in fact, probably the most important single factor in achieving the overall objective of restoring the rate of profit at a level acceptable for business. By and large this objective has been achieved. Organized labor in most capitalist countries, with the exception of Scandinavia, is at the lowest point of its power and influence in the last thirty years, and its situation is still deteriorating rapidly. Some of the reasons for this decline are structural: for example, the fading away of traditional manufacturing, where the strength of the unions was concentrated, and the parallel expansion of a weakly unionized service economy. Other factors have to do directly with the transformation of labor markets, as noted under (e) above: women, often because of the sexism of the labor unions, are less unionized: many immigrants do not feel that the unions represent them; the informal economy detracts from the socializing effects of the workplace. However, organized labor has also been weakened as a result of targeted policies by both governments and firms, engaging in a deliberate effort at achieving what is perceived as a historical objective that would dramatically increase the freedom of capital to steer the economy and society.[42] Thus, Reagan's tough handling of the 1981 air traffic controllers' strike in the US, ending up with the de-registration of their union (PATCO), and the placement of the names of all the strikers in a blacklist to ban them from future Federal government employment, sent out a powerful signal that was well heard by business. Similarly, Thatcher's merciless repression of the coal miners' strike in the UK ushered in a new era of management-labor relations that put the British Trades Union Congress on the defensive. The historical reversal of the capital–labor power relationship, encapsulated in the gradual decline of the trade union movement, is the cornerstone of the restructuring of capitalism in the 1980s.

(2) *A substantial change in the pattern of state intervention, with the emphasis shifted from political legitimation and social redistribution to political domination and capital accumulation.*[43] Although in the "Keynesian" model regulation of capitalist growth was also a key objective, the means by which such regulation was exercised included widespread expansion of the welfare state, as well as both direct and indirect creation of public sector jobs, stimulating demand and contributing to the reproduction of labor power. The new forms of state intervention are much more directly focused on capital accumulation, and give priority to domination over legitimation in the relationship between state and society, in response to the emergency situation in which the system found itself in the 1970s. However, in contradiction of the ideological self-representation of the restructuring process by its main protagonists, what we are witnessing is not the withdrawal of the state from the economic scene, but the emergence of a new form of intervention, whereby new means and new areas are penetrated by the state, while others are deregulated and transferred to the market. This simultaneous engagement and disengagement of the state in the economy and society is evident in several mechanisms that express the new form of state support of capitalism:

(a) Deregulation of many activities, including relaxation of social and environmental controls in the work process.
(b) Shrinkage of, and privatization of productive activities in, the public sector.
(c) Regressive tax reform, favoring corporations and upper-income groups.
(d) State support for high-technology R&D and leading industrial sectors which form the basis of the new informational economy. This support usually takes the dual form of financing infrastructure and research, and favorable fiscal policies.
(e) Accordance of priority status to defense and to defense-related industries, combining, in pursuit of the objectives of the new state, the reinforcement of military power and the stimulation of a high-technology dominated defense sector. Following an old formula of Herbert Marcuse, I will call this trend the rise of the "warfare state." Defense spending and the development of new defense industries is also a fundamental way of creating new markets to compensate for

retrenchment in other public-sector expenditures, as well as for the loss of demand resulting from the lowering of wages in the production process.

(f) Shrinkage of the welfare state, with variations within and between countries according to the relative power of affected groups.

(g) Fiscal austerity, with the goal of a balanced budget, and tight monetary policy. These are key policies for the new model of capitalism, as the fundamental means of controlling inflation. However, while fiscal conservatism is an integral component of the new capitalism, recent historical experience shows the possibility of huge budget deficits resulting from the contradictions consequent on the implementation of the model in a given country, in particular in the US.

(3) *The third major mechanism of the restructuring of capitalism is the accelerated internationalization of all economic processes, to increase profitability and to open up markets through the expansion of the system.*

The capitalist economy has been, since its beginnings, a world economy, as Braudel and Wallerstein have reminded us.[44] However, what is new is the increasing interpenetration of all economic processes at the international level with the system working as a unit, worldwide in real time. This is a process that has grown steadily since the 1950s and has accelerated rapidly in the 1970s and 1980s as an essential element of the restructuring process. It embraces capital movements, labor migration, the process of production itself, the interpenetration of markets, and the use of nation states as elements of support in an international competition that will ultimately determine the economic fate of all nations.

The internationalization of capitalism enhances profitability at several levels:

(a) It allows capital to take advantage of the most favorable conditions for investment and production anywhere in the world. Sometimes this translates into low wages and lack of government regulation. In other instances, penetration of key markets or access to technology are more important considerations for the firm. But the fact remains that the increasing homogenization of the economic structure across nations allows for a variable geometry of production and distribution that maximizes advantages in terms of opportunity costs.

(b) By allowing round-the-clock capital investment opportunities worldwide, internationalization dramatically increases the rate of turnover of capital, thus enhancing profit levels for a given profit rate, although at the cost of increasing instability built into the system.

(c) The internationalization process also opens up new markets, and connects segments of markets across borders, increasingly differentiating societies vertically while homogenizing markets horizontally. This expansion of demand through new markets is absolutely crucial in a model that relies on the reduction of wages in the core countries, since the loss in potential demand has to be made up by the incorporation of whichever new markets may exist anywhere in the world. This is particularly important in the transitional period of restructuring, when wages have to be kept at the lowest possible level to increase profits and attract investment, while keeping demand high enough to justify new investment.

The process of internationalization offers dynamic expansion possibilities that could substantially benefit the capitalist system. But it can also pose fundamental problems to individual units of that system, be they firms or countries, which are faced with new, tougher competition from the new actors which are incorporated into the system and quickly learn the ruthlessness of the game. This has been the case for the US which has lost market share, in both its domestic market and the international economy, to Japan and the newly industrialized countries. Given the interdependence of economic processes and national policies, the internationalization process prepares the ground for future major crises: on the one hand, any significant downturn has immediate repercussions worldwide, and is thus amplified; on the other hand, competition constantly provokes the threat of protectionism which could wreck the very basis of the system. A system in which the interests of the totality are not necessarily the interests of each competitive unit in every moment in time could become increasingly disruptive. When the "creative destruction" process[45] takes place at the international level, the intermixing of national interests with competitive strategies becomes explosive.

The overpowering of labor by capital, the shift of the state toward the domination–accumulation functions of its intervention in economy and society, and the internationalization of the capitalist system to form a worldwide interdependent unit working in real time are the three fundamental dimensions of the restructuring process that has given birth to a new model of capitalism, as distinct from the "Keynesian" model of the 1945–75 era as that one was from "laisser-faire" capitalism.[46]

These three processes are present in most countries' recent economic policies, but their relative importance may vary considerably according to each country's history, institutions, social dynamics, and place in the world economy. Thus, the UK has emphasized the overpowering of labor as the rallying cry of the Thatcher government; the US has made the emergence of a new "warfare state," based upon high-technology development, the centerpiece of its economic recovery; Japan has saved itself much of the pain of the restructuring process by riding the crest of the internationalization wave. However, since the capitalist system is a world system at the level of the mode of production (although certainly not at the level of societies), the different dimensions of the restructuring process are interconnected across the various regions of the international economy.

Also, the actual practice of restructuring is full of contradictions. Not only social but economic as well. For instance, in the case of the Reagan Administration in the US the dramatic defense build up, combined with a regressive tax reform and the political inability to dismantle Social Security, led to the biggest budget deficit in American history, under one of the most ideologically committed Administrations to fiscal conservatism. The budget deficit was financed to a large extent by foreign capital, attracted by high interest rates, driving up the dollar's exchange rate. Together with declining competitiveness of American manufacturing, this evolution resulted in catastrophic trade deficits that weakened the American economy. The twin mega-deficits have spoiled to a large extent the benefits of restructuring for American capitalism and will, most likely, lead to austerity policies in the 1989–91 period that could trigger a world recession. While our purpose here goes far beyond economic forecasting we want to emphasize that the process of restructuring is by no means exempt of contradictions. While fiscal austerity was a must of the new model, and as such was formulated by its supply-side defenders, it could not actually be implemented because the political support for the boldest extremes of restructuring could not be marshalled. The artificial implementation of the model (on the basis of debt-financed military expenditures, a policy we have labeled "perverted Keynesianism"[47] could lead to its demise or to its sharpening through reinforced austerity policies, ushering in a new crisis.

However, in spite of these contradictory trends, a new model of capitalism has emerged that could outlast the forthcoming crises. One of the reasons for its likely durability, we hypothesize, is that it has encompassed in its expansion the informational mode of development that was bursting into life in a process of historical simultaneity. It is the interaction and the articulation between the informational mode of development and the restructuring of capitalism that creates the framework shaping the dynamics of our society and our space.

The Articulation between the Informational Mode of Development and the Restructuring of Capitalism: Reshaping the Techno-Economic Paradigm

The historical coincidence of the restructuring of capitalism and the rise of the informational mode of development has created a structural convergence resulting in the formation of a specific techno-economic paradigm at the very roots of our social dynamics. Because political and organizational decision-makers are always primarily concerned to perpetuate the interests they represent, and therefore concerned with the process of restructuring, it is under the dominance of that process that the merger has taken place. However, the two components of the paradigm are distinguishable only analytically, because while informationalism has now been decisively shaped by the restructuring process, restructuring could never have been accomplished, even in a contradictory manner, without the unleashing of the technological and organizational potential of informationalism.

Given the complexity of the articulation process, I will differentiate between the two dimensions that compose the informational mode of development: the *technological* and the *organizational*. Both have been fundamental in giving rise to a new form of capitalism which, in turn, has stimulated and supported the technological revolution and has adopted new organizational forms.

New *information technologies* have been decisive in the implementation of the three fundamental processes of capitalist restructuring.

(1) *Increasing the rate of profit* by various means:

(a) Enhancing productivity by the introduction of microelectronics-based machines that transform the production process.

(b) Making possible the decentralization of production, and the spatial separation of different units of the firm, while reintegrating production and management at the level of the firm by using telecommunications and flexible manufacturing systems.

(c) Enabling management to automate those processes employing labor with a sufficiently high cost level and a sufficiently low skill level to make automation both profitable and feasible. These jobs happened to be those concentrated in the large-scale factories that had become the strongholds of labor unions, and better remunerated labor, during the industrial era.

(d) Positioning capital in a powerful position *vis-à-vis* labor. Automation, flexible manufacturing, and new transportation technologies provide management with a variety of options that considerably weaken the bargaining position of the unions. Should the unions insist on preserving or improving their levels of wages and benefits, the company can automate or move elsewhere, or both, without losing its connections with the market or with the network of production. Thus, either by using automation to substitute for labor, or by extracting concessions by wielding the threat to automate or relocate, capital uses new technologies to free itself from the constraints of organized labor.

(2) New technologies are also a powerful instrument in weighting the accumulation and domination functions of state intervention. This occurs on two main levels:

(a) On the one hand, rapid technological change makes obsolete the entire existing weapons system, creating the basis for the expansion of the "warfare state" in a political environment characterized by states striving for military supremacy and therefore engaging in a technological arms race that can only be supported by the resources of the state.

(b) On the other hand, the strategic role played by high technology in economic development draws the state to concentrate on providing the required infrastructure, downplaying its role in redistributional policies.

(3) The process of *internationalization of the economy* could never take place without the dramatic breakthroughs in information technologies. Advances in telecommunications, flexible manufacturing that allows simultaneously for standardization and customization, and new transportation technologies emerging from the use of computers and new materials, have created the material infrastructure for the world economy, as the construction of the railway system provided the basis for the formation of national markets in the nineteenth century. In addition, the economic effects of new technologies are also crucial in the formation of an international economy. Their effects on process condition the international competitiveness of countries and firms. Their effects on new products create new markets in which the harshest competitive battles are fought, with new economic actors trying to short-circuit the sequence of development by leapfrogging into state-of-the-art high-technology markets through dramatic efforts of national development. The new technological division of labor is one of the fundamental lines of cleavage in the emerging international economic order.

The *organizational* components of the informational mode of development are also fundamental features in the restructuring process. Three major organizational characteristics of informationalism may be distinguished, each one of them affecting the three dimensions of the restructuring process.

(1) There is a growing *concentration of knowledge-generation and decision-making processes in high-level organizations* in which both information and the capacity of processing it are concentrated. The informational world is made up of a very hierarchical functional structure in which increasingly secluded centers take to its extreme the historical division between intellectual and manual labor. Given the strategic role of knowledge and information control in productivity and profitability, these core centers of corporate organizations are the only truly indispensable components of the system, with most other work, and thus most other workers, being potential candidates for automation from the strictly functional point of view. How far this tendency toward widespread automation is actually taken in practice is a different matter, depending on the dynamics of labor markets and social organization.

This concentration of information power in selected segments of the corporate structure greatly favors the chances of the restructuring process in the three dimensions presented:

(a) Productive labor can be reduced to its essential component, thus downgrading the objective bargaining power of the large mass of functionally dispensable labor.

(b) The rise of the technocracy within the state displaces the traditional integrative functions of the politically determined bureaucracy, establishing a tight linkage between the high levels of the state and the corporate world through the intermediary of the scientific establishment. The rise of the meritocracy, using the notion advanced by Daniel Bell, establishes new principles of legitimacy in the state, further removing it from the political controls and constituencies represented by the diversity of social interests.

(c) As technology transfer becomes the key to competition in the international economy, that process is controlled by knowledge holders in the centers of the dominant scientific and corporate organizations. It follows that the effective accomplishment of the internationalization process requires access to these knowledge centers, ruling out the adoption of an isolationist stance, which would only lead to the technological obsolescence of those economies and firms holding it.

(2) The second major organizational characteristic of informationalism concerns the *flexibility* of the system and of the relationships among its units, since flexibility is both a requirement of and a possibility offered by new information technologies.[48] Flexibility acts powerfully as a facilitator of the restructuring process in the following ways:

(a) It changes capital–labor relationships, transforming a potentially permanent and protected worker status into a flexible arrangement generally adapted to the momentary convenience of management. Thus, temporary workers, part-time jobs, homework, flexitime schedules, indefinite positions in the corporate structure, changing assignments, varying wages and benefits according to performance, etc., are all creative expedients of management that, while they increase tremendously the flexibility and thus the productivity of the firm, undermine the collective status of labor vis-à-vis capital.

(b) In the restructuring of the state, organizational flexibility contributes to the formation of public–private partnerships and to the blurring of the distinction between the public and private spheres. Segments of the welfare state are being shifted to the private sector, corporations are being brought into the formulation of public policies, and a selective interpenetration of state and capital is diminishing the autonomy of the state, along the lines of the "recapitalization" of the state, characteristic of the restructuring process.[49]

(c) Flexibility is also a necessary condition for the formation of the new world economy, since it is the only organizational form that allows constant adaptation of firms to the changing conditions of the world market.[50]

(3) A third fundamental organizational characteristic of informationalism is the shift from *centralized* large corporations to *decentralized* networks made up of a plurality of sizes and forms of organizational units.[51] Although networking increases flexibility, it is actually a different characteristic, since there are forms of flexibility that do not require networks. These networks, which could not exist on such a large scale without the medium provided by new information technologies, are the emerging organizational form of our world, and have played a fundamental role in ensuring the restructuring process:

(a) They are the prevalent form of the informal economy, as well as of the sub-contracting practices that have disorganized and reorganized the labor process, enhancing capital's profitability.[52]

(b) They have provided the model for the constitution of the new warfare state, as will be argued in chapter 6, on the basis of the interaction between different specialized government agencies, the defence industry, high-technology firms, and the scientific establishment.

(c) They are the organizational form used by major multinational corporations that have established variable strategic alliances to compete in the international economy.[53] Unlike the tendency of the industrial mode of development toward oligopolistic concentration, in the informational era large corporations set up specific alliances for given products, processes, and markets: these alliances vary according to time and space, and result in a variable geometry of corporate strategies that follow the logic of the multiple networks where they are engaged rather than the monolithic hierarchy of empire conglomerates.

Networks, on the basis of new information technologies, provide the organizational basis for the transformation of socially and spatially based relationships of production into flows of information and power that articulate the new flexible system of production and management. The restructuring of capitalism has used the adaptive potential of organizational networking to find breathing room for its "creative–destructive" energy, hitherto constrained by the social and political bonds inflicted upon it by a society reluctant to be but a commodity. The libertarian spirit of capitalism finally found itself at home at the last frontier where organizational networks and information flows dissolve locales and supersede societies. Informationalism and capitalism have historically merged in a process of techo-economic restructuring whose social consequences will last far beyond the social events and political circumstances that triggered the decisions leading to its development in the 1980s.

From this historical synthesis, new social forms and new spatial processes have emerged. My inquiry will explore the territory thus constituted. It will take us into the new world being made up from the contradictions of our past and the promises of our future through the conflicts of our present.

2

The New Industrial Space

The Locational Pattern of Information-Technology Manufacturing and its Effects on Spatial Dynamics

Introduction

The development of new industries, spearheaded by the producers of information technologies, along with the crisis of old line manufacturing, is transforming the economic landscape of the United States; and similar processes are under way in most countries of the industrialized world. This technological revolution has very definite spatial dimensions, with far-reaching consequences for the future of cities and regions. This chapter explores the locational pattern of information technology manufacturing and its effects on spatial dynamics.

In recent years, a growing body of research has focused on the location of high-technology industries, the factors conditioning their spatial pattern, and the consequences of this pattern for regional development.[1] This chapter will build on the results obtained by this research while also attempting to elaborate a broader analytical framework which will incorporate as coherently as possible what we already know of the new industrial space.[2] The perspective presented here starts from the assumption that traditional location theory fails to deal with the novel technological and economic conditions of the new industrialization process.[3] Furthermore, more refined models of regional economic analysis, such as the product cycle–profit cycle model,[4] overlook the historical specificity of the new information-based industries, reducing their spatial logic to a simple manifestation of the stage of the industry in its life cycle. Taking a different view, I argue, with other scholars,[5] that the specific characteristics of the new industries lead to a new and original spatial logic, whose development will reveal itself even more clearly in the future as the organization of knowledge-based production continues to expand in our societies. In turn, this distinctive spatial logic has implications for the inter-regional and international division of labor which affect the world economy, and ultimately, the world itself.[6]

Before presenting the analytical perspective in some detail, it seems useful to summarize the main facts of what we already know on the location of high-technology manufacturing in the US. After reviewing some recent studies on the subject, I will propose an analytical framework whose main elements will then be examined in regard to the available empirical evidence.

Information-Technology Manufacturing and Industrial Location: An Overview

The Spatial Distribution of Information-Technology Manufacturing

Any discussion on the relationship between high-technology industries and spatial structure must be grounded in empirical observation of where such industries are located and what the factors are that seem to be at the roots of their location pattern. However, there are considerable theoretical and methodological problems in appraising the results of such empirical studies. The production of information-technology devices is generally defined in terms of the popular descriptive label "high technology," and questionable operational definitions of high technology bias the findings. Inadequate statistical sources limit the possibilities of refining the analysis. Spatial units of analysis (regions, states, metropolitan areas) are so broad that aggregation of data confuses contradictory coexisting trends, blurring the actual profile of the phenomenon. It is also difficult to distinguish the cumulative effects of long-term location patterns from recent trends emerging from the new industries. In sum, the first impression given by the data on the location of the so-called high-technology industries is one of confusion and indeterminacy in the observed spatial trends. Nevertheless, it is important to start from this overall picture, however complex, in undertaking the task of making analytical sense of the processes constituting the new industrial space.

The most comprehensive empirical study to date is the research by Ann Markusen, Peter Hall, and Amy Glasmeier,[7] and its spin-off, Glasmeier's doctoral dissertation.[8] They define high-technology industries on the basis of a greater-than-average proportion of engineers and scientists in the sector's labor force. Having selected 100 four-digit industrial sectors on this criterion, they studied the distribution of jobs and plants for each sector among 223 metropolitan areas of the US in 1972 and 1977, the most recent year for which Census of Manufacturing data were available in 1985. They also performed a statistical analysis of the main variables associated with the location of these industries.

The first conclusion reached by this study is that the popular sunbelt/snowbelt distinction regarding high-technology development is meaningless. Although California, Texas, and Arizona appear among the states with the largest concentrations of high-technology jobs, so do New England, New Jersey, and Illinois. Furthermore, four of the top five states, ranked in terms of absolute number of high-technology jobs, are states of the old manufacturing belt: Illinois, Pennsylvania, New York, and Ohio (see tables 2.1 and 2.2). Confronted with this finding, one wonders if there is actually a new emergent industrial space or if, on the contrary, the sheer size of the old manufacturing belt means that it simply reproduces itself on the basis of the new industries. To explore this issue, we have to take into consideration *simultaneously* the absolute size of each industry and the share of high-technology industries in each regional economy, as measured by location quotients. By combining the two criteria we arrive at those states which both contain the majority of jobs in

Table 2.1 Leading high-tech states, 1977
(a) In order of absolute high-tech employment

Rank	State	Jobs (000)	Location quotient
1	California	641.3	1.49
2	Illinois	360.3	1.15
3	New York	336.8	0.89
4	Pennsylvania	314.3	0.94
5	Ohio	295.1	0.88
6	Texas	285.7	1.33
7	New Jersey	232.3	1.23
8	Massachusetts	204.6	1.43
9	Michigan	169.4	0.86
10	Connecticut	160.0	1.65
11	Indiana	153.5	0.89
12	Wisconsin	128.8	1.00
13	Florida	119.0	1.39

(b) In order of location quotient

Rank	State	Location quotient	Jobs (000)
1	Arizona	1.80	45.9
2	Connecticut	1.65	160.0
3	Kansas	1.63	62.8
4	Maryland	1.60	48.5
5	Colorado	1.57	52.9
6	California	1.49	641.3
7	Massachusetts	1.43	204.6
8	Florida	1.39	119.0
9	Oklahoma	1.38	53.9
10	Texas	1.33	285.7
11	Utah	1.30	22.9
12	New Jersey	1.23	232.3
13	Louisiana	1.22	56.4

Source: Glasmeier (see note 8).

Table 2.2 Top ranked metropolitan areas, job and plant levels and change, 1972–7

Rank	SMSA	Plants, 1977
1	Los Angeles–Long Beach, California	3,732
2	Chicago, Illinois	3,029
3	Detroit, Michigan	2,291
4	New York, New York/New Jersey	2,149
5	Boston–Lowell–Brockton–Lawrence–Haverhill, Massachusetts	1,484
6	Philadelphia, Pennsylvania/New Jersey	1,455
7	Anaheim–Santa Ana–Garden Grove, California	1,118
8	Newark, New Jersey	1,077
9	Cleveland, Ohio	1,037
10	Nassau–Suffolk, New York	963
11	Dallas–Fort Worth, Texas	942
12	San Francisco–Oakland, California	933
13	San Jose, California	856
14	Houston, Texas	840
15	Minneapolis–St Paul, Minnesota/Wisconsin	740

Rank	SMSA	Jobs, 1977
1	Los Angeles–Long Beach, California	279,293
2	Chicago, Illinois	255,051
3	Boston–Lowell–Brockton–Lawrence–Haverhill, Massachusetts	144,720
4	Philadelphia, Pennsylvania/New Jersey	136,891
5	San Jose, California	106,002
6	Anaheim–Santa Ana–Garden Grove, California	92,726
7	Newark, New Jersey	92,078
8	Dallas–Fort Worth, Texas	87,658
9	Detroit, Michigan	87,180
10	Houston, Texas	81,577
11	New York, New York/New Jersey	80,980
12	Milwaukee, Wisconsin	69,741
13	Minneapolis–St Paul, Minnesota/Wisconsin	68,664
14	Cleveland, Ohio	66,344
15	Nassau–Suffolk, New York	66,335

Rank	SMSA	New plant change 1972–7
1	Anaheim, California	464
2	Los Angeles, California	367
3	San Jose, California	339
4	Dallas, Texas	276
5	Chicago, Illinois	224
6	Houston, Texas	204
7	Boston, Massachusetts	191
8	Minneapolis, Minnesota	158
9	San Francisco, California	151
10	Detroit, Michigan	145
	Median gain	9

Rank	SMSA	Net job change 1972-7
1	San Jose, California	31,909
2	Anaheim, California	30,612
3	Houston, Texas	18,932
4	San Diego, California	16,782
5	Boston, Massachusetts	15,173
6	Dallas, Texas	12,067
7	Worcester, Massachusetts	9,893
8	Oklahoma City, Oklahoma	8,363
9	Lakeland, Florida	8,132
10	Phoenix, Arizona	7,976
	Median gain	248

Rank	SMSA	Percent plant change
1	Lawton, Oklahoma	600.00
2	St Cloud, Minnesota	214.29
3	Laredo, Texas	150.00
4	Santa Cruz, California	137.50
5	Champagne–Urbana, Illinois	118.18
6	Oxnard, California	114.55
7	Fort Meyers, Florida	110.00
8	Billings, Montana	100.00
9	Cedar Rapids, Iowa	100.00
10	Panama City, Florida	100.00

Rank	SMSA	Percent job change
1	Lawton, Oklahoma	2,266.97
2	St Cloud, Minnesota	1,265.08
3	Boise, Idaho	729.31
4	Santa Rosa, California	360.58
5	Lakeland, Florida	266.69
6	Lubbock, Texas	237.44
7	Topeka, Kansas	237.35
8	Laredo, Texas	220.84
9	Savannah, Georgia	204.78
10	McAllen–Pharr–Edinburg, Texas	181.54

Source: Markusen, Hall, and Glasmeier (see note 2).

Table 2.3 States ranked according to their combined position on a scale of (a) high-technology industries location quotients and (b) their number of high-technology manufacturing jobs (states ranking among the top ten on both criteria)

Rank	State
1	California
2	Connecticut
3	Massachusetts
4	Texas
5	Illinois
6	New Jersey
7	Florida

Source: Markusen, Hall, and Glasmeier (note 2) (my elaboration of their database)

the new industries and seem to be specialized in these industries. Thus, if we select the states that in 1977 were both among the top ten in terms of high technology jobs and had location quotients higher than one, we obtain the ranking given in table 2.3. At a very general level of observation, these states seem to represent the hard core of high-technology manufacturing under the terms defined by the Markusen, Hall, and Glasmeier study. This impression is confirmed by a closer look at the internal composition of the industrial sectors that account for most of the high-technology manufacturing jobs in these states: semiconductors, computers, aircraft, telecommunications equipment, space, and defense-related industries. Simply reading through this list of high-technology-prone states gives an idea of the geographical, social, and historical diversity of the new industrial space. Any coherent pattern in industrial location will have to be found at a deeper analytical level.

Similar findings can be cited concerning the distribution of high-technology industries among the metropolitan areas. There is an important difference between those areas that show a concentration of high-technology jobs because of the sheer size of their industrial history, and those newer areas that have both a strong quantitative high-technology base and a rapid rate of growth in these sectors. Thus, if we rank the top ten areas in absolute number of high-technology jobs *and* the top ten areas in terms of rate of growth in high-technology jobs between 1972 and 1977, and again combine the two rankings, we come up with the following top five metropolitan areas: San Jose, California; Anaheim, California; Boston, Massachusetts; Houston, Texas; and Dallas, Texas. While this short list also shows a regional and social diversity, the shift from the state level to the more disaggregated level of the metropolitan areas gives more specific information about the particular spatial features of high-technology location. For example, while Los Angeles–Long Beach had the highest number of high-technology jobs in

1977, Anaheim appears to be the main growth engine for the new industries in Southern California. Also, it would seem that areas such as Chicago and Philadelphia retain their quantitative importance in these high-technology statistics more because of the use of new technologies in the modernization of traditional manufacturing than because of their capacity to retain a significant share of the information-technology producer industries.[9]

Why do high-technology industries locate where they do? According to the regression analysis performed by Markusen, Hall, and Glasmeier, four series of variables explain a sizable proportion of the variance in the distribution of industrial sectors among metropolitan areas:[10]

(1) Amenities (good climate, good educational options, high (?) housing prices).
(2) Access features (airport access, freeway access).
(3) Agglomeration economies (presence of business services; location of headquarters of *Fortune* 500 corporations).
(4) Socio-political factors (importance of defense spending, low percentage of blacks in the resident population).

Other factors frequently cited in the literature, such as wage rates, levels of unionization, or presence of a major university, do not seem to hold a statistical relationship with high-technology location, although these observations will need further qualification as the analysis progresses.

In spite of their interest and importance, the data provided by the Markusen, Hall, and Glasmeier study have two major methodological shortcomings from the point of view of our own analytical purpose. First, since their calculations concern entire sectors, this database does not permit a distinction to be made between innovative functions and assembly-line plants within the same high-technology industry. Given the sharp division of labor within each industry and the extreme differentiation among segments of its labor force, we need to introduce additional criteria to understand the differential spatial dynamics of different segments of the industry. Secondly, the definition of high-technology industries in terms of the proportion of skilled technical labor does not allow differentiation between high-technology producers and high-technology users, since many old line manufacturing companies are also increasing the proportion of engineers and scientists employed in order to be able to use new technologies, regardless of the characteristics of their final products. Although the spatial impact of technological modernization in manufacturing is a very important matter, it is analytically crucial to distinguish it from the spatial logic of the new, information-based industries. The fact that the definition of high technology used in the Markusen, Hall, and Glasmeier study cannot capture this crucial distinction could account for the quantitative importance in their results, in terms of high-technology jobs, of some old industrial areas, such as Illinois and Ohio.

Thus, while the data commented on here present a most interesting overview of the effects of technological change on manufacturing in general, they are not sufficient for an understanding of the potential new spatial dynamics that could exist within the new information-technology industries.

As stated in chapter 2, our hypothesis is that the core of the current technological revolution lies in the development of new information technologies, particularly microelectronics, computers, and telecommunications as well as in biotechnology, with its basis in genetic engineering. From this perspective, studies of particular industries which are clearly a part of the new informational economy, such as semiconductors, computers (hardware and software), and genetic engineering, are crucial to understanding the new spatial logic, if it actually exists. What we lose in comprehensiveness, we gain in deeper insight, thus enhancing the chances of forming the empirical grounding of an analytical model capable of making progress in explaining the process of formation of the new industrial space.

The Evolution of the Locational Pattern of the Semiconductors Industry

Semiconductors manufacturing remains the archetype of information-technology industries. Since it is also the industry on which we have the most detailed information, a synthesis of the main trends of its typical spatial behavior could be a useful step toward understanding the locational pattern of information-technology producers.

First of all, Storper's data[11] show that employment in semiconductors is heavily concentrated in four states: 72.5 per cent of all employment in the industry in 1980 was in California, Massachusetts, Arizona, and Texas. This has been the case since 1969; though not all four states at the top have remained the same, California has been ahead throughout and increased its lead over the years (see table 2.4).

A more recent analysis by Scott and Angel[12] shows a similar tendency, although, according to their calculations, Massachusetts has not been among the top four states since the early 1970s, while New York has maintained a significant share, mainly because of production associated with IBM (see table 2.5). It is important to notice the differences in trend between areas highlighted by Scott and Angel's data: New England and the Mid-Atlantic suffered a significant decline in their shares after an early lead (New England accounted for over 29 per cent of total semiconductors employment in 1958). In contrast, Texas and Arizona displayed impressive gains during the 1970s, and California gradually increased its share to become the undisputed leader in the 1980s. Figure 2.1, elaborated by Scott and Angel, compares the strikingly different evolution in semiconductors employment in, variously, the Mid-Atlantic (New Jersey, New York, Pennsylvania), Massachusetts, and Silicon Valley (Santa Clara County), showing a clear advantage for the last.

These observations emphasize the need for a historical perspective on the formation of the spatial pattern of the industry in generating some hypotheses

Table 2.4 Location of the semiconductor industry

	Production Employment[a] 1980		Production Employment Census, 1977			Value-Added 1977			Establishments 1977	
		%		000	%		$000	%		No.	%
First State	CA	30.4	CA	18.1	28.5	CA	1,172.6	34.4	CA	180	33.0
Second State	AZ	18.3	TX	13.0	20.4	TX	568.6	17.2	NY	59	10.8
Third State	TX	14.6	PA	8.0	12.6	NY	422.4	12.3	MA	46	8.44
Fourth State	MA	9.2	AZ	7.0	11.0	PA	359.9	10.5	TX	36	6.6
Top Four States		72.5		46.1	72.5		2,523.5	74.0		321	58.8
Total	102.99			63.5			3,409.6			545	

[a]SIC 3674 and part of SIC 3679; author's statistics.
Sources: State Industrial Directories, Key Plants, Marketing Economics Incorporated, New York, 1980. Sources gathered and elaborated by Storper (see note 1).

about its underlying logic. To pursue this perspective further, we will turn to Servet Mutlu's pioneering doctoral dissertation, which surveys in great detail the sequence of events that put semiconductors on the economic map of the US.[13]

The first significant fact in this sequence is that the development of semiconductors was actually missed out on by the big companies, which were in the business of making electronic components on the basis of vacuum tube technology. Even when these companies converted to semiconductors in the late 1960s, it was mainly to produce them for their own manufacturing processes, basically focused on consumer durables. They remained located in their original sites in the north-east: Westinghouse in Pittsburgh, Sylvania in Long Island, RCA in New Jersey, and General Electric in northern New York. Since the development of semiconductors was to a large extent

Table 2.5   Percentage distribution of employment in SIC 3674 (semiconductors and related devices) for census divisions and selected states, 1958–1982

	1958	1963	1967	1972	1977	1982
New England	29.1	18.0	n.a.	10.7*	10.6	n.a.
Massachusetts	n.a.	11.2	9.4	4.8	4.4	4.4
Mid-Atlantic	34.5	34.2	30.8	21.8	21.7	16.4
New Jersey	n.a.	6.5	6.2	3.5	2.3	1.9
New York	n.a.	8.1	8.5	5.3	10.6	9.0
Pennsylvania	n.a.	19.6	16.1	13.0	8.8	5.5
East-north-central	n.a.	n.a.	3.1	9.2	2.3	1.9
West-north-central	n.a.	n.a.	0.5	0.8	0.7	n.a.
South Atlantic	n.a.	n.a.	3.5	2.1	2.9	n.a.
Florida	n.a.	n.a.	3.4	1.4	2.6	3.2
East-south-central	n.a.	n.a.	n.a.	0.2	n.a.	n.a.
West-south-central	n.a.	n.a.	3.1	n.a.	14.5	n.a.
Texas	n.a.	n.a.	3.1	18.3	14.5	13.3
Mountain	n.a.	n.a.	6.3	n.a.	n.a.	n.a.
Arizona	n.a.	9.3	6.3	5.8	14.5	10.7
Pacific	n.a.	n.a.	17.5	n.a.	n.a.	n.a.
California	15.9	19.9	17.5	21.0	27.6	28.7

Source: All data for the years 1958 and 1963 taken from US Department of Commerce, Bureau of the Census, Census of Manufactures. All data for the years 1967, 1972, 1977, and 1982 taken from US Department of Commerce, Bureau of the Census, County Business Patterns (except where marked by an asterik which indicates that the source is the Census of Manufactures). Data collected and elaborated by Scott and Angel (see note 12).

dependent on innovation, and none of these companies chose to invest in electronics research, they were gradually pushed aside by the competition.

The only established large firm that could have dominated the innovation process and taken on the leadership of the new industry was obviously ATT–Western Electric, since the New Jersey-based Bell Laboratories were at the very source of the invention of the transistor in 1947, as well as of most of the original R&D in the field of semiconductors. Yet, threatened with anti-trust law suits (particularly the one brought by the Department of Justice against Western Electric in 1956) Bell decided to diffuse its knowledge, organizing conferences to communicate its findings, and liberally licensing the applications of its discoveries. Bell Laboratories, in fact, heavily dependent as it was on government research contracts, became a national research facility. In the long term this turned out to be a brilliant commercial strategy, since telecommunications, largely dominated by ATT, eventually became the highway system of the electronic age. However, it was probably not a conscious decision, but rather a combination of legal and institutional constraints with the research dynamics generated at Bell. This is in fact one of the crucial, new characteristics of a science-based industry: it is very difficult

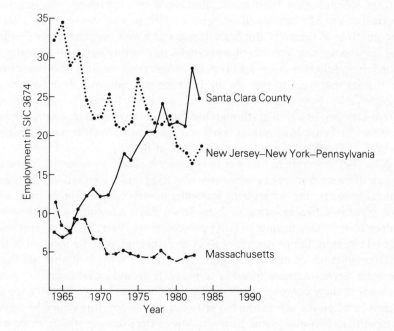

Figure 2.1   Distribution of employment in SIC 3674 (semiconductors and related devices), 1964–1983
Source: US Department of Commerce, Bureau of the Census, County Business Patterns, in Scott and Angel (see note 12)

to play the innovation game and at the same time set up organizational constraints that would undermine the vitality of the research effort, and ultimately its ability to connect with social and commercial applications. Those companies who behaved in such a way as to restrain the process of communicating innovations were left behind in the technological competition, and ultimately lost markets as well.

Interestingly enough, the direct industrial development resulting from Bell's technological discoveries took place elsewhere, when Bell's researchers set up shop in other areas of the country, emphasizing the crucial role of humanly embodied research in the development of the new information-technology industry. Noble Prize winner William Shockley, one of the inventors of the transistor, was appointed Professor of Electrical Engineering at Stanford University by Frank Terman, an entrepreneurial Provost who, in 1951, founded the Stanford Industrial Park and gave high priority to supporting technologically advanced companies. Shockley was a native of Palo Alto, a fact that made his recruitment easier. Yet it was the initiative of the university which created the conditions for bringing together the innovative capacity of one of the leading scientists with the university support and business environment necessary to generate industrial spin-offs and further technological innovation. Shockley's own company was not very successful, since he insisted in engaging himself in what proved to be a dead-end new line of research. But his students and junior partners, more flexible and open to the new avenues of semiconductors technology, quit Shockley to found Fairchild, the source (direct or indirect) of most of the innovative companies that were to provide the basis for the industrial development of Silicon Valley. Spin-offs of Fairchild included Intel, Signetics, and Advanced Micro-Devices. In a similar, though less famous, development, one of the key elements in Texas Instruments' early start in semiconductors was the hiring in 1953 of Gordon Teal, a leading scientist at Bell.

ATT–Bell was able in this way to organize by itself the scientific research milieu in which discoveries were made that triggered the growth of a new and crucial industry; the subsequent spin-offs, however, were not its own, and took place in different locations. New Jersey did not become a major center for semiconductors, in spite of Bell's pre-eminence there, the asset represented by Princeton, the proximity of RCA at Princeton, and the location of the IBM production center in southern New York. Why is it that all these elements never clustered together to generate an industrial complex? First, each one of these companies and institutions constituted a world apart, too arrogant to solicit the others and too self-confident to feel threatened by future competition. Secondly, some basic conditions were lacking which, as we will see, are necessary for the location of advanced electronics industries: the pool of electrical engineers and technicians was not large enough, military markets were simply not present in the region, New York–New Jersey was an area which had strong labor unions, and venture capital was not keen on direct industrial investment, being traditionally channeled through Wall Street. Thus, the world's greatest institution in electronics research could not generate its own manufacturing complex, in spite of its location in a Stanford-like semi-rural area, in the vicinity of the great metropolis, and close to a major university. The seeds of invention were spread by the winds of risk-taking enterprises toward more fertile ground.

A third series of cases revealing the complex dynamics in the historical evolution of semiconductors location is represented by those large companies that dominated semiconductors production from the origins of the technology, constituting isolated, self-sufficient production systems: IBM, Texas Instruments, and Motorola.

IBM started semiconductors production for its own captive market in computer-making. It organized its own production space, with three major research centers in Yorktown Heights, New York; San Jose, California; and Zurich, Switzerland, along with four large plants with integrated production and R&D facilities in East Fishkill, New York; Burlington, Vermont; Manassas, Virginia; and Endicott, New York. Three distinctive features characterize IBM's locational pattern in semiconductors manufacturing in the US.

(1) IBM controlled the rate of obsolescence of the new technology through its dominance of and consequent vertical integration in the computer market. This enabled the company to automate assembly operations from the beginning, thus reducing labor costs without having to disperse production facilities. Therefore, only a relatively small share of production took place off-shore (in semiconductors, not in computers, production of which was decentralized worldwide very early). The two plants located in semi-rural areas (Vermont and Virginia) were the smaller ones: the cost of labor does not seem to have been a major factor in IBM's location.

(2) Access to science and technology was provided by the company itself through its research personnel, network of consultants, and research contracts. Thus, physical proximity to major research centers was not an important criterion, and the location of one of the high-level centers in San Jose was mainly linked to the expansion of the early electronics complex in Silicon Valley.

(3) IBM developed an ethos of isolation and self-sufficiency in relation to its environment, with facilities settled on a campus-like principle. The location of semiconductors production was in fact determined by that of the firm's computer factories and research centers, themselves historically dependent upon the proximity to the market for business services represented by Manhattan, a market to which IBM used, in its early stages, to lease and maintain its machines, requiring daily service contact. This pattern of indifference to its environment (made easier to maintain by a paternalistic policy of high salaries and in-house career prospects which kept IBM's employees away from unions) resulted both in the location of IBM in

environments hardly typical of later high-technology agglomerations, and in the absence of a complex of technologically advanced industries springing up around IBM's production sites.

A different, and very interesting case, is offered by the development of Texas Instruments (TI) in Dallas, and the different courses taken by expansion of semiconductors production, in largely unrelated processes, in Dallas and Austin. Dallas's role in the semiconductors industry appears to be the result of the location of Texas Instruments, following a logic relatively close to IBM's isolationist tactics. In the 1930s, Texas Instruments was a small Dallas company engaged in the oil exploration business. It expanded its electronics capabilities during World War II when it converted itself to the fabrication of anti-submarine detectors. After the war, Texas Instruments decided to build on the recent discovery of the transistor in developing its research and production activities in electronic components, mainly aiming at the markets that could develop from its Navy contacts. In 1953, as mentioned above, TI hired Gordon Teal, a leading semiconductors researcher from Bell Laboratories. By 1956 TI had become a leader in silicon transistors, with most of its production geared to military markets. In 1957 Jack Kilby, from TI, co-invented the integrated circuit, simultaneously with Bob Noyce at Intel. Later, TI diversifed its production, becoming a large producer of hand calculators and computers. For a long period, it remained located in Dallas, and in nearby Texas communities, with the major exception of a new plant in Attleboro, Massachusetts, in the early 1970s.

Texas Instruments' location pattern represents a combination of IBM's type of behavior, and of the model represented by a high-technology industrial complex. TI used its isolation in Dallas to generate its own research milieu, taking advantage of its strength in the local market, only challenged by McDonnell Douglas for electronics engineers. It also used its financial and technological capacity to recruit on a nation-wide basis. Yet it did not have the resources that IBM had. So its expansion benefited from a series of factors that were related to its Dallas location: connection with military markets; cheap labor, both skilled and unskilled; a good business climate; and, since the early 1970s, the role of Dallas as a major center of air transportation. However, TI did not generate any significant spin-off activity in Dallas, because the company's policy prevented dissemination of technological know-how to suppliers and customers. To move from the growth of TI to the development of semiconductors production in Texas, then, required a diversification of the new industry and stimulation of the creation of a production complex with scientific and commercial externalities.

At this point, the focus of the action shifted to Austin, which boasted the best university in the state, and where a small number of high energy physics firms had created the germ of a high-technology industrial base. Austin eventually became a major center of semiconductors and electronics manufacturing. Its development was sparked off by the decentralization of the technical branch plants of major electronics companies, with IBM taking the lead in 1967, followed by TI itself, Lockheed, Intel, Control Data, Motorola, Rolm, Hughes, and others. Around these companies developed a network of smaller high-technology firms which provided specialized services.[14] In the 1980s, two major electronics research consortia located in Austin, attracted by good conditions offered by the state government and by the quality of the university. One was MCC, oriented toward microelectronics research and bringing together the technological and financial resources of ten major corporations. The other was SEMATECH, a billionaire facility funded by the Defense Department and operated by major corporations to develop new technologies in semiconductors manufacturing, with the aim of supporting American companies against Japanese competition in technology. Thus, while Austin started as a locus for several decentralized technical branch plants, it was able, unlike Dallas, to generated a network of ancillary companies, and to engage in the upgrading of its technological basis, with government support. Interestingly enough, then, Texas Instruments and Texas do not seem to have shared a common fate in high-technology development, although the accidental location of Texas Instruments in Dallas did generate the first electronics production complex in the state, and provided the sample of the possibilities open to Texas, should the Lone Star be willing to engage itself on the new frontier of manufacturing. Texas Instruments in Dallas, and the Austin industrial complex, represent two locational models, linked in their historical development but clearly distinct in their functional and spatial logic.[15]

An even more clear case of discrepancy between the logic of a major company and that of a region is offered by the expansion of Motorola (the second largest semiconductors company in the US) in Phoenix, Arizona. Here again, Motorola's location in Phoenix (away from its original base as an auto radio producer in Chicago) was accidental, apparently motivated by the advantages of good weather and a pleasant environment in attracting highly skilled engineers. A key factor was the personal preference of David Noble, Vice President for Electronics, who convinced the company to set up an engineering research laboratory in Phoenix in 1949. He took the risk of staking the laboratory's future on the potential of the transistor, shortly after its discovery. According to the case study on Motorola conducted by Glasmeier,[16] by the early 1970s the company was prominent in all aspects of the integrated circuit industry. It then started moving some of its assembly operations off-shore to Mexico, South Korea, and Malaysia, while setting up more advanced facilities in Austin, Texas, and in Chandler, a Phoenix suburb. Yet Motorola's know-how had no real spin-off effects in the Phoenix area. The development of electronics in Phoenix was basically linked to the location there of branch plants of large electronics companies, such as Honeywell, GTE-Microcircuits, Intel, and Sperry. Motorola, nevertheless, remained the dominant employer, with 22,000 workers in Pima County in 1984. Its employment policy included a requirement for all its employees to sign an oath barring the use by them of any knowledge generated while working for the company; in exchange, it was generous toward its skilled personnel.

Among the reasons for Motorola's isolationist attitude Glasmeier cites the following:

(1) The consolidation of purchases of large inputs within the company, precluding local linkages.
(2) The fact that much of the volume of Motorola's inputs is represented by standard materials, such as silicon and special chemicals, delivered by out-of-state suppliers.
(3) New equipment is provided by manufacturing representatives of national companies.
(4) Motorola's market is worldwide, and this limits downstream linkages in the region.

In the absence of local linkages, in both its production and its markets, and with a policy aimed at discouraging new start-ups by former employees, Motorola stands by itself in Phoenix, without being able to spur a process of locally based autonomous technological development. Because of this isolation *vis à vis* its industrial environment, it is dependent on its own scientific and manufacturing potential. Such aloofness, as Glasmeier points out, is detrimental to competitiveness in an industry that is shifting from standardized production into customized products, a trend that requires continuous innovation and strong linkages within a diversified industrial milieu.

A single company, then, however large or technologically well equipped, is not able to generate an industrial milieu reaching beyond its own organization if it does not allow spin-offs and establish backward and forward linkages. The most it can do is to lend visibility to an area which given the proper conditions for high-technology development, could then attract other industries. This is what happened in Arizona. Lacking the scientific base for autonomous innovative development, Phoenix could not become a leading technological center outside Motorola. But, being an ideal location in terms of cheap labor, a pro-business environment, and access to military markets, Arizona became a case of "mitigated success:" a very large complex of advanced manufacturing in standardized electronics products.

It is apparent, then, that the largest companies pioneering in semi-conductors production were not able to create a dynamic of development around them. When the regions where they located were eventually able to develop an advanced technological industrial base, other factors largely autonomous from the companies' presence were generally responsible. As Mutlu writes, "the heart of the American semiconductors industry beats elsewhere."[17] It beats in Silicon Valley (Santa Clara County, California), and along Route 128 near Boston. Why is this so? Although the story is now familiar, it is worthwhile emphasizing those of its elements that bear analytical significance.

In semiconductors, Boston came first. In 1958, of the 55 firms producing semiconductors, 13 were located in Massachusetts, and only 7 in California. Yet by 1967, the San Jose Metropolitan Area employed more workers in semiconductors manufacturing than all of New England. To understand how this came about it will be necessary to explain both the distinguishing characteristics of Boston and Silicon Valley in relationship to the rest of the country, and the differences between the two areas that could account for Silicon Valley's eventual dominance in spite of its late start.[18] The most important common characteristic of the two areas is the fact that they host the top research-oriented university complexes in the US, particularly in electrical engineering and computer sciences, organized around MIT and Harvard in the Boston area, and around Stanford and the University of California at Berkeley in the San Francisco Bay area. As table 2.6 shows, 43 of the 64 science-based electronics firms in the Boston area in 1965 were spin-offs of other research facilities, and 24 of these spin-offs came directly from universities, including 21 from MIT alone. In the case of Silicon Valley there is an even more direct and evident link between the origins of advanced research and manufacturing in semiconductors and the deliberate effort made by Stanford University to develop an industrial park oriented toward high technology. The business-oriented policy of Stanford in the area of electronics received a major boost from Frederick Terman, a professor of engineering who joined Stanford in the 1940s after having directed a military-oriented research program at Harvard, to become Dean and, later, Provost. Under his tenure Stanford not only built an outstanding electrical engineering program and established close ties with the electronics companies, but also played a pioneering role in the formation of a Stanford Industrial Park in 1951, providing low-rent space for 99-year leases of university-owned land to high-technology companies that would benefit, and benefit from, the university. Lockheed's aerospace research facility was one of the first to locate here. From Stanford's Faculty and student body came the majority of researcher/entrepreneurs who started up semiconductors firms in the early stages of formation of the Silicon Valley complex, either directly, or as spin-offs of companies such as Fairchild, itself a creation of William Shockley's Stanford disciples.

The second feature common to the Boston and San Francisco areas is the existence of an active and organized network of financial firms specialized in channeling venture capital toward promising small businesses. This financial sector, boosted by the Small Business Investment Act of 1958, played a major role in the development of a network of small, innovative semiconductors

Table 2.6 Origins of science-based firms in greater Boston, c.1965, by technical area[a]

Company Origin	Electronics	Communication systems, etc.	Computer hardware	Data processing	Instruments	Other	All companies
MIT	21	9	5	5	12	31	(49)
Harvard	3	1			4	4	(7)
Another local university						3	3
Non-local university						3	3
Government laboratory	2	1			1	1	3
Another company	17	4	6	2	10	28	
Total "Spin-offs"	43	15	11	7	27	100	109
Formed a subsidiary	1			1	2	9	
Formed independently	19	10	3	5	8	54	
Other	1						
Total "non-spin-offs"	21	10	3	6	10	63	78
Total, all origins	64	25	14	13	37	135	187

Source: D. Shimshoni, "Regional Development and Science Based Industry," in J.F. Kain and R. Meyer, eds, *Essays in Regional Economics* (Cambridge Mass., Harvard University Press, 1971). pp 111–14, 119. (Cited by Servet Mutlu, see note 13).
[a]A science-based firm is defined as having 20% or more of its employees in R&D. A company can be in more than one technical area. The sample covers 187 firms out of a total of 406 science-based firms in the greater Boston area c.1965.

companies in the two areas. In the early stages of the semiconductors industry, there were low entry barriers in the field of innovative technology production. Because of the relatively small amount of capital required to manufacture a product whose main value came from the knowledge embodied in it, venture capital and personal savings were the main sources of financing in the formative years of Silicon Valley and Route 128. Yet venture capital firms do not spring up in all areas. They require a local society with a profusion of individually wealthy households able and willing to invest outside the traditional avenues of the stock market. Inside knowledge about developments in a new industry, made easy to gain given the local connections of venture capital firms, is a crucial factor that can be exploited by these firms to give them the advantage over the stock exchange or the larger financial institutions. San Francisco and Boston were both particularly suited to the development of such entrepreneurial financial systems. Once the network of venture capital firms was in place, and with the development of the new industry, capital from other sources flowed into it, generally from much larger investors, in particular the pension funds. Ultimately, Wall Street based investment firms joined the rush. But the important element is that, regardless of the origins of the funds, most investment for companies starting up was channeled through the venture capital firms which became a pivotal organizational element of the electronics complex in both Boston and San Francisco.

It is important to emphasize that while venture capital is still a major element in the creation of new firms, its significance has declined in the 1980s under the new conditions of high-technology industries. On the one hand, the capital requirements for entry into the semiconductors business have dramatically escalated, because of the very great research efforts necessary to compete, and the high cost of new semiconductors manufacturing equipment; on the other hand, the downturn of the industry in the mid-1980s diverted much investment attention toward more promising ventures, including the high returns once more available in a speculative, volatile stock market. Yet the organizational linkage between a specific source of high risk–high return financing and the development of semiconductors companies was crucial in the formation of the two major industrial complexes of Santa Clara County and Boston, and set the stage for their joint development as innovative milieux.

A third characteristic common to the two areas, although by no means exclusive to them, is their position as major regional centers and nodal points in a national and international network of telecommunications and air transportation. This enables firms to develop through spatial dispersion in distant locations while maintaining the location of their headquarters and key production facilities close to the core of high-technology centers, actually forming networked milieux of production.

Another feature often cited as common to both areas, although with particular emphasis for Santa Clara County, is their pleasant environment, rich cultural life, proximity to urban amenities and outdoor recreation, and, in the case of Silicon Valley, good weather all year around. In sum, "quality of life:" a crucial asset in attracting the highly educated, demanding personnel that are so important for the development of information-based industries. Yet these images are too vague and too subjective to admit consideration of the so-called "quality of life" factor as a truly distinctive feature of high-technology complexes. Mild weather is certainly not an attribute of New England winters. Sophisticated urban atmosphere does not really describe the rather dull suburban world of Silicon Valley. Active cultural life is generally a correlate of the presence of major universities in an area. The very notion of the attributes of suburbanism as "quality of life" would be challenged by hard-core New Yorkers. While the orchards and beautiful weather of Santa Clara County or the pleasant rural atmosphere of suburban Boston could certainly be an attractive location for nature-loving professionals, a vast number of other places in the United States, including many locations relatively close to major metropolitan areas, would fit the requirements of environmental quality. In fact, the causality seems to operate in the other direction. Most places were quite beautiful before being hit by the first waves of industrialization and urbanization. So, what we are considering are *new* areas of development, which, because they rely on a highly educated, well-paid labor force, could be kept in better environmental condition than the earlier industrial areas, in spite of chemical pollution and traffic jams. Housing prices and industrial real estate prices act as a deterrent for the location of non-desirable activities or lower-income populations. Services catering to a resident population with high social status improve the quality of life in the area for people and activities able to afford it. So, the "quality of life" of high-technology areas is a *result* of the characteristics of the industry (its newness, its highly educated labor force) rather than the *determinant* of its location pattern.

One crucial characteristic of the location of the semiconductors industry that applies in specific and different ways to each of the two leading areas is its relationship to the military markets. In the early stages of the industry these markets were without doubt decisive for its development, although from the mid-1960s to the early 1980s the share of the military in semiconductors sales dramatically decreased. In the formative period of information-technology centers, the assurance of large military markets, more interested in performance than in cost, was the bedrock on which the industry set itself up. In this regard, California clearly enjoyed an advantage. The existence of a complex of large military installations inherited from the Pacific War, the proximity to weapons testing sites in the western deserts, good weather allowing for planes and missiles testing all year round, and the connection to the Los Angeles complex of airframe manufacturers created the basis for a customized relationship between the electronics industry and its military clients. All the data indicate the pre-eminence of California as recipient of the largest proportion of military contracts; Massachusetts did not have the same privileged access to military contracts and the hypothesis has often been formulated that this is what caused the displacement of the center of the semi-conductors industry toward California during the 1960s. In fact, the process seems to be more complex than this. MIT received many very large military contracts, and during World War II played a much greater military role than Stanford. The main northern California connection to weapons-oriented research, the Lawrence Livermore National Laboratory operated by the University of California, did not spin off much industrial development, given the secrecy of its research; neither did its eastern counterpart, the MIT-operated Lincoln Laboratory. It is important to distinguish between military research and military-oriented production, and only in the latter does California appear to have had a historical advantage, maybe accounting for the shift of the semiconductors industry from east to west. Yet once the high-technology complex of Massachusetts took off on its own, based more on computers than on semiconductors, large military markets were accessible to the firms located there, and by the mid-1980s the Route 128 complex was more dependent on military markets than Silicon Valley. In sum, then, Boston – and New England in general – also benefited from military contracts from the very beginning, and the firms there moved more extensively into these markets, regardless of their connection with the military establishment, once their information-generating capability was sufficiently attractive to the Defense Department. On the other hand, the concentration of the military markets in California since the 1950s may have played a role in shifting the main center of semiconductors production westwards, while Boston remained very much on top of the world map of information technology.

There is one further factor to be discussed which is often mentioned as an area of contrast between the two regions, and proposed in explanation of Silicon Valley's prominence in semiconductors: namely, the presence of strong labor unions in Massachusetts, and their absence in Santa Clara County. In fact, the empirical data do not hold up this interpretation. Santa Clara County did have a significant union presence (although proportional to its low industrial base) in the automobile, canneries, transportation, communications, and hospital sectors, *before the growth of the electronics industry.* As with the "quality of life" argument, causality works in the opposite direction: semiconductors, because of its very specific labor requirements, and because it is a new industry, is little unionized anywhere in the world, and therefore the extent of unionization is lower in those areas where it becomes dominant.[19] This interpretation seems to be confirmed by most international experience in the development of the semiconductors industry, including areas with a long labor union tradition, such as Scotland. Furthermore, semiconductors developed first in Massachusetts, in the 1950s and early 1960s, in the heyday of the unions' strength in the Boston area; by the time

Boston's loss of dominance to California at a later stage took place, industrial restructuring had already significantly eroded union power in New England, partly because of the development of the electronics industry.

Most of the locational characteristics that seem to be related to semi-conductors production, then, were common to the two major seedbeds of innovation. Those that do not appear to be distinctive of these two areas, also differ between them. Thus it becomes possible to see a tentative pattern in the development of the two locations. Their differential evolution seems to be the result partly of the more direct connection of California to military markets in the 1950s and 1960s; partly of the higher synergetic capabilities of Silicon Valley; and finally, of the ability of Silicon Valley industrialists to build a political business organization that did not face opposition in the region, unlike their counterparts on Route 128 who had to face an old industrial society with conflicting interest groups.[20] The important point, though, is the dominance of *both areas* as centers of technological innovation in the information-based manufacturing industries.

Finally, a crucial element in the locational pattern of the semiconductors industry is the sharp spatial distinction between its innovative production functions, its advanced manufacturing functions and its assembly operations. This has become the central theme for all researchers concerned with the spatial behavior of the new industries.[21] Scott and Angel have provided empirical support for this hypothesis by making a distinction between integrated circuits manufacturing establishments (an indicator of advanced research functions performed in the firm), and discrete devices manufacturing establishments (which tend to be concentrated in the standardized production of less advanced products).[22] As table 2.7 and maps 2.1 and 2.2

Table 2.7 Shipments of discrete semiconductor devices and integrated circuits in 1982 for selected states

| | Discrete devices (transistors, diodes and rectifiers) | | Integrated circuits | |
	(%)	$m	(%)	$m
Arizona	n.a.		6.3	
California	21.8		33.3	
Florida	n.a.		3.1	
Massachusetts	12.5		2.4	
New Jersey	2.4		1.0	
New York	1.9		n.a.	
Pennsylvania	12.5		n.a.	
Texas	n.a.		16.2	
Total US shipments		1102.3		7298.4

Source: US Department of Commerce, Bureau of the Census, *Census of Manufactures,* 1982 (Elaborated by Scott and Angel, see note 12).

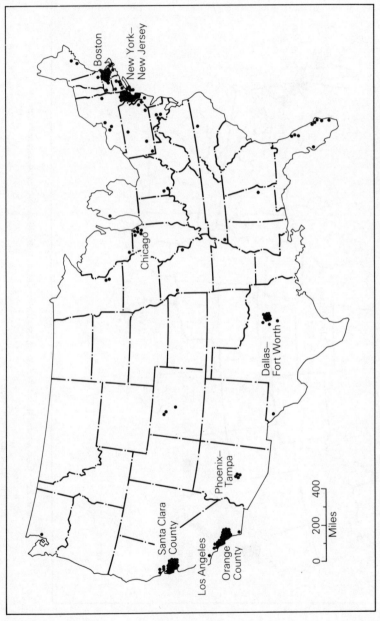

Map 2.1 Geographical distribution of discrete device manufacturing establishments in the US in 1982

Source: Scott and Angel (see note 12)

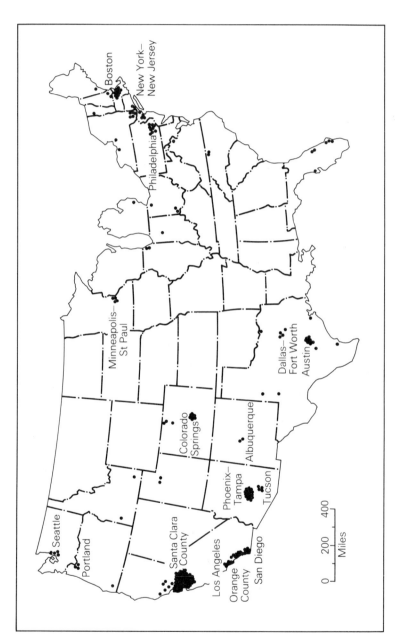

Map 2.2 Geographical distribution of integrated circuit manufacturing establishments in the US in 1982

Source: Scott and Angel (see note 12)

show, integrated circuit producers are much more selective in their location, with California, and particularly Silicon Valley, emerging as the core production center, with Massachusetts, Arizona, Texas, and, to a lesser extent, Pennsylvania, New York–New Jersey, and Colorado, holding a solid position in the new industry. Furthermore, the ability of semiconductors production to segment itself between distant spatial locations has made this industry the pioneer of worldwide decentralization; since 1962 it has moved production facilities abroad, first for assembly operations, later for testing and custom design, and in the near future wafer production will follow suit.[23]

Thus, while the semiconductors industry, spearhead of information-technology manufacturing, does show a distinct spatial pattern, that pattern's complexity, its moving boundaries, and its variation throughout its evolution, render inadequate any simplistic images or hasty generalizations, and call for a theoretically based analytical model capable of grasping the new relation-ship between production and space. Before trying to propose some elements of such an analytical perspective, it will be useful to observe, at a preliminary, descriptive level, the early location pattern of other key industries represent-ative of the current technological revolution.

Computerlands: The Spatial Location of the Computer Industry in its Early Stage

The computer industry is much larger and more diversified than the semiconductors industry. It represents the key linkage between the prod-uction of information technology and its widespread use. Unlike semicon-ductors, it has been dominated, since its beginning, by large companies such as IBM (an industrial universe by itself), Digital, Control Data, Honeywell, Sperry, Burroughs, and Hewlett-Packard, and the initial location of these firms largely determined the spatial profile of the industry in its later stages. For the purpose of this overview, we will focus on the early stages of development of the industry in the 1960s and 1970s, looking for recurring elements that might provide some clues in the process of building an empirically grounded analytical model.[24]

At first sight the evolution of the locational pattern of computer hardware production looks much like that of semiconductors. Tables 2.8 and 2.9, elaborated by Servet Mutlu, show both the autonomy of the industry in relation to the old manufacturing belt and its tendency to cluster in some areas. By ranking order, the largest concentrations of employment in computers manufacturing in the 1970s were: California, Massachusetts, Minnesota, New York, and, well behind, Florida, Texas, Pennsylvania, and Arizona. If we observe the location quotients, indicating spatial specialization, and their evolution over time, we find the largest relative concentration of employment in San Jose Standard Metropolitan Statistical Area (SMSA) as

Table 2.8 Distribution of employment in the electronic computing equipment industry (SIC 3573), by census regions

	1958[a]		1963[a]		1967		1972		1976	
	% of total employment	location quotient	% of total employment	location quotient	% of total employment	location quotient	% of total employment	location quotient	% of total employment	location quotient
US Total Employment (000s)	50.9		96.4		96.9		144.8		176.0	
New England	3.46	0.39	3.63	0.43			12.09	1.59	12.08	
Massachusetts	1.50	0.37	3.22	0.81			10.44	3.17		3.81
Boston SMSA	1.60	0.66	2.28	1.32						
Middle Atlantic	43.86	1.74	35.06	1.46	25.09	1.15	16.55	0.90	15.62	0.62
New York	38.17	3.29	27.90	2.55			13.33	1.51	9.64	1.22
New York-north-eastern New Jersey SMSA	2.34	0.22	2.90	0.28	2.43	0.25	2.97	0.35	3.37	0.46
Pennsylvania			4.85	0.57			2.07	0.28		
East-north-central			27.59	1.04	4.65	0.16	4.56	0.18		
West-north-central			12.03	2.01	19.00	6.04	14.01	2.22		
Minnesota							6.70	0.46	10.76	
South Atlantic									11.35	
Florida									4.15	2.25

Region								
West-south-central								
Texas	11.52						3.88	
Mountain								0.65
Arizona							3.08	
Pacific								5.71
California			1.51	28.25		3.47		
San Jose SMSA				10.77	15.17		12.19	14.34
San Francisco-Oakland SMSA						1.23		
Los Angeles-Long Beach SMSA	4.59	0.99		9.74	2.37		7.86	1.86
Anaheim-Santa Ana-Garden Grove SMSA							5.79	2.14
San Diego SMSA							2.19	5.334

Sources: For 1958–72, US Bureau of the Census, *Census of Manufactures*, issues for the respective years; for 1976, *Country Business Patterns* (Washington DC, US Government Printing Office, 1978) (processed). Sources gathered and elaborated by Servet Mutlu (see note 13).

[a]Includes accounting machines as well (SIC 3571).

Table 2.9 Location of plants of the main American computing equipment manufacturers

Company	1966 Location		Employment code[1]	1978 Location	
IBM	Burlington[a]	VT	D	*Computers*	
	Endicott[b]	NY	E	Endicott[d]	NY
	Kingston[b]	NY	E	Kingston	NY
	Lexington	KY	D	Poughkeepsie[d]	NY
	Poughkeepsie[b]	NY	E	Brooklyn	NY
	Rochester[e]	MN	D	Burlington[d]	MA
	San Jose[d]	CA	D		
				Small information handling systems and associated peripheral equipment	
				Boca Raton[d]	FL
				Rochester	MN
				Menlo Park[e]	CA
				Peripherals	
				San Jose[d]	CA
				Los Angeles[e]	CA
				Los Gatos[e]	CA
				Boulder[d]	CO
				Endicott[e]	NY
				Kingston[e]	NY
				Mohawsic[e]	NY
				Poughkeepsie[e]	NY
				Burlington[e]	MA
				Gaithesburg[e]	MD
				Manassas	VI
				Raleigh[d]	NC
				Tucson[d]	AZ
				Federal systems	
				Owega[d]	NY
				Manassas[d]	VI
				Gaitherburg[d]	MD
				Houston[f]	TX
				Huntsville[f]	AL
				Cape Kennedy[f]	FL
				Westlake[f]	CA
				Atlantic City[f]	NJ
				Morris Plains[f]	NJ
				Components	
				Burlington[d]	VT
				Manassas[d]	VI
				East Fishkill[d]	NY
				Endicott	NY

Table 2.9 Continued

Company	1966 Location	Employment code[1]	1978 Location	
Burroughs[h]	Detroit	MI	D	*Computers*	
	Paoli[d]	PA	B	Santa Barbara	CA
	Pasadena[d]	CA	D	Pasadena	CA
	Plainfield[c]	NY	C	Proctor	
	Plymouth	MI	E	Fredyfifrin	PA
				Dowington	PA
				Plymouth[g]	
				Peripherals	
				Tireman	MI
				Westlake	CA
				Federal systems	
				Paoli	PA
				Components	
				Carlsbad	CA
				Hollywood	CA
Control Data	Cambridge[c]	MN	A	*Computers*	
Corp.	Chatsworth[a]	CA	A	Minneapolis	MN
(CDC)	La Jolla[a]	CA	B	St Paul	MN
	Minneapolis[b]	MN	D		
	Philadelphia	PA	B	*Peripherals*	
	Rockville[a]	MN	B	Campton	KY
	St Paul	MN	D	Washington	DC
	Spring Grove[c]	MN	A	Minneapolis	MN
	Warren[a]	Mi	B		
General	Phoenix	AZ		(exited in 1970)	
Electric	Palo Alto[e]	CA			
Honeywell	Brighton	MA	D	*Computers*	
	Denver	CO	C	Brighton[d]	MA
	Lawrence	MA		Bilterica	MA
	Lowell	MA		Lawrence[d]	MA
				Phoenix[d]	AZ
				Santa Clara	CA
				(microprocessors)	
				Peripheral equipment	
				Northboro	MA
				Lawrence	MA
				Components	
				Santa Clara	CA

Table 2.9   Continued

	1966		Employment code[1]	1978	
Company	Location			Location	
National	Dayton[b]	OH	E	*Computers*	
Cash	Hawthorne[b]	CA	E	San Diego	CA
Register	Ithaca[a]	NY	D	Wichita[g]	KS
(NCR)				Columbia[g]	SC
				Terminals and	
				subsystems	
				General Purpose	
				Terminals	
				Ithaca	NY
				Retail Terminals	
				Cambridge	OH
				Millsboro	DE
				Financial Terminals	
				Dayton	OH
RCA	Camdem	NY	E	(exited in 1971)	
	Palm Beach Gardens	FL	D		
	Van Nuys	CA	D		
Sperry-Rand	Blue Bell	PA	D	*Computers*	
	Elmira[a]	NY	D	Roseville	MN
	Long Island City	NY	D	St Paul	MN
	St Paul	MN	D	Bristol	TN
	Utica	NY	D	*Small business*	
				systems and	
				peripherals	
				Bristol	TN
				Salt Lake City	UT
				Irvine	CA
Sperry-Rand				*Peripherals and*	
				memory systems	
				Cupertino	CA
				San Jose	CA
				Santa Clara	CA
				Sunnyvale	CA
				Federal systems	
				Clearwater	FL

[a]Only products belonging to SIC 35712 manufactured.
[b]Products of both SIC 35711 and 35712 manufactured.

early as 1972, in spite of the early dominance of New York and Minneapolis–St Paul in the computer industry. We also find a rapid growth of the computer industry in Massachusetts in the 20-year span between 1956 (location quotient 0.37) and 1976 (location quotient 3.81). The industry's development in Arizona and Florida is also striking, while Texas does not perform as well in computers as it does in semiconductors. While Minnesota maintains its significant share of the industry, New York's declines over time, probably because of the worldwide decentralization pattern of IBM. What is the significance of these data?

New York actually means IBM. It emphasizes the characteristics of this firm as a global company, constructing its own environment and inter-linking its different locations. The original reason for the location of IBM in New York can be traced back to the early nature of the firm's operations. Because early IBM machines were so expensive, and computer knowledge so rare, the machines were leased to businesses, with IBM providing service, maintenance, and repair. This meant that close proximity to the large concentration of business and accounting firms in New York was crucial at the beginning of the firm's history. Later, when IBM had achieved domination of the computer market, displacing the initial leader Remington-Rand (makers of the Univac-1, the first commercial computer delivered to the US Census Bureau in 1951) cash-shortage problems (linked to the leasing nature of the business) led to its decision to concentrate most of its production in the facilities it already owned, to avoid new expenditure in plant building. Because of the vertical integration of research and production functions within the firm, and the proprietary nature of its innovation, no industrial milieu developed locally around IBM in suburban New York.

The emergence of a major center of the computer industry in Minneapolis–St Paul, Minnesota, can be likened to the isolated development of semiconductor production in Dallas around Texas Instruments' pioneering activity. The origins of both Remington-Rand (later Sperry-Rand, and since 1986 Unisys), and Control Data can be traced back to a group of particularly

---

cComponents and products belonging to 357112 manufactured.
dHas both laboratories and manufacturing facilities.
eHas only laboratories.
fOperations.
gMinicomputers.
hCirca 1975.
iEmployment code: A: under 100 employees; B: 100–499; C: 500–999; D: 1,006–4,999; E: 5,000 and over.

Sources: For 1966, Fortune, Plant and Product Directory, 1966, Vol. II (1966); Wickham Skinner and David C.D. Rogers, Manufacturing Policy in the Electronics Industry (Homewood, Il, Richard Irwin, Inc., 1968), pp. 109–21; Company Annual Reports: IBM, Employment Fact Sheet, various issues; Burroughs Corporation, Burroughs Corporate Management Systems (Detroit, 1973); Burroughs in Brief (circa 1978); CDC, Committee on Corporate Social Responsibility, Our Corporation's Contributions to Solving Social Needs (1972); CDC, Contact, 3, 9 (August 1977). Sources gathered and elaborated by Servet Mutlu (see note 13).

skilled Navy engineers who created a firm after World War II: Engineering Research Associates. They set up in St Paul because through their Navy contacts they obtained financial support and infrastructural facilities from a businessman in that city. This is not to say that the location of information-technology producers is totally accidental. For instance, a key element in the development of the computer industry in the Twin Cities, founded on this initial technological basis, was the ability of the University of Minnesota to upgrade its engineering and computer sciences programs, and to provide locally the necessary personnel for the industry, overcoming the limitations of a location not outstandingly attractive measured against the traditional image standards for "quality of life." Also, Minneapolis had a long industrial tradition in miniaturization associated with the manufacture of hearing devices; and there was a penny stock market which helped to raise capital for the new companies.[25] The relative isolation of the Minnesota computer seedbed allowed companies (particularly Rand) to enjoy the lack of competition in the *local* labor market for skilled engineers and technicians, while still working within a large, diversified *national* labor market, to which they were selling a transportation- and cost-insensitive product.

As the industry grew and became more competitive, particularly with the introduction of microcomputers in the 1970s, it expanded to take in additional locations, many of which coincided with the preferred locations of semiconductors manufacturing. Again, the major exception was Minnesota, which took the course of further specialization in computers, with the major development of, among others, Cray, the leading manufacturer in super-computers. By as early as 1976 California accounted for about one-third of total US employment in computers manufacturing, with Silicon Valley alone providing about 12 per cent. In the meantime, New York – in other words, IBM – which in 1958 accounted for 38 per cent of total computer-based employment, had fallen in the ratings to offer only 9.6 per cent in 1976. Furthermore, the majority of computer employment in California, particu-larly in Silicon Valley, is made up of non-production workers, thus concentrating in a few areas the upper tier of the industry. Massachusetts also enjoyed a tremendous expansion in computer manufacturing, increasing its share of total employment from 1.6 percent in 1958 to 12 percent in 1976. [26] Texas and Arizona, on the other hand, leading states in semiconductors employment, lagged behind in the development of their computer industry, emphasizing their mixed character as states with cheap technical labor, and new high-technology centers, the latter feature being still far from dominant. While some of the new locations of the computer industry that emerged during the 1970s seemed to be directly geared toward aerospace and military markets (San Diego, Florida), the main factors that appeared to have formed its locational pattern in the growth period were:

(1) The vertical integration of semiconductor manufacturers, linking the two industries spatially, particularly after the development of the micro-

processor in 1971.[27] In the 1980s, for instance, both Silicon Valley and Route 128 have larger numbers of jobs in the computer industry (both hardware and software) than in semiconductors.

(2) The growing dependence of the industry on the availability of engineers and computer scientists.

(3) The existence of a milieu of innovation, based on the exchange of information and personnel, in areas originally organized around semi-conductors production.

While these factors were leading the computer industry toward concentration in certain areas offering access to technological information and skilled labor, other elements were working toward its worldwide decentralization. Unlike semiconductors, the computer industry decentralized part of its production from the very beginning, in search of markets rather than of cheap labor. IBM set up shop in Europe as early as the 1950s, and most other companies followed as soon as their resources enabled them to do so. Within specific countries, IBM, and other computer companies, located in semi-peripheral regions to take advantage of cheaper labor and government support for regional development – Scotland in the UK, the Midi in France.[28]

A pattern seems to emerge which is distinctive of the computer industry: concentration of research and innovation in a few centers, often vertically integrated with other electronics industries; worldwide markets, insensitive to transportation costs, penetrated by setting up local production facilities to establish a direct relationship to the clients and circumvent trade tariffs; location of assembly plants in areas with cheap technical labor relatively close to some major market. Again, as in the case of the technological origins of semiconductors technology at Bell Laboratories, it has to be noticed that the first industrial milieu of the computer industry did not develop around the pioneering research institution, in this case the University of Pennsylvania, where the first computer was produced for the Army in 1946. Though Pennsylvania does have a computer industry, as much as Texas, for instance, does, it never reached the level of other areas, such as Minnesota, Massachusetts, or California, where scientific innovation is embodied in a network of business organizations. Information-technology production, while being a science-based industry, *remains an industry*, and can only be understood as such. It is the combination of management and research that is reshaping the industrial world. Computers manufacturing does not exactly replicate the spatial distribution of the semiconductors industry; but its locational logic does.

Is Knowledge Placeless? Computer Software, Genetic Engineering, and Beyond

The computer software industry is the fastest growing information-technology sector (with under $1 billion sales in the late 1970s, it is expected to reach 20 billion by 1990), and the ultimate expression of scientific labor-intensive activity. It sells pure knowledge, fabrication being reduced to the minimum material expression, and in theory, therefore, could be an absolutely footloose activity. Yet, according to one of the few locational studies on the industry, [29] by the mid-1980s about 20 percent of employees of all 4,000 firms producing software in the US at that time was concentrated in California; and it was estimated that software employment in that state would increase by 230 percent in the decade 1985–95. Other states with a disproportionately high share of software production are Massachusetts, Texas, and Washington. Within California, although greater Los Angeles accounted for the largest proportion of total employment (about 50 percent of software jobs in California) because of the sheer size of the area, the San Francisco Bay area had the highest relative concentration of these jobs, with over 35 percent of the state total, having increased its leadership during the 1970s. And yet, most of the California software firms interviewed in the study declared that proximity to the market was not the major concern for their location. What seems to account for the location of software firms, particularly for the most technologically advanced of them, are the social and cultural characteristics of the area, in terms valued by their professional employees. According to the study cited:

Eleven out of twenty-eight interviewees said that lifestyle is of major importance. Many firms located where their founders have lived for some time before founding the firm. Many of these firms, plus some others, located where the lifestyle choices of prospective good employees converged with preferences of the firm's founders. These firms said explicitly, and many implied, that they located near available good employees. Another three mentioned "creative atmosphere" as a factor for a full range of business and cultural reasons.[30]

Nevertheless, as argued above, the notion of lifestyle is ambiguous and subjective. Lifestyle for whom? And why is a "desirable" lifestyle associated with some cities or regions rather than with others? Standard preconceptions immediately flash glittering images of sunny California, the Arizona desert, or a daring sail across Seattle Sound. Yet it is very doubtful that the southern charm of New Orleans could attract information-technology production in substantial terms, or that the spectacularly beautiful Ozarks region will ever become a major center of microelectronics. The case of the software industry gives us the chance to try to understand what "lifestyle" or "quality of life" mean in this precise context. The important point is that the reference to such subjective preferences as a determinant of the industry's location underscores the crucial importance of highly skilled scientific labor for the existence of the industry itself. Without software inventors and writers prepared to live in a particular location there would be no such industry. Here the old notion of "milieu" seems to be analytically useful. New York has always been the center of the writing and publishing industry, as Los Angeles kept its early lead in the film production business. Originally, New York's publishing success relied on its vibrant, socially diverse, big-city atmosphere, which attracted intellectuals and creators. Los Angeles was the biggest city with year-round good weather for shooting film. But in each case the original, historical rationale became less important than the milieu that blossomed and expanded over time. The more an industry depends upon information-trained, information-oriented labor, the more this labor itself depends for its development on its continuing relationship with a creative milieu able to generate new ideas and new techniques through the interaction of elements spatially clustered in its inner network. This is why the image of the wired software writer, working in his or her mountain refuge, connected to Silicon Valley over the phone line, is fundamentally a bright advertising spot from futurologists. Software production is heavily dependent on the existence of a consolidated milieu of electronics research and manufacturing, where exchange of ideas and of people is far more important than the beauty of the environment. Once a highly paid, highly educated labor pool is concentrated in a place, its members generally take care of keeping the place beautiful and of improving the social and cultural quality of the area, helped by the protective barrier of real estate prices. And even when the quality of life deteriorates, advanced electronics in general, and software writing in particular, continue to concentrate in the same areas because of the invaluable access to the milieu that generates both the information and the job opportunities. The very basis of computer software production location is an industrial research milieu, generated by an advanced electronics center, often connected to major universities, in the vicinity of a major metropolitan area containing corporate headquarters, around which business services develop.

The connection between science and industry is even more evident in what some experts like to call the "next industrial revolution:" genetic engineering.[31] It is too early to assess the potential of this field and even more problematic to understand its future connection to a new form of science-based manufacturing. In 1977, only 18,489 workers in the US were employed in "manufacturing biological products" (SIC 2831), and only a tiny proportion of these were related to genetic engineering. In 1983, the top 50 American biotechnology companies employed only 6,000 people.[32] We are witnessing the infancy of an industry that could become a major economic force.[33] In 1987, biotechnology in the US is a $3.2 billion industry.[34] The US Office of Technology Assessment predicted that between 1981 and the end of the century, genetic engineering could replace manufactured products worth $27 billion. Dr Glick, President of Genex Corporation, asserts that the market will in fact be worth around $40 billion by the year 2000. When one of the leading genetic engineering firms, Genentech, went public in 1980, its founders, most of them former academic scientists, instantly became multimillionaires. Major pharmaceutical, medical, and energy companies, as well as Wall Street firms, are actively searching for new potential investments in the field. Because the industry is still young, yet already established on solid commercial ground, high returns are expected in a market which still offers relatively low financial barriers to entry. The progression of the industry has been very fast in the last decade. In 1977 only three new biotechnology firms were started up; in 1978 there were 6, and the figure rose to 9 in 1979, 18 in 1980, and 33 in 1981.[35] During the 1980s, the new specialist firms were joined by large pharmaceutical and chemical companies which started to invest in biotechnology, either in their own research departments or by absorbing or contracting with smaller, innovative firms, and by 1987 Cetus' *Bioscan* database identified 512 biotechnology plants in the US.[36] Beyond the smokescreen of science fiction fantasies, biotechnology is becoming a major information-technology industry. The core of this industry, and the truly revolutionary technology, lies in genetic engineering.

The development process of this industry and its spatial pattern are, interestingly enough, very similar to those that characterized the most dynamic firms in semiconductors, computers, and software, namely, small businesses starting as spin-offs of major universities and medical research facilities. While the scientific origins of genetic engineering can be traced back to 1953, when the discovery of the first model of DNA was made by Crick and Watson at Cambridge University, UK, the development of the industry took place only after the discovery in 1973 by Herbert Boyer from the University of California at San Francisco and by Stanley Cohen from Stanford University, on the basis of research by Stanford biologist Paul Berg, of the techniques of gene-splicing, enabling the production of recombinant DNA. However, both the development of this science, and that of its industrial applications, were possible only because of substantial Federal government funding from the National Science Foundation and from the National Institute of Health to medical centers and universities. In 1953 Federal funding accounted for 56.9 percent of all basic research in biotechnology; this proportion increased to 66.5 percent in 1984, when over 48 percent of this went to universities.[37] Thus, the majority of the new companies leading research and production in genetic engineering originated as spin-offs from faculty members and researchers associated with the research centers that were (and are) in the forefront of this scientific field: University of California at San Francisco, Stanford University, Harvard, MIT, Cal Tech in Pasadena, California, Cold Spring Harbor Laboratories in Long Island, New York, University of California at Berkeley, and the National Institute of Health in Washington DC. The three leading firms in the developing stage of the new industry certainly fit the pattern: Genentech (south San Francisco), and Cetus (Berkeley, later moved to nearby Emeryville) were spin-offs from the Stanford and University of California scientific networks: Biogen, with its headquarters in Geneva and its main research activities in Massachusetts, was founded by Nobel Prize-winner Walter Gilbert, a Harvard professor of biology. Most of the new companies have clustered around the Boston–Cambridge area, in the San Francisco Bay area, in the New York–New Jersey area (linked to Cold Spring Harbor, to Princeton University, and to the major hospitals in New York); and around the Washington DC–Baltimore area, closely bound up with the national medical facilities located there.[38] Of all biotechnology companies in the US, 24.4 percent are located in California, 10.6 percent in Massachusetts, and 15.9 percent in New York–New Jersey.[39] Table 2.10, constructed by Hall, Bornstein, Grier, and Webber[40] provides an analysis of the locational pattern of biotechnology firms in the top seven metropolitan areas which account for 44 percent of all biotechnology operations and 60 percent of the firms founded after 1970 (these are assumed to be the most strongly science-based). The location quotients for these areas show their capacity to attract the new industry on the basis of their scientific potential. Thus, the higher location quotients are for Trenton PMSA, which includes Princeton; for Washington DC, which includes various national medical research facilities; for the San Francisco and Oakland PMSAs, which include the University of California campuses at San Francisco and Berkeley; and for the San Diego MSA, linked to the advanced biological research of the University of California at San Diego.

In fact, most of the new companies were directly created by Faculty members. A 1984 survey of 20 percent of all biotechnology companies found 345 scholars represented in these companies. Fifteen members of MIT's biology Faculty were found to have created six different companies.[41] Edward Blakely, in his study on biotechnology in California[42] reports the close links between universities, scientists, and the new biotechnology firms, with northern California accounting for 60 percent of all such firms in the state on the basis of its strong university connections. Firms in northern California are clustered around Palo Alto (site of Stanford), and in the East Bay (around Berkeley).

There is, then, ample evidence that, in the case of biotechnology and genetic engineering, universities and other scientific institutions, such as major research-oriented hospitals, are the principal determinants of location. To be more precise, they are in fact the "mining sites:" the name of the new mineral is knowledge. Universities, Harvard for example, tried to become directly involved in the new and profitable business, but were prevented from doing so by the majority of the Faculty, fearful of the dangers that commercial considerations might interfere in the conduct of scientific research. Nevertheless, business continued as usual for individual Faculty members in all research universities, who more and more often were trying to transform their discoveries into industrial development and personal gain. This evolution illustrates the increasingly intimate connection between advanced university

Table 2.10 US Biotech plants, leading metropolitan areas, 1987

	Total manufacturing plants		Biotech Plants		Post-1971 Biotech plants		Pre-1971 Biotech plants		Location quotient		
	(1982) No.	% of US total	No.	% of US total	No.	% of US total	No.	% of US total	All Biotech plants	Post-1971 plants	Pre-1971 plants
New York CMSA	39100	10.9	74	14.5	29	10.9	5	29.4	1.3	1.0	2.7
New York PMSA	19534	5.5	22	4.3	7	2.6	2	11.8	0.8	0.5	2.2
Newark PMSA	4175	1.2	17	3.3	8	3.0	1	5.9	2.8	2.6	5.0
San Francisco CMSA	10526	2.9	65	12.7	42	15.8	2	11.8	4.3	5.4	4.0
Oakland PMSA	2883	0.8	21	4.1	13	4.9	1	5.9	5.1	6.1	7.3
San Francisco PMSA	3095	0.9	25	4.9	17	6.4		0.0	5.6	7.4	0.0
San Jose PMSA	3326	0.9	16	3.1	11	4.2	1	5.9	3.4	4.5	6.3
Boston-Lawrence NECMA	6798	1.9	41	8.0	28	10.6	1	5.9	4.2	5.6	3.1
Philadelphia CMSA	8700	2.4	32	6.3	19	7.2	0	0.0	2.6	3.0	0.0
Philadelphia PMSA	7495	2.1	17	3.3	12	4.5		0.0	1.6	2.2	0.0
Trenton PMSA	454	0.1	11	2.1	6	2.3		0.0	16.9	17.9	0.0
Washington MSA	2388	0.7	24	4.7	17	6.4	2	11.8	7.0	9.6	17.6
San Diego MSA	2522	0.7	18	3.5	13	4.9			5.0	7.0	0.0
Seattle–Tacoma CMSA	3669	1.0	14	2.7	10	3.8		0.0	2.7	3.7	0.0
Seattle PMSA	3077	0.9	13	2.5	10	3.8		0.0	3.0	4.4	0.0
USA total	358061	100.0	512	100.0	265	100.0	17	100.0	1.0	1.0	1.0

Source: Hall, Bornstein, Grier and Webber (see note 36).

research and the hottest stocks in the market.[43] Scientific knowledge, at least in some key areas, is now clearly a directly productive force and the source of major profits. In other words, science itself has become an industry.

Thus, in this the purest example of an information technology industry, we observe that the key element in the development of genetic engineering is its relationship to a scientific milieu; a milieu which, in this particular case, itself developed an initial market through government-sponsored contracts to health research institutions.[44] This has clearly been the case in its early stages; will we observe a similar process in the more mature phases of the industry? There are reasonable grounds for hypothesizing that this will be the case for research laboratories, which will either be located in the vicinity of a national or international research community, or absorbed into the closed world of some pharmaceutical or agricultural giant, ready to form a kind of "Bio-Bell Laboratories." The fabrication and diffusion of the products generated by this industry will have no specific space. Its impact will be felt across a broad spectrum of manufacturing and agricultural activities; there will also be applications in energy and, above all, in health services and medical sciences. The real output of genetic engineering, as for electronics, is less a product than a process. In the latter case, it is the process of symbolic information; in the former, the process of information inscribed in living matter.

From specifically located seedbeds of information-technology production emerges a new, pervasive, placeless logic of industrial activity, transforming the economy, the workplace, and the consumer markets, without attaching itself to a particular location. New information technologies organize the space of production along a hierarchy of activities and functions, made up of *networks* and *flows*, which takes the social division between intellectual and manual labor to its extreme limit. To understand this process, whose empirical manifestations we have surveyed without actually explaining, we need a more systematic, explicit, analytical framework to enable us to unveil the logic underlying the formation of the new industrial space.

Investigating the Spatial Pattern of Information-Technology Industries: An Analytical Framework

As argued in chapter 1, the core of the current process of technological change lies in the invention, development, and use of new information technologies. Accordingly, the industries producing information-technology devices are the ones responsible for the new historical trends in the process of restructuring industrial location. Information-technology industries constitute a specific form of productive organization, deriving their specificity from the distinctiveness of their raw material (information), and from the singularity of their product (process-oriented devices with applications across the entire spectrum of human activity).[45] The analytical perspective put forward here contends that the specific spatial pattern of information-technology industries is the result of these two fundamental characteristics. This is not to deny the importance of other factors, such as profit-seeking as the ultimate principle of any capitalist corporation, in determining spatial behavior. Rather, it is to highlight the technological means by which such profit can be obtained as the distinctive feature of the new industries which sets them apart from the old line manufacturing industries. In other words, technology mediates the relationship between the economic rationality embodied in the firm and the attributes of a given space, thus determining locational patterns and the resulting spatial structure.

Let us explore the specific connections between these two fundamental characteristics of information-technology industries and their spatial requirements. First, the reliance on information of these industries means that their basic factor of production is the quality of labor; more precisely, of their scientific and technical labor.[46] Furthermore, this labor requires an organizational environment in which its innovative capacity can be utilized to the full. There are two levels to this organizational environment: the micro-environment of the firm or institution in which the process of innovation occurs; and the macro-environment formed by the network of interactive relationships among innovative organizations and individuals that generate added value in the process of information creation as an outcome of the interaction between the producers.[47] We will call this macro-environment a *milieu*, understood as a specific set of social relationships of production and management, based upon some common instrumental goals, generally sharing a work culture, and generating a high level of organizational synergy.[48] If this analysis is correct, then the spatial logic of information-technology industries will be determined in the first place by the location of innovative labor *and* by the territorial conditions for the formation of innovative milieux.

The second major characteristic of the new industries, namely their production of *process-oriented devices*,[49] has two major spatial consequences. To some extent they contradict each other, underlining the complexity of the spatial logic we are trying to analyze. On the one hand, since the value of the industry's output depends largely on the processing capability embodied in the product, regardless of transportation costs or of general conditions of production, information-technology industries can locate almost anywhere, provided that they keep their access to the sources of innovation, namely innovative labor and a supportive environment.[50] On the other hand, since the effectiveness of the processing devices depends on their capacity to adapt to the users' needs, the general trend in information technology is toward customized devices, and consequently its spatial logic will increasingly depend upon the location of its users. This does not necessarily mean that the industry will have to locate close to its customers: for instance, if an industry has a worldwide market for its customized product, its main locational constraint will be good access to a telecommunications network and to air transportation.[51] If a firm works instead for a very specific client requiring continuous interaction on the use, maintenance, and specification of the processing device (as is frequently the case in defense-related information technologies), then spatial proximity does become a locational requirement. Thus, what seems to characterize the industry is not so much a general, footloose indifference to location as a greater dependence on the spatial characteristics of its markets, because of the intimate relationship between the product of the industry and the process of its users.[52]

A third fundamental spatial implication stems from the *combined* effect of these two basic characteristics: it is the very distinct *internal segmentation of the production process*.[53]

On the one hand, the production of information can be separated from its material support. From this follows a sharp division of labor within the industry, leading to very different requirements in type of labor, and therefore, at least potentially, to different locations for each type, or labor "pool." For instance, in the case of semiconductors manufacturing, so widely discussed in the literature, there are five distinct operations, which can easily be differentiated in time and space[54]: research and design of the circuit, which requires, in general, advanced research engineers and scientists; mask-making, that is, engineering the circuit that will go into the chip and reducing it through lithography, an operation requiring skilled engineers and technicians; wafer fabrication (diffusion), a process in which the circuits receive their material support in the form of wafers which undergo a series of chemical treatments before being divided into individual chips, a process that requires skilled manual workers and quality-control supervision; assembly of the chips to form electronic components (integrated circuits or discrete semiconductor devices), a routine, labor-intensive operation, that can either be performed by unskilled workers or easily automated; finally, testing, a capital-intensive, widely automated process, the main problem of which is quality control. The more pronounced in the electronics industry is the shift from standardized production to custom-designed devices, the more highly skilled, state-of-the art operations increase their strategic importance in the overall production process; yet in all cases, and in all products of the industry, there is a need for material production. This combination leads to very sharply differing labor requirements for each stage of the work process, and allows for separate and distinct organizational environments for each operation. Although in some other information-technology industries the separation between different phases in the production process is less clear than in semiconductors, there remain, as a general trend, basic divisions between knowledge-based research and design, advanced manufacturing, unskilled assembly work, and testing. Some industries, such as computer software and genetic engineering, are almost purely information-production processes, to the point where the very notion of manufacturing loses meaning. Other industries, on the contrary, retain a strong component of skilled factory work; this is the case in robotics and in automated machine-tool industries.[55] In all cases, it is the specific combination of creating information-processing devices and fabricating their material support that determines the process of production in the industry and therefore its labor requirements, which constitute a major determining factor of its location pattern.

Given this strict internal division of labor within the industry, the process-oriented characteristic of its product allows for the spatial differentiation of the various distinct production functions. This is in the first place because of the low sensitivity of the industry to traditional factors influencing location, such as transportation costs or access to bulky raw materials, which makes possible a multilocational pattern in which each production function maximizes its own particular relationship to the spatial conditions of production (particularly labor) or to the location of its markets.[56]

Secondly, information-technology industries are the pioneers in using their products in their own processes of production and management, thereby taking advantage of breakthroughs in automation, telecommunications, and miniaturization of components, to enable themselves to maintain the functional unity of production and management without requiring spatial proximity between the different segments of the organization.[57]

From these three fundamental characteristics of information-technology industries stem four basic spatial processes which I contend to be distinctive of these industries in reflecting a new form of production and a new type of product. These four processes are:

(1) A sharp spatial division of labor within the industry, with each phase of production having distinct labor and functional requirements that translate into specific and different spatial manifestations.

(2) The domination of the industry's technical, social, and spatial hierarchy by the functions of information generation, structured around milieux of innovation which possess specific spatial attributes and are concentrated in a few, exclusive locations.

(3) A process of decentralization of different production functions, reproducing the hierarchical pattern of the industry's internal structure and of its spatial logic.

(4) With the exception of the higher-level innovative milieux, information-technology industries are characterized by extreme flexibility in their actual locations. This flexibility is the result of the close relationship of the industry with its markets, under the conditions of continuous variation in the location of those markets.

The trend toward customized production and the pervasiveness of the industry's products combine to favor a general pattern of centralized generation of technological innovation and decentralized application of the products embodying the processes resulting from such technological discoveries. Figure 2.2 attempts to represent schematically the system of relationships proposed in this analytical framework.

Information-technology industries do not, then, share one single locational pattern; yet they do collectively express a distinctive spatial logic, in a rather

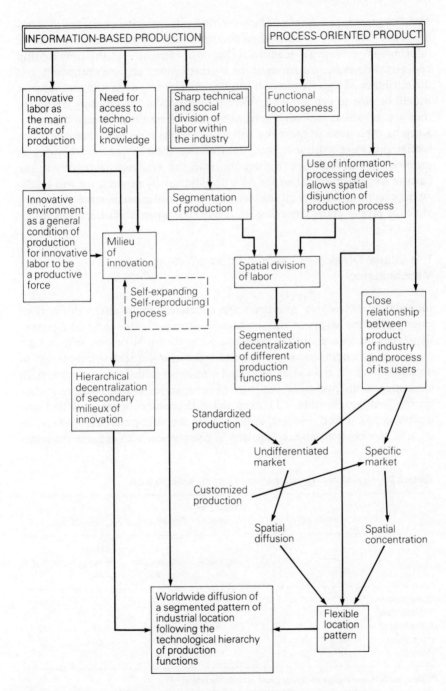

Figure 2.2 System of relationships between the characteristics of information-technology manufacturing and the industry's spatial pattern

complex process of interaction between their fundamental characteristics and the basic processes of the economic structure. The actual location of information-technology manufacturing will depend on the relationship between the specific functions of the industry, along the lines proposed, and the attributes of a given space. If this analytical framework is of any value, it should be able to explain why different segments of the industry are where they are, as well as to predict general trends in their future spatial dynamics. Keeping these goals in mind, we will try to address separately each one of the spatial processes outlined here, confronting their hypothetical logic, as proposed in this analytical framework, with the available evidence. On the basis of the results obtained for each specific spatial process, we will finally attempt to bring together all the elements in a broader perspective which may yield the profile of the emerging relationship between production and space.

The Spatial Division of Labor in Information-technology Manufacturing

Information-technology industries are characterized by sharp distinctions among different stages of the production process.[58] This internal differentiation results in a distinctly polarized occupational structure, with a high proportion of engineers, scientists, and technicians, a sizable proportion of unskilled workers, and a relatively small number of skilled manual workers, in opposition to the pyramidal structure of occupations in traditional manufacturing.[59] Although table 2.11 does not differentiate between skilled and unskilled production workers, it does show the substantial over-representation of professionals and technicians in comparison with average manufac-

Table 2.11   High-technology occupational structure: selected areas

	All US		Massachu-setts	Silicon Valley	Santa Cruz	
	High-tech (%)	Manu-facturing (%)	High-tech (%)	High-tech (%)	Manu-facturing (%)	High-tech (%)
Management	11	7	9	13	7	9
Professional/ Technical[a]	29	12	34	43	14	32
Production	48	70	40	30	68	50
Clerical	12	11	17	14	11	9

[a]Sales workers are included under professional/technical
Sources: Gordon and Kimball, table VI (see note 3); Carnoy (see note 60).

turing industries.[60] In addition it shows a significantly higher proportion of technical labor in the areas with a higher level of technological sophistication, Silicon Valley and Massachusetts. This polarized occupational structure is also characterized by divisions of gender and ethnicity, with women and ethnic minorities being significantly over-represented in unskilled production jobs.

The internal differentiation of the work process, and thus of labor requirements, in information-technology industries, results in a correspondingly sharp spatial differentiation of the various stages of the production process.[61] Higher-level functions tend to be concentrated in certain privileged locations, attracting to those areas the upper tier of the labor force, while assembly functions, employing unskilled labor, are scattered over more and varied locations. Advanced manufacturing occupies an intermediate position, generally clustered around innovation functions in the early stages of the industry, later decentralizing to specific locations on the basis of isolated pools of skilled manual workers, in areas not too far away from the firm's innovative center. This pattern applies to both units of production within a given firm, and to different firms, with their respective locations following the technological hierarchy between the firms. Spatial differentiation occurs among regions, countries, metropolitan areas, and even among specific locations within the same metropolitan area. The technical and social division of labor in information-technology industries not only allows for their spatial segmentation, but actually causes it. Furthermore, it is my hypothesis that the spatial logic of each different segment of the industry not only differs from, but contradicts, that of the others. In other words, the spatial characteristics required by each stage of production and by each type of labor force tend to be reciprocally exclusive, leading to extremely different spatial manifestations of information-technology manufacturing. The new industrial structure will be characterized by locational sprawl, distinct spatial segments, with functional interconnections between the elements of the structure maintained by the means of communication links. Before elaborating on the consequences of this spatial logic, let us examine the evidence supporting the hypothesis of the spatial division of labor in information-technology industries.

First, we will try to assess whether there exists a spatial differentiation among high-technology industries according to their specific occupational levels: namely, are high-technology industries characterized by higher technical levels in their occupational profile disproportionately concentrated in some areas? Amy Glasmeier has tested this hypothesis by conducting a statistical analysis of the distribution of nine occupational categories within five key high-technology industries among the 50 states, in 1977 and 1980.[62] The industries studied were chemicals, non-electrical equipment, electrical equipment, transportation equipment, and professional and scientific instruments. According to Glasmeier:

The results of the analysis for all five industries indicate that the hypothesized spatial division of labor is confirmed in the occupational distribution of employment in high-tech industries. Concentrations of technical, administrative, and professional workers, are present in similar places, while production workers are found in different locations. In general, these results confirm the hypothesis that workers engaged in design and prototype activities are spatially associated with professional and administrative employees . . . The sample high-tech industries also exhibit the tendency for assembly workers to be segmented from both production and technical workers . . . Service workers are found in relatively constant proportions across locations. High-technology industries clearly exhibit a spatial division of labor. States with high proportions of technical and administrative jobs have low proportions of production workers.[63]

Secondly, what is the evidence in support of my contention that there is a spatial differentiation among functions within the same industry, according to the technological level of these functions? Scott and Angel have provided the most accurate empirical test to date of this hypothesis, by comparing the structure and behavior of semiconductor firms located in Silicon Valley to that of firms located in other areas.[64] The group of firms located in Silicon Valley, they found, tended to have a higher percentage of employees engaged in R&D activities, as well as to produce semiconductor wafers with a larger average diameter (an indicator of technological sophistication in the production process). In addition, Scott and Angel performed a similar analysis for two different groups of semiconductor companies: discrete device producers and integrated circuit producers. In general, their earlier findings hold good only for the integrated circuit producers, meaning that the spatial hierarchy of production between Silicon Valley and other locations applies only in the technologically advanced segment of the industry. In other words, the more information-based an industry is, the clearer is the trend toward a hierarchical pattern of segmented location. A general summary of Scott and Angel's findings is presented in table 2.12. As they write:

The correlation coefficients forcefully corroborate our assessment of Silicon Valley as a center of research-intensive, and engineering-intensive forms of leading edge semiconductors production, and above all, complex unstandardized device production. Semiconductor production outside Silicon Valley is more likely to involve high-volume routinized manufacture of standardized integrated circuits and low-technology discrete devices.[65]

This analysis takes one step further the logic of the spatial division of labor in information-technology manufacturing. Not only are there different locations for different functions, but the spatial distribution of the industry follows a very discontinuous pattern, with the concentration of high-level functions in a few locations, most notably Silicon Valley in the case of semiconductors. On the other hand, less sophisticated functions are increasingly dispersed, both nationally and internationally. Yet this locational sprawl must be interpreted within the framework of the technical division of labor within the industry, as shown in maps 2.1 and 2.2, where integrated circuit plants are shown to follow a more concentrated and selective pattern of location than less technologically advanced discrete semiconductor devices.

Other studies of semiconductor manufacturing location at different points in time all reveal the same tendencies; in particular, research conducted by Michael Storper, by Anna Lee Saxenian, and by Servet Mutlu.[66] These studies show that, in addition to their inter-regional division of labor, information-technology industries also pioneered the new international division of labor. There is a vast research literature on this topic, showing how information-technology industries, particularly semiconductors, were among the first to divide their production process over a worldwide variety of locations.[67] Taking advantage of miniaturization, of the light weight of the devices produced, and of advances in air transportation and telecommunication networks, assembly operations in semiconductors and computers began to be relocated offshore in the early 1960s, particularly to cheap labor areas in south-east Asia, and later Mexico. While internationalization of production by multinational corporations was nothing new, the distinguishing feature of this phenomenon was the separation worldwide of the different individual operations of one particular production process within one firm, giving rise to the idea of the "world factory." Although some experts considered this process to be characteristic of the earlier stages of the industry, and expected widespread automation of assembly lines to lead to the "relocation back north" of most plants, most researchers disagree, for reasons we will discuss below. And indeed, the data for the past twenty years show an

Table 2.12 Percentage distribution of semiconductor establishments according to location and type

	Silicon Valley		Non-Silicon Valley		Total	
	Sample[a] (%)	Population[b] (%)	Sample (%)	Population (%)	Sample (%)	Population (%)
Discrete device producers	8.3	5.6	28.3	38.3	36.6	49.3
Integrated circuit producers	31.7	25.3	31.7	30.8	63.4	56.1
Total	40.0	30.9	60.0	69.1	100.0	100.0

[a]Sample of 60 establishments.
[b]The population consists of the 517 establishments (out of a total of 590) that were classifiable by type.
Source: Scott and Angel (see note 12).

increasing tendency for the production of US electronics firms to be located offshore.[68] Information-technology manufacturing is in fact spearheading the formation of a new hierarchical space of production, spread across the world, segmenting countries and differentiating locations, with the connections necessary to the economic and functional logic of the process maintained by the new means of communication. This new industrial space is represented by a variable geometry as firms, regions, and countries move up and down the technological ladder.

Spatial division of labor in these industries also affects labor sub-markets and plant location within individual metropolitan areas. Real estate prices and residential segregation create spatially distinct labor markets and work sub-cultures, as shown by Saxenian[69] and by Keller[70] for Silicon Valley, and by Storper[71] for the "ghetto–peasant worker" communities created in Oregon around decentralized electronics production facilities. Firms' research and design centers tend also to be spatially separate from the main production facility, even when they are in the same area. Yet with a continuous process of deeper spatial differentiation at the inter-regional and international levels taking place, there is a trend toward internal homogenization of technological production functions within each metropolitan area. For example, while what assembly work remains in Silicon Valley tends increasingly to be automated, gradually lowering the proportion of unskilled immigrant workers in its labor force (while employing increasing numbers of foreign *engineers*), the new industrial communities in the western United States resulting from decentralization, such as those analyzed by Storper in Oregon, tend increasingly to specialize in the middle-to-bottom end of the production process.

The reasons behind this strict spatial division of labor in information-technology industries seem to stem from three main factors:

(1) The development of new information technologies, focused on processes of programmable manufacturing and on transmission of information, creates the material conditions for the decentralized location pattern of the industries themselves. Miniaturization of devices means low weight and low transportation costs. Computer automation of manufacturing makes possible high-quality standardization of parts than can be assembled anywhere. Computer-aided flexible manufacturing enables production to be adjusted to market requirements without the different production functions being spatially proximate. Telecommunications and on-line information systems allow for coordination of management of spatially distant units. A dense air transportation network makes possible when necessary quick personal contacts, as well as shipments of equipment and output.

(2) Social control of labor has always been a major condition for the competitiveness of any industry, but it is even more important for information-technology industries whose fate depends on innovation and on the

appropriate timing of such innovation. Any major disturbance in the labor process will slow down the pace of innovation and could result in the firm's loss of its competitive edge. Given the sharp differentiation of the various segments of labor within the industry, processes of social control for each segment are correspondingly different, requiring distinct social spaces for their implementation. In other words, what helps to integrate the high-level engineers into the company's life and work is not necessarily what would be appropriate (or affordable) to achieve similar bonds for workers in isolated rural communities, for immigrants in the US, or for Third World women in offshore locations. Workers' integration into firms depends above all on work culture. In the case of information-technology industries, the differentiation of the labor process into distinct stages leads to a similar differentiation in work sub-cultures, and each of these is likely to be more effective when operating in a specific, isolated space.

(3) Finally, different functions of production and segments of labor in the industry exclude each other in spatial terms, because the upper level of the industry is so valuable, so unique, so irreplaceable, that the locations where such labor performs its functions tend to increase dramatically in quality, and even more in value and price, so becoming exclusive and ruling out the location there of lower-level functions and of strategically less important labor. The mechanisms at work in this process are, on the one hand, real estate prices, and on the other hand, residential and industrial zoning regulations. Local governments, supported by well-to-do residents and business groups (sometimes opposed to each other), tend to draw a restrictive line *vis-à-vis* the activities that are welcome in the privileged land around the high-level information-technology industrial centers. Once a given area of land is declared privileged, demand explodes while supply is limited. Thus, the market achieves the exclusion of lower-level workers – sometimes too fast, outpacing the gradual upgrading of the industrial complex. At the same time, in the less desirable areas, with a low-skilled labor force and scarce technological capabilities, real estate prices are low, representing no barrier to growth, and local governments strive to lure into their area industries labeled "high-technology," regardless of their true technological level. In this way, the spatial division of labor is self-reproductive and self-expansionary. Increasingly valuable spaces first segregate and later expel functions and people that are not worth the cost of keeping them in the gold mines of our technological age. As jobs and economic growth depend more and more upon the performance of high-technology industries, localities fighting for their survival try to compensate for their lack of technological skills by offering convenient conditions for the bottom end of the production process. Functional hierarchy and social segregation are fundamental features of the new industrial space.

The analysis presented here has considerable implications for the method of investigating the relationship between information-technology manufacturing and the spatial structure of the industry. On the one hand, we cannot establish any such relationship until we have decided which particular functions of the industry we are considering, since each stage of the production process has a specific pattern of location, sometimes contrary to that of other stages. On the other hand, if there is one factor common to all elements of the process of high-technology manufacturing, it is precisely their spatial differentiation, along with the fact that their distinct locations are functionally connected by a social and technological hierarchy. The process of industrial decentralization of information-technology producers will tend to reproduce this spatial hierarchy on a larger scale. We will now turn to analyze the spatial pattern specific to each stage of production in the information-technology industries, focusing on the dynamics between concentration and decentralization of their different functions.

Milieux of Innovation

The higher-level production functions of information-technology industries are concentrated in a few selected areas which we will term *milieux of innovation*.[72] By a milieu of innovation we understand a specific set of relationships of production and management, based on a social organization that by and large shares a work culture and instrumental goals aimed at generating new knowledge, new processes, and new products. Although the concept of milieu does not necessarily include a spatial dimension, I will argue that, in the case of information-technology industries, spatial proximity is a necessary material condition for the existence of such milieux, because of the nature of interaction in the innovation process.

There are two different (albeit inter-related) questions concerning the spatial dimension of innovative milieux: these concern their genesis and their structure. That is, how and why they are formed in particular locations? and why and how do they continue to function as specific units of production and innovation?

In terms of the first question, that is, their coming into existence, the informational milieux of innovation are not very different from other industrial milieux of our recent past. They result from the spatio-temporal convergence of the three fundamental elements of production: labor, capital, and raw material.[73] The specific characteristics of the new industries result from the specific characteristics of these three elements in this particular case. Their raw material is information. Technical labor in these industries, because of its unique capacity for symbol processing, will require special methods of generation and reproduction. The nature of this industrial activity will also influence the type of capital invested during the formative stage of the innovative milieu: given the high risk of the investment, depending upon relatively unpredictable technological discoveries, it will be either of a venture capital nature (although not necessarily managed by venture capitalists), expecting high returns, or capital invested on a long-term profit-seeking strategy by a major corporation or institution engaged in a quest for technological superiority, and able to afford a loss on the investment. Different sources of technological and scientific information, of scientific and technical labor, and of adequate capital supply, as well as the combination of all three elements, will determine the different forms taken by milieux of innovation and consequently, their location patterns.

The basic raw material on which the new industries work is innovative technological information. Such information can be found in four different types of organizational environments that are not mutually exclusive:

(1) Leading universities and higher education institutions.
(2) Government-sponsored R&D centers.
(3) Corporate R&D centers linked to technologically advanced large corporations.
(4) A network of R&D centers in an established industrial complex which collectively produce innovative research, creating the critical mass of knowledge necessary to become an autonomous source of generation of technological discovery. These complexes take two forms:
    (a) a traditional manufacturing complex that moves into information technology to keep pace with technological change, as is the case with the aerospace and defense industries;
    (b) the new industrial innovative milieux of information-technology producers, once they become established as such on the basis of any of the sources of information cited above.

The first condition for the development of information-technology industries is access to one of these sources of innovative information. Yet while this is naturally the fundamental condition of production for the new industries, it alone cannot account for the information of an innovative *industrial* milieu since, in principle, the diffusion and communication of science and technology do not require spatial proximity. Nevertheless, as we will see, the spatial dimension becomes an important material condition in linking the source of information to other key components of the production process, namely innovative labor and high-risk capital.

The second major element required for the formation of a milieu of innovation is a large pool of scientific and technical labor. It is important to note that this factor cannot be equated with the first one, access to information, even if information is most often embodied in labor, for there are situations in which one could exist without the other. Examples of this are an isolated research center without connection to a large labor market, such as Los Alamos or Sandia Laboratories in Albuquerque, New Mexico; or a large pool of good quality engineers with little access to companies or institutions able to generate major technological discoveries, such as may be found in some mid-western industrial areas whose high-quality engineering schools export their best graduates to the advanced centers of industrial innovation in the north-east or California. The scientific and technical labor market usually grows up on the basis of major academic institutions, such as the complexes around MIT–Harvard–University of Massachusetts in the Boston area, Stanford–Berkeley–UC San Francisco in the San Francisco Bay area, or Cal Tech–UCLA–USC in Los Angeles. The development of the labor market around the initial nucleus of high-quality professional schools is fostered by a number of conditions which enhance the quality of life for skilled labor, making it attractive to migrate to such areas of opportunity. Among these conditions, good housing and urban services, high-quality educational facilities and urban amenities, including provision for sophisticated leisure and consumption requirements, seem to be important elements in continuing attraction of engineers and scientists to a given area. These conditions relating to the "quality of life" are an important factor in maintaining the attractiveness of a milieu of innovation; however, they are the consequence, rather than the cause, of a sophisticated labor market, as argued above. Furthermore, should they deteriorate, the ultimate fate of the milieu of innovation still depends upon its industrial vitality. For instance, the process of environmental deterioration in Silicon Valley, its skyrocketing housing costs and the gridlock of its highway system, while creating increasing difficulties for residents, have not destroyed its appeal for the most highly qualified electronics engineers from all over the world. As in all truly innovative milieux, the best labor concentrates in the places "where the action is," then trying to make its environment as pleasant as possible. The main factor in the formation of a large technical and scientific labor market is the presence of job opportunities in the most advanced segments of the industry, which amounts to saying that the main factor in attracting highly skilled labor is the location of the milieu itself. The labor requirements for the formative stages of the milieu are generally fulfilled by the presence of good-quality academic and vocational institutions able to train a large pool of skilled personnel. Such institutions also tend to be located in areas of high social status and good urban amenities, able to attract and retain highly valued scientific and technical labor.

The third major element conducive to the formation of an innovative industrial milieu is the availability of investors ready to risk capital in an always uncertain discovery-based activity. While not all information-technology industries can be considered high-risk investments, the early stages of milieux of innovation depend upon the expansion of companies whose products, and even whose future as businesses, are somewhat unpredictable.

These particular features of the investment process lead to three specific sources of funding for the industry:

(1) Long-term investment in R&D by a large company whose assets and position in the market enable it to rationalize its returns over a long span of time, compensating for potential monetary losses with the technological edge which, overall, the company will enjoy as a result of its investment in research.

(2) Direct investment or indirect financing by government in R&D aimed at performance of the product, regardless of cost, as, for example, in the case of Department of Defense subsidies for the development of new technologies for military purposes. There is also a more subtle, and in fact more important way, in which government interests in technological innovation affect the financial basis of the new industries: this is by providing large-scale, secure, profitable markets for untested technological products. While this is not, technically speaking, a source of capital, guaranteed markets eliminate risk, transforming high-risk investments into low-risk ventures and allowing firms to use standard financial sources in spite of the high-risk nature of their business.

(3) The third, and originally the most popular source of high-risk, high-return financing for innovative firms is venture capital, either formal, through investment firms, or informal, that is, from individuals staking their savings on the opportunity represented by a promising start-up. Some high-risk investments (which, for the present analytical purpose, can be taken to mean venture capital) are also made by local commercial banks seeking a high return on the basis of their direct knowledge of a new industry. Without venture capital and the network of financial intermediaries between capital firms and new information-technology companies, much of the dynamism of the new industrial milieux would have never existed. Nevertheless, it is important to differentiate between the functions and origins of venture capital during the initial stages of innovative milieux on the one hand and, on the other, in the later, more mature phases of these industrial areas. In the milieux' formative stages, venture capital firms develop on the basis of the ability of their financial entrepreneurs to identify promising industrial ventures, and to spread the risk among a plurality of small investors betting on the expectation of high returns. In the mature stage, when larger investments are required, and the existence of an established milieu of innovation makes the investment safer, venture capital firms tend to be the financial channels through which major investors, such as pension funds and investment banks, often operate. What is crucial in both cases is the presence of a network of financial intermediaries specializing in transferring resources to the new industries, on the basis of a degree of inside knowledge as to the potential of specific technological projects. In this fundamental sense, the network of

venture capital firms is an indispensable part of the industrial milieu itself.[74]

The important implication for our research purposes is that while capital flows are placeless, the organizational conditions of high-risk investment do have a substantial spatial component: large corporations finance their own research facilities, whose location depends upon the internal logic of the corporation; government contracts, particularly for military expenditure, are biased toward certain regions and metropolitan areas; and venture capital, as argued above, depends upon the existence of a local network of financial firms, itself the expression of a wealthy, entrepreneurial society. Let us examine in some detail the specific spatial implications of these different modes of financing the development of innovative milieux.

Large corporations tend to locate their R&D laboratories close to their headquarters, creating a symbiotic relationship between strategic management and high-level industrial innovation.[75] This is the case for IBM in suburban New York, for ATT and Bell Laboratories in New Jersey, Texas Instruments in Dallas, Motorola in Phoenix, Sperry-Rand, Control Data, and Cray, in Minneapolis-St Paul, Hewlett-Packard in Palo Alto, and so on. It is also the case that, given the global reach of these corporations, they tend to spread their research facilities over a few different locations: for example, IBM's laboratories in San Jose and Zurich are technological centers in their own right. In all cases, the spatial implication of this form of financing, with its corollaries of secrecy and proprietary information (including ATT's Bell after ATT's divestiture) is the confinement of innovation within the boundaries of a given corporation, thus closely following the corporation's own spatial pattern. Considering the broader implications of this trend for the spatial structure of the industry, the connection between headquarters location and R&D centers accounts for the formation of innovative industrial milieux in the largest metropolitan areas, such as New York or Philadelphia.

Concerning direct government financing and indirect financing through guaranteed markets, particularly in defense, there is ample evidence of regional concentration in the distribution of Federal, including military, expenditure, in favor primarily of California and the south-west, but also including Boston, Seattle, Philadelphia, New York–New Jersey, and St Louis among the top beneficiaries of defense and aerospace research funding.[76] It is vital to keep in mind that defense spending favors regions and cities, for cultural, political, functional, and strategic reasons, only to the extent to which these areas are able to provide valuable technological innovation. The existence of a financial source, including defense spending, is an important but not sufficient condition in the formation of an innovative milieu. In other words, defense funding follows the source of information, although it is a very important factor in the development of an original source of technological information into a fully fledged milieu of innovation.

Venture capital is also dependent upon local social and economic characteristics, particularly in the early stages of development of the network of financial intermediaries.[77]A combination of three elements seems to account for favorable conditions for venture capital firms to develop:

(1) A wealthy area with abundance of upper-income households able and willing to invest some of their savings in high-return placements.
(2) An area that is a significant financial center but has no stock exchange or commodities market, since the existence of such powerful financial networks tends to siphon off regional savings from local financial institutions. In other words, what is required is a financial center important enough to generate a network of financial intermediaries but where there is still room for the small investor.
(3) Venture capital firms thrive in areas that have a sound, fast-growing economy, where there is a collective memory of entrepreneurial success, as well as new opportunities opened up by the existence of innovative industrialism.

Interestingly enough, some of the best developed venture capital networks, relative to the size of the regional economies, are in Boston, San Francisco, southern California, and, to a lesser extent, in Texas, that is, in areas that seem to possess the characteristics we have indicated, as opposed to New York or Chicago, traditional financial centers basically geared toward corporate investment (see figure 2.3). In the mature stage of an innovative milieu, in Boston or the San Francisco Bay area, for instance, corporate investment flows in, particularly from New York and Los Angeles, but still generally channeled through the network of venture capital firms established in the formative stage, basically because of their knowledge of the potential of each new development in the industry. In the end, while successful innovative industries go public to raise capital in the stock exchange market, the

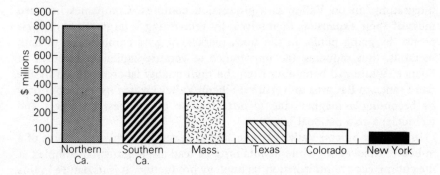

Figure 2.3   Venture capital invested in companies 1985 ($m)
Source: Electronics Business, 1987

dynamism of the milieu remains largely dependent upon the ability of high-risk investors to keep financing quantum-leap innovations. In fact, most of these high-risk investments in the 1980s tend to be made by corporations, including foreign industrial investors, because of the high cost barriers to entry in terms of the capital to undertake major research programs, particularly in microelectronics.

An industrial complex becomes a milieu of innovation when it is able to generate within itself a continuous flow of the key elements that constitute the basis for innovative production of information technologies, namely: new scientific and technological information, high-risk capital, and innovative technical labor. By way of illustration, let us consider the typical case of Silicon Valley, elaborating on the information already provided by Saxenian, Rogers and Larsen, and other researchers.[78] Stanford University's Faculty and graduates played a crucial role in providing the basic technological information on which a group of companies relied during the 1950s. Stanford and Berkeley, with the addition, years later, of the engineering programs at San Jose State University and the University of Santa Clara, provided a very large pool of high-quality electrical engineers. Military markets and government contracts supported the necessary research in the initial stages; and venture capital was decisive in the creation of many innovative companies, including Apple Computers. But during the 1970s the situation changed substantially as Silicon Valley grew and matured as a self-sufficient industrial milieu. Most of the information by this time was generated by the companies' own research efforts; this included the invention of the integrated circuit in 1957, of the planar process in 1959, and of the microprocessor in 1971. Furthermore, this information was diffused and enhanced by informal exchanges between engineers of different companies, as well as continuous spin-offs from existing companies. The military markets' share of the industry's total output plunged, and commercially oriented research became far more important than defense-related subsidized research programs. While markets expanded worldwide, numerous sub-contracting networks developed locally, further integrating Silicon Valley as a production complex. Companies financed most of their expansion themselves, by reinvesting a large share of their profits, by going public in the stock market, or by a combination of both methods, thus reducing the importance of venture capital as a source of finance. While still benefiting from the high-quality labor produced by the San Francisco Bay area universities, Silicon Valley created its own labor pool by becoming a magnet able to attract some of the best engineers and technicians on a national scale.

In this way Silicon Valley became able to generate all the ingredients of a milieu of innovation, while maintaining its lead as an industrial complex at the cutting edge of information-technology production. It is its nature in this respect, as a self-sufficient, self-generating system, that constitutes the strength of a milieu of innovation beyond the ups and downs of business cycles. Around this superior technological capacity, Silicon Valley generated a network of auxiliary companies, as well as a wealth of scientific and business contacts and, ultimately, a distinctive local culture. The concept of "agglomeration economies" does not capture the specificity or the richness of this set of social relationships, because the external economies of an informational production unit are quite different from those of the previous forms of industrialization.[79] For instance, there is little need of spatial proximity because of transportation costs; but there is much need to be able to exchange personal views on last night's software breakthrough, or on a recent visit to Japan. This notion of an innovative industrial milieu is closer to the situation of writers and artists, or stock exchange traders, in New York, or to film and television producers and actors, or financial consultants, in Los Angeles, than to the concentrations of textile or steel mills in the early industrial cities.[80]

Once a milieu of innovation takes shape, it develops its own dynamics, and becomes largely independent of the factors that once converged to give rise to its creation in a particular locality. After coming into being, a milieu of innovation will develop less on the basis of the original locational factors than on that of the overall dynamics of the industry. Nevertheless, it is crucial to understand the original location in terms of bringing together the key factors necessary for the development of innovation in informational production. Where a milieu of innovation locates depends upon the existence in one place of all three main factors as described (information, labor, capital) and upon the process of linking all three factors by the initiative of some key economic or social actors. It is in this sense that the figure of the entrepreneur (capitalist, individual, or institutional) becomes crucial.[81] For instance, the consciously positive attitude of Stanford University toward the creation of an industrial complex of electronics companies was decisive in bringing together the various favorable factors that were present in the San Francisco Bay area for the potential formation of an innovative milieu. It is both the existence of the key factors and the deliberate action by some subjects/entrepreneurs to build an industrial complex, that are necessary to form a milieu of innovation. A very similar story can be told concerning the formation of Boston's Route 128 as the second major center of technological innovation, although in this case the initiative was far more decentralized, and basically took the form of a number of young engineers and scientists starting up their companies on the basis of an entrepreneurially minded academic environment.[82]

Once a milieu is in existence, its evolution closely follows that of the industries clustered in it. Saxenian, in her latest research[83] differentiates three stages in the development of Silicon Valley: the entrepreneurial stage of the 1960s; the era of corporate consolidation and branch plants in the 1970s; and the emergence of networked production in the 1980s. Networked production refers to the formation of a series of linkages among firms and among industries in a given spatially contiguous production complex, under the

Table 2.13   Jobs in electronics industry (excluding defense and aerospace) in Santa Clara
County, by sector (annual averages)

	1975		1985		1995[a]	
	(000)	(%)	(000)	(%)	(000)	(%)
Computers	23.0	25	63.1	28	86.4	30
Communications Equipment	10.2	11	25.2	11	32.8	11
Semiconductors	19.6	21	45.5	20	43.2	15
Other electronic components	13.4	15	35.8	16	39.4	14
Instruments	16.9	18	31.8	14	44.5	15
Wholesale electronics	2.5	3	6.6	3	9.9	3
Software development	0.5	1	6.3	3	18.9	6
Research and development	6.1	7	8.1	4	16.2	6
Total	92.2		222.4		291.3	

[a]Projection.
Source: California Employment Development Department.

dominance of system firms. In spatial terms, the first stage represented a
period of concentration, leading to the formation of the milieu; the second
stage saw a process of decentralization of low-level manufacturing activities,
while Silicon Valley continued to grow on the basis of higher-level
production functions; the third stage witnessed the re-integration of manufacturing into the Silicon Valley firms, but through automation of assembly
and testing. Throughout all three stages, Silicon Valley maintained, and even
expanded, its technological leadership, adding new layers of complexity to its
industrial structure, but always concentrating the highest technological
functions. The net result has been an endless expansion of employment, in
spite of downturns in the electronics industry, such that of 1984–6. Table 2.13
and figure 2.4 indicate the trend. Saxenian's latest research reveals that
between 1980 and 1986, about 50,000 new high-technology jobs were created
in Silicon Valley, more than any other area in the US, ranking second in
terms of absolute number of jobs with 234,000 after Los Angeles (297,000),
but before Boston (175,000) and Orange Country (114,000).

Silicon Valley and Route 128 have maintained their early technological
lead in high-technology manufacturing, continuously enhancing their R&D
capabilities, and transforming their industrial organization to cope with the
trends of international competition.

The process by which a particular milieu is formed, and therefore the
characteristics of the area in which it is located, greatly influence the final
outcome of the process, that is, the structure and dynamics of the milieu of innovation itself. In other words, the combination of different sources of
innovative information, of different pools of skilled labor, and of different
investors of high-risk capital, will result in the formation of *different types of*

milieux of innovation, whose location could therefore take place in very different areas. In order to illustrate our approach we will proceed to analyze the relationship between these different sources of information, capital, and technical labor, on the one hand, the location of R&D centers in the US on the other. Admittedly, this is only a very rough, approximate idea of what we understand by milieux of innovation; and moreover, since the data on which we rely concern all R&D, and not just R&D by information-technology producers, we are clearly underplaying the specific nature of the new industry as opposed to traditional manufacturing activities. Corresponding adjustments will therefore have to be made in the interpretation of the data. Nevertheless, we start from the safe assumption that the research function is particularly prominent in information-technology industries; this is especially relevant when the matter in hand is the location of their innovative milieux. It is therefore plausible that there exists some relationship between the spatial logic of information-technology innovative centers and that of R&D centers in general. In any case, at this stage of our investigation we are dependent on the best empirical source available concerning the geography of R&D in the US, namely the research carried out on this subject over a number of years by Edward J. Malecki.[84] While referring to the original

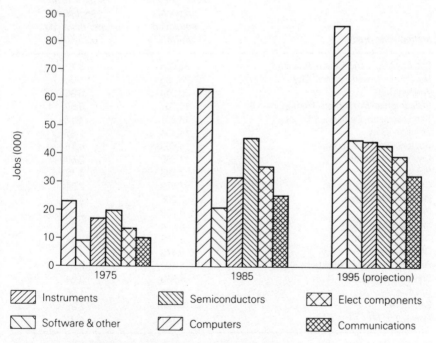

Figure 2.4   Santa Clara County: jobs in electronics, by sector
Source: California Employment Development Department

sources to explain the methodology underlying his data collection, we need to present our own methodology in analyzing that database for the specific purposes of this research.

On the basis of Malecki's data (see tables 2.14–2.16), we have constructed a series of indicators concerning the different potential sources of technological information, high-risk capital, and scientific/technical labor. For each one of these indicators, we have ranked the US metropolitan areas and picked out the top 20 of each ranking. As a criterion for selection we have used absolute values of the variables rather than weighted measures, such as location quotients, or standardized values. The reason for taking this methodological option is our concern with defining the factors that gave birth to the actual innovative milieux that structure industrial space. It is the sheer volume of information generated, of capital invested, and of technical labor available in a given location, that is actually crucially important for the overall spatial structure of information-technology industries, rather than the ability of an

Table 2.14   Location of scientists and engineers employed in R&D or administration of R&D; top 20 metropolitan areas, 1977

Metropolitan area	Number of scientists and engineers employed in R&D	R&D scientists and engineers per thousand population
Los Angeles–Long Beach–Anaheim	32,085	3.13
New York–Newark–Jersey City	26,395	1.65
Washington	20,244	6.95
Philadelphia–Wilmington–Trenton	19,701	3.50
San Francisco–Oakland–San Jose	18,201	4.12
Chicago–Gary	14,834	1.95
Boston–Lawrence–Lowell	14,653	4.16
Detroit–Ann Arbor	11,659	2.50
Seattle–Tacoma	7,683	4.19
Cleveland–Akron–Lorain	7,529	2.51
Houston–Galveston	7,006	3.25
Pittsburgh	6,732	2.80
Minneapolis–St Paul	5,824	2.95
Dallas–Fort Worth	5,568	2.34
Denver–Boulder	5,476	4.42
Hartford–Springfield–Waterbury	5,400	3.21
San Diego	4,939	3.64
St Louis	4,781	1.98
Baltimore	4,726	2.28
Rochester, NY	4,721	4.91

Source: Malecki (see note 75).

area to become innovative on a limited basis, without in fact being able to generate a self-expanding milieu of technological discovery. However, the adoption of this methodological criterion will also introduce a bias in our data in favor of the largest metropolitan areas, a bias that will have to be taken into account in our interpretation.

Furthermore, to attempt a more systematic observation of the location pattern of R&D centers, we have combined the scores of each metropolitan area with respect to the different scales representing sources of information, sources of capital, and sources of research labor. Since areas ranked among the first 20 do not overlap on all indicators, we have analyzed the relative positions of 42 metropolitan areas that can be considered, by various criteria, as forming the backbone of US R&D. Thus, we have been able to assign to each metropolitan area three scores, summarizing its relative position *vis-à-vis* the three main components of a milieu of innovation. Finally, we have combined the three scores to give one global score which is proposed as representative of the rank-order of each metropolitan area in terms of its overall R&D potential. Because of the cumbersome procedures necessary to arrive at this synthetic measure, the reader is referred to the final note to this chapter for the methodological explanation and justification (see p. 366). For present purposes, in order to be able to elaborate on these findings, it is important to note, first, that this analysis is purely illustrative of a research perspective, and therefore does not pretend to set the ranking presented here as hard evidence beyond the significance of Malecki's original findings; secondly, that measurement is limited to that of relative rank-order, and the use of metric numbering is simply an indication of the supposed magnitude of the differences between levels in the scales, not at all a quantitative measure of

Table 2.15 Metropolitan complexes of research and development[a]

Concentrations of both laboratories and employment, 1977

Austin, TX
Boston–Lawrence–Lowell
Denver–Boulder, CO
Huntsville, AL
Lafayette, IN
Madison, WI
Philadelphia–Wilmington–Trenton
Raleigh–Durham, NC
San Francisco–Oakland–San Jose
Washington, DC–MD–VA

[a]Concentration refers to a value over one standard deviation above the average for 177 metropolitan areas.
Source: Malecki (see note 75).

Table 2.16 Location quotients for Federal and private R&D in 50 SMSAs, 1977

Urban area	Total DoD and NASA[a] ($m)	Federal R&D location quotient	Total private R&D Labs[b]	Private R&D location quotient	Speciali- zation in Federal or private R&D
Los Angeles–Long Beach–Anaheim	2,916.3	2.83	446	0.96	Federal
Boston–Lawrence–Lowell	791.1	2.24	264	1.66	Both
San Francisco–Oakland–San Jose	724.1	1.59	187	0.91	Federal
Seattle–Tacoma	548.6	3.03	36	0.44	Federal
Washington	484.0	1.61	214	1.58	Both
Philadelphia–Wilmington–Trenton	432.1	0.77	282	1.11	Private
Dallas–Fort Worth	431.8	1.72	56	0.49	Federal
St Louis	372.1	1.58	71	0.67	Federal
New York–Newark–Jersey City	311.3	0.19	978	1.33	Private
San Diego	284.9	1.81	53	0.75	Federal
Baltimore	228.6	1.07	64	0.66	Federal
Houston–Galveston	210.0	0.86	99	0.89	Private
Detroit–Ann Arbor	183.2	0.39	124	0.59	Private
Orlando	156.5	2.70	4	0.15	Federal
New Orleans	143.2	1.32	8	0.16	Federal
Santa Barbara	141.1	5.07	23	1.83	Both
Cincinnati–Hamilton	139.4	0.86	54	0.74	Federal
Melbourne–Titusville–Cocoa	121.6	5.27	13	1.25	Both
Albany–Schenectady–Troy	85.5	1.08	23	0.64	Federal
Salt Lake City	84.7	1.09	22	0.63	Federal
Binghamton	83.3	2.76	8	0.59	Federal
Bridgeport–New Haven	82.4	1.02	46	1.27	Private
Hartford–Springfield	77.7	0.46	89	1.16	Private
Minneapolis–St Paul	69.5	0.35	53	0.59	Private
Denver–Boulder	60.4	0.43	49	0.93	Private
Huntsville	57.1	2.01	13	1.01	Federal
Dayton	55.1	0.66	32	0.85	Private
Phoenix	50.7	0.42	35	0.64	Private
Columbus	48.1	0.45	44	0.92	Private
Atlanta	43.3	0.24	35	0.44	Private
New London–Norwich	33.6	1.34	5	0.44	Federal
Syracuse	30.9	0.48	22	0.76	Private
Albuquerque	28.0	0.73	10	0.58	Federal
Tampa–St Peterburg	26.5	0.20	14	0.23	Private
Pittsburgh	22.5	0.10	105	1.01	Private
Fort Wayne	21.4	0.58	10	0.60	Private
Pensacola	21.1	0.79	6	0.50	Federal
West Palm Beach	20.5	0.45	8	0.39	Federal
Biloxi–Gulfport	19.1	1.13	2	0.26	Federal
Kansas City	16.8	0.13	37	0.64	Private
Austin	16.6	0.42	18	1.01	Private
Cleveland–Akron–Lorain	16.3	0.06	150	1.76	Private
Indianapolis	16.1	0.14	32	0.63	Private
Buffalo	14.1	0.11	62	1.04	Private
Chicago–Gary	12.1	0.02	390	1.13	Private
Pittsfield	11.6	1.24	3	0.71	Federal

Table 2.16   Continued

Urban area	Total DoD and NASA[a] ($m)	Federal R&D location quotient	Total private R&D Labs[b]	Private R&D location quotient	Speciali- zation in Federal or private R&D
Nashua	11.2	1.12	8	1.76	Private
Utica–Rome	10.5	0.33	12	0.80	Private
Miami–Fort Lauderdale	4.7	0.02	25	0.24	Private
Milwaukee–Racine	0	0	88	1.24	Private

[a]Source: [25, 45].
[b]Source: [4].
Source: Malecki (see note 76).

the statistical intervals between ranks. With all these necessary caveats, we can now look at table 2.17 and try to understand the geography of R&D in the US as it relates to the development of industrial milieux of innovation.

Let us first describe our observations in terms of the spatial location of R&D centers, as they result from the combined criteria we have derived from our analytical model. Los Angeles stands out at the top in a class by itself. This may be surprising, but in fact its ranking is the direct consequence of the combination of a strong corporate basis, government funding (for defense and aerospace work), large, major universities, and a very large pool of technical labor. Since we know from the general literature that this trend has become more marked since 1977, it is probable that, in the mid-1980s, the greater Los Angeles area (including, of course, Orange County) holds, at least quantitatively, the largest concentration of industrial R&D in the US; maybe, with Tokyo–Yokohama, the largest in the world. After Los Angeles comes a group of four major centers of innovation which, in the rank-order given by our elaboration of Malecki's data, are: New York–New Jersey, San Francisco–Oakland–San Jose, Philadelphia–Wilmington–Trenton, and Boston–Lawrence–Lowell. These four represent a mixture of the old and the new industrial R&D centers. On the one hand, the close connection between corporate headquarters and R&D facilities, demonstrated by Malecki in another study, accounts for the renewed importance of old, large metropolitan centers, such as New York and Philadelphia, as R&D locations. On the other hand, the new information-technology centers, such as Boston and San Francisco, are quickly taking up a leading role, on the basis of their strong university presence, their government funding, and their ability to generate a diversified industrial research milieu; it is in fact the last element which is statistically responsible for their presence among the top five areas. This group of just five metropolitan areas appears to form the core of industrial R&D in the US, clearly exhibiting a pattern of concentration that is likely to have consequences for the future manufacturing landscape of America.

Table 2.17 Ranking of 42 metropolitan areas according to their potential as sources of technological innovation, by potential in generating information capital, research labor, with indication of their combined score (ranks only shown for top 20 areas)

Metropolitan Area	Sources for sources[a]				
	Sources of information	Sources of capital	Sources of research labor	Total combined score	Overall rank
Boston	4.25	3.5	3.5	11.25	4
New York–New Jersey	3.33	5.0	1.0	9.33	2
San Francisco–Oakland– San Jose	3.75	4.5	2.5	10.75	3
Los Angeles	3.0	1.5	0.5	5.0	1
Philadelphia– Wilmington–Trenton	4.33	5.0	2.0	11.33	5
Washington, DC–MD–VA	5.0	15.0	3.0	23.0	6
Chicago	7.33	14.0	3.0	24.33	7
Cleveland	16.0	16.0	10.0	42.5	16
Detroit–Ann Arbor	14.0	10.5	4.0	38.5	10
Pittsburgh	2.0	17.0	6.0	43.0	
Houston–Galveston	16.6	11.0	11.0	38.6	11
Hartford–Springfield	20.6	18.0	16.0	54.6	
Milwaukee	21.0	18.5	25.0	64.5	
St Louis	19.33	10.5	9.0	38.83	12
Baltimore	11.33	12.5	9.5	33.33	8
Buffalo, NY	22.0	20.0	25.0	67.0	
Denver–Boulder	11.0	22.5	7.5	41.0	14
Dallas–Fort Worth	22.66	11.5	7.0	41.1	15
Cincinnati–Hamilton	23.0	17.0	25.0	65.0	
Minneapolis–St Paul	18.33	21.5	6.5	46.33	18
San Diego	13.66	14.0	8.5	36.16	9
Huntsville, AL	13.0	25.0	25.0	63.0	
Dayton, OH	18.66	25.0	−25.0	68.66	
Newport–Hampton	20.33	25.0	25.0	70.33	
Portland	18.66	25.0	25.0	68.66	
Knoxville	22.33	25.0	25.0	72.33	
Salt Lake City	22.66	22.5	25.0	70.16	
Sacramento	20.33	25.0	25.0	70.33	
Davenport	23.33	25.0	25.0	73.33	
Madison	14.25	25.0	12.5	51.75	19
Seattle	20.33	14.5	4.5	39.33	13
Champaign–Urbana	21.33	25.0	12.5	58.83	
Austin	16.25	25.0	12.5	53.75	20
Rochester, NY	22.0	25.0	25.0	72.0	
Bridgeport–New Haven	23.33	25.0	25.0	73.33	
Lafayette, IN	18.75	25.0	25.0	68.75	
Raleigh–Durham	18.75	25.0	12.5	56.25	
Orlando, FL	25.0	19.5	25.0	69.5	
New Orleans	25.0	20.0	25.0	70.0	
Santa Barbara, CA	25.0	20.5	25.0	70.5	

Table 2.17   Continued

	Scores for sources[a]				
Metropolitan Area	Sources of information	Sources of capital	Sources of research labor	Total combined score	Overall rank
Melbourne, FL	25.0	21.5	25.0	71.5	
Albany, NY	25.0	22.0	25.0	72.0	

[a]Low score indicates higher potential: level of measure is ordinal. (For scores and procedure for calculating the scores, see note 150.)
Source: Author's elaboration of Malecki's data.

Among other considerations, while New York–New Jersey is still losing manufacturing jobs, even in high technology, it is hardly lagging behind in terms of R&D capabilities, if only because of the sheer size of its financial, institutional, corporate, and technical labor resources.

The leading group is followed by two special cases: Washington DC–Maryland–Virginia, and Chicago, which represent the two opposite poles of the government–corporate spectrum. To some extent, it is clear that R&D is located in Washington because of the Federal government agencies, and that Chicago's R&D is the direct spin-off of headquarters location in the capital of the midwest, as well as of its now fading manufacturing past. Will these two locations be able to shift into the new generation of R&D? This will very much depend on the future of government intervention in research and on the ability of old manufacturing industry to generate new forms of innovation. Activity over the past decade since the mid-1970s suggests that spin-offs from government research centers are in fact generating technological development in Maryland and Virginia, while Chicago is trailing in such developments, despite its strong university base.

Moving down our list, there follows a mixture of areas that combine a university base with a very strong traditional manufacturing structure which is in the process of being revitalized through stepped-up R&D efforts: Baltimore (with outstanding research universities, particularly in health sciences, and the military connection to Johns Hopkins' Applied Physics Laboratory); San Diego, a center for biotechnology, computer industries, and defense-related informational production; Detroit–Ann Arbor, where a large research university complex helps the automobile industry in its transition to robotics and new materials, not forgetting tanks; Houston–Galveston, where the connection is between oil capital and government-supported aerospace research and industrial development; St Louis and Seattle, where the aircraft industry still thrives, supported by government and a solid network of local universities. Denver–Boulder and Dallas–Fort Worth seem to have different stories: while both have medium-level universities (if we include Texas A&M in the Dallas sphere), and well-developed technical labor markets, Denver has government-sponsored research facilities but low research funding, while Dallas relies on its advanced corporate structure funded by government. Next on the list, Cleveland, with the remnants of strong corporate industrial R&D, and Pittsburgh, and advanced university research in robotics and artificial intelligence, witness the persistence of the old manufacturing belt, although not at a level commensurate with its industrial past; Minneapolis remains a major computer industry center and relies on its large, technically oriented public university system to keep pace with industrial research. Finally, Madison and Austin are clear examples of the research vitality that major public universities can generate in an isolated setting. They also demonstrate, however, that university quality by itself cannot generate an industrial complex: Madison was not able to do so in the 1980s, while Austin became a substantial electronics manufacturing area on the basis of government support and corporate decentralization of production facilities.

Outside our list of the top 20 there remain some significant technological centers, such as North Carolina's "research triangle" around the Raleigh-Durham metropolitan area. The 1977 data could not provide the quantitative basis to justify a ranking for this area among the top 20, given our bias toward the effect of absolute size of labor, research facilities, and funding in constituting an innovative milieu. Nevertheless, the "research triangle" does constitute an innovative milieu in the 1980s, on the basis of an original combination of university facilities and government sponsored R&D.[85]

The summary comments above are intended simply to lay the ground for some more analytical conclusions reached on the basis of our elaboration of Malecki's findings. The first of these concerns the necessary distinction between the geography of industrial R&D in the broad sense, as shown here, for the 1976–7 period, and the location of leading information-technology industrial milieux of innovation. Boston and Silicon Valley appear much less clearly dominant in Malecki's data than in the literature specializing in information technology. In fact, Malecki himself provides the explanation, and some empirical data, for this discrepancy. He analyzes the location of headquarters and R&D laboratories for a sample of 54 electronics firms, as shown in table 2.18.[86] The findings are striking: 36 out of the 54 firms have an R&D laborartory either in the Boston area or in California, and the main reason for the other 18 firms *not* having such a facility in either area is related to the location of their headquarters elsewhere. It therefore seems plausible that the location of milieux of innovation in information technology follows the general determinants presented in our analytical framework, but with further determining effect on their spatial location: namely, R&D information, capital, and labor are increasingly targeted to the specific recipient industries. In other words, there seems to be a difference between redesigning the

Table 2.18 Locational characteristics of R&D in three US industries, from a sample of 85 firms

Number of R&D locations	Number of firms	Firms with a laboratory in the headquarters' area	Firms with a laboratory in the Boston area or California	Firms with headquarters in the Boston area or California
Aerospace				
1	1	1	0	0
2–4	4	4	1	0
5	3	2	3	1
6	3	3	3	1
All aerospace firms	11	10	7	2
Electrical and electronics products				
1	18	16	7	6
2	15	12	10	2
3–5	9	8	8	3
6–10	8	8	7	1
11–36	4	4	4	1
All electronics firms	54	48	36	13
Instruments				
1	11	8	6	4
2	4	4	2	1
3–5	5	5	4	2
All instruments firms	20	16	12	7
All firms	85	74	55	22

Source: Malecki (see note 84).

automobile or steel industries and fostering new breakthroughs in electronics and biotechnology. Thus, within a common matrix of technological and institutional determinants of R&D location there is some specialization in R&D concerned with the new technological frontier that translates into specific spatial locations.

Nevertheless, the importance of R&D facilities in the very large, older metropolitan areas, along with the presence of information-technology manufacturing in these areas, when considered in absolute numbers, calls attention to the diversity of milieux of innovation, away from the simplistic images of the sunrise regions and to the complex reality of the multifaceted process of new industrial development. Because of the variable geometry of sources of information, capital, and labor, linking corporations, government, universities, and industrial complexes, we are clearly in the presence of a variety of high-level innovative milieux that develop along the lines of the specific factors proposed by our analytical framework. To focus more specifically on the innovative milieux of information-technology producers, we can construct a typology on the basis of information already cited, by combining the different structural elements that converge in their formation. Such a typology might provide a basis for comparing innovative information-technology milieux with the location pattern of the overall industrial R&D system, so as to generate some hypotheses on what is specific to the new industrial milieu of innovation.

Type 1, represented by areas such as Silicon Valley and Boston's Route 128, is historically based on a combination of university research, government markets, venture capital, university-produced skilled labor, and start-up companies, ultimately generating through their interaction a self-sustaining milieu. This is the kind of milieu of innovation on which we have focused our analysis, because it is the more distinctively original in the current stage of industrialization, and because it remains the most dynamic configuration in the process of technological development. Yet there are other potential combinations of information, capital, and labor, that have in reality come together to form different kinds of innovative milieux.[87]

Type 2, exemplified by the Los Angeles–Orange Country complex or, on a much smaller scale, by Phoenix or Dallas, directly links large corporations and government funding around defense-related industries that originally recruit from a network of good local engineering schools, to become subsequently a pole of attraction for skilled personnel nationwide.[88]

Type 3, represented by IBM's New York or ATT's New Jersey locations, organizes a self-sustaining milieu behind the closed doors of a very large, innovative corporation. In this particular case it would be difficult to consider that there exists a milieu of innovation as a specific spatial entity. In fact, it is the corporation itself in each case that constitutes the milieu, its component parts sometimes scattered in different locations around the world and interacting via on-line systems. Yet it is important to recognize that the location of such major centers of information-based industrial development do organize the new spatial structure of production, even if the process of innovation takes place generally in a secluded space, and local spin-offs are few.[89]

Type 4, whose closest resemblance could be the Austin, Texas area, mixes the domination of technical branch plants of large corporations, and some level of spin-off able to generate a relatively autonomous dynamic of locally induced firms.[90] In the survey conducted by Amy Glasmeier on 70 high-technology firms in Austin in 1987,[91] half of the firms were manufacturing establishments. Of these, only 4 percent were research oriented. However, 37 percent of them were engaged in some form of R&D on the basis of the technologies of their parent corporations or other outside firms. Austin, until the mid-1980s, was the typical example of a milieu of innovation resulting from the decentralization of corporate R&D to be complemented with a network of ancillary firms.

Type 5, which could be illustrated by the rise of the computer industry in Minneapolis–St Paul, represents an original combination of corporate development, government markets, and self-generation of technological information.[92]

These types do not cover all the variations of innovative milieux that exist in practice, but they provide some standards by which to estimate the originality of other areas. For example, North Carolina's Research Triangle is close in its structure and dynamics to type 1 (Silicon Valley), but with the major difference of a much greater reliance on government contracts and guidance. Pittsburgh and Philadelphia could probably fit well in the same category as Minneapolis (type 5), maybe with the additional features of an even stronger university research basis, particularly in computer software and robotics (Carnegie–Mellon in Pittsburgh), and of a much more highly developed corporate environment.[93]

It is my contention that all types of milieu of innovation are equally at the forefront of the constitution of the new industrial space; and further, that they are all likely to become yet more prominent worldwide because of the cumulative character of knowledge-based uneven development. However, functioning and dynamics of each type of milieu vary according to the specific structure of each. The more a milieu generates its own internal structure, independent of a small group of large corporations or government facilities, the more it fosters its synergetic potential, ultimately enhancing its technological leadership. Where government support plays a leading role in the growth of an innovative milieu, the resources for industry development are larger, accelerating the pace of the milieu's growth; yet, in these cases, milieux tend to be rather unstable and to go through sharp ups and downs, following the uncertain path of government policies.

In terms of the spatial dynamics of innovative milieux, government dominance tends to restrain tendencies toward offshoring, particularly in defense-related industries, and to foster tendencies toward disproportionate concentration in certain areas and regions. Where large corporations are predominant, the linkages of the milieu with the overall international chain of production are emphasized. The highest technological specialization tends to occur in those milieux which rely on a spatially concentrated, functionally decentralized, network-based structure that draws its strength from those very informational/economic externalities that are attached to its clustering pattern.

We are now in a position to assess how the location pattern of informational milieux of innovation has in fact developed over time in relation to the spatial distribution of industrial R&D in general. Ideally, we should be able to compare Malecki's findings to a similar database referring specifically to information-technology industrial R&D. Since no such comparable database is available, we must rely on the general knowledge of the new industries' behavior, particularly in electronics, as presented in a variety of studies already cited.

By and large, the new milieux of innovation occur as specific developments of existing dominant R&D locations. The main reason for this historical overlap is the crucial importance of large metropolitan areas in mobilizing productive resources, including innovative technological capabilities. However, there are three main differences between the traditional R&D areas, as studied by Malecki, and the new emerging centers of innovation:

(1) The technological dominance in information-based industrial R&D, both quantitative and qualitative, has shifted to Silicon Valley and Boston. Their technological advance is the result of a concentration there of all key factors that are fundamental to the process of innovation, as well as of the cumulative character of the knowledge-based process of uneven development. Yet this dominance is not overwhelming, in contrary to what is generally believed, and is in fact shared with at least two other forms of information-based technological centers.

(2) The second type of major center, as described above, is the technological capacity installed in large corporations headquartered in major metro-politan areas such as New York–New Jersey. This is not simply the reproduction of the previous R&D model, but is the spatial expression of the control of innovation by global corporations. In this case, IBM, or ATT, is more important than the area where it is located. The continuity of metropolitan dominance does not mean a continuation in type of industrial milieu.

(3) The third type of center, whose main exemplar is Los Angeles–Orange County, witnesses the entry into the new industrial history of major conglomerates of government programs and large corporations, creating the basis for what may be in the future the fastest and largest

accumulation of technological development, generally organized around defense-related goals.

Thus, the continuity of a pattern of R&D centered on the largest metropolitan areas disguises the shifts in the relative weights of these areas in the new technological era, as well as the very different sources of their developmental potential. Milieux of innovation structure themselves by articulating a major technological revolution to industrial production through the web of relationships among three of the major historical forces of our experience: large corporations, the state, and social networks. They bear the marks of these forces' changing strategies and interests as they unfold according to their developmental logic in the restructuring of the relationship between technology and space.

Decentralization of Production

Information-technology industries are characterized by a strong tendency to decentralize their production operations, both functionally and spatially. This decentralization occurs both within firms and among firms specializing in different segments of the industry. It is important to differentiate between decentralization of production and the spatial dispersion of the industry. The latter is a process that takes place as the industry expands and seeks out new locations and new markets. The former concerns a specific characteristic of the industry's behavior, that has manifested itself since the early stages of its development, as an expression of structural features of information-technology producers. There seem to be four factors that are most important in accounting for the tendency to organize production in a decentralized pattern:[94]

(1) Labor requirements are specific, and different, for each segment of the production process, and there is great difficulty in obtaining and reproducing these very different types of labor in the same functional and spatial unit.[95]
(2) The nature of the product gives it a functional freedom from location: it is indifferent to transportation costs, given its high value/low volume ratio. Different components of the production process can locate in different areas and ship their intermediate output back and forth between those areas.[96]
(3) The industry, being a producer of information-processing devices, is also the main early user of its own products. Advanced devices able to process and telecommunicate information allow for the spatial separation of functions that are reintegrated in the same process of production and management by on-line information systems and programmable manufacturing tools.[97]

(4) The process-orientation of the informational product establishes a very close connection between the industry and the users of its products, since such information processing devices become crucial components of the final product or activity to which they are destined.

The fourth of these factors draws a sharp distinction between standardized production and customized production in the informational industries which is worth discussing in some detail.[98] Those products that are standardized have ubiquitous markets; their production can be centralized, while distribution is potentially decentralized worldwide. The general tendency in the industry, on the other hand, is toward a greater emphasis on customized production, which also accounts for the higher-value products. Customized production, with the associated requirement for a close interaction between producers and users of information-processing devices, translates into strong market dependency in terms of the industry's location pattern. However, the spatial implications of this market dependency may vary according to the characteristics of the market itself. Two main cases must be considered. In the first case, given the general applicability of information-processing devices, most products of the new industry have markets everywhere. In this case, decentralization of production takes place according to the strategies of market penetration, with the only exception being the higher-level R&D functions, which generally remain concentrated in the milieux of innovation. On the other hand, if markets are highly specific, the nature of a process-oriented, customized product requires a very close relationship between the industry and its market, leading to spatial clustering around the market itself, sometimes requiring spatial reintegration of the entire production process. In such cases, market conditions reverse the process of decentralization. This is the case, in particular, with defense-oriented information-technology producers, which tend to cluster around major military–industrial complexes, and end up generating an innovative milieu articulated to the defense complex.[99]

In sum, market conditions in information-technology industries, determined by the process-orientation of their production, call for a *flexible location pattern*, able simultaneously to cater to a worldwide market, to penetrate a specific regional market, or to develop a customized, localized relationship in a given place, according to the changing conditions of an expanding market. Thus, the tendency toward decentralization of production takes place in a context in which flexibility is the most important requirement in the relationship between the industry and its spatial location.[100]

Finally, it is important to keep in mind that decentralization of production, when it occurs, takes place under the commanding logic of the spatial division of labor, with an occupational, functional, and organizational hierarchy separating the different production units and their locations.[101]

On the basis of these hypotheses, we can go on to analyze some of the available empirical evidence on the decentralization of production for US information-technology producers, at both the international and the inter-regional level.

Spatial decentralization of information-technology production industries is exemplified by the behavior of American semiconductor companies, the core of high-technology manufacturing, since the early 1960s. Jeffery Henderson has analyzed the locational pattern of US chip makers, as they spread out their plants in the US, Scotland, and south-east Asia.[102] Table 2.19, constructed by Henderson on the basis of his interviews with company managers, shows the sharp division of labor among research and design functions, concentrated in the innovative milieux of the US; skilled production functions (wafer fabrication), somewhat decentralized in Scotland for the companies studied; assembly and testing, localized in areas such as Hong Kong and Singapore; and finally, predominantly assembly operations in the new periphery, including the Philippines, Malaysia, and Indonesia. Beyond the spatial division of labor, which we have already analyzed, what is significant is the spatial segmentation of the industry, including the shipment back and forth of the various components of its output between different locations. Chips designed in the US go into wafer fabrication in Scotland, then into assembly in south-east Asia, and then, very often, back to Scotland or to the US for final testing and distribution to their markets. Henderson emphasizes the crucial importance of specific labor characteristics in each stage of the production process. The main reason for semiconductors companies to locate in Scotland is the high quality of technical labor trained by Scottish universities, together with the long tradition of skilled industrial workers in the area. In addition, the salaries of these Scottish engineers are 40 percent lower than those of their equivalents in California. Such competitive advantage overrode the supposed concern that companies might have felt about a region with a long tradition of unionzation and class struggle. Once located in Scotland, US companies designed a number of policies aimed at taming labor militancy, such as introducing special advantages for their personnel, and locating in new towns and other isolated areas, bypassing when possible the older industrial agglomerations.

Saxenian's study of Silicon Valley companies[103] shows the same pattern of hierarchical decentralization of production, with control and R&D functions in Silicon Valley, advanced manufacturing in the US, Europe, and Japan, and assembly operations in the Third World (see table 2.20).

Labor force characteristics, together with government support for business, seem to have played a major role, at least originally, in the location of semiconductor companies in south-east Asia. Particularly important was the ability to tap a large pool of unskilled young women, with little protection regarding their health and working conditions. These women provided, and

Table 2.19 American semiconductor companies manufacturing in Scotland and other European and Asian locations

Nature of Operation and Labour Processes

Company	USA	Scotland	England & Wales	France	Germany	Switzer- land	Israel	Japan	Hong Kong	Malaysia	Korea	Singapore	Philippines	Indonesia	Thailand	Taiwan
National Semiconductor	c,rd,w t,ms,m	d,w	r,m				w		a,t, m	a,t		a,t,d,m, r	a	a	a,t	
Motorola	c,rd,w, a,t,ms, m	w,a,t		w,a	w,t	d,r,m	d	w,d	d,t, r,m	a	a		a			a
General Instrument	c,rd,w, ms,m	w	d,m,r	m						a						a,t
Hughes Aircraft	c,rd,w, ms,m,a, t	w,a,t, (ms)	d,r,m						(a)				(a)			
Burr-Brown	c,rd,w, a,t,ms, m	w,a,t, d														

c – corporate control
rd – research & development
d – design centre
ms – mask making
w – wafer fabrication
a – assembly

t – final testing
m – marketing
r – regional/national headquarters
( ) – operation under sub-contract arrangement

Source: Henderson (see note 56) on the basis of interviews with company executives; company reports and data collected by Henderson.

still do provide, the bulk of the workers required for labor-intensive assembly operations, during the industry's period of rapid expansion.[104]

Allen Scott has also conducted a detailed study on the decentralization of US semiconductor manufacturers to south-east Asia.[105] Table 2.21 shows the growing number of such plants in the region, and table 2.22 the growing proportion of semiconductors manufacturing production conducted offshore. Scott reiterates the importance of cheap, unskilled labor in this trend. He also points out the influence of two major institutional factors in the decentralization process: first, US Tariff Schedule legislation, which provided favorable conditions for the firms to reimport output produced offshore; and second, the relative demilitarization of the semiconductors market which enabled it to circumvent the Defense Department's prescription that defense-related manufacturing take place on US soil.

Nevertheless, while labor conditions are important in explaining the *origins* of the process of decentralization in semiconductors production, market-related strategies seem to be a major factor in the *persistence* of this pattern.[106] In the first place, protectionist trends and the dramatic expansion of electronics markets over the long term place a premium on the location of plants within the areas that will become large markets. This clearly applies to western Europe, where Scotland holds the largest concentration of semicon-

Table 2.20   Location of facilities of 11 Santa Clara County-based firms, by phase of production (plants in operation or under construction in 1980)

Location	Phase of production[a]			
	Control	R & D	Advanced manu-facturing[b]	Assembly
Santa Clara County	11	11	35	1
Pacific north-west and south-west	0	0	34	3
Rest of US	0	0	12[c]	0
Europe and Japan	0	3	15[d]	0
Third World	0	0	0	29

[a] This division of the production process is sometimes arbitrary in the case of many older facilities with mixed uses. In particular, all R & D includes prototype production lines and assembly, so therefore includes manufacturing and assembly in the research lab. The guideline for allocation thus is the dominant process occurring in a plant. If the two are of equal importance (e.g. control and R & D are often in the same building), the plant is counted twice; otherwise all plants are counted only once.

[b] Advanced manufacturing refers to wafer fabrication for semiconductor production. Since two of the firms included are electronics, not solely semiconductor firms (Hewlett-Packard and Varian), the term manufacturing is used.

[c] This number would be only three if Hewlett-Packard and Varian were not included.

[d] Facilities established in Europe and Japan are mainly through joint ventures and co-production agreements, and typically are established in order to gain access to foreign markets.

Source: Saxenian (see note 66).

Table 2.21 US semiconductor production and imports under tariff codes 806.30 and 807.00

Year	Value of all US shipments in SIC 3674 ($m)[a]	Total 806.30/807.00 imports ($m)[a]	Total 806.30/807.00 imports as % of US shipments in SIC 3674	Total 806.30/807.00 imports from Asia ($m)[a]	Total 806.30/807.00 imports from Asia as % of total 806.30/807.00 imports
1969	1572.9	127	8.1	77	60.6
1970	1501.2	160	10.7	90	56.3
1971	1599.6	178	11.1	98	55.1
1972	2704.8	254	9.4	170	66.9
1973	3647.7	413	11.3	297	71.9
1974	4305.1	684	15.9	479	70.0
1975	3276.9	617	18.8	469	76.0
1976	4473.8	879	19.6	721	82.0
1977	5322.6	1120	21.0	974	87.0
1978	6435.4	1478	23.0	1300	88.0
1979	8266.7	1916	23.2	1667	87.0
1980	10500.8	2506	23.9	2205	88.0
1981	11701.5	2825	24.1	2458	87.0
1982	12429.9	3131	25.2	2787	89.0
1983	–	3383	–	2876	85.0

[a]All values in current dollars.
Sources: US Department of Commerce, Bureau of the Census, *Census of Manufactures,* and *Annual Survey of Manufactures;* US International Trade Commission (1980, 1981, 1984, 1985); US Tariff Commission (1970); Flamm (see note 23). Data collected by Scott (see note 105).

Table 2.22 Principal sources of assembled semiconductor devices imported into the United States under tariff items 806.30 and 807.00

Year	Hong Kong	Indo-nesia	Korea	Malay-sia	Phili-ppines	Singa-pore	Taiwan	Thai-land	All Asia ($m)[a]
1969	49.2	–	22.9	–	–	9.8	14.8	–	228
1970	44.6	–	23.2	–	–	17.9	8.9	–	254
1971	32.7	–	30.9	–	–	23.6	12.7	–	270
1972	25.4	–	26.9	–	–	37.3	10.4	–	452
1973	19.4	–	23.6	8.3	1.4	33.3	12.5	–	740
1974	17.1	–	22.9	21.4	2.9	22.9	12.9	–	977
1975	11.8	–	17.1	30.3	5.3	26.3	7.9	–	858
1976	13.1	–	20.7	25.6	7.3	28.0	7.3	–	1240
1977	8.0	1.1	21.8	27.6	6.9	24.1	9.2	1.1	1567
1978	6.8	1.1	17.0	34.1	9.1	22.7	5.7	3.4	1948
1979	4.6	2.3	13.8	33.3	11.5	23.0	4.6	2.3	2212
1980	4.5	2.3	10.2	34.1	15.9	25.0	4.5	3.4	2518
1981	3.4	2.3	9.2	34.5	18.4	23.0	4.6	4.6	2536
1982	3.4	2.2	8.9	36.0	20.2	19.1	4.5	3.4	2800
1983	1.2	2.4	16.5	36.5	21.2	12.9	4.7	4.7	2876

[a]All values in constant dollars.
Sources: Calculated by Allen Scott (see note 105) from table 3.7 in Flamm (see note 23).

ductors plants, dominated by US companies thus avoiding the 17 percent EEC tariff on imports. Similar reasons lie behind the development of US-owned electronics production in Ireland, and behind ATT's 1987 decision to locate a design and production facility of advanced integrated circuits in Madrid. Also, US electronics companies in Asia have as their prime target for the 1980s the penetration of crucial and heavily protected markets: mainly Japan (the second largest market in the world), but also Korea, one of the fastest growing, and China. In fact, market conditions are confusing the traditional distinction between the locational behavior of merchant manufacturers and that of the so-called "captive producers," large companies such as IBM and ATT, producing semiconductors for in-house use. While the former typically used decentralization in their early stages, the latter kept most of their production (of semiconductors, not of computers) onshore, close to their own in-house markets. With the expansion of world markets, increasing competition in them, and the trend toward vertical integration, large companies set up production facilities in countries such as Spain and Korea, to establish a firm connection with European and Asian markets, once the basic conditions in terms of local provision of technical labor could be fulfilled. ATT is a good example of a firm practicing this strategy.

Furthermore, the customized relationship between producers and users of semiconductors adds to the reasons for the presence of US companies in those areas that have undertaken a process of industrialization based on intensive use of information technologies. Thus, while the potential for automation of assembly work has provoked considerable speculation about the "relocation back north" of formerly decentralized production functions,[107] there is little evidence of this phenomenon.[108] On the contrary, countries such as Taiwan, Korea, Hong Kong, and Singapore, have upgraded the technological level of their production,[109] and wafer production has started in south-east Asia.[110] Automation of assembly and testing is taking place, but in the same decentralized plants. Western European branch plants are also upgrading their technological capabilities, with customized integrated circuit design taking place in the 1980s in several European countries.[111] Indigenous firms are now joining American companies in local production, although most south-east Asian firms are actually engaged in sub-contracting for US firms, and European companies on the whole, are still limited to protected government and other specialized markets.[112] Nevertheless, overall, market relationships have reinforced the pattern of decentralized production originally built around the quest for specific types of labor.

This process of renewed decentralization gathers momentum given its technological feasibility on the basis of breakthroughs in telecommunications, air transportation networks, and computer-integrated flexible manufacturing. Yet because of the consequent dependence on telecommunications and transportation, most decentralized facilities are clustered in medium-to-large metropolitan areas, close to an airport, and well connected with the US, in a location pattern that is as typical of Europe as of Asia. Scott's study shows the pattern of metropolitan concentration of US semiconductors firms in a few areas such as Singapore, Kuala Lumpur, Penang, Manila, Hong Kong, Taipei, Kaohsiung, and Seoul-Inchon.[113] The study by Breheny, Cheshire and Landgridge points to a similar tendency for British-based US companies.[114] Decentralization of production for information-technology industries is also an inter-regional phenomenon in the US. Saxenian provided one of the first systematic observations of this phenomenon in her 1980 study of a sample of electronics companies in Silicon Valley (see table 2.23).[115] Most of the plants decentralized are advanced manufacturing facilities, generally excluding R&D functions; some companies, such as Intel, did decentralize complete sets of operations, including design functions, but their most advanced research centers always remained in Silicon Valley. Although areas to which companies decentralize are very diverse, a tentative pattern appears from the data collected by Saxenian. The western states are the preferred region for firms decentralizing from Silicon Valley, with an oft-cited criterion for choice of location being a maximum distance from Silicon Valley of three hours by air. Further criteria for selection specify a medium-size city in a semi-rural area with a sufficient level of urbanism and cultural sophistication to attract engineers and technicians with the area's "quality of life," including a rich social life in beautiful surroundings. Proximity to a university is valued, but not so much in terms of a functional need for research (the company brings that with it) as in terms of the cultural and social life associated with it, precluding the isolation that would be attached to a truly rural environment. Of course, an abundant work force, with a suitable level of education and skills, is a must. Educated, unemployed women are the workers preferred by decentralized electronics plants (Saxenian writes of a bias toward employing wives of graduate students in university towns). Companies tend to avoid locating a decentralized facility in the same area as other companies, in order to improve their bargaining position as main employer, both toward the labor force and toward local governments. Although some agglomerations still develop notwithstanding, it is interesting to note that while high-level production facilities in electronics tend to cluster in milieux, whose innovative capacity depends upon interaction and synergistic creativity, their decentralized advanced manufacturing operations look for relative isolation *vis-à-vis* other industrial plants. This seems to be the reason for the characteristic pattern of decentralized production facilities: location in middle-sized towns in newly industrializing regions.[116]

The study by Markusen, Hall, and Glasmeier provides some contradictory evidence on the decentralization process.[117] They calculated an entropy index for 100 industrial sectors, and then observed the variation of the indexes between 1972 and 1977. According to their findings, while military-related sectors and bulk material processors actually increased their spatial concentration, most rapid growth sectors "showed a modest tendency toward decentralization from original growth centers." Areas with the largest rates of growth in high-technology jobs were precisely those adjacent to states that had the largest concentrations of high-technology industries. Nevertheless, at the same time, some of the most innovative industries did not exhibit a similar trend toward decentralization. Thus, while semiconductors plants spread over the country, semiconductors jobs became more concentrated over the 1972-7 period. Also, high-technology centers such as California increased their share of semiconductors jobs and plants, as well as for computer manufacturing jobs and plants, between the early 1960s and 1977.[118]

Table 2.23   Location of advanced manufacturing facilities of Santa Clara County firms, 1980

Firm	Plant Locations
Hewlett-Packard[a]	McMinnville, Corvallis, Oregon; Boise, Idaho; Fort Collins, Greely, Loveland, Colorado Springs, Colorado; Everett, Spokane, Vancouver, Washington; Roseville, California; Raleigh, North Carolina.
National Semiconductor	Salt Lake City, Utah; Tucson, Arizona; Vancouver, Washington.
Fairchild Camera & Instrument	South Portland, Maine; Worpingers Falls, Massachusetts, Tulsa, Oklahoma (planned).
Intel Corporation	Aloha, Oregon; Chandler, Arizona; Austin, Texas.
Varian Associates[a]	Salt Lake City, Utah; Florence, Lexington, Kentucky; Grove City, Ohio; Geneva, Illinois; Beverly, Danvers, Lexington, Woburn, Massachusetts.
Advanced Micro Devices	Austin, Texas.
American Microsystems, Inc.	Pocatello, Idaho.
Signetics	Orem, Utah.
Intersil	Ogden, Utah.
Memorex[a]	Plano, Texas.
Zilog	Boise, Idaho.
Spectra Physics[a]	Eugene, Oregon.
Siltec[a]	Salem, Oregon.

[a]Not a semiconductor firm.
[b]For semiconductor firms, advanced manufacturing is the same as wafer fabrication. For other firms, the process varies.
Source: Interviews; San Jose Mercury News, Business Section; collected and elaborated by Saxenian (see note 66).

These findings could support two related hypotheses. First, for information-technology industries decentralization of production is a function not of the "age" of the industry, but of the structural characteristics manifested by the industry since its early stages. Therefore, while the period 1960–77 could show a spatial sprawl of industries characterized by a higher than average technological level, the decentralized pattern of information-technology producers simply expanded in size without reversing its location pattern. The original centers of the industry maintained, or even increased, their share, as the continuous upgrading of technological innovation reinforced the role of the higher-level production functions.

Secondly, the decentralization off-shore of low-skilled jobs, and therefore of labor-intensive plants, has been taking place since 1962 at least. Since the entropy index refers only to US counties, it follows that it cannot account for this phenomenon. So, the more an industry decentralizes off-shore, the more its process of decentralization will be under-estimated by a US-specific analysis. As we have observed, off-shoring is especially characteristic of electronics in general, and of semiconductors in particular. This could explain the seemingly contradictory observations of jobs on the one hand and plants on the other: if labor-intensive plants decentralize off-shore, when the industry expands the spatial dispersion of plants in the US will be less than proportional to the expansion of jobs. Thus the growth of the industry on-shore will be biased toward the upper-level productive functions, with most jobs concentrated in the technologically advanced areas. This interpretation seems to fit the available evidence.

Glasmeier's analysis of the trends in decentralization of production also carries this central idea of the selective character of the process.[119] The bulk of new jobs created in the south are in low-skilled production and branch plants from the innovative firms of California and the north-east. According to Glasmeier's data, analysis of the industries on occupational lines to discriminate between higher and lower technological levels within the industry reveals that only 10 states appear to be technological high spots: Arizona, California, Colorado, Connecticut, Florida, Massachusetts, New Jersey, New York, Texas, and Washington. Most of the expansion of high-technology industries in other areas is accounted for by economic and technological subsidiaries of major centers of the new industrial structure. Yet, this new core does not bear out the popular image of a sunbelt/frostbelt opposition, nor does it correspond to the cleavage between old and new areas of industrialization. Some of the traditional industrial regions, such as New England and New Jersey, have transformed themselves into new manufacturing centers, clearly showing that the profile of the new industrial space does not result from some fixed geographical attributes, but from the relationship between the structure of the information-based industry and its socio-economic environment.

In sum, the decentralization of production is a recurrent trend of behavior in technologically advanced industries, and generally takes place within the hierarchical logic of the spatial division of labor among production functions, occupational skills, and organizational levels of the firm. This process of decentralization does not seem to be related to the age of the industry but to its structure since the early stages of its development. Decentralization occurs internationally, inter-regionally and intra-regionally, in a complex web of interaction that reorganizes the industrial landscape while reintegrating its functional and economic logic into a single system.

Growth of Information-technology Industries and Spatial Diffusion of their Location Pattern

Given the remarkable growth of information-technology industries in the past two decades, it is only natural that they should have dispersed their activities over regions and countries. The 1986 study cited above by Markusen, Hall, and Glasmeier found a strong tendency in most of the high-technology sectors they examined in the US to disperse among counties between 1972 and 1977. The extent of their dispersion seemed to be directly related to their rate of job growth. Glasmeier's updated database drawn from the 1982 Manufacturing Census confirms the trend over a longer period.[120] Semiconductors plants were present in 1972 in 120 counties, and in 1977 in 182. Computer manufacturing plants were present in 203 counties in 1977. Similar trends of industrial sprawl can be observed in western Europe, as the new industries continue to thrive, in spite of temporary downturns such as the 1984–6 slump.

A crucial question arises concerning the specificity of the location pattern of information-technology industries once they start dispersing across different regions. In fact, most evidence points to the fact that while production of information-technology devices takes place in an increasing number of places, the proportion of this activity that is concentrated in the main technological centers continues to grow. Furthermore, the spatial diffusion of information-technology production follows, broadly, the spatial logic of the pattern described and analyzed above.

If we consider again the findings of the Markusen, Hall, and Glasmeier study, we see that the most innovative industries were only moderately dispersed, as compared with the "average high-technology industries." Indeed, semiconductors, and other electronic sectors, such as resistors, telephone equipment, and most military-related industries, became more concentrated between 1972 and 1977. Computer manufacturing jobs and plants in 1977 were geographically more heavily concentrated, with the ten top states accounting for 76 percent of jobs and 75 percent of plants;

California alone boasted 30 percent of jobs and 35 percent of plants – an increase of 353 percent in the number of plants since 1967. In semiconductors, the top states maintained their shares of plants between 1963 and 1977, with California actually increasing its lead by 264 percent, compared to a US average increase of 152 percent in 1963–77.[121] Glasmeier's calculations for 1977–82 confirm the trend.

Thus, while the sheer size of the information-technology sector, after two decades of growth at a phenomenal rate, gives rise to its spatial sprawl, the industries remain disproportionately concentrated in the areas that were already the hubs of high-technology activity in the 1960s. There is a cumulative process of uneven development associated with the concentration of information generation and corporate control in the key milieux of innovation.

Furthermore, the spatial diffusion of the industry follows the processes, analyzed above, of hierarchical division of labor and decentralization of production. Specifically, the process of spatial diffusion manifests four main features. First of these is the generation of *secondary milieux of innovation* which articulate themselves to the seedbeds of technology in an asymmetrical, interdependent relationship. These secondary milieux are truly innovative production complexes that specialize in specific technological areas and tend to rely on a network of small, entrepreneurial start-up firms. Gordon and Kimball have analyzed the formation of such a milieu in Santa Cruz, California, since the late 1970s, in close association with nearby Silicon Valley.[122] Yet, as they make clear, Santa Cruz is much more than a set of ancillary firms for Silicon Valley. Most of the firms there tend to engage in innovative R&D for products that they sell, generally, to Silicon Valley companies; they sub-contract most of their production work to other California companies, so that they constitute truly a milieu of innovation of the second order, thus making more complex the chain of interdependence linking innovation, manufacturing, and markets. Secondary milieux of innovation are being generated in areas such as North Carolina's Research Triangle, Colorado Springs, Santa Barbara, and Salt Lake City. The important feature in each case is the direct relationship of these milieu to the higher-order innovation centers, sometimes represented by complexes, such as Route 128 or Silicon Valley, but often also organized around the inner world of large corporations, such as IBM or Motorola.

The second distinctive feature is the decentralization of technical branch plants, subsidiaries of companies located in predominant technological centers. Glasmeier, who has emphasized the role of these plants in the decentralization of high-technology industries, writes:

Technical branch plants represent a new tier in the corporate hierarchy and can be characterized as stand alone profit centers that have spun out of existing concentrations of older and newer vintages in search of pools of technical labor, as well as other factors, such as access to newly developing high-tech agglomerations and final markets. These units are organized often along product lines and are sites where both design and production are carried out.[123]

Thus, they are complete production units, with a large degree of initiative, yet organizationally and technologically dependent on the parent firm. Booming high-technology areas such as Austin and Phoenix are based mainly upon a concentration of large technical branch plants. For instance, Austin's industrial development was based on the location of such plants from IBM, Lockheed, TI, Intel, Control Data, Motorola, Rolm, Tandem, Sperry-Rand, Hughes, and more, attracted to Austin by a good university training large numbers of engineers, relatively cheap labor, good environmental quality, easy air connections, and a direct relationship with the expanding Texas market.

Industrial complexes built around technical branch plants are largely autonomous in their dynamics, yet they remain dependent on the primary milieux of innovation with respect to strategic decisions and access to new discoveries. There are, however, exceptions: for instance, in the case of Austin, the location of the electronics consortium MCC has provided the possibility of access to cutting-edge innovation in advanced microelectronics.[124] It is expected that the location of SEMATECH, a Defense Department-funded major research facility on manufacturing technology for semiconductors, approved in 1987, will further reinforce the potential for high-level research in Austin, which until now has been very limited.[125] Nevertheless, most of MCC's research findings, as well as, most likely, SEMATECH's technology, will constitute proprietary information that is likely to be diffused within the participant corporation networks rather than through the Austin complex.

Technical branch plants are also present in the high-level technological milieux, such as Silicon Valley or Boston, but here they tend to be subsidiaries of a parent company located in a different high-level milieu, set up in the alternative center in an attempt to tap into a competitor's local resources. An example of this would be Intel's branch plant near Boston.

Thirdly, manufacturing continues to be decentralized to less industrialized, relatively isolated areas. This process accounts for the majority of high-technology development in the southern United States, as well as for the location of American companies in the Third World. The evidence reviewed shows that the more industrial sprawl takes place, the more pronounced becomes the separation between advanced manufacturing and assembly manufacturing. The latter is increasingly rare in the US. The distinction between these two tiers of manufacturing tends to be sharper at present in the off-shore production process, with different levels of skill concentrated in different locations in Europe, Asia, and Latin America. For the present analytical purpose it is important to observe the reproduction of the spatial division of labor between different production functions off-shore, with the implication this carries that when information-technology industries expand over the world they do so according to their specific spatial logic.

The fourth feature that would seem to be suggested by the third is that the original milieux of innovation are irreproducible and that the new industrial space is going to be increasingly polarized inter-regionally and internationally. This is indeed the position clearly stated by Gordon and Kimball:

Global high-technology headquarters, once established, are not replicable. First: they were formed under specific historical conditions and circumstances that no longer pertain. Their emergence, far from being reducible to a single, easily replicated origin, was dependent precisely upon the favorable confluence of diverse and complex sources of growth whose simulation, particularly in competition with established headquarters locations, would require new, and impossibly risky governmental and business strategies as well as the concentration of extraordinarily vast resources. Second: rather than other areas creating anew the conditions which made the headquarters successful, the latter's infrastructural advantages act as a magnet for new businesses and skills which continue to be attracted to such areas rather than locating elsewhere. Third, the conversion of competitive entrepreneurial places into dominant technology headquarters renders their duplication unnecessary.[126]

Along similar lines, Oakey also provides a convincing argument about the self-expanding logic of Silicon Valley's pre-eminence.[127]

I tend to concur with these interpretations, yet with two important qualifications. First, the continuous technological upgrading of the industry considerably enhances the technological level of secondary milieux of innovation and technical branch complexes. It also expands the number and size of such complexes. More and more medium-level technological developments can take place away from the upper-level centers of innovation. Thus, the spatial division of labor should be seen no longer as a simple split between innovation and production, but rather as a separation of different levels of innovation and the emergence of different forms of linkage between innovation and production functions. Secondly, the more information-technology products become customized, programmable devices, the more crucial in all sectors is the direct connection between industrial producers and industrial users. While this trend has not reversed the dominance of high-level milieux of innovation, it has nevertheless created an incentive for information-technology producers and technological services to locate close to the major markets, namely the major metropolitan areas, including those of them in the old industrial regions. This is even more evident in the booming European market, where large metropolitan areas are acting as magnets for the location of Japanese and American information-technology firms, superseding the traditional rationale of location in underdeveloped European regions to take advantage of governmental incentives. Most of these new developments take the form of upgraded technical branch plants, including a complete ensemble of production functions. In some cases, research and design centers are being set up for customized prototype production in conjunction with the revitalization of the traditional industrial structure.[128]

The spatial diffusion of information-technology industries, then, basically expands the logic embedded in its structural characteristics. But it also places their location pattern in the context of the unfolding dynamics of economic restructuring and international competition.

Conclusion: The Dynamics of Information-technology Producers and the Transformation of the New Industrial Space

The main theme of this chapter has been the specific nature of the spatial location pattern of information-technology producers, a specificity which stems from the articulation of the structural characteristics of the industry with the dynamics of the firms and institutions that engage in its development. If the analysis presented here is correct, it should hold, in its main elements, for information-technology industries in other national contexts, as well as for future stages of the industry in the United States. This does not necessarily mean that the industry would continue to locate in similar places. The proposition concerns, rather, the replication of the spatial logic of the new productive organizations, namely their characteristic relationship to space, consequent on the dynamics of their process of production and their strategies as firms. To pursue the empirical verification of this proposition would require a comparative, historical, and prospective framework of analysis, and is clearly beyond the limits of this book. The present purpose is limited to defining the profile of a distinctive location pattern, so that its reproducibility can be tested, and the accuracy of the analytical model eventually perfected. Besides, we have made a methodological choice that informs this whole book, namely, to focus on the spatial transformation induced by new information technologies *in the United States*, as a way of testing the broader analytical framework proposed. Accordingly I have in general refrained from analyzing processes in other societies, the description of which could make the content of this book unnecessarily cumbersome at the current stage of development of the theory. Nevertheless, in concluding the treatment of the emergence of the new industrial space, on the basis of the US experience, it seems intellectually useful to consider the validity of the location pattern we have found for information-technology producers in other areas and, even more important, in the subsequent stages of the industry's development.

The only country with a mature information-technology industry at a comparable technological level to that of the US is Japan; and systematic data on Japanese firms' spatial behavior are too sparse to be able to conduct an adequate comparison. At first sight, however, it would seem that the pattern of location of the electronics industry in Japan is quite different from that pertaining in the US. From the beginning, most information-technology industries were located in the greater Tokyo metropolitan area;[129] and until recently, the industry did not present much international and inter-regional division of labor. Of course, geographic specificity has to be taken into consideration along with industrial specificity. Japan being smaller than California, one could hardly expect the same level of spatial differentiation among productive functions and types of firms as exhibited by electronics industries in the US. Yet if the characteristics of each national territory dominate and supersede those of the industry, it would be difficult to argue that we are in the presence of a new logic of industrial space. In fact, the Japanese experience has been more diversified, evolving as it did in different stages of technological development, and has recently become somewhat closer to the location pattern found in America. The key fact in this respect is that, in its initial stage, the Japanese electronics industry did not start from autonomous generation of new technological information.[130] It developed on the basis of manufacturing better information-technology products derived from discoveries made in the US and, to some extent, in Europe.[131] Therefore, since manufacturing quality and low production costs were crucial in gaining a competitive edge in the early stages of the new industry, it was essential to locate in the heart of the Japanese manufacturing areas, where skilled production with skilled workers could take place. There was little room for risking low-quality work in cheaper offshore locations. Besides, governmental support (particularly that of MITI) to large Japanese corporations was vital in the technological upgrading of the industry, as well as in its positioning in domestic and international markets, and Japanese government policy strongly supported location of economically strategic industries on Japanese soil. Given the high concentration of large corporations and government-sponsored research centers in the Tokyo–Yokohama area, this was the obvious location, linking research and manufacturing with the largest domestic market.

Nevertheless, when the industry matured, reaching higher technological status, and dramatically increasing its volume of production and exports, it expanded on the basis of a trend toward decentralization of production inside Japan. This trend has been evident since the early 1970s.[132] The main beneficiary of the process has been the hitherto underdeveloped southern island of Kyushu, which in the mid-1980s accounted for about 40 per cent of Japanese production of integrated circuits, with particularly heavy concentration around the Oita Prefecture.[133] Most of the decentralization concerned technical branch plants of the large corporations, including some American firms. The government also attempted to foster spatial dispersal of R&D by creating the "science and technology city" of Tsukuba,[134] about 60 km north of Tokyo, where in 1988 7,000 researchers worked on advanced research programs, most of them joint ventures between government and corporations.

In the third stage of development, when the Japanese electronics industry raised itself, economically and technologically, to the level of its US counterpart and became a world leader in information-technology production, its location pattern drifted in the direction of that we have found to be typical of the American information-technology industry. First, in a joint initiative between MITI and a number of regional Prefectures, the "technopolis program" was launched, its goal the development of 14 decentralized industrial milieux of innovation and production.[135] These "technopolises" try to reproduce the combination of elements present in Silicon Valley: university and government research centers, manufacturing companies, venture capital, government markets, and a concentration of high-level technical labor, in the hope of generating dynamic synergy among the different factors.[136] Although it is still early to assess the effects of the program, it is already possible to note the significant self-identification of the Japanese industry with the location pattern of milieux of innovation presented in this chapter. In fact, these technopolises are secondary milieux, still dependent on the Tokyo-based higher-level centers. Also, the decentralization of scientists and engineers is only made possible because of the development of a telecommunications infrastructure aimed at linking all milieux on-line, allowing researchers to work together in real time. Another factor favoring decentralization of innovation is a good inter-regional transportation network, based on the bullet-train, which, by increasing the accessibility of Tokyo, makes bearable the engineers' exile from the centers of power and consumption.

Secondly, when cut-throat international competition, the emergence of the newly industralizing countries (NICs) in the electronics market, and new protectionist measures indicated the possibility of a future threat to Japanese hegemony in the world market, the major corporations, among them NEC, Hitachi, and Toshiba, increasingly resorted to the strategy used by their American counterparts years before: offshoring lower-level production functions to the Pacific Rim, particularly to Taiwan, Singapore, Thailand, and Malaysia, to reduce production costs on the basis of cheaper labor, cheaper land, and fewer government taxes and regulations.[137] These plants are, of course, directly dependent on their parent companies. While originally they used to ship their finished products back to Japan, they are now exporting directly to the final markets, in a truly integrated world production chain.

Finally, to circumvent protectionism in other countries, Japanese companies have started to assemble, and sometimes to produce, in their key foreign markets, particularly the US and Europe, in a move parallel to that of American companies in the 1960s.[138]

In spite of obvious geographical contrasts, then, the main difference between the spatial behavior of the US and Japanese electronics industries seems to be related to the time difference in reaching a stage of development at which the firms' strategies had to face similar problems. From this point onwards, similarities in location strategies seem to be greater than the differences resulting from the two countries' specific history and geography. While there are still a great many differences between the American and Japanese industrial location patterns, given their very diverse respective starting points, the unfolding spatial logic of Japanese electronic firms does seem to result from the interaction between the specific structure of their production process and their industrial strategy, along lines not too distant from the spatial behavior observed in the case of the US.

Will this spatial logic persevere in the current stage of development of information-technology industries? Only by answering this question, even tentatively, can we make the distinction between the description of a temporary phenomenon and the analysis of a new process. To address the issue, within the limits of this study, I will conclude by considering the restructuring of the electronics industry during the 1980s and the spatial implication of the trends there displayed.

In 1984–6 the US electronics industry experienced its most serious slump ever, to the point of calling into question standing assumptions on the growth prospects of "sunrise" sectors. Silicon Valley was significantly hurt, with over 12,000 lay-offs, including substantial numbers of researchers and engineers. Vacancies for R&D and industrial space in the Valley jumped to a stunning 35 percent in 1986, a sign that the growth anticipated by the developers had not materialized.[139] The industry did not fully recover its dynamism until late 1987, and even then the potential for future crises was still present, as acknowledged by most observers of the industry. Three major factors appear to account for this crisis:[140]

(1) A process of "creative destruction," in the Schumpeterian sense, in which excess capacity developed by less competitive firms is eliminated, while resources are reoriented toward more productive uses. This is part of the typical cycle of a booming industry reaching a mature stage, a phenomenon that can be understood in the classical terms of the product cycle–profit cycle model. It is not, however, a primary cause of this crisis, which seems to stem mainly from other, more powerful factors.

(2) Increasing international competition, particularly from the Japanese electronics companies, based on lower production costs, higher manufacturing quality, and sustained effort in technological innovation. The arrival of new NIC and European producers in the market forced US companies to revise their structure of production costs as well as their marketing strategies.

(3) The difference in pace between the rate of technological innovation and the rate of diffusion and utilization of information technology in the economy and society at large. This was perhaps the crucial factor. Without wider use of information-technology devices it is impossible for

the electronics industry to keep growing at the same rate and still find markets. But at the same time the drive to innovate is the main competitive strategy hitherto used by information-technology producers, and capital-intensive investments and massive research efforts continue to be the main instruments for winning market shares. It follows that more costly investments and increasingly sophisticated technology need to generate higher returns in a market that, in fact, provides decreasing opportunities for such super-profits to match the expectations of the industry.

This "applications gap" is a particularly serious obstacle to the continuous growth of information-technology producers, because it is deeply entrenched in both the institutions of society and the organization of the industry. Without a massive re-equipping of traditional manufacturing, an upgrading of the educational system, and the appropriation by people and organizations of the full potential of information technologies, the pace of the industry will slow down in the near future, both technologically and economically. It is true that during the 1980s military markets came to the rescue of information-technology producers in the US; high-technology industries experienced a process of remilitarization after a long period of overwhelming dominance by commercial applications. Nevertheless, the military option can hardly be a way out of the potential structural crisis, because of its negative effects on technological diffusion, its limited commercial spin-offs, and its high dependence on budgetary constraints and political conjunctures. The expansion of military markets in the 1980s may have eased the downturn of the industry and allowed it to pick up momentum again, but it cannot absorb in the long term the tremendous productive potential that is boiling up in information technology's cauldrons.

In practice, electronics companies and government industrial polices (at both federal and state level) have tried to respond to the crisis through a number of strategies, leading to a major process of restructuring in the information-technology industries. Most of these new strategic policies can be grouped under four headings:[141]

(1) Establishment of closer and broader linkages with industrial sectors and final users of the technology. Examples are the effort by the computer industry massively to penetrate the school system, or the emphasis of electronics companies on the development of "mechatronics," in connection with the restructuring of old line manufacturing.
(2) Renewed efforts to automate electronics manufacturing, thus lowering production costs. Skilled non-research labor is the main target of cost-saving strategies in the production process. US companies seem to be engaging themselves in a blend of Japanese-inspired emphasis on manufacturing quality and their own traditional concern in finding cheaper sources of labor.

(3) Focus on the technological upgrading of the industry's products, targeting particularly the software component of the new systems, an area in which US science and technology retains a clear technological edge, although still being unable to use effectively the potential of the newest hardware. This strategy includes stepped-up research budgets, joint ventures with universities, sponsored corporate consortia on key technological fields (such as MCC), government-sponsored industrial research facilities, (such as SCI or SEMATECH), and a general call for government support in funding research and providing markets, sometimes on the grounds of protecting national security interests.

(4) An appeal to government support in opening up world markets and helping to protect US markets, under the disguise of free-trade ideology outraged by unfair competition.

The final impact of these strategies on the industry and its spatial manifestation will depend on the broader process of the restructuring of electronics worldwide. Dieter Ernst, having examined this process in detail, foresees four major developments:[142]

(1) A substantial decline of US semiconductors merchant firms will occur relative to huge, diversified electronics systems companies, the so-called "captive producers."

(2) Strategic alliances built around a few major systems corporations will become a key feature of global competition.

(3) There will be a major shift of wafer fabrication capacities to Asia and, more generally, a development of advanced manufacturing capability in that area of the world.

(4) Neo-mercantilist policies will proliferate, increasing protectionism in all economic regions.

Most of the available information points in these directions. However, my purpose here is not to indulge in economic forecasting but to analyze the spatial logic of information-technology industries. For the sake of this analysis, I will assume that the trends presented by Ernst take place, and try to elaborate on their potential spatial implications.

The emphasis on new linkages to be established with traditional manufacturing and information-based service activities is already fostering spatial relocation of some technical branch plants in a closer spatial relationship with the industry's markets.[143] This is also increasingly true for some customized design and prototype production focused on particular applications. The main beneficiaries of this move are large metropolitan areas with a concentration of information services, and old industrial regions in the process of converting their manufacturing basis. Yet only areas that can retain their nodal role in the economy, such as New York, or that are engaged in upgrading the industry's competitiveness in the world economy, such as

Michigan, are actually able to attract electronics industries organized around new strategic linkages.

Protectionist tendencies at the world level accentuate the linkage-induced decentralization of production, adding to the pattern an international dimension, as the need to penetrate growing markets dictates location inside the boundaries of each major economic region. While early decentralization of US electronics companies in Europe favored peripheral areas, such as Scotland or Montpellier, more recent developments tend to be concentrated in large industrial metropolitan areas, business centers, or a combination of both, such as Paris, Milan, Madrid, and Munich;[144] the formerly dominant concentrations of US companies in Scotland and Ireland are likely to be overshadowed by the new, linkage-oriented locations.

The drive toward automation, in terms of both labor cost-saving and manufacturing quality, definitely downplays the importance of cheap, unskilled labor as a location factor. Taking this to its logical extreme, decentralization to the Third World could come to a halt, even eventually be reversed. In fact, a more complex pattern is taking shape, in line with the new industrial strategy:[145] existing offshore locations are being automated and upgraded, and it seems likely, as predicted by Ernst, that advanced manufacturing will eventually take place in Asia. The reason for this development sees to be two-fold: first, the need to penetrate future potential markets, such as China, Korea, and India; secondly, the learning curve of workers in south-east Asian locations and the training of engineers by local institutions makes it possible to upgrade manufacturing and save costs on skilled labor, while keeping in place the existing industrial structure. So the pattern of decentralized production is likely to persist, still along the lines of the technical division of labor, yet with the important qualification of the upgrading of the low end of the technological spectrum. Purely routine tasks will most likely be entirely automated, not so much to save unskilled labor (given its low cost in new potential locations around the world) as to ensure high and consistent quality and smooth production.

The process of technological upgrading, the key element if the US industry is to keep its competitive edge, translates spatially into the reinforcement of high-level innovative milieux, as well as the development of secondary milieux in direct relationship with major centers of innovation. These high-level milieux (Silicon Valley, Boston, North Carolina's Research Triangle, Minneapolis, etc.) concentrate an increasing share of technological knowledge, to the point where we can foresee their evolution into providers of technological services, engaging mainly in design and prototype production, with an attenuation of their manufacturing basis. This trend was already apparent in Silicon Valley in 1987.[146] Companies from all over the world set up shop in Silicon Valley, in many cases by acquiring existing companies, to take advantage of the new technological developments produced there in order to manufacture products resulting from the Valley's discoveries in different, more convenient locations. Thus, in spite of increasingly acute urban problems and occasional economic downturns, these higher milieux will continue to thrive, and are unlikely to be replaced or even replicated at the same level of innovative potential, because of the cumulative character of knowledge generation and the industrial learning process. Only targeted efforts, supported by governments on a very large scale, are able to set up new high-level milieux of innovation in other areas of the world, and even this will become more and more difficult to achieve as the pace of scientific and technological discovery accelerates. High-level milieux of innovation reinforce their own dominance and their exclusiveness on the basis of their self-expanding synergy.

In sum, the spatial implications of the restructuring process in the electronics industry do not reverse the locational logic I have presented and analyzed. In fact, they develop it and give it specific form. Milieux of innovation continue to command the chain of interdependencies, and, if anything, they become more exclusive, more secluded, and more central in the overall production process. Secondary milieux of innovation are developing and will continue to do so, but more as an expression of the process of decentralization of some aspects of innovation functions than as a diffusion of the industry's original seedbeds throughout the country and the world. Decentralization of production still takes place along the lines of the specific requirements of each stage of the labor process. Market-oriented location becomes increasingly important at both domestic and international levels, further decentralizing production to ensure linkages with users of information technology. Spatial division of labor, on the basis of technological level and corporate control functions, is still the pervasive and distinctive characteristic of information-technology industries, although increased automation, upgrading of manufacturing operations, and new technological discoveries have extended the scope of this division both toward the upper end (increasingly exclusive milieux of innovation) and toward the lower end (offshoring of advanced manufacturing).

Thus, although the industry is extending its presence into new locations (for instance, to older manufacturing regions via the "mechatronics connection"), its spatial logic seems to be rooted in its structural characteristics, though the actual location pattern of the industry results from the interaction of that structurally determined logic with the specific orientations of the industry in the changing pattern of world competition. Nevertheless, a major trend in the process of industrial restructuring could decisively effect that spatial logic itself, along with everything else in the world of information-technology producers. I refer here to the evolution, predicted by various authors,[147] toward global strategic alliances between a few major system corporations, together with the dependence of US merchant firms on these large corporations. Could this trend decisively affect the economic, technological, and spatial structure of the industry as I have presented it? Economically, without any doubt, because such is precisely the meaning of the restructuring process. Technologically, less so, because the large corporations have a strong interest in maintaining and enhancing the creativity and synergistic potential of milieux of innovation, while wishing to capture that potential in their corporate structures. Very much in the way that IBM keeps Intel thriving technologically, while making it increasingly dependent commercially, large corporate systems are taking over the world of information technology using a non-traditional approach: the emphasis is on networks and sub-contracting, not on mergers and takeovers. The instruments of domination are technological specification, price-cutting competition, and access to large, secure markets. Large corporations, American as well as Japanese and Europeans, tread a thin line between subduing innovative companies and not destroying their technological potential and entrepreneurial dynamism. Thus, milieux of innovation such as Silicon Valley or Route 128 are becoming increasingly dependent on worldwide corporate conglomerates that internalize their innovative potential in their commercial strategies. In so doing, they do not transform the spatial logic of information-technology industries. IBM, or ATT, or Phillips-Signetics also operate, and will operate, on the basis of spatial division of labor, exclusive milieux of innovation, and decentralization of the production process.[148] Yet there is a major change in the making: the spatial logic of information-technology producers is being drawn inside the organizational structure of large corporations. The internationalization of production, the social and spatial separation of innovation functions, the relocation of production as a basis for market-oriented downward linkages – all these processes increasingly take place within the corporate structures, either inside the corporation itself of within the networks through which the corporate system controls its inputs and expands its output.[149] The emergence of a dominant corporate world in the information-technology industry does not preclude the spatial logic stemming form the industry's structure: it internalizes it, institutionalizing in a network of flows interconnected at a global level the new socio-spatial division of labor. Control over the production of information technology is tantamount to structural domination of the new industrial space.

3

The Space of Flows

The Use of New Technologies in the Information Economy, and the Dialectics between Centralization and Decentralization of Services

Introduction

It would seem obvious that the most direct impact of information technologies on the economy and society, and therefore on their spatial structure, occurs in the realm of information-processing activities. Such an elementary observation nevertheless has far-reaching consequences for social and spatial organization, because the processes of production, distribution, and management of advanced economies rely increasingly on knowledge generation, information exchanges and information handling. The dramatic changes in information technology deeply affect the core of our system, and in so doing lie at the very roots of its pattern of spatial change. The use of information technology by organizations, and particularly by large private corporations and large-scale public bureaucracies, may be the most important immediate source of technological change in our cities and regions. However, the spatial form taken by this change is far from simple. While the prophets of technological determinism have forecast the general dissolution of cities and metropolitan areas in an undifferentiated territorial sprawl, with all communication conducted by satellites and optic fiber networks, the actual processes at work are much more complex because technology is only an instrument, albeit a very powerful one, of the process of organizational restructuring dictated by economic, social, and institutional changes. So, between the new information technologies and the emerging spatial structure, there are a number of fundamental mediating factors: the evolution of services; the rise of the information economy; the impact of automation on office work and office workers; the new organizational, and thus locational, logic of large corporations and public bureaucracies; and the interaction of all these elements with the existing spatial structure and with the social environment in which all these trends articulate with one another. It is this complexity that I will try to reconstruct in this chapter, in order to explain in its final section the dialectics between centralization and decentralization of information-processing activities and the consequences of this process for the overall social and spatial structure. But before we are able to understand the actual meaning of this new spatial logic, we need to examine the impact of office automation in the context of the expansion of an information economy, a process which is at the very core of the shift of employment and output toward service activities.

The Structural Shift to Services and the Rise of the Information Economy

The fundamental transformation of the economic structure in advanced industrial societies, and particularly in the US, is expressed in the continuing shift toward service activities as a source of employment and generation of output.[1] In 1986, in the US, services accounted for 71 per cent of total employment and 68 per cent of GNP.[2] This trend has led to the characterization of such societies as "post-industrial,"[3] a notion that confuses rather than helps the identification of the new historical trends. The notion of post-industrialism is purely negative: it refers to the fact that manufacturing is no more at the center of the economy. This itself is open to question, yet, even accepting that position, we would still need to define what is at the core of the new social and economic dynamics. On both counts (the implicit under-estimation of the structural role of manufacturing industries, and the descriptive negativism of characterizing a major social trend as "post-"), the notion of post-industrialism recognizes, without truly explaining, a major social transformation.[4] It is important to assess this transformation analytically if we are to be able to understand the extent of the impact of information technologies on our socio-spatial structure.

On the one hand, although manufacturing activities have seen their relative importance decline steadily over time, the rise of services cannot be directly correlated with the "demise" of manufacturing.[5] The dramatic increase in service jobs in recent decades (see table 3.1) has taken place mainly as a result of job transfers from agriculture,[6] and of the entry into the labor market of new kinds of workers, particularly women, who account for the great majority of all new jobs in services during the period 1975–85, filling over 82 percent of all new jobs created during that period. There is a direct relationship between the rise of services and the feminization of the labor force.[7]

On the other hand, the declining proportion of jobs in manufacturing, as well as its shrinking share of GNP, do not eliminate its strategic importance in the overall economic picture, in very much the same way as the shrinkage

Table 3.1 Percentage distribution of the labor force by industry sectors and intermediate industry groups 1870–1980

Sectors and industries	1870	1900	1920	1940	1950	1960	1970	1980
Extractive	52.3	40.7	28.9	21.3	14.4	8.1	4.5	4.5
Agriculture	50.8	38.1	26.3	19.2	12.7	7.0	3.7	3.6
Mining	1.6	2.6	2.6	2.1	1.7	1.1	0.8	0.9
Transformative	23.5	27.9	32.9	29.8	33.9	35.9	33.1	29.8
Construction	5.9	5.8		4.7	6.2	6.2	5.8	6.2
Food				2.7	2.7	3.1	2.0	1.8
Textile				2.6	2.2	3.3	3.0	2.1
Metal				2.9	3.6	3.9	3.3	2.7
Machinery	17.6	22.1		2.4	3.7	7.5	8.3	5.2
Chemical				1.5	1.7	1.8	1.6	1.3
Misc. manufacturing				11.8	12.3	8.7	7.7	10.5
Utilities	a	a	a	1.2	1.4	1.4	1.4	1.4
Distributive services	11.5	16.9	18.7	20.4	22.4	21.9	22.3	23.9
Transportation	5.0	7.3	7.6	4.9	5.3	4.4	3.9	6.6
Communication				0.9	1.2	1.3	1.5	1.5
Wholesale				2.7	3.5	3.6	4.1	3.9
Retail	6.5	9.5	11.1	11.8	12.3	12.5	12.8	11.9
Producer services	b	b	2.8	4.6	4.8	6.6	8.2	9.5
Banking				1.1	1.1	1.6	2.6	1.7
Insurance				1.2	1.4	1.7	1.8	1.9
Real Estate				1.1	1.0	1.0	1.0	1.6
Engineering					0.2	0.3	0.4	0.6
Accounting					0.2	0.3	0.4	0.5
Misc. business services				1.3	0.6	1.2	1.8	2.4
Legal services					0.4	0.5	0.5	0.8
Social services	3.4	5.1	8.7	10.0	12.4	16.3	21.9	24.3
Medical					1.1	1.4	2.2	3.3
Hospitals				2.3	1.8	2.7	3.7	4.1
Education	1.5	2.3	2.8	3.5	3.8	5.4	8.6	7.7
Welfare				0.9	0.7	1.0	1.2	1.0
Non-profits					0.3	0.4	0.4	0.6
Postal services				0.7	0.8	0.9	1.0	0.7
Government	0.8	1.0	2.2	2.6	3.7	4.3	4.6	4.7
Misc. social services					0.1	0.2	0.3	2.3
Personal services	9.3	9.4	8.1	14.0	12.1	11.3	10.0	10.8
Domestic Serv.	7.4	6.1	4.1	5.3	3.2	3.1	1.7	1.3
Hotels				1.3	1.0	1.0	1.0	1.1
Eating and drinking	2.0	3.4	4.0	2.5	3.0	2.9	3.3	4.4

Table 3.1 Continued

Sectors and industries	1870	1900	1920	1940	1950	1960	1970	1980
Repair				1.5	1.7	1.4	1.3	1.5
Laundry				1.0	1.2	1.0	0.8	0.4
Barber and								
beauty				—	—	0.8	0.9	0.7
Entertainment				0.9	1.0	0.8	0.8	1.0
Misc. personal								
services				1.6	1.2	0.4	0.3	0.4

[a] Utilities included in distributive services.
[b] Finance, insurance, and real estate included in trade.
Source: 1870–1970 US Census; 1980: "Special Labor Force Report 244," U.S. Department of Labor Bureau of Labor Statistics, 1981. Compiled by Singelman (see note 6) and updated by Baran (see note 48).

of the proportion of farmers and agricultural workers to less than 3 percent of total US employment does not preclude agriculture continuing to play a very important role in the economy, both directly, through the provision and pricing of its products, and indirectly, through the manufacturing and service activities it generates. Pursuing this line of reasoning, Cohen and Zysman have argued convincingly the close linkages between manufacturing and service activities.[8] They point out that many service activities, particularly in producer services, the most dynamic in output generation, are in fact support activities to the management, production, and distribution of manufactured goods. In fact, they argue, when a national economy, such as the US, overlooks such linkages, increasingly specializing in services, the loss of competitiveness in manufacturing leads to correspondingly increasing losses in services to the point where service growth cannot compensate in either quantity or quality for the jobs and wealth lost in the process of de-industrialization.

An alternative vision to the classical, and misleading line of argument, Colin Clark's mechanistic and evolutionary distinction between primary, secondary, and tertiary sectors, is to consider the economic structure as made up of *processes*, in which service activities connect agriculture and manufacturing with the consumption of goods and services, and with the management of organizations and institutions of society. Only from this perspective will we be able to understand the diversity of services, a diversity in fact so extreme that it forbids considering services as a single, homogeneous sector of economic activity. Joachim Singelman proposed a few years ago a typology of services that still appears to be the most useful characterization of the different activities arbitrarily merged under the label.[9] Table 3.1 documents the evolution of employment in the US between 1870 and 1980 using Singelman's typology, updated to include the figures of the 1980 Census. A reading of this table shows the great differences among types of services in their relative share of total employment. Thus, between 1960 and 1980, distributive services grew moderately, although still accounting for 23.9 percent of the labor force in 1980. Personal services actually declined, from 11.3 percent to 10.8 percent, with the major exception of eating and drinking activities, which employ 4.4 percent of the labor force – more than agriculture. Producer services almost doubled, while still employing, overall, fewer workers than personal services. And social services literally exploded, jumping from 10 percent in 1940 to 24.3 percent in 1980. Even during the crisis years of the 1970s, the decline in education employment has been more than compensated by employment growth in hospitals and medical services, which in 1980 reached 7.8 percent of the labor force. These trends have continued in the same direction during the 1980s, increasing the gap between expanding service industries and moderate job creation in other sectors. According to calculations by Peter Hall, between 1980 and 1985 4,219,700 new non-farm jobs were added to the US economy.[10] Of these, only 33,200 were in manufacturing, and 3,477,800 were in services. However, within services there were major disparities. For instance, communications grew by over 400,000 jobs, while commerce (wholesale and retail together) actually lost over 66,000 jobs (see table 3.2). Table 3.3 shows the dissimilarity of the evolution of the various types of services in the 1970–84 period in terms of contribution to GNP, with finance, insurance, and real estate, and "other service industries" (including health and education), dramatically increasing their share. Together, these two categories account for 30.7 percent of 1984 GNP, well above the 21 percent accounted for by manufacturing.

The lesson to be drawn from this disparity is very simple: *there is not a service sector*. There are a number of activities, employing people and generating income, that go beyond the extractive and manufacturing activities, and which increase their diversity as our societies grow in complexity.[11] The so-called "services" have grown out of a variety of functional demands and social pressures, many of which derive from social mobilization and political concessions, as I suggested years ago.[12] A substantial part of employment in services, particularly in social services and personal services, is in fact, a way of absorbing the surplus population generated by increased productivity in agriculture and industry, in a society that still requires salaried work to survive, even if we could achieve greater collective output with less collective work. This is why, as Stanback writes:

Productivity is a key issue in assessing the role of services in our economy. There is little evidence of a strong, cumulative shift of demand from goods to services. Yet the shift toward greater shares of employment in services is well established. For services taken as a whole, gains in productivity have failed to match those in non-service activities. Consequently, economic growth has been accompanied by disproportionately large increases in service sector jobs.[13]

Table 3.2 Employment changes by SIC single-digit headings, divisions, 1975–80, 1980–5

(a) 1975–80

	New England	Mid-Atlantic	E.-N.-Cent.	W.-N.-Cent.	S. Atlantic	E.-S.-Cent.	W.-S.-Cent.	Mountain	Pacific	Total US
TOTAL thousands	857.8	1360.0	2071.2	1130.5	2742.5	881.9	2310.5	1180.9	3199.2	15734.5
Mining	1.2	−0.3	10.2	11.7	7.8	15.7	171.2	49.1	14.9	281.5
Construction	12.7	13.6	67.1	37.9	156.4	23.2	186.8	92.6	167.4	757.9
Manufacturing	223.9	38.0	79.9	149.0	414.7	120.7	345.9	141.8	526.6	2039.9
Transportation	31.0	99.6	175.2	121.4	187.9	77.2	166.2	95.7	161.8	1116.0
Transportation	27.1	85.9	152.2	100.9	134.5	58.0	119.7	66.3	108.9	852.6
Communication	3.9	13.7	23.0	21.4	53.4	19.2	46.5	28.6	52.9	262.6
Wholesale/retail	168.0	236.7	442.1	222.3	627.4	169.4	494.6	252.5	782.1	3395.1
Finance, Insurance, Real Estate	60.7	109.9	162.3	71.9	163.4	39.3	134.9	75.0	250.9	1068.3
Services	281.7	814.9	906.8	414.9	721.2	283.7	554.1	347.6	1110.3	5435.2
Government	78.6	47.4	227.6	101.4	463.7	152.7	256.8	127.4	185.8	1641.4
Industry	237.8	51.5	157.2	198.6	578.9	159.6	703.9	283.5	708.3	3079.3
Service	620.0	1308.5	1914.0	931.9	2163.6	722.3	1606.6	897.4	2490.9	12655.2
Goods-handling	432.9	374.1	751.5	520.9	1340.8	387.0	1318.2	602.3	1599.3	7327.0
Information-handling	424.9	985.9	1319.7	609.6	1401.7	494.9	992.3	578.6	1599.9	8407.5
Ratio: serv./ind.	2.6	25.4	12.2	4.7	3.7	4.5	2.3	3.2	3.5	4.1
info./goods	1.0	2.6	1.8	1.2	1.0	1.3	0.8	1.0	1.0	1.1

Table 3.2 Continued

	(b) 1980–85									
	New England	Mid-Atlantic	E.-N.-Cent.	W.-N.-Cent.	S. Atlantic	E.-S.-Cent.	W.-S.-Cent.	Mountain	Pacific	Total US
TOTAL thousands	381.3	39.4	−147.9	19.1	1745.1	265.6	811.8	476.7	628.6	4219.7
Mining	0.7	−7.3	−16.3	−8.1	−23.7	−6.8	−15.4	−44.0	8.8	120.2
Construction	93.2	155.0	31.7	14.8	236.9	24.2	109.8	60.9	102.3	828.8
Manufacturing	64.4	−276.2	−138.0	−39.1	158.6	18.7	−19.0	86.3	177.5	33.2
Transportation	58.0	66.4	91.4	56.6	161.8	68.0	52.2	52.2	140.3	746.9
Transportation	25.1	−2.4	40.7	17.1	48.1	28.0	17.4	21.3	64.8	260.1
Communication	32.9	68.8	50.7	39.5	113.7	40.0	34.8	27.0	44.3	451.3
Wholesale/retail	−55.3	−195.1	−137.0	−66.9	250.5	58.1	120.3	70.5	−111.6	−66.4
Finance, Insurance, Real Estate	105.5	159.4	122.2	63.2	224.8	47.8	159.0	101.8	153.4	1137.3
Services	152.8	204.5	225.5	100.2	794.7	105.3	354.4	119.7	198.2	2255.4
Government	−38.2	−67.4	−327.3	−101.7	−58.5	−49.7	50.4	33.3	−1.0	−560.1
Industry	158.4	−128.4	−122.6	−32.4	371.8	36.1	75.4	103.1	280.5	741.9
Service	222.9	167.8	−25.3	51.5	1373.4	229.5	736.4	373.6	348.0	3477.8
Goods-handling	128.2	−325.9	−218.9	−82.2	670.4	122.2	213.2	194.9	233.7	935.6
Information-handling	253.1	365.3	71.0	101.3	1074.7	143.4	598.6	281.8	394.9	3284.1
Ratios: serv./ind.	1.4	NA	0.2	NA	3.7	6.4	9.8	3.6	1.2	4.7
Info./goods	2.0	NA	NA	NA	1.6	1.2	2.8	1.4	1.7	3.5

Source: Bureau of Labor Statistics, calculated by Peter Hall (see note 10).

Table 3.3 Components of United States Gross National Product

Services	Current $					1972 $ B				
	1970	1975	1980	1983	1984	1970	1975	1980	1983	1984
Total GNP	993	1,549	2,632	3,305	3,663	1,086	1,234	1,475	1,535	1,639
Agriculture, forestry, fisheries	29	53	77	73	91	34	37	40	39	45
Manufacturing	252	358	582	685	776	261	290	351	354	391
Transportation	39	55	99	115	130	43	46	52	47	50
Communication	24	40	67	92	103	26	36	52	59	63
Wholesale trade	68	117	190	229	265	72	88	104	114	130
Retail trade	98	149	238	307	337	104	122	142	152	165
Finance, insurance, real estate	142	216	399	543	598	155	188	236	254	265
Other service industries	114	186	342	478	529	127	148	189	207	219

Source: Quinn (see note 2).

Table 3.4 confirms this statement for the period 1968–78, on the threshold of the technological revolution in information processing. However, here again we find substantial differences among "services." Thus, while communications exhibited spectacular productivity growth during the period under consideration, "other services" (particularly health) and government showed a dismal performance, largely accounting for the low productivity growth overall of the US economy (manufacturing increased by 2.34 percent). Even finance, insurance, and real estate had a lower than average productivity growth, because its major increase in output was accompanied by a significant increase in employment. Yet, this does not imply that service activities, and particularly producer services and social services, are "parasite economic

Table 3.4   Output, employment and productivity growth rates in the US economy 1968–78 (%)

Industry	Output: Constant $ gross product originating	Full-time and part-time employees	Productivity: gross product originating per hour worked
All industries	2.89	1.90	1.41
Private non-farm economy	3.11	2.15	1.42
Agriculture forestry and fishing	1.8	1.18	0.68
Mining	1.40	3.68	−2.29
Construction	−0.54	1.96	−2.28
Manufacturing	2.44	0.34	2.34
Communications	8.36	2.39	5.84
Electric, gas and sanitary services	3.26	1.69	1.59
Wholesale trade	3.97	2.68	1.63
Retail trade	3.06	3.37	0.76
Finance insurance and real estate	4.22	3.50	0.99
Services	3.82	3.37	0.77
Business	5.88	5.95	0.69
Health	4.82	7.04	−1.44
Other	2.82	1.6	1.41
Government	1.31	1.02	0.56

Source: Economic Perspective on Trends in the United States Economy, 1968–1978, US Industrial Outlook, 1981, US Department of Commerce, Bureau of Industrial Economics. Compiled by Baron (see note 48)

activities." The contribution of most services to overall economic growth and social well-being is fundamental. But, until now, the characteristic nature of their labor processes and the institutional framework of service activities (many of them linked to the public sector) made it difficult to obtain the same productivity increases in services that took place in agriculture and manufacturing over the whole of this century. There is a fundamental contradiction building up in advanced economies: on the one hand, support activities, and particularly the handling of information, are at the core of productivity increases in the whole economy;[14] on the other hand, until very recently, many of the information-processing activities were labor-intensive and prone to low labor productivity.[15] Increased productivity in the economy as a whole was being disguised by the expansion of low-productivity, yet indispensable, service activities, particularly in information-handling. This is what explains the apparent mystery illustrated by figure 3.1, constructed by the Bureau of Labor Statistics: between 1948 and 1982, labor output increased substantially, as did, although to a lesser extent, "multifactor productivity" (which accounts for elements other than labor and capital). However, the productivity of capital remained stable.[16] In other words, the overhead costs of production for capital skyrocketed. This trend is partly due to the expansion of government and public services, both in defense and in social expenditures. But a substantial part of these overhead costs is attributable to the management of costs of production, that is, to the processing of information, that for a long time has been difficult to mechanize and rationalize, and even more difficult to automate.[17] Thus, at the center of the expansion of employment in services lies the explosion of information-processing activities.[18]

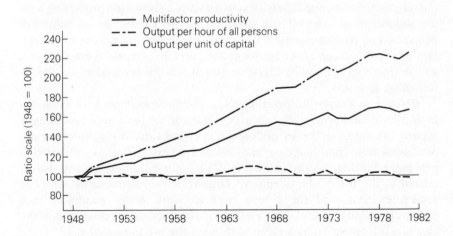

Figure 3.1   Indices of output per hour of all persons, output per unit of capital and multifactor productivity in the private business sector, 1948–1982
Source: Bureau of Labor Statistics

Marc Porat, in his pioneering work on the subject,[19] estimated that by 1970 46 percent of the US work force was employed in the information sector. Building on Porat's work, Kling and Turner have estimated that in 1980 50.5 percent of the US work force was employed in information-handling, up from 41 percent in 1960.[20] Peter Hall estimated that 8 million of the 15.6 million new non-farm jobs generated in the US in 1975–80, and almost 3.3 million of the 4 million new jobs created in 1980–5, were information-handling jobs. This is a most useful catergorization[21] because it cuts across the outmoded distinction between manufacturing and services to address the actual job content of a given occupation, thus avoiding the misleading practice of classifying as manufacturing workers the clerks of an automobile maker company. Kling and Turner have evaluated the distribution of the information work force by occupational categories, showing the increasing relative importance of professionals and semiprofessionals, the stabilization of the proportion of clerical workers (still representing 42.4 percent of the work force in 1980), and the decreasing proportion of sales and supervisory, and of blue-collar workers. It is this information-oriented work force which constitutes the quantitative and qualitative basis of advanced economies. The application of the information generated and processed by this labor force to all sectors, be they extractive, manufacturing, or services, is the main generator of productivity growth and income.[22] Our economies are to be categorized not as "post-industrial," but, as I argued in the first chapter of this book, *informational*, that is to say, the production of surplus derives mainly from the generation of knowledge and from the processing of necessary information. It is the surplus of productivity realized in manufacturing, agriculture, and producer services that allows the secular tendency to the growth of output per unit of input to continue.[23] Service activities mix information processing with the support of production and distribution, the satisfaction of consumer demands, and the management of organizations and institutions of society. Behind the expansion of the service sector, directly in terms of employment, and indirectly in terms of its effects on output, lies the development of the information economy.[24]

However, in a major historical paradox, the more societies have expanded their information-processing activities, the lower has been their productivity growth, because, unlike in high-technology manufacturing, information-processing organizations did not and/or could not extensively use information processing for their own restructuring. With a number of exceptions, mainly related to the use of the telephone, large-scale organizations in advanced economies continued for a long time to work under conditions and procedures close to those of the early periods of industrialization, and in the case of government bureaucracies to those of the pre-industrial age.[25] To be sure, since the mid-1960s some new trends toward greater capital intensity in the service industries did appear, notably in air transport, pipeline and rail transportation, communications, and public facilities.[26] But capital intensity remained low in the core of information industries, even in the financial sector until well into the 1970s.[27] The lack of information-processing technology in the information-processing organizations serving the economy and society at large was (and still largely is) the stumbling block for the unleashing of productive forces in our informational age. When the institutional context of the 1970s and 1980s forced corporations and governments into fully-fledged restructuring, the timely discoveries in information technology of the preceding three decades were at last put to work.[28] The result was the beginning of a dramatic transformation of information-handling activities, and therefore of office work,[29] that is perhaps the true equivalent in our societies to what manufacturing represented *vis-à-vis* craft production during the first industrial revolution.

Office Automation and Organizational Change in the Information Industries

The development of the information economy relies on large-scale organizations, be they private corporations or public bureaucracies.[30] Although small businesses continue to play a dynamic role in investment and job creation,[31] their role is auxiliary in relation to processes that depend largely on the commanding heights of the economy.[32] Both the internal and the external linkages of large organizations have expanded at a dramatic rate in the past quarter of a century, and they continue to do so. Added flexibility in the system, whether by means of decentralization of units of large corporations or by multiple connections with small firms, only increases the number and complexity of the exchanges on which the day-to-day management of the economy is based. In 1985, US offices processed about 500 billion documents, and the volume of paperwork is increasing by 72 billion additional documents per year.[33] It is clear that without a substantial technological overhaul, the system's capacity has arrived at breaking point. Accordingly, in recent years, the bulk of information-technology devices are being installed in the service sector. For instance, in 1982, 80 percent of all computing, communications, and information-technology equipment sold in the US went to services.[34]

The impact of this trend is most significant, and most strongly felt, in relation to office work. By office work, following the definition of the Office of Technology Assessment (OTA), we understand "the processing and use of information for the purpose of tracking, monitoring, recording, directing, and supporting complex human activities."[35] In this context, office automation, again in the OTA's terms, refers to "the application of microelectronic information technology and communication technology to office work."[36]

Two major streams of new information technologies are converging to revolutionize office work and corporate organizations: the computerization of information processing, and the multifaceted application of telecommunications to information exchange. Although for the sake of clarity I will distinguish here between the two processes, they have interacted throughout the evolution of automation, and the most significant recent development is their actual merger into information systems.[37]

The computerization of office work has gone through three different phases.[38] In the first one, mainframe computers were used for batch processing of data, to build corporate databases; centralized computing, handled by specialists in electronic data-processing centers, formed the basis of a system characterized by rigidity and hierarchical control of information flows; data entry operations required substantial efforts since the goal of the system was the accumulation of large amounts of information in a central memory; work was standardized, routinized, and, in essence, de-skilled for the majority of clerical workers, in a process analyzed, and denounced, by Harry Braverman in his pioneer work.[39]

The following stages of automation, however, quite substantially changed this situation in the office and in office work.[40] The second phase, spurred on by the diffusion of microprocessors and the personal computer,[41] is characterized by the emphasis on the handling of microcomputers by the end users, that is the employees in charge of the actual work process; although they can be supported by centralized databases, they interact directly in the process of generating information without the intermediation of computer experts. In fact, by the mid-1980s, the two forms of computerization were merging, under the dominance of the second, with databases being managed mainly through decentralized information-handling processes.

The third phase introduces a more qualitative difference: it relies on networking and integrated office systems, where multiple microcomputers interact among themselves and with mainframes, in a web of generally horizontal exchanges.[42] The process is interactive, and the flows multi-directional. This third phase is made possible by the development of telecommunications. The current impact of telecommunications on the office originates in the dramatic expansion of transmission capacity in recent years, on the basis of the digitization of the telephone network, the use of satellites (which make the cost of transmission independent of the distance involved), microwave systems, coaxial cable, cellular telephony, and, above all, the trend toward the use of laser signals and the installation of optic fiber lines, giving substantially increased carrying capacity as well as much greater speed and accuracy of transmission. It is the combination of these different communication systems, and their gradual integration in an Integrated Service Digital Network (ISDN) which that is projected to become universal, which provides the capability for flexible communication of both voice and data between information-processing units, from anywhere to anywhere, most often simply by using the standard telephone line.[43] It is the merger of computers and telecommunications in the same network that gives birth to *information systems* (IS), which constitute the true foundation of office automation and have already become indispensable tools in the management of our economy and of our society.[44]

New technologies being introduced in the late 1980s will enhance even further the information-processing and transmission capabilities of the automated office.[45] Particularly notable examples are optical character recognition (OCR), already widely used in banking, and speech recognition (SR), which could by the mid-1990s entirely transform the accessibility of sophisticated computing to non-specialist users. Also, the current development of optical disks as storage devices, and more generally the potential of photonics, as well as more powerful chips, will open the way for ultrapowerful microcomputers, rendering less valid the current distinction between mainframe, mini- and microcomputers, and fully decentralizing the information-processing capability. Another major development, related to advances in artificial intelligence, is the setting up of expert systems that synthesize the accumulated knowledge in particular fields (for instance, medical or legal specialties), for use directly by professionals in the field. Coupled with access to centralized or decentralized databases, expert systems allow processing of valuable information by the professionals themselves, bypassing numerous steps of information retrieval and preparation and thus of clerical work.

The effects of these technological changes on office work and office workers are fundamental and complex, and they are not yet fully identified, in part because the process of technological change is only beginning and is rapidly accelerating in pace. However, there are a number of case studies that point consistently toward some fundamental trends.[46] I will leave aside, for the moment, the impact of these trends on employment and on working conditions, aspects that will be analyzed in some detail in chapter 4. Focusing here on the organizational consequences of office automation, the first observation is that there is no such thing as a pure technological effect. The actual effects of automation depend largely on the product of the service industry, as well as on the management of the industry at a particular time. Thus, within one industry, insurance for instance, the underwriting and the selling of the policy do not follow the same logic and are not affected in the same way by automation.[47] Furthermore, life insurance and health insurance also present different effects, given their different markets. Therefore, any specific analysis of office automation will have to consider the interaction between the process and the product, and between the technology and the industry.[48]

With these caveats in mind we can, nevertheless, emphasize some generally observed trends that have particular relevance for the present subject of inquiry. There is a clear tendency to automate the lower end of clerical jobs, those routine tasks that, because they can be reduced to a number of standard steps, can be easily programmed. There is also a movement toward decentralizing as much as possible the process of data entry, gathering the information and entering it into the system as close as possible to the source. For instance, sales accounting will be increasingly connected to automated scanning and storage at the cashier's point-of-sale machine. Bank branches' automated telling machines (ATMs) will be used to update bank accounts' movements constantly without intermediate accounting operations. Insurance claims will be directly stored in memory with respect to all the elements that do not call for a business judgement; and so on. All these trends lead to the elimination of a substantial amount of routine clerical work, and thus, potentially, of clerical jobs (although the matter of the elimination of clerical jobs is a function of social organization and of employment policies, not a direct consequence of technology, and thus will vary among companies and according to varying economic policies).

On the other hand, while routine operations are automated, higher-level operations are concentrated in the hands of skilled clerical workers, middle managers, and professionals, who will make informed decisions on the basis of a considerable amount of information contained in their centralized files. So, while at the bottom of the process there is increasing routinization and automation of data entry, at the middle level, there is reintegration of several tasks into an informed decision-making operation, generally processed, evaluated, and performed by a team made up of clerical workers with some level of autonomy in reaching their decision. Thus, the latest stage of office automation, instead of simply rationalizing the task (which was characteristic of the first phase of batch-processing automation), actually rationalizes the process, because the technology allows the integration of information from many different sources and its redistribution, once processed, to different decentralized units of execution. The pathbreaking studies by Baran and by Baran and Teegarden on the insurance industry have provided systematic evidence of this fundamental process that contradicts the simplistic, Orwellian image of centralized, inflexible office automation.[49] As Baran and Teegarden write:

The first stage of automation in the insurance industry tended to increase office fragmentation, centralize production by narrow function, heighten occupational sex segregation, and make many routine keyboarding functions spatially footloose. More recently however, the greater sophistication of the technologies and transformed market conditions are dictating a new organizational logic which promises to reverse many of the earlier trends. . . . This evolution can be characterized as the gradual movement from functional approaches to systems approaches, that is, from automating discrete tasks (e.g.: typing, calculating) to rationalizing an entire procedure (e.g.: new business insurance, claims processing), to reorganizing and integrating all the procedures involved in a particular decision or product line . . . . As a result, the work process is, in many cases, being functionally reintegrated. Workers who were formerly divided into functional units are being integrated into divisions which serve a particular subset of customers, often on the basis of geographic location and/or market segments.[50]

A similar trend has been observed by Hirschhorn in his case studies of banks.[51] While routine operations are now being processed increasingly by

ATMs (often by the forced procedure of closing down bank branches and replacing them with automatic machines), the remaining bank clerks are being retrained into the business of selling services to the customers, thus upgrading the work content of a smaller number of employees, and taking a more aggressive, marketing-oriented attitude toward clients.

In another study of the banking industry conducted for the Office of Technology Assessment, Paul Adler obtains similar findings.[52] As the OTA reports:

With computerization, the process of fabricating accounts, the principal activity of the bank, was made internal to the computer. These procedures had previously been done manually, or with the assistance of mechanical accounting machines. The role of human operators then changed from one of doing banking to one of surveillance of the computing as it does banking. Adler points out that "A series of tasks formerly considered the very essence of bank work have been eliminated, including accounting imputation and adjustment, classification of documents, multiple entries of data, manual data search, and supervision by signature . . . . Accountants now diagnose and rectify residues and anomalies listed by the computer system. New types of errors – and fraud – appear." [53]

The automation of tasks is increasingly penetrating the sphere of decision-making, not so much to save labor as to save time, and reach quick decisions in a global financial world where minutes might cost millions. The most important example of this trend, of course, is the automation of stock exchange markets around the world, enabling them to trade in real time at an increasingly faster speed of decision, on a "launch on warning" system of electronically processed financial indicators. The consequences of this process are dramatic and far-reaching. The "Presidential Task Force on Market Mechanisms," appointed by President Reagan to investigate the causes of the collapse of the New York Stock Exchange on 19 October 1987, concluded that the most important single factor immediately behind the crash (apart, of course, from the structural reasons concerning the imbalance of the US economy) was computerized trading by large institutional investors, particularly pension funds. More specifically, the Task Force referred to two computer-trading techniques, portfolio insurance and stock index arbitrage, by which computers can generate transactions that result in orders to sell huge amounts of stock under a number of programmed circumstances. Prompted by a downward market trend, automatic selling orders dramatically amplified that trend and set in motion the 508-point collapse of the Dow Jones index.[54]

In sum, the penetration of computer-and-telecommunications information systems is altering the dynamics of office work and of the information economy in all its dimensions. Quinn has summarized the effects of technology in six major areas:[55] increasing economies of scale; increasing economies of scope; increasing output complexity; furthering functional competition (that is, integrating several industries and activities around a major function, for example, the sales of financial services by department stores such as Sears[56]); enhancing international competitiveness; and increasing wealth through higher productivity in services. In a word, what is facilitated by information technologies is the interconnection of activities, providing the basis for the increasing complexity of service industries, which exchange information relentlessly and ubiquitously. The old separation among different businesses, different markets, different industries, and different organizations disappears in technological terms. Whatever becomes organizationally and legally possible can be technologically implemented, because of the versatility of the technological medium. Such evolution, of course, does not supersede the logic inherent to each specific organization, but minimizes the friction between decision and execution of the organizational goals. What results is the amplification of the problems, conflicts, and errors in the outcome of organizational decisions, but also of the successes and achievements of the strategies and policies that the organization assumes. The technological basis of information systems increasingly frees organizations from their bureaucratic inefficiencies, but brings them into direct confrontation with their built-in shortcomings and strategic failures.

 A fundamental effect of a technologically driven organizational logic of this kind is that the operations of many organizations become timeless, because information systems communicate with each other on programmed time patterns, either non-stop in real time or, on the contrary, delayed and recorded. There is a shift, in fact, away from the centrality of the organizational unit to the network of information and decision. In other words, *flows, rather than organizations*, become the units of work, decision, and output accounting. Is the same trend developing in relation to the spatial dimension of organizations? Are flows substituting for localities in the information economy? Under the impact of information systems, are organizations becoming not only timeless but also placeless? These are fundamental questions and require detailed consideration.

Telecommunications, Office Automation, and the Spatial Pattern of Information-processing Activities

Introduction: The Metropolitan Dominance of the Service Economy

Examination of the empirical data on the spatial effects of telecommunications and automation on office work and service activities shows how ill-founded are the simplistic assumptions about the potential for decentralization of activities and businesses under the impetus provided by new technologies able to overcome spatial distance while maintaining communication. There is no direct effect of communication technologies on the location of offices and services. Their effects are mediated through trends in

The Space of Flows 143

the evolution of service and information activities, and through the changing organizational logic of corporations. Stanback, Noyelle, and their co-workers have systematically studied over a number of years the relationship between the expansion of the service economy and its impact in American cities.[57] Their findings can be summarized in a number of fundamental trends:

(1) Producer services are increasingly concentrated in nodal large metropolitan areas.
(2) These services are further increasingly concentrated within the central business districts (CBDs) of large metropolitan areas.
(3) Both of these tendencies are particularly pronounced for advanced corporate services, as established for the 1970s by Robert Cohen's research. Cohen also showed that the booming sunbelt remained largely dependent on the old established base of headquarters and corporate services in New York, Chicago, San Francisco, and Los Angeles. In particular, the predominance of New York in all advanced corporate services (banking, insurance, financial services, legal services, accounting and auditing, advertising, publishing, consulting, and so on) was, and still is, overwhelming.
(4) There has been a growing tendency toward the suburbanization of secondary offices of major corporations, as well as of some headquarters, unable to or uninterested in sustaining the cost of land and office space in the highly priced CBDs. Most of this suburbanization has occurred in the largest metropolitan areas.
(5) Consumer services, by and large, have followed the suburbanization of middle-class residents, while the high-level entertainment services have stayed in the established elite cores of central cities.
(6) Public services, particularly in health and education, tend to follow the spatial distribution of the population they serve, thus becoming increasingly suburbanized. However, some of these services (major hospitals, for example) can also be export-oriented, and in these cases they tend to dominate a given area, generally in their former location in the inner city.

What Noyelle and Stanback's work shows is, on the one hand, that the spatial consequences of the expansion of the service economy are contradictory, leading at the same time toward centralization and decentralization of activities; and on the other hand, that these processes follow a logic that depends on the function of each organization, and on the hierarchical relationships among the different functions. In order to understand the role played by the use of new technologies in the spatial patterning of information-processing service activities, we must consider their interaction with the characteristics of such activities. I will proceed with this analysis by focusing in turn on the process of centralization and on the different processes of decentralization, attempting in conclusion a synthetic integration of my observations in the formulation of a new spatial logic.

Telecommunications and the Centralization of Information-intensive Industries

At the core of the service economy lies the expansion of information-processing activities. These activities are organized around a nucleus of information-intensive industries whose organizational and spatial logic occupies the top of the functional and economic corporate hierarchy. According to the thorough study of the matter by Drennan,[58] these information-intensive industries (see table 3.5 for an operational definition) accounted in 1985 for 13.9 percent of all US jobs and about 13 percent of GNP. Altogether they were responsible for almost as many jobs as manufacturing (17.6 million in information-intensive industries versus 18.8 million in manufacturing), and they were growing during the 1980s at a much faster rate than the average GNP. Data collected by Drennan show the dramatic expansion between 1975 and 1984 in banking, finance, securities, and insurance. It can be argued convincingly that the emergence of information systems was the technological prerequisite for the dramatic growth of these industries, and that the process will accelerate in the foreseeable future. In turn, it is the growth of these information-intensive industries that drives the demand for advanced information technologies. Consequently, the spatial impact of these technologies will be most clearly manifested in the location of these industries. However, following our methodology of inquiry, in order to assess the impact of new communication technologies, we need first to examine the location patterns of information-intensive industries themselves.

Drennan found that in 1984 there was a significant concentration of these information-intensive jobs in the core counties of the 24 largest metropolitan

Table 3.5   Information-intensive industries

SIC Code	Industry
—	Central administrative offices, all industries
45	Air transportation
47	Transportation services
60	Banking
61	Credit agencies
62	Security and commodity brokers and services
63	Insurance carriers
64	Insurance agents, brokers and services
67	Holding and other investment offices
73	Business services
81	Legal services
82	Educational services (private)
86	Membership organizations
89	Miscellaneous services (engineering and accounting)

Source: US Department of Commerce, Bureau of the Census, County Business Patterns, US Summary, 1983, 1985, elaborated by Drennan (see note 58).

areas: they accounted for 39 percent of information-intensive jobs, while their share of total private employment was only 27 percent, with New York, Los Angeles, and Chicago on top of this list (see table 3.6). Banking is one of the most concentrated industries: one-third of all commercial and savings banks deposits are located in the five largest metropolitan areas, and New York alone has 17 percent of all deposits. Law firms in the top five

Table 3.6 Population, employment, and information-intensive industries' employment, 24 metropolitan areas and United States

Metropolitan Area	Population[a]	Total employment[b]	Information-intensive industries' employment		
			No.	% of total	Rank order
New York	17,677	8,448	1,773	21.0	1
Los Angeles	12,373	5,773	944	16.4	10
Chicago	8,035	3,695	670	18.1	4
Philadelphia	5,755	2,653	404	15.2	
San Francisco	5,685	2,961	524	17.7	5
Detroit	4,316	1,872	247	13.2	
Boston	4,027	2,065	405	19.6	2
Houston	3,566	1,735	276	15.9	
Washington	3,430	1,965	360	18.3	3
Dallas	3,348	1,772	285	16.1	
Miami	2,799	1,274	220	17.3	6
Cleveland	2,788	1,256	167	13.3	
Atlanta	2,380	1,238	200	16.1	
Pittsburgh	2,372	984	150	15.2	
Baltimore	2,245	1,092	184	16.9	7
Minneapolis–St Paul	2,231	1,212	175	14.4	
San Diego	2,064	933	154	16.5	9
Denver	1,791	986	164	16.6	8
Phoenix	1,715	782	123	15.7	
Milwaukee	1,568	763	106	13.9	
Columbus	1,279	614	93	15.1	
Indianapolis	1,195	583	74	12.7	
San Antonio	1,189	530	84	15.8	
Memphis	935	437	55	12.6	
Total 24 areas	94,763	45,623	7,837	17.2	
United States total	235,671	106,891	14,856	13.9	
24 areas as % of US total	40.2	42.7	52.8		

[a] 1984; [b] 1983.
Source: Population data from US Bureau of the Census, *Statistical Abstract of the United States*, 1986. Total employment (actual) and information-intensive industries employment (partly estimated) from US Department of Commerce, Bureau of Economic Analysis, *Survey of Current Business*, May 1985, October 1985, and August 1986. Elaborated by Drennan (see note 58).

metropolitan areas earned 39 percent of the receipts of all law firms, and 40 percent of all law firms with more than 50 employees were in the core counties of those five largest metropolitan areas. Here again, New York ranks first with 179 large law offices. For securities and commodities offices, the concentration is even heavier, as one might expect: New York, with 261, and Chicago, with 107, together account for one-third of all large securities firms. Table 3.7 summarizes the data on the relative concentration of information-intensive industries in the top ten areas, as measured by location quotients. Washington DC, New York, and Boston dominate the pack, while, significantly enough, Los Angeles is not among the top ten, emphasizing the greater decentralization of information-intensive industries in southern California (toward Orange County).[59] What is significant is the positive location quotient exhibited by all major metropolitan areas in proportion to the average of information-intensive employment for the US as a whole. Thus, Drennan's recent work on the 1980s, confirming the trends observed by Cohen, Stanback and Noyelle,[60] among others, for the 1970s, suggests that information-intensive industries are disproportionately concentrated in metropolitan areas, in the largest metropolitan areas, and in the cores of the largest metropolitan areas. Since these industries are the main users of new information technologies, it will be important to establish the role played by such technologies in the process of spatial centralization of these industries.

Mitchell Moss has systematically researched this question over a number of years.[61] His data show the close relationship among the internationalization of trade and finance, the centralization of such activities in a few global cities (New York being foremost among them), and the development of the telecommunications infrastructure in these cities. In fact, only through the revolution in telecommunications technology does it become possible to exercise co-ordination and control functions from a given location in a metropolitan CBD over the entire nation or the global economy. On the other hand, the deregulation of telecommunications, with the divestiture of ATT, has made investment in telecommunications even more sensitive to demand. Since the main source of this demand is in the information-intensive industries concentrated in the cores of the largest metropolitan areas, it is in such areas and core locations that most of the new telecommunications infrastructure has been concentrated.

Therefore, in order to exploit the global reach of telecommunications, organizations must locate in certain areas where they will have access to an advanced infrastructure at relatively affordable costs (affordable because of the economies of scale permitted by the extensive use of telecommunication facilities by a large number of customers). Thus, concentration of information industries attracts telecommunications investment which in turn reinforces the pattern of centralization for information-based activities. Furthermore, under the current legal framework in the US, new communication lines have to follow the rights of way already established; and the inter-

Table 3.7 Relative concentration of information-intensive industries, top 10 areas

Population rank	Metropolitan area (rank order)	Information-intensive employment Location quotient	Employment/population ratio	% population college graduates
9	Washington	2.62	58.3	31.9
7	Boston	2.26	56.2	22.6
1	New York	2.06	48.0	19.5
5	San Francisco	1.93	52.6	25.0
13	Atlanta	1.74	53.8	23.8
	Mean (unweighted) – top five		*53.8*	*23.8*
4	Philadelphia	1.69	46.2	17.0
18	Denver	1.59	55.8	25.9
14	Pittsburgh	1.43	41.0	14.1
3	Chicago	1.42	46.1	17.8
11	Miami	1.33	45.6	16.1
	Mean (unweighted)		*50.4*	*21.0*
	United States	1.00	45.7	16.2

Source: Data on percentage of college graduates from US Bureau of the Census, *State and Metropolitan Area Data Book 1986.* Elaborated by Drennan (see note 58).

city rights of way generally follow the lines of railroads built during the nineteenth century. Thus, the new optic fiber networks are in fact connecting the major areas that were already nodal points during the last century, although when demand is important enough, for example in some new sunbelt locations, they too become integrated into the network.

The creation of a new telecommunications infrastructure in the US is taking place at three levels: (a) long-distance communication; (b) intra-regional communication; and (c) local networks.[62] Concerning *long distance*, the major development is the construction of several optic fiber networks (by different competing companies: ATT, Sprint, MCI) which, because they need to carry a high volume of communication to be profitable, concentrate on communications between the largest metropolitan areas. Thus, the higher the level of existing corporate concentration in an areas, the better and the cheaper the new telecommunications equipment. Satellite-based networks have the edge on optic fiber in terms of versatility of communication flows, being able to communicate, at the same cost, from anywhere to anywhere. However, although optic fiber networks depend on flows that connect two points through a line, their carrying capacity and accuracy are much greater, in particular when satellite signals need to go through the saturated air space of metropolitan CBDs. Therefore, the setting up of optic fiber networks also contributes to reinforcing the inherited pattern of centralization of information-intensive industries.

At the *regional level*, the new companies resulting from ATT's divestiture are also turning to optic fiber, and to the establishment of new facilities for the regionally based organizations. New York also leads in these new developments.[63] By 1984 it accounted for one-third of all optic fiber networks installed in the US. During the 1980s several major telecommunications projects have been developed in the New York area, basically to serve the business agglomeration in Manhattan. The most important project of its kind in the entire world, the Teleport of New York epitomizes the trend. It was developed by the Port Authority of New York and New Jersey, on land leased by the City of New York, and in co-operation with a private partner, Teleport Communications Inc., owned by Merrill Lynch and Western Union. The Port and the City each receive a percentage of the company's profits. The Teleport will provide access to communications satellites through 17 earth stations located on Staten Island, and hooked through an optic fiber line with Manhattan and, in the future, other locations. In addition, Teleport has a developed a 100-acre office park generally used for decentralized back office organizations. The teleport concept is being equated to the harbours of the industrial era, and in the mid-1980s there were under way about 20 similar projects in 12 states in the US. Other intra-regional systems are also being set up, particularly in the New York area, relying on coaxial cable, microwave, digital termination systems, and, increasingly, cellular mobile radio, which extends the office into its transportation vehicles.

At the *local level*, "local area networks" (LANs) and "smart buildings" are establishing telecommunications equipment as an integral part of the structure of the built environment for the office. Increasingly, developers provide built-in telecommunications facilities and wired automated equipment, which are economical because they are shared among different tenants of a particular building or area.[64] This is the best example of the direct relationship with location in a given place as a means of access to the placeless communications network. Telecommunications equipment accounts for most of the increasing capital investment by companies in office workers. According to Jonscher, in 1977 US businesses were investing twice as much capital per worker in blue-collar staff as in white-collar staff.[65] By 1982 the ratios for both had become similar. The "wired city" is now a reality, not only through cable or telephone line networks, but through a variety of telecommunications technologies that lend extraordinary versatility to the system. In addition, it is a business-oriented "wired city," rather than one focused on the "electronic home."[66] As Moss writes:

The emerging telecommunications infrastructure is an overwhelmingly urban-based phenomenon. Although most discussions of new communication technologies emphasize the opportunities presented for decentralization, large cities are the hubs of the new telecommunications systems in the U.S. and are the sites for the most advanced applications of information technology . . . . Although new communications technologies permit geographic dispersal, the economics of the new infrastructure are oriented towards those urban regions that are major information centres . . . . Contrary to much of the popular folklore, new communication technologies have not led to the decline of cities. Rather, new communications technologies have enhanced those cities that serve [in Gottman's words] "the important function of hosting transactional activities."[67]

Interestingly enough, most of the business communications travel a short distance: 60 percent of all communications are intra-facility, and only 8 percent "travel" over 500 miles.

The first impact of the development of telecommunications infrastructure on the location of information-intensive industries, then, is to reinforce their centralization in the higher nodal points of the informational economy, namely, the CBDs of the largest metropolitan areas. (Indeed, it is only because of the existence of automated telecommunications and on-line equipment that offices located in a very few areas are able to extend their global reach without comparable diversification of location.) New York, and particularly Manhattan, is the best illustration of this tendency. In 1958, 35 percent of the city's private jobs were in information-intensive industries. In 1982 the proportion had jumped to 54 percent.[68] The role of telecommunications and office automation in facilitating such concentration while reinforcing the control of New York corporations over the world economy has been crucial.[69] In addition, around the concentration of headquarters of large corporations, whose physical proximity is vital as a way of sustaining the social milieu on which business decisions rely, a constellation of ancillary services has developed, both in business services and in consumer services, from printing and copying to business bars and restaurants. Manhattan hosts an immense concentration of information-technology equipment, as the necessary material condition for processing all the information centralized and decided upon in the Manhattan offices. For instance, to take a simple indicator, in 1984 there were more word processors in Manhattan than in the whole of western Europe. Using another indicator, constructed by Moss in one of his studies, the penetration of facsimile machines for the top US cities (see figure 3.2), shows the overwhelming proportion of these machines to be installed in New York, and in addition a disproportionate concentration of fax machines in major information-industry cities such as San Francisco, Washington DC, Atlanta, and Boston.

The reasons for the persistence of this centralized locational pattern for the top level of information-intensive industries are still the same as those pointed out years ago by the literature on office location:[70] importance of trusted

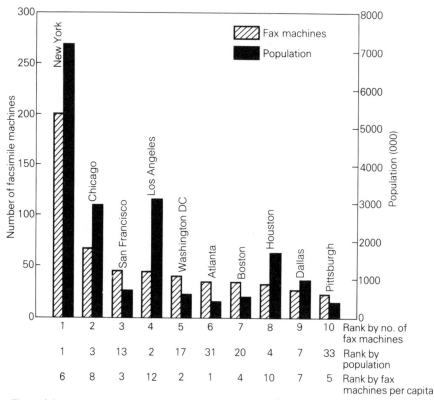

Figure 3.2   Penetration of facsimile machines for top US cities
Source: Official Facsimile Users Guide, 1985; Moss (see note 62)

person-to-person contacts in the decision-making process at the highest level; existence of a business social milieu with strong cultural connotations; prestige of location in a given place; importance of the fixed assets represented by the real estate owned by companies in the CBDs, assets that could be devalued in case of a massive exodus from the area; consolidation of a network of ancillary services around major firms and organizations, a network that provides diversity and versatility of supplies, and which becomes an indispensable working tool for the corporations, at the same time as it is spatially and functionally linked to their concentration. None of these elements is new, and they are largely independent of the development of information technologies, although the telephone was crucial in allowing the formation of such concentrations, as well as making possible vertical communication inside the skyscrapers.[71] However, what is new is that advanced information technologies have made it possible for these concentrations of high-level information-based organizations to operate from the same location while increasing the volume of information they process by a multiple factor, as a result of the large scale of the operations commanded from a particular corporate milieu. In this sense, the large corporation and its network of ancillary services, the world city, the CBD, and information systems based on telecommunications and computers, are all inextricably linked elements of the same system. Raymond Vernon predicted many years ago that the development of telecommunications and air transportation would lead toward increasing concentration of high-level services in a few cities, and particularly in the major metropolitan areas such as New York.[72] He has been proved right.

However, this process is not without its contradictions, nor is it the only spatial trend associated with the new information technologies. On the one hand, the inner cities of large metropolitan areas concentrate not only the corporate headquarters and their support networks, but also the destitute and overexploited segments of the population resulting from the unbalanced restructuring of economy and society, in an increasingly explosive socio-spatial contradiction that will be analyzed in chapter 4.[73] On the other hand, alongside the centralization and metropolitanization of information industries, there is also a process of decentralization of service activities over regions, urban areas, and locations within the major metropolitan areas; and this decentralization is being helped, and sometimes even stimulated, by new information technologies. It is this two-fold process of simultaneous centralization and decentralization, both elements associated with the same techno-economic dynamics, which explains the complexity of our analysis. Beyond a mere formal characterization of the process in terms of concentration/deconcentration of population and activities, we must be able to assess what is being centralized, what is being decentralized, why, and how. Only then we will be able to trace connections between the two processes and come to an understanding of the emerging socio-spatial logic.

Information Technology, Organizational Restructuring, and the
Spatial Decentralization of Office Activities

During the last two decades a process of spatial decentralization of service
activities generally, including the information-processing industries, has
taken place in the United States, although the activities that have been
decentralized are specific in terms of their content and function within the
hierarchy of services. It is received wisdom that new information and
transportation technologies have made this possible; here I will try to assess
the precise role played by technology in these developments. However, we
must differentiate among levels of spatial decentralization, since these differ
both in their origins and in their implications. Decentralization of services is
taking place on at least three different levels: between regions; from
metropolitan to non-metropolitan areas and small cities; from inner cities to
the suburbs of metropolitan areas. In addition, two potential trends will be
discussed, in spite of their current limited impact: the offshoring of service
activities; and the decentralization of office work at home (the so-called
"telecommuting").

Regional decentralization of information-processing activities   Peter Hall has
calculated the regional pattern of distribution of service and informational
jobs for the periods 1975–80 and 1980–5.[74] At a very aggregate level, but in an
analytically useful regional typology, he distinguishes four regional clusters:
the old manufacturing belt (including New England, the mid-Atlantic, and
east–north–central regions); the rural middle (consisting of the west–north–
–central and east–south–central divisions); the sunbelt (south Atlantic,
west–south–central, mountain and Pacific divisions); and what he labels the
"new perimeter," supposedly the new dynamic composite of US economic
geography, made up from the combination of the sunbelt and New England.
53.5 percent of the 15.7 million new non-farm jobs generated during 1975–80
were in information processing. Three out of five of these jobs were created in
the sunbelt and two-thirds of them in the "new perimeter." The period
1980–5 further intensified this regional differentiation, with 96 percent of
all new non-farm jobs created in these years falling in the "new perimeter."
Information-processing jobs accounted for 77.8 percent of all new US jobs in
this period, and of these, 73.2 percent were created in the "new perimeter,"
and 71.6 percent in the sunbelt. Given the former concentration of
information jobs in the older industrial areas of the north-east and north-central regions, there is clearly a major regional restructuring under way.
However, this must be qualified by the analysis of table 3.8, which provides a
more disaggregated view of the trends at the level of individual regions.
According to Hall's index of information jobs/goods-producing jobs, the mid-
Atlantic region (around New York–New Jersey) clearly stands out as the

region with the highest concentration of new information-handling jobs in 1975–80; a trend that, although the index is not calculated in the table, appears even more pronounced for 1980–5. So if, rather than adding New England to the sunbelt to forge the "new perimeter," for the period 1980–5 we add the mid-Atlantic region to the sunbelt, we account for 82.6 percent of all new information-handling jobs. It would seem that the "new perimeter" for information employment should include New York–New Jersey instead of New England. The major decline in share of information jobs has been suffered by the midwest.

In any event, the dramatic increase in the proportion of new information jobs in the sunbelt, and particularly in the south Atlantic region, for the whole decade 1975–85, indicates a clear regional shift in the dynamism of the information-processing sector, as well as in services in general. While we lack the precise data to enable us to identify which activities are being shifted, Peter Hall, recalling findings by Noyelle and Stanback,[75] speculates about three potential sources for the regional decentralization of service and information activities. First is the need to serve the growing population of the sunbelt, given the links of many of the services to residentially based factors. In turn, the decentralization of population to the sunbelt is itself a function of decentralization of economic activities at large, including manufacturing. Secondly, he points to the emergence of a series of new, regionally based industries, such as retirement and tourism, in the south Atlantic region; and his third factor is the dynamism of new regional centers, including such cities as Miami, Atlanta, Houston, Denver, and Phoenix, which have been able to attract corporations to cheaper, more suitable business environments. To these I would add another hypothesis concerning the linkage between manufacturing and information-processing activities. Given the massive scale of the decline in manufacturing jobs in the old manufacturing belt, that decline cannot be compensated for by information-processing jobs except when they deal with higher command and control functions, as is the case in New York. However, the vitality of a number of medium-level information-handling processes is associated with the production and distribution of goods. With a substantial number of manufacturing jobs shifting to the sunbelt and to the "new perimeter," and with the distribution of goods following an expanding population, the linkage factor will tend to induce a similarity in the locational pattern of many information-processing activities to the tendencies shown by the new manufacturing industries.

In sum, it appears that there is a process of regional decentralization of information activities linked to second-rank business services, to producer services of the new industrial perimeter, and to consumer and personal services for the expanding population of the sunbelt areas. Information technologies do play a role in facilitating this movement because the new nodal areas would be unable to compete with the established metropolitan

Table 3.8 Employment changes by SIC single-digit headings, divisions, 1975–80, 1980–5 (% rate of change during the period)

(a) 1975–80

	New England	Mid-Atlantic	E.-N.-Central	W.-N.-Central	S. Atlantic	E.-S.-Central	W.-S.-Central	Mountain	Pacific	Total US
TOTAL	10.8	10.0	14.1	19.6	23.4	20.7	33.0	35.6	32.4	21.0
Mining	38.7	−0.5	13.2	27.7	7.2	20.9	71.3	44.2	36.7	37.3
Construction	7.3	2.8	11.8	13.8	22.4	16.8	39.8	45.5	37.1	21.3
Manufacturing	17.2	1.1	1.7	12.1	15.8	9.7	26.1	33.6	25.7	11.1
Transportation	15.1	12.6	25.7	38.5	30.1	40.5	37.9	52.9	27.7	27.8
Communication	27.7	19.9	44.0	58.9	42.3	61.0	49.5	82.1	33.9	40.6
Wholesale	3.6	3.8	6.8	14.7	17.4	20.1	23.7	28.4	20.1	13.7
retail	16.8	8.2	13.4	15.0	24.0	18.7	28.7	31.3	34.7	20.0
Finance, Insurance, Real Estate	22.6	12.1	22.9	23.9	26.7	21.6	37.2	44.6	43.6	26.1
Services	33.2	33.0	41.0	44.1	40.3	52.2	53.0	56.1	66.3	44.7
Government	10.4	1.9	9.0	8.6	17.6	17.2	16.5	15.8	8.2	11.0
Industry	16.1	1.3	3.0	12.8	16.9	10.3	34.6	38.5	27.9	13.6
Service	20.1	13.6	20.3	22.1	26.1	26.6	32.4	34.7	33.9	24.2
Goods-handling	16.8	5.1	8.5	16.3	21.1	15.2	32.9	37.1	31.3	17.6
Information-handling	21.5	15.6	22.8	23.7	26.2	29.0	33.1	34.1	33.6	25.4
Ratios: serv./ind.	1.2	10.5	6.8	1.7	1.5	2.6	0.9	0.9	1.2	1.8
Info./goods	1.3	3.1	2.7	1.5	1.2	1.9	1.0	0.9	1.1	1.4

(b) 1980–85

	New England	Mid-Atlantic	E.-N.-Central	W.-N.-Central	S. Atlantic	E.-S.-Central	W.-S.-Central	Mountain	Pacific	Total US
TOTAL	7.0	0.3	-0.9	0.3	12.1	5.2	8.7	10.6	4.8	4.7
Mining	16.2	-12.6	-10.7	-15.0	-20.5	-7.5	-3.7	-27.5	1.4	-11.6
Construction	50.0	30.4	5.0	4.7	27.7	9.5	16.7	20.6	16.5	19.2
Manufacturing	4.2	-7.8	-3.0	-2.8	5.2	1.4 12.8	-1.1	15.3	6.9	0.2
Transportation	24.5	7.5	10.6	13.0	19.9	25.4	8.6	18.9	18.8	14.6
Transportation	20.1	-0.5	8.2	6.3	10.6	18.3	4.8	14.5	15.0	8.8
Communication	29.4	18.5	14.1	23.7	31.5	34.9	14.3	20.8	14.0	20.8
Wholesale/Retail	-4.7	-6.2	-3.7	-3.9	7.7	5.4	5.4	6.7	-3.7	-0.3
Finance, Insurance, Real Estate	32.1	15.6	14.0	17.0	29.0	21.6	31.9	41.9	18.6	22.1
Services	13.5	6.2	7.2	7.4	31.7	12.7	22.2	12.4	7.1	12.8
Government	-4.6	-2.6	-11.9	-7.9	-1.9	-4.8	3.1	3.6	0.0	-3.4
Industry	9.2	-3.1	-2.3	-1.9	9.3	2.1	2.8	10.1	8.7 4.8	2.9
Service	6.0	1.5	-0.2	1.0	13.2	6.7	11.2	10.7	3.5	5.4
Goods-handling	4.3	-4.2	-2.3	-2.2	8.7	4.2	4.0	8.8	3.5	1.9
Information-handling	10.5	5.0	1.0	3.2	15.9	6.5	15.0	12.4	6.2	7.9
Ratios: serv./ind.	0.7	NA	0.1	NA	1.4	3.2	4.0	1.1	0.4	1.9
Info./goods	2.4	NA	NA	NA	1.8	1.5	3.8	1.4	1.8 4.8	4.2

Source: Bureau of Labor Statistics. Calculated and elaborated by Hall (see note 10)

centers were it not for their access to communication and information networks that keep them in close and constant contact with their command and control centers, as well as, for the minority of headquarters in the sunbelt, in direct connection with their national and international markets. Having achieved a minimum density of information complexes, and counting on regional patterns of investment in telecommunications and data processing, the new economic centers lay claim to the advantages of a newer, more flexible, and generally cheaper business environment, with the accessibility to the mainstream of the economy through their integration in the network of information flows.

Suburbanization of business and office activities   While the cores of the dominant metropolitan areas still maintain their function as locations for most of the command and control centers of the economy, a major process of suburbanization of services, and particularly of office activities has been taking place since the late 1960s in most metropolitan areas in the US.[76] The new suburbanization process is in fact business-led rather than purely residential, although the population too is increasingly suburban. What characterizes this new wave of suburbanization is that it relies on the formation of relatively dense business and commercial sub-centers, trans-forming the metropolitan areas in into multinuclear, multifunctional spatial structures, organized around what Leinberger and Lockwood label new "urban villages."[77] The scale of this phenomenon is unprecedented and constitutes the most important single trend in the transformation of America's built environment. Table 3.9 documents the process of office suburbanization for the 1970s and for 1984 respectively. In the latter year, data computed by Dowall and Salkin for the 19 metropolitan areas under ana-lysis showed that, on average, suburban office construction accounted for 59.3 percent of all new office space in these areas. And the trend is accelerating through the 1980s: between 1982 and 1985 Manhattan gained 23 million square feet of office space, but its share of office space for the whole metropolitan area fell from 67 percent to 60 percent. In 1986 the New York metropolitan suburbs were the location for 261.1 million feet of office space, as compared to 317.6 million for Manhattan. The trend is even more pronounced in the second major metropolitan area of the US, Los Angeles, where the downtown share of the metropolitan area's office market has dropped from 60 percent to 34 percent of new office construction. The new business complex in Orange County (Costa Mesa–Irvine–Newport Beach) contained in 1986 21.1 million square feet of office space; still behind downtown LA with 36.6 million square feet but already the third largest business complex in California.[78]

These new suburban office centers tend to be quite different from their inner-city predecessors. They are generally low-density, either with low-rise buildings or, in the case of major centers, with skyscrapers scattered over a very large area, separated by areas of landscaped open space. Parking lots and the automobile dominate the scenery. In fact, such massive suburban decentralization is closely associated with the expansion of the metropolitan freeway system and the use of the automobile as the prevalent mode of commuting: in 1980, nationwide, 86 percent of all commuting trips were by car, compared with 69.5 percent in 1960. This requires parking space that only an automobile-oriented suburban development can provide, in terms of both physical availability and affordable cost.

It is, then, undeniable that offices are decentralizating, mainly to the suburbs of the largest metropolitan areas. This is taking place both through relocation of existing companies and through new businesses deciding to locate in the suburbs. Let us examine what is being decentralized, and why, and what is the specific effect of the new information technologies on the process.

Table 3.9 Office-dominated industry employment growth in central city and suburban locations: 50 largest and 50 small and mid-sized SMSAs, 1967–1977 (000s)

	Finance, insurance, and real estate		Services		Government	
	Number	% change	Number	% change	Number	% change
Largest SMSAs						
Central city	422	23.5	1177	34.6	1107	44.5
Suburbs	375	172.5	2028	134.2	509	67.3
North-east						
Central city	−16	−2.4	171	14.7	210	36.5
Suburbs	141	152.9	496	109.9	118	42.7
North-central						
Central city	90	20.5	182	20.9	215	37.4
Suburbs	149	176.2	578	151.9	142	96.1
South						
Central city	157	46.2	477	69.9	395	63.3
Suburbs	76	153.0	470	161.0	190	79.0
West						
Central city	192	52.1	347	50.6	288	40.3
Suburbs	62	338.8	485	120.0	60	65.0
Small/Mid-sized SMSAs						
Central city	17	25.0	146	63.5	28	18.3
Suburbs	11	123.5	201	99.0	14	28.6

Source: Phillips and Vidal (1983), tables 6, 7, 9, as compiled by Dowall and Salkin, (see note 79).

Dowall and Salkin have reviewed the available information on this question, and they point to several factors favoring the decentralized location or relocation of office activities.[79] In the first place, they cite the dominance of large, multifunctional, multilocational corporations, whose internal linkages become more important than linkages to their spatial environment. Units of these companies that can be decentralized will be, while maintaining their connections with the other units of the corporation. This functional linkage of the centre and decentralized units is only possible because of the existence of telecommunications and automation technologies that establish an information system able to link the company internally and with its inputs and markets through the communications network. Nevertheless, if corporate structure and information technologies allow for the process of decentralization, with particular emphasis on suburbanization, they do not explain why companies would relocate or locate initially in the suburbs, or, to a lesser extent, in smaller areas. Here a number of inter-related factors emerge to account for most of the preferences for a suburban site over the traditional downtown location:[80]

(1) Land prices and office rents in the suburbs are lower than in downtown locations. Leinberger and Lockwood report that in 1980, the price for suburban office space oscillated between $10 and $50 per square foot, while in downtown areas it jumped to between $50 and $1,000 per square foot.[81] Similarly, office rents were in the range of $18–$42 per square foot for downtown space, while prestige, high-rise suburban office space could be had for between $15 and $24 per square foot.

(2) Suburban offices are more accessible to their workers, most of whom live in the suburbs, and make commuting by car easier.[82]

(3) For retail offices, delivering services directly to the population, suburban locations simply follow the increasing suburbanization of the resident population, as with service activities in general.[83]

(4) One of the most important factors for suburban decentralization is the search for specific labor markets, as a result of the transformation of the labor process by automation, and the redefinition of the type of workers required in the automated office.[84] As we will see, suburban, educated, married women, working part-time or, in any case, for a wage under their level of skill, appears to be the most significant and sought-after labor source for the new type of office work. The case study reported below on the insurance industry will illustrate and elaborate this point. It is important to emphasize here that access to labor markets also works as a negative factor for downtown location, since the new skills required by the automated office are unlikely to be found (or at least, such is the perception of most companies) among the population of minorities that increasingly constitutes the bulk of inner-city residents in the large metropolitan areas.

The process of office decentralization is differentiated according to the different types of office functions and their place in the hierarchy of the corporation. Dowall and Salkin follow the distinction made by Thorngren [85] among orientation, planning, and programming functions in office work, corresponding to the more rigorous traditional sociological distinction of the functions of enterprises among decision, organization, and execution.[86] Nelson adds a more empirical classification separating headquarters, divisional branches, back offices, and retail offices.[87] Tendencies toward spatial decentralization clearly vary according to the three functions and the four categories of office activity. Headquarters of corporations continue, by and large, to be situated in the CBDs of the metropolitan areas, although metropolitan dominance has been eroded in terms both of metropolitan areas themselves and of competition from the suburbs. In 1963 New York City housed 147 of the *Fortune* 500 corporations' headquarters; in 1978 the figure was down to 104. Chicago and Pittsburgh respectively lost six and seven headquarters of major corporations in the same period, while the numbers of headquarters of major firms in Los Angeles, Houston, Atlanta, and San Francisco rose.[88] However, most often, when headquarters relocate they do so over short distances, to the suburbs of the same area.[89] They do so to escape the high costs of doing business in the CBD, and also they are attracted toward the areas where most of their managers and professionals live. Consequently, there is a clear tendency for business suburbanization to take place in upper-middle-class residential areas, such as the Princeton Corridor in the New York–New Jersey area, or the Perimeter Center in the northern suburbs of Atlanta.

Divisional branch offices value connections with the region they serve, or, when they are product divisions, connections with their headquarters.[90] They tend to concentrate in the CBDs of second-tier metropolitan areas or in the suburbs of the largest metropolitan areas. Air transportation links are a fundamental locational factor in this case, since telecommunication linkages do not preclude the need for frequent personal contacts among the managers, as well as for access to courier delivery of important documents.

Retail offices locate according to their need for access to their client base. Consequently they tend to be spatially diffused, following a segregated location pattern specific to each market segment. The higher the social status of an area, the higher the likelihood of increasing density of retail office location. Thus, while retail offices are located wherever there is a concentration of residence and of business, they also tend to follow a pattern of decentralization and suburbanization because of the growing dynamism, both residentially and commercially, of the metropolitan suburbs.

Back offices, in which most of companies' organization and execution work, increasingly automated, is concentrated, are functionally the most footloose office activity, because their main connection is to the company's decision centers, and this is a connection that can easily be maintained through automated information systems.[91] This being the case, it becomes uneconomic to maintain large back-office operations, which generally occupy a lot of space, on expensive downtown sites. Accordingly, back offices account for the bulk of the office decentralization that has taken place since the late 1960s.[92] Most of this decentralization, as we have seen, has taken place into the suburbs of the metropolitan areas, and the main reason for this seems to relate to the presence of a labor market that fulfils the needs of the automated office. The following case study of the insurance industry will clarify this important point, as well as providing a more precise view of the spatial division of labor within the corporation.

On the basis of Barbara Baran's analysis of the impact of office automation on the insurance industry,[93] Jean Marion Ross has analyzed the spatial implications of this transformation, on the basis of both secondary data and her own survey of 37 insurance companies.[94] She shows that the origins of the process lie in the restructuring of the industry as a consequence of increasing deregulation of financial services, putting increasingly competitive pressure on a traditionally regulated industry. Information technologies have played a major role in such restructuring, making insurance the most highly automated white-collar industry. In fact, the characteristics of the industry are particularly suited for information systems: scale economies favor consolidation of information-processing activities, while the requirement of market proximity favors decentralization of sales and service activities. The impact of information technologies on the new spatial pattern of the industry is two-fold. First, telecommunications technology increases the spatial mobility of the industry and lowers the cost of transmission between companies' units. On-line information processing allows geographical separation of activities without losing accessibility to the customers. Secondly, large-scale office automation, particularly in data entry and back-office operations (as described above, on the basis of Baran's study) restructures the occupational profile, increasing the need for skilled clerical labor. This appears to be a major factor in the relocation of back offices, a trend confirmed by Nelson's study of office location in the San Francisco Bay area.[95] The argument is as follows: the reintegration of tasks in the work process, through the use of automated data entry and standardization of routine procedures, calls for the remaining clerical workers to have a higher level of skill, and for team work. Team work is facilitated by similar cultural, ethnic, and gender characteristics in the components of the team. Therefore, insurance companies have increasingly targeted as their preferred labor pool the vast numbers of educated, married women, who can afford to be less demanding in terms of wages, and who will provide skills in information-processing activities at a lower cost than would be incurred by employing men, who were traditionally charged with the more analytical tasks of the

Table 3.10   Survey results: spatial change of insurance employment

Question/response	No. of responses	% response
(I) Spatial change of operations within the past 10 years		
Total responses	33	
Yes	22	66.7
No	9	27.3
Planned	2	6.1
(II) Structural trends in the organization of activities		
Total responses	23	
Consolidation of functions	8	34.8
Dispersion of functions	4	17.4
Both	11	47.8
(III) Has there been an increase in the number of operations in small urban or suburban settings?		
Total responses	24	
Yes	16	66.7
No	8	33.3
(IV) Criteria affecting choice of location		
Total responses	22	
Labor cost	12	54.5
Labor force quality	11	50.0
Land/rental cost and availability	12	54.5
Market proximity	7	31.8
Other	3	13.6

Source: Telephone survey of 37 insurance companies, July 1984, by Ross, (see note 94).

business. These women tend to be white and suburban (in one instance, an insurance company targeted a suburban location because of the abundance of educated women of "Dutch and German descent"); their social and cultural homogeneity is supposed to help team work. For many of these women an important factor in looking for a job is to keep time available for family life and child-rearing, and part-time work and/or a location relatively close to their suburban residence is therefore crucial – for them and for the company. Also, easy access by automobile and controlled parking space are key elements in attracting safety-conscious women, likely to be reluctant to commute to downtown areas in the evening hours, as is required by the shift-working of many back offices.

Altogether, back-office work in the insurance industry is being massively decentralized, mainly to the suburbs of the large metropolitan areas. Table 3.10 reports the findings of Ross's survey, indicating the high frequency of the decentralization/relocation process, which has affected over two-thirds of the surveyed companies in the 10 years covered. Of the factors cited as influencing choice of location, land/rental cost and access to labor are clearly

Table 3.11   Insurance employment shifts by city type, 1970–1981

	Percent of SIC 63, 1981	Percent of SIC 63, 1970	Percent change in SIC 63, 1970–81	Percent change in total employment 1970–81
Central cities[a]	32.7	39.1	2.5	3.7
Middle cities[b]	16.6	17.7	14.3	9.7
Small cities[c]	24.3	22.0	35.6	29.7
First ring[d]	13.9	8.1	113.4	34.5
Non-metropolitan[e]	4.9	3.6	67.6	9.3
All other	7.6	9.5	59.6	13.1
Total	100.0	100.0	22.7	30.7

[a] Counties with primary cities ≥ 500,000 population in 1980
[b] Counties with primary cities of 250,000–500,000 population in 1980
[c] Counties with primary cities of 50, 000–250,000 population in 1980
[d] Counties adjacent to or in the same SMSA as central or middle cities
[e] Counties with no city ≥ 50,000 population in 1980

Source: County Business Patterns, 1970 and 1981; compiled by Ross (see note 94).

predominant. It is important to emphasize that labor considerations concern both cost and quality, a finding that is also reported by Kroll and by Nelson in their studies on the San Francisco Bay area. That is to say, the automated office is not looking for cheap labor, but for skilled clerical labor as inexpensive as possible. It is the skill/cost ratio that determines the choice of suburban locations over the potentially even cheaper labor to be found among the inner-city minority populations. In the San Francisco Bay area, insurance companies, and back offices in general, decentralize from San Francisco to the outer suburbs of the East Bay, around Walnut Creek and Concord, skipping Oakland, in spite of the proximity and better infrastructure of this predominantly black city. Indeed, according to Ross, 70 percent of companies are dissatisfied with central city locations, and their main complaint concerns the low quality of the labor force, resulting from the deficiencies of the educational system as suffered by minorities in the public schools of the inner city.

    The consequences of these structurally determined locational preferences can be perceived in the overall trend toward decentralization of insurance employment, as shown in Table 3.11. Although in 1981 central cities were still holding 32.7 percent of US insurance employment, the first-ring suburbs showed a dramatic increase in their employment share between 1970 and 1981, followed by non-metropolitan and "other" areas. Thus, office automation at the same time pushes toward the decentralization of back offices, and, to a lesser extent, of headquarters, while making it technologically feasible.

Trends toward further decentralization of office work The process of decentralization of business and office activities is not limited to the metropolitan suburbs, although to date they account for the largest proportion of the phenomenon. New communication technologies make it possible in principle to relocate operations, particularly back offices, in remote locations, be they non-metropolitan areas, rural localities, or foreign countries.

The trend has been particularly important in the shift of employment shares toward small cities and non-metropolitan areas.[96] In a well publicized move, Citicorp relocated and consolidated a share of its nationwide back-office operations to Sioux Falls, South Dakota, from where most Citibank credit card operations are now managed. And Blue Shield of Northern California moved claim-processing operations to small communities in the California central valley, including Woodland, Sonora, and Turlock. These moves triggered speculation about the dramatic potential for general relocation and dispersal of CBDs' business concentrations. Indeed, during the 1970s small and medium-sized metropolitan areas displayed the highest growth rates in finance, insurance, and real estate jobs. However, as a look back at table 3.9 will remind us, the respective absolute shares of new jobs in the same period still bear no comparison: 797,000 FIRE jobs in the largest SMSAs versus 28,000 in the small and medium-sized SMSAs. Table 3.11 shows a somewhat similar pattern for the insurance industry in 1970–81. While small cities always had a significant share of insurance employment (22 percent in 1970), because of the decentralization of insurance services relative to the industry's customers, the high rates of growth in the non-metropolitan and "all other" categories translate into a mere 12.5 percent of total employment in 1981. So, although the increasing role of small metropolitan areas and non-metropolitan areas in office work is analytically significant, and demonstrates the increasing geographical flexibility provided by information technologies, it does not appear that it will reverse substantially in the near future the overwhelmingly metropolitan character of office location, and the dominance of the largest metropolitan areas.

A number of factors account for the limits of demetropolitanization. Some of them are of a technical nature: the radial pattern of power transmission lines in the US, for examples, which makes remote locations much more vulnerable to power failures, threatening the information systems on which the entire process of decentralization relies; the lack of adequate telecommunications facilities in small areas because of the sufficient market there for sophisticated networks; and insufficient air transportation connections to meet the need for quick personal access to the decision-making centers. The myth of generalized spatial diffusion is confronted with the reality of small communities at a disadvantage in the new communications infrastructure because of their low potential as markets for that infrastructure. The development of technology is dominated by the interests of its providers, in this case determined by the pre-existence of a spatial hierarchy of business locations.

Intense speculation about the future of office work has also been aroused by the offshoring of some routine information-handling operations by American companies to Third World countries,[97] particularly in the Caribbean and Asia, where keyboarding of raw documents is performed by local workers for wages that are between 6 and 20 times lower than those that would be paid in the US. This is a qualitatively most significant phenomenon. I have personally observed the working of one such company in Beijing in 1987. A small Chinese software company finances its development operations by obtaining foreign currency from data entry performed in Beijing for Californian companies. The data are generally law records, sent by several California law firms by air cargo. The documents are keyed onto magnetic tape by temporary workers, teenage girls from high schools who are supposed to obtain their "computer training" through this work for several months, in exchange for a "salary" equivalent to US $15 per month. Quality control and supervision are performed by a male software technician who organizes and supervises the work of about 25 teenagers. The women do not know a word of English, and they transcribe each letter as an ideogramme. The rate of error seems to be lower than in equivalent operations in the US.

Most operations of this kind, however, take place in the Caribbean, fostered in recent years by the Caribbean Basin Initiative Act approved by the US Congress for geopolitical reasons. Barbados, Jamaica, and Haiti have been the main locations for offshoring of data entry work, often used by airlines to process their coupons. Mexico is also a growing location for these activities, as are India, Singapore, and China. While air transport is often used for the exchange of documents for magnetic tapes, some facilities involve one-way or two-way telecommunication links to transmit information where time is a high-priority element in processing. Jamaica is investing heavily in telecommunications facilities, particularly in facsimile transmission, in order to attract US investment in this new, clean industry. Future development of optical character readers and scanning devices could give a boost to the offshoring of routine office jobs. However, in spite of the striking images evoked by this trend, its quantitative importance is very limited. According to the OTA report, in 1985 fewer than 3,000 workers in the Caribbean were employed by US firms on data-entry operations, and just 2,000 more such were predicted for the following decade. Including Mexico and Asia, fewer than 10,000 jobs seem to be involved in the operation overall. In fact, much of the Third World is not suitable for this kind of decentralization of office work because of the inadequacy of telecommunications infrastructure and the unreliability of air connections. This is in fact why the Caribbean was targeted as the expansion area, close to the concentration of business on the US east coast, and enjoying good links with the US on the basis of the communications infrastructure set up by the tourist industry. But even in the closer and more reliable areas, offshore decentralization of office work will remain a marginal phenomenon because the nature of activities that can be decentralized corresponds precisely to those tasks that can be easily automated and will be automated during the 1990s. The same process of technological change that made telecommunicated offshoring possible will cause the phenomenon to be superseded as information-processing capabilities develop further the capacity to operate without requiring a significant amount of unskilled labor.

A more important debate is taking place concerning the extent and potential of the ultimate decentralization of office work: "telecommuting," or, more properly defined in OTA terms, "home-based automated office work."[98] This refers to the ability of workers to perform their work from their homes, using computers connected to information systems networks. Alvin Toffler's prophecy of the "electronic cottage" has fueled speculation that as many as 15 million jobs could be operated from remote locations, including homes, by 1990.[99] However, the data currently available completely contradict such expectations. Around 1985, estimates of the numbers of home-based office workers using electronic equipment ranged between 10,000 and 30,000 for the entire US.[100] Moreover, this includes casual, overtime work; salaried workers "telecommuting" as their main employment for a given company probably number less than 5,000 scattered in experimental programs initiated by about 200 companies in the whole country. These workers fall into two different groups.[101] On the one hand, there are professionals whose job flexibility allows them to perform work from home; and on the other hand, there are clerical workers performing data entry operations, who accept the requirement of higher output for lower pay in exchange for being able to stay home. Most of the workers in the second category are women who stay home to take care of children (although some studies show that many of them eventually find they need to pay for day care for their children in order to be able to perform their work at home). Corporations involved in these experiments are mainly in the financial services and computer business sectors. As Gretzos argues,[102] their main motivation for conducting these experiments seems to be the potential for control of future unionization of clerical office workers, a matter of concern for corporations beginning to face the discontent of the new service working class made up of women clerical workers. This is also the reason why labor unions staunchly oppose home-based work. The findings of case studies conducted on the issue [103] tend to show higher productivity of workers, a tendency toward self-exploitation (putting in more hours of work than are claimed for), and yet higher satisfaction with the work because of increased autonomy in terms of time and space. However, management tends to dislike such arrangements because they largely take workers' activity beyond their control and threaten the traditional organization of the office. The development of home work is also inhibited by the existing legal framework, as it makes fiscal regulations and health and labor legislation more difficult to enforce.

The combination of routine legal obstacles, union hostility, and lack of fundamental motivation on the business side, seem to account for the negligible development of telecommuting in the US during the 1980s. However, the real question for the evolution of the spatial structure, is the extent to which this situation could be reversed. It is obvious that the widespread application of telecommuting on the basis of information technologies could considerably modify not only office work itself, but also the communication and transportation flows in the metropolitan areas, deeply affecting the overall urban system. An assessment of the possibilities here must take into consideration, again, the increasingly bifurcated profile of the occupational structure in information-processing activities. For professionals and managers, electronically-based work at home is already a reality, in the sense that many professionals work overtime at home, increasingly using computers, while still going into the office every day to work. This is , in fact, the continuation of a trend that has always existed for the managerial –professional labor force, with the addition of two relatively new factors: the much greater quantitative importance of this professional stratum; and the facility to access the information network system from home, or from other locations, such as from a hotel room by portable computer during a business trip, that makes professional work a potentially non-stop activity. On the other hand, routine clerical work performed at home, on a full-time or, more often, part-time basis, generally by women combining paid work and unpaid family duties, will tend to develop if workers' control over their labor conditions in the office becomes an important factor, as it will if clerical unionization develops. Unskilled homework is more likely to be associated to the growth of an exploitative underground service economy than with the free worker controlling her or his premises and time. More likely than this is the expansion of electronic home work related to the growth of independent contractors and freelancers, the basis of small business growth in the service sector, for whom automatic information-processing offers the possibility of greater efficiency without investment in hiring employees. But this development, which will probably account for most of business uses of electronic equipment in domestic premises in the next few years, can hardly be equated with telecommuting or to the images generally associated with the electronic cottage. It actually means that small businesses, operating from their various locations, including homes when locations are mixed, will be equipped with information systems machines. The potentially crucial development is the possibility for increasing connections among small businesses, and among corporations and their small business ancillary suppliers, through networks of information systems.[104] Rather than decentralized salaried work at home, we could be witnessing the expansion of sub-contracting and networking, with information technologies reinforcing and making materially feasible the trend toward decentralization of production and organizational flexibility that is one of the main features of the current business dynamics.

Overall, then, we observe a major trend toward spatial decentralization of office work and business activities. This decentralization occurs among regions, among metropolitan areas, from metropolitan areas to smaller cities and rural areas, to a limited extent abroad, and, in the future, to the domestic premises. The most important decentralizing trend is taking place within the largest metropolitan areas, from central cities to suburbia and, increasingly, beyond to exurbia and the creation of multifunctional, multinuclear spatial structures. *This process is not undifferentiated.*[105] It follows a hierarchical and functional logic, with lower-level activities being decentralized to secondary suburban locations, and market-oriented facilities being dispersed close to their segmented markets. New directional centers are also being created, shifting regional and metropolitan locations, thus further complicating the geometry of the corporate structure. Ancillary services follow this decentralization, forming new agglomerations that crystallize at nodal points of the communications structure. However, such major decentralization, best expressed in the process of suburbanization of offices and services, is taking place simultaneously with the reinforcement of centralization of decision-making in the corporate cores of major CBDs, and within the framework of metropolitan dominance reinforced by the new telecommunications infrastructure. It is the dialectics between these processes of centralization and of decentralization that fundamentally characterizes the new spatial logic resulting from the transformation of office activities by the use of new information technologies.

Conclusion: the Information Economy, the New Corporate Structure, and the Space of Flows

Information-processing activities increasingly play a structurally determining role in advanced industrialized countries, be it in services, manufacturing, or agriculture. Our economies should be characterized as information economies, rather than as service economies. Information-processing activities are currently undergoing a profound transformation under the combined effect of organizational changes, economic restructuring, and technological innovation. New spatial forms, and even more important, a new spatial logic, emerge as the result of these transformations.

At the organizational level, four major trends combine to produce a new corporate structure: the growing dominance of the large corporation; the decentralization of management; the sub-contracting of operations to a constellation of ancillary small and medium-sized businesses; and the networking of corporations linking their elements to each other and to their auxiliaries. The result is the formation of a complex, hierarchical, diversified organizational structure that is characterized by a variable geometry depending upon time, place, and realm of activity.

Deregulation, crisis management, and stepped-up worldwide competition have led corporations, and their dependent units, to engage in cost-saving, product diversification, creation of new markets, and reorganization of the labor process, in order to increase profits and win market shares in a new and increasingly challenging environment. As a result, increasing productivity of both labor and capital becomes the bottom line on which will depend the fate of each corporate conglomerate in the struggle for survival.

Major innovations in information technology provide a powerful tool for organizational change and economic restructuring, while at the same time imposing constraints and introducing new processes of management and labor in the workings of business organizations. Increasing automation of routine operations, reintegration of tasks at a higher level, emphasis on decision-making on the basis of expert systems, networking of units within the corporation and between economic units; all these technological trends converge on the growing importance of communication networks and interactive patterns in the life and death of organizations. While technology in the main amplifies the logic built into the organization itself, rather than creating it, it does so at such a fundamental level that it allows for a growing independence of the internal relationships of the organization *vis-à-vis* its external environment. Although the increasing automation of internal procedures allows the corporation to concentrate on the moment of decision from which everything else follows, the velocity and complexity of management tasks in a system of multiple interaction mean that the internal system must be able to process the instructions received from the high level of decision making without referring back to it after the initial input into the system. From this follows a very decentralized, but also extremely hierarchical, division of labor among the different units of the corporate conglomerate and its surrounding network. These complex, decentralized systems are heavily centered, and new information technologies make it possible for them to be at the same time flexible and hierarchical. Moreover, the design of the information systems will generally reflect these hierarchies and priorities in terms of access to information and processing capacity.

The spatial dynamics of information activities express this complex organizational and technological pattern. It is characterized, simultaneously, by the persistent centralization of high-level activities in the CBDs of the largest metropolitan areas, and by the decentralization of back offices to smaller areas, and, above all, to the suburbs of major metropolitan areas. In addition, some limited suburban and regional decentralization of headquarters locations bears witness to the pervasive presence of information activities in the overall economic geography. Together with the two above-mentioned trends, decentralization of retail services, particularly to the suburbs, reflects the three-fold tendency toward concentration of decision, automation of organization, and diffusion of customized activities across segmented markets. The regional shift of activities, population, and jobs proceeds by reproducing the same basic spatial logic on an expanded geographic scale, as other areas of the national territory are brought into the new developmental dynamics.

In this complex territorial development process, neither centralization nor decentralization is dominant. *What is crucial is the relationship between the two processes.* On the one hand, what matters is what is centralized and what is decentralized. High-level decision-making is increasingly centralized; organizational management is basically decentralized within major metropolitan areas; and service delivery and customized information retrieval and delivery are diffused throughout the territory. On the other hand, the fundamental characteristic of all these spaces is their interrelationship by means of communication flows. Centralized decision-making can only operate on the basis of customized provision of services and retrieval of information. Back offices are the material basis for decision-making, and large-scale information-processing organizations can only work on the basis of instructions received from the center. The constellation of services linked to each stage of the process of each industry also depends on access to the corresponding level of the communication network. Thus, the linkages of the intra-organizational network are the defining linkages of the new spatial logic. The space of flows among units of the organization and among different organizational units is the most significant space for the functioning, the performance, and ultimately, the very existence of any given organization. The space of organizations in the informational economy is increasingly a *space of flows*.

However, this does *not* imply that organizations are placeless. On the contrary, we have seen that decision-making continues to be dependent upon the milieu on which metropolitan dominance is based; that service delivery must follow dispersed, segmented, segregated markets; and that large-scale operations in back offices are highly dependent upon specific pools of labor that are concentrated in some suburbs of large metropolitan areas. Thus, each component of the information-processing structure is place-oriented.

Nevertheless, the organizational logic of corporations and their satellite activities is fundamentally dependent upon the network of interaction among the different components of the systems. While organizations are located in places, and their components are place-dependent, the *organizational logic is placeless*, being fundamentally dependent on the space of flows that characterizes information networks. But such flows are structured, not undetermined. They possess directionality, conferred both by the hierarchical logic of the organization as reflected in instructions given, and by the material characteristics of the information systems infrastructure. Organizations establish flows according to their hierarchy within the limits set by the telecommunications and computer infrastructure existing at a particular time in a particular place. The space of flows remains the fundamental spatial dimension of large-scale information-processing complexes.

The consequences of this conclusion are far-reaching, because the more organizations depend, ultimately, upon flows and networks, the less they are influenced by the social contexts associated with the places of their location. From this follows a growing independence of the organizational logic from the societal logic: a trend that we could call "bureaucratization" in the Weberian sense, that is, the predominance of the rationality of means over the rationality of goals. Because access to the network of flows is the basic condition for the performance of any organization, this access will have to take precedence over any other requirement originating from the inputs from a particular location of one of the components of the organization at any given point in the network. In more concrete terms: the interests of a local business elite, or of a local resident working class, or of a local market, will be constantly subordinated to the need for the organization to be connected simultaneously with the financial markets, the pool of professional labor, the strategic alliances in the world economy, and the ability to install and update the necessary technology, to mention just some of the potentially key internal requirements, all of which are dependent upon interactions in the space of flows. Since most organizations (or conglomerates of organizations) tend to connect and interact with other systems, the key element for an organization is, increasingly, to preserve those connections. The organizational flows are connected in a macro-space of flows.

Yet most of these flows are directional, and these directions have a socially specific, place-based component. For instance, the decisions of top financial institutions headquartered in New York are not entirely alien to the social milieu of life and decision-making of the New York-based business elite. However, the more heavily interdependent the world economy and the national economy become, the more information technologies are required to handle instant decision processes, and the more the logic of global organizations, materialized in a series of programmed instructions transmitted to the communications network, becomes largely independent from the cultural values and personal preferences of any particular elite group. While the structural logic embedded in the pattern of flows cannot be entirely abstracted from its originators, given the diversity of sources and the changing pattern of manifestation of dominant interests there is an increasing tension between the individual characteristics of the decision-makers in the corporate world and the structure of flows materialized in the communication networks and the repertoire of computerized instructions. Thus, the dialectics between centralization and decentralization, the increasing tension between places and flows, could reflect, in the final analysis, the gradual transformation of the flows of power into the power of flows.

4

Information Technology, the Restructuring of Capital–Labor Relationships, and the Rise of the Dual City

Introduction: The Impact of New Technologies on Labor and Cities

The impact of new technologies on the level of employment, the quality of work, and the condition of labor, is at the core of the social debate over the technological revolution. As cities are made of and by people, and most people are workers, the relationship between technology and labor is decisive in shaping the urban dynamics.

In order to explore systematically the complex web of interactions between high technology, labor, and cities, I will first address the effects of new technologies on the general level of employment and on the occupational structure. I will then locate the specific impact of technology within the broader restructuring process undergone by labor in recent decades, drawing implications for social stratification and income distribution. On the basis of these analyses it will then be possible to assess the transformation of urban social structure into one that I will characterize as "dual," in a sense that I will try to define precisely in terms of several analytical dimensions, on the basis of case studies of New York City and Los Angeles. Throughout this intellectual journey the central methodological question to be considered is the ability to determine the specific role of high technology in the complex interplay among economic and institutional processes that lies at the roots of a new socio-spatial configuration that I will call the "dual city." The thesis I will try to sustain is that while new technologies are by no means the causal factor in the process leading to the new socio-spatial form, they are a major contributing variable in terms of their instrumental role in the overall process of restructuring of labor. While these trends could be altered, and ultimately reversed, the historical rigidity of spatial forms threatens to consolidate this urban process beyond the time horizon of current economic and technological policies. In this sense, the restructuring of labor could be embodied in our social and spatial organization under the impetus of the technological imperative. Let us examine, in analytical order, the different elements underlying the potential formation of the dual city.

High Technology, Employment, and the Transformation of the Occupational Structure

The potential impact of new technologies on work and employment represents the main source of both hopes and fears for the economy and for people. On the one hand, productivity gains made possible by the diffusion of the technological revolution throughout all sectors of activity could pave the way for economic rejuvenation, leading to a new era of innovation and growth.[1] On the other hand, it is feared that the widespread use of labor-saving process-oriented technologies will worsen unemployment, both functional and structural, at a historical moment when hundreds of thousands of jobs, particularly in manufacturing, are being lost.[2] The debate goes beyond the matter of the quantity of jobs to raise the issue of the quality of work in the new technological environment.[3] Is automation de-skilling workers and reducing them to mindless appendages of computers?[4] Or, on the contrary, is there a process of task reintegration taking place that provides workers with greater autonomy in decision-making and enhances the role of judgmental capacity in the work process?[5] In other words, is technology serving people or further alienating workers, or both? If both, which are the conditions determining each potential outcome of the process of technologyical change?

This polemical background makes it particularly difficult to conduct a serious, objective assessment of the matter in the absence of methodologically indisputable empirical research on a comparative basis, and over a sufficiently long span of time.[6] This is why, while I introduce the subject for the sake of the specific research purpose of this work, it will be necessary to proceed with great caution, pinpointing, one after another, the different questions underlying the general issue of the relationship between information technologies and employment. Indeed, a major reason for the intellectual confusion surrounding this debate is the tendency to tangle several issues in a single question, with that question generally being presented in such a way as to suggest a preconceived answer.

At the most elementary level, it is clear that information technologies, when introduced in the work process, both in factories and in offices, considerably reduce working time per unit of output. Scattered evidence, on the basis of case studies, points in this direction, for instance, studies by Hunt and Hunt on the impact of robotics, and by Maeda, Cockroft, Drennan, and Roessner et al., on office automation.[7] However, labor reduction induced by process technology could be offset by new demand for the products, generated by lower prices and improved quality resulting from technological change. Added demand could also result from the new inputs necessary to the new production processes, as well as from the development of new products made possible by the application of new technologies. Furthermore, for a given firm or for a given national economy, technological innovation may result in enhanced competitiveness, thus enabling that economic unit to win market shares, and thus ultimately to increase employment by providing for a much larger demand, thus requiring a substantially higher output. The transformation of reduced working time into job losses is certainly not the result of technology but of a given form of social organization that cannot be considered historically immutable. After all, in comparison with earlier stages of industralization, workers in advanced industrial societies work fewer hours, produce substantially more output, and receive much higher pay. Productivity increases, as a result of both technological innovation and social change, rather than long, hard working hours, are the fundamental basis for economic growth and social well-being.[8]

The complexity of the issue requires a cautious approach of the kind taken by Kaplinsky in his survey of international experience of the relationship between microelectronics and employment.[9] He carefully emphasized the need to differentiate the interpretation of the findings according to various different levels of discourse, of which he defined eight: process level, plant level, firm level, industry level, region level, sector level, national level, and meta level (meaning the discussion of effects according to specific techno-economic paradigms). After reviewing the evidence for each one of these levels, he concluded:

Insofar as the individual studies offer any clear statement on the issue, it would appear that the quantitative macro and micro studies are drawn to fundamentally different conclusions. Process and plant level investigations generally seem to point to a significant displacement of labour. On the other hand, national level simulations more often reach the conclusion that there is no significant employment problem on hand.[10]

We find a similar level of uncertainty when reviewing available evidence for the United States. Flynn summarized about 200 case studies of the employment impacts of process innovations between 1940 and 1982.[11] According to his conclusions, it appears that while process innovations in manufacturing eliminated high-skill jobs and helped to create low-skill jobs, the opposite was true for information-processing in offices, where technological innovation suppressed low-skill jobs and created high-skill ones. Flynn concluded that the effects of process innovation were variable, depending upon specific situations of industries and firms.

At the industry level, the analysis by Levy and others of five industries showed divergent effects of technological innovation:[12] in three of the industries (iron mining, coal mining, and aluminum), technological change increased output and resulted in higher employment levels; in the other two industries (steel and automobiles), growth of demand did not match reduction of labor per unit of output, and job losses resulted. A matter which this study did not investigate is the consideration that automobiles and steel are both industries in which the loss of American competitiveness has reduced market shares for US firms; here we have pinpointed the crucial role of nontechnological factors in determining the evolution of demand and output, and thus of employment levels.

At an aggregate level, a number of simulations, using input–output methodology, constitute the most comprehensive attempt to evaulate the impact of technology on employment, measuring direct and indirect effects over a period of time. Howell evaluated the employment effect of industrial robots on 86 industrial sectors between 1986 and 1990.[13] He concluded that the number of jobs displaced by robotics would range between 168,000 (assuming low diffusion) and 718,000 (assuming fast diffusion). The latter scenario amounts to a displacement level equivalent to about 0.7 percent of total US employment and 3.7 percent of US manufacturing employment, on 1986 figures.

The most ambitious and widely cited study at the national level is the simulation performed by Leontieff and Duchin to evaluate the impact of computers on employment for the period 1963–2000, on the basis of a dynamic input–output matrix of the US economy.[14] They found, in their moderate secenario, that 20 million fewer workers would be required in the year 2000 to fill the expected number of jobs required to achieve the same output, while keeping constant the level of technology. This figure represents a drop of 11.7 percent in required labor. However, according to their calculations, the impact is strongly differentiated among industries and occupations. Interestingly enough, services, and particularly office activities, are predicted to suffer greater job losses than manufacturing, as a result of massive diffusion of office automation. Consequently, clerical workers and managers would see their prospects of employment significantly reduced by new information technologies, while those for professionals would increase substantially, and craftsmen and operatives would maintain their position in the labor force. The methodology of the Leontieff–Duchin study, has, however, been strongly criticized,[15] because it relies on a number of assumptions that, on the basis of limited case studies, maximize the potential impact of computer automation, while limiting technological change to the effect of computers.

However, should reductions in labor requirements materialize, it is unlikely that they would be compensated for by high-technology employment induced by demand for new capital goods. High-technology employment projections show these industries growing very fast, but still representing a very small proportion of all new jobs: less than 6 per cent for 1982–95, according to estimates from the Bureau of Labor Statistics (see table 4.1). Following the same line of argument, Gordon and Kimball have shown that high-technology industries will not be able to replace the jobs lost, particularly in manufacturing, because of technological obsolescence and economic restructuring.[16] Employment in electronics in the US tripled between 1960 and 1980, increasing from 1.6 percent of the total labor force in 1965 to 2.1 percent in 1974, and to 2.9 percent in 1986. In that year, with 2,731,000

Table 4.1 Employment and employment growth, by high-tech industries and occupations: 1982–1995

Industries and occupations	Employment, 1982 (000s)	Employment growth, 1982–95[a] (000s)	(%)
All industries[b]	91,950	25,795	28.1
High-tech industries[c]			
Group I (48 industries)	12,350	4,263	34.5
As % of all industries	13.4	16.5	
Group II (6 industries)	2,543	867	34.1
As % of all industries	2.8	3.4	
Group II (28 industries)	5,691	2,029	35.7
As % of all industries	6.2	7.9	
All occupations[d]	101,510	24,600	25.2
High-tech occupations[e]	3,287	1,508	45.9
As % of all occupations	3.2	5.9	

[a]Data for 1995 based on moderate-trend projections.
[b]Employment covers all wage and salary workers.
[c]Group I includes industries where the proportion of workers employed in high-tech occupations[e] is at least 1.5 times the average for all industries. Group II includes industries with a ratio of R & D expenditure to net sales at least twice the average for all industries. Group III includes manufacturing industries in which the proportion of workers employed in high-tech occupations is equal to or greater than the average for all manufacturing industries; two manufacturing industries that provide technical support to high-tech manufacturing industries are also included.
[d]Employment covers all civilian workers.
[e]Engineers, life and physical scientists, mathematical specialists, engineering and science technicians and computer specialists.
Source: Richard W. Riche, Daniel E. Hecker, and John V. Burgan, "High Technology Today and Tomorrow: A Small Slice of the Employment Pie," *Monthly Labor Review,* 106 (November 1983), tables 2 and 4.

workers in the industry, electronics accounted for twice as many jobs as the automobile and the iron and steel industries combined. And yet, electronics in 1986 represented only 12 percent of the total number of manufacturing jobs and 2.9 percent of total US employment. In 1984, eating and drinking places were employing almost twice as many people as electronics, government six times as many and non-government services seven times as many; and this situation will not change in the foreseeable future. The main high-technology electronics industries together are expected to create about 830,000 new jobs between 1984 and 1995. This figure, as Gordon and Kimball write,

constitutes less than half the number of the manufacturing jobs lost in the US economy between 1980 and 1983. High-technology industries will continue to expand more rapidly than total employment but nevertheless are expected to contribute less than 9% of all new jobs in the period 1982–95. In other words, all but a small proportion of the new jobs established in the foreseeable future will originate in spheres outside high-technology industry while high technology itself will have little impact on reducing unemployment in the US, Western Europe or the Third World.[17]

However, the real issue is not the direct trade-off between jobs eliminated by labor-saving technologies and jobs created in high-technology industries, but the overall effect of technological innovation on economic growth and thus on employment in all activities, including services, on the basis of surplus productivity generated in factories and offices and translated into greater demand and greater output. Robert Z. Lawrence has argued that information technologies have a positive effect on employment in a number of ways: by stimulating production and employment in the capital goods sector; by increasing productivity, thus alleviating disputes over redistribution; and by extending productivity increases to the service sector.[18] He considers it unlikely that the impact of information technology on the economy will be disruptive, for at least three major reasons: first, because their introduction proceeds at a relatively slow pace: increases in output per worker attributable to information technology will not be more than 1 per cent per year; secondly, because high rates of investment in new technology will probably take place during expansionary phases of the business cycle, in which disruption is less frequent; and thirdly, and most importantly, the strongest impact will be during the 1990s, when the rate of growth of the labor force will substantially decline (from 3.5 percent in 1970–82 to 2.3 percent in 1982–90 and 1.4 percent in 1990–5). Assuming these conditions, he proceeds with a simulation of employment growth in the US, after which he concludes:

the decline in the US labor force growth of 2.1% is more than twice the rise in output per manhour, but would probably be the maximum due to a rapid increase in information technology. The U.S. economy needs to be no more successful at creating jobs than it has been in the past to absorb the labor potentially displaced by information technology.[19]

Lawrence's analysis, along with a number of other studies, underscores the fundamental flaw in the simulation models used by researchers who come up with predictions of significant job losses, including that built by Leontieff and Duchin: namely, that most of these models assume a fixed level of final demand and output. This is precisely what past experience of technological innovation seems to reject as the most likely hypothesis.[20] If the economy does not grow, it is obvious that labor-saving techniques will reduce the amount of working time required (even on this hypothesis by a somewhat limited amount – less than 12 percent in the Leontieff–Duchin calculations). But in the past, rapid technological change has generally been associated with an expansionary trend that, by increasing demand and output, has generated the need for *more* working time in absolute terms, even if it represents less working time per unit of output. However, in an internationally integrated economic system, expansion of demand and output will depend on the competitiveness of each specific economic unit. Since quality and production costs, the determinants of competitiveness, will largely depend on product and process innovation, and thus on technology, it is likely that faster technological change for a given firm, industry, or national economy, would result in a higher, not a lower, employment level. This is in line with the findings of the Young and Lawson study on the effect of technology on employment and output between 1972 and 1984.[21] In 44 of the 79 industries they examined, the labor-saving effects of new technologies were more than compensated for by higher final demand, so that, overall, employment expanded.

In the most carefully designed recent study, the Bureau of Labor Statistics forecast the impact of technological change on 378 industries and 562 occupations in 1995.[22] Almost all of the 350 occupations with more than 25,000 workers showed employment growth in the simulation. Only 11 occupations showed absolute declines in the number of projected jobs, under the impact of new technologies, and they were concentrated in four areas: office workers performing data entry; communications workers displaced by automation of telecommunications; trucks and tractor operators, linked to containerization and warehouse automation; and gas service station operators. Overall, job losses in the occupation analyzed would amount to 251,000, that is, about 1.6 percent of total employment growth projected for 1984–95.

Thus it seems that, as a general trend, there is no systematic structural correlation between the diffusion of information technologies in the labor process and the evolution of employment levels. Jobs are being displaced and new jobs are being created, but the quantitative relationship between the losses and the gains varies among firms, industries, sectors, regions, and countries, depending upon competitiveness, firms' strategies, government policies, institutional environments, and relative position in the international economy. The specific outcome of the interaction between high technology and employment is largely dominated by macroeconomic factors and economic strategies.

Overall, in the US it does not seem that the aggregate level of employment will be negatively affected by the impact of process-oriented information technologies. Nevertheless, if new jobs are created on the basis of technologically driven productivity and its stimulating effect on demand and output, they are of very different kinds from those phased out by techno-economic restructuring, particularly in manufacturing. Fast-growing high-technology industries are characterized, as reported in chapter 2, by a bipolar distribution

Table 4.2   High-technology occupational structure: gender, ethnicity and race

Occupation type	White female (%)	Minority (male and female) (%)	White male (%)
	(a) US high-technology industry		
Production	38.4	24.4	37.2
Technical	15.8	14.3	69.9
Professional	11.9	8.4	79.7
	(b) Santa Clara County		
Production	30.2	46.4	23.4
Technical	16.7	28.0	55.3
Professional	13.3	14.4	72.2
	(c) Santa Cruz County		
Production	48.4	29.4	22.2
Technical	25.3	23.0	51.7
Professional	24.0	12.7	63.4

Sources: *1980 EEOI Summary Report of Selected Establishments from the Technical Services Division, OSP,* Equal Employment Opportunity Commission; R. Gordon and L. Kimball, *Small Town High Technology: The Industrialization of Santa Cruz County,* (1985). The authors are very grateful to Lenny Siegel, Pacific Studies Center, Mountain View for supplying the EEOI raw data from which the US and Santa Clara, figures are calculated.
Compiled and elaborated by Gordon and Kimball (see note 28).

of skills and wages,[23] specified by gender and race, as illustrated in table 4.2, elaborated by Gordon and Kimball.

Concerning the evolution of the occupational structure at large, the projections of the Bureau of Labor Statistics for 1982–95[24] provide some fundamental clues to understanding the emerging social structure (see tables 4.3, 4.4, and 4.5). The bulk of new jobs correspond to low-skilled occupations in the service sector: 779,000 building custodians, 744,000 cashiers, 719,000 secretaries, and so on. While some of the fastest growing categories, as shown in table 4.4, do represent the rise of high-skill occupations related to the process of technological development, their share in the total of new jobs is still limited. Computer systems analysts boast an 85.3 percent growth rate for 1982–95, but this adds only 217,000 new jobs, while the 27.5 percent increase in building custodians translates into 3 million new jobs. A similar argument could be sustained in terms of the projections of job growth by sector. BLS projections for 1982–90 attributed a 27 percent expansion to computers and peripherals, and only 16 percent to "restaurants and other retailing," but these growth rates translated into 200,000 new jobs for the computers sector, and 3 million jobs for "restaurants and other retailing," on top of the 17 million jobs already existing in the latter sector. Similarly, the rate of growth

Table 4.3 Forty occupations with largest job growth, 1982–1995[a]

Occupation	Change in total employment (000s)	% of total job growth	% change
Building custodians	779	3.0	27.5
Cashiers	744	2.9	47.4
Secretaries	719	2.8	29.5
General clerks, office	696	2.7	29.6
Salesclerks	685	2.7	23.5
Nurses, registered	642	2.5	48.9
Waiters and waitresses	562	2.2	33.8
Teachers, kindergarten and elementary	511	2.0	37.4
Truckdrivers	425	1.7	26.5
Nursing aides and orderlies	423	1.7	34.8
Sales representatives, technical	386	1.5	29.3
Accountants and auditors	344	1.3	40.2
Automotive mechanics	324	1.3	38.3
Supervisors of blue-collar workers	319	1.2	26.6
Kitchen helpers	305	1.2	35.9
Guards and doorkeepers	300	1.2	47.3
Food preparation and service workers, fast-food restaurants	297	1.2	36.7
Managers, store	292	1.1	30.1
Carpenters	247	1.0	28.6
Electrical and electronic technicians	222	0.9	60.7
Licensed practical nurses	220	0.9	37.1
Computer systems analysts	217	0.8	85.3
Electrical engineers	209	0.8	65.3
Computer programmers	205	0.8	76.9
Maintenance repairers, general utility	193	0.8	27.8
Helpers, trades	190	0.7	31.2
Receptionists	189	0.7	48.8
Electricians	173	0.7	31.8
Physicians	163	0.7	34.0
Clerical supervisors	162	0.6	34.6
Computer operators	160	0.6	75.8
Sales representatives, non-technical	160	0.6	27.4
Lawyers	159	0.6	34.3
Stock clerks, stockroom and warehouse	156	0.6	18.8
Typists	155	0.6	15.7
Delivery and route workers	153	0.6	19.2
Bookkeepers, hand	152	0.6	15.9
Cooks, restaurants	149	0.6	42.3
Bank tellers	142	0.6	30.0
Cooks, short order, speciality and fast-food	141	0.6	32.2

[a]Includes only detailed occupations with 1982 employment of 25,000 or more.
Data for 1995 are based on moderate-trend projections.
Source: Bureau of Labor Statistics.

Table 4.4   Twenty fastest growing occupations, 1982–1995[a]

Occupation	Growth in employment (%)
Computer service technicians	96.8
Legal assistants	94.3
Computer systems analysts	85.3
Computer programmers	76.9
Computer operators	75.8
Office machine repairers	71.7
Physical therapy assistants	67.8
Electrical engineers	65.3
Civil engineering technicians	63.9
Peripheral EDP equipment operators	63.5
Insurance clerks, medical	62.2
Electrical and electronic technicians	60.7
Occupational therapists	59.8
Surveyor helpers	58.6
Credit clerks, banking and insurance	54.1
Physical therapists	53.6
Employment interviewers	52.5
Mechanical engineers	52.1
Mechanical engineering technicians	51.6
Compression and injection mold machine operators, plastics	50.3

[a]Includes only detailed occupations with 1982 employment of 25,000 or more.
Data for 1995 are based on moderate-trend projections.
Source: Bureau of Labor Statistics.

of secretarial jobs for 1982–90 (28.3 percent) was far below that for data processing mechanics (92.3 percent) but translated into about 700,000 more secretaries, in comparison with 77,000 additional data processing mechanics. Rumberger and Levine have analyzed the wages and skills components of these occupational categories on the basis of BLS projections.[25] Their findings, some of which are displayed in table 4.6, show that occupations with the highest growth in absolute numbers, accounting for the majority of new jobs, are concentrated in low-skilled, low-paid activities with low educational requirements, while three out of the five fastest-declining occupations have high relative earnings.

Bluestone and Harrison have compared the wages and working conditions attached to maufacturing jobs displaced by the restructuring process with those prevailing in the bulk of new manufacturing and service jobs. On the basis of BLS data they report that, in 1982, the average weekly wage was $310 in the declining industries but only $210 in the fastest-growing industries. According to their study, "it was necessary to create 163 electronic components jobs to compensate for the wage bill loss of 100 steel workers. Similarly it takes almost two department store jobs or three restaurant jobs to

Table 4.5   Twenty most rapidly declining occupations, 1982–1995[a]

Occupation	Decline in employment (%)
Railroad conductors	−32.0
Shoemaking machine operatives	−30.2
Aircraft structure assemblers	−21.0
Central telephone office operators	−20.0
Taxi drivers	−18.9
Postal clerks	−17.9
Private household workers	−16.9
Farm laborers	−15.9
College and university faculty	−15.0
Roustabouts	−14.4
Postmasters and mail superintendents	−13.8
Rotary drill operator helpers	−11.6
Graduate assistants	−11.2
Data entry operators	−10.6
Railboard brake operators	−9.8
Fallers and buckers	−8.7
Stenographers	−7.4
Farm owners and tenants	−7.3
Typesetters and compositors	−7.3
Butchers and meatcutters	−6.3

[a]Includes only detailed occupations with 1982 employment of 25,000 or more.
Data for 1995 are based on moderate-trend projections.
Source: Bureau of Labor Statistics.

make up for the earning loss of just one average manufacturing position."[26] Gordon and Kimball advance a similar argument, indicating that in 1984 the average hourly wage of an electronics production worker was $8.89, compared with $13.09 in steel, and $12.54 in the automobile industry.[27] They also report usual starting wages in operative work in electronics in the range of $3.50–$5.50 per hour. Comparable trends in electronics manufacturing are documented by Carnoy for Silicon Valley, Scott for Orange County, and Gordon and Kimball for Santa Cruz, California.[28]

A similar pattern in the evolution of the occupational structure is observed by Michael Teitz in his analysis of prospects for the California economy when he writes:

Electronics, especially production of semiconductors and products derived from them, requires a labor force that differs markedly from that in traditional manufacturing. The proportion of skilled technical and professional workers tends to be much higher than the average in manufacturing, and they are paid correspondingly well. However, production work is highly routinized and selectively low-skilled. Its pay has been below average for manufacturing and it tends to draw on female and immigrant labor

Table 4.6 Employment, education, and relative earnings in the greatest declining and growing occupations, 1982–1995

	Employment (000s)			Relative earnings[a] (%)	Modal education[b] (years)
	1982	1995	1982–95		
Declining occupations					
Farm laborers	1,211	1,019	192	53	<12
Private household workers	1,023	850	173	30	<12
College and university faculty	744	632	112	136	17+
Farm owners and tenants	1,407	1,304	103	119	12
Postal service clerks	307	252	55	122	12
Total	4,692	4,057	635	78	–
Growing occupations					
Building custodians	2,828	3,606	778	69	<12
Cashiers	1,570	2,314	744	49	12
Secretaries	2,441	3,161	720	67	12
General clerks, office	2,348	3,044	696	67	12
Sales clerks	2,916	3,601	685	52	12
Total	12,103	15,726	3,623	61	–

[a]Average weekly earnings during 1979 of workers in each occupation relative to the average weekly earnings of all workers.
[b]Level of education completed by the majority of workers employed in each occupation in the spring of 1980.
Sources: Employment data from Geoge T. Silvestri, John M. Lukasiewicz, and Marcus F. Einstein, "Occupational Employment Projections Through 1995," *Monthly Labor Review* 106 (November 1983), table 1; earnings and education data calculated from the 1980 Public Use sample, US Bureau of the Census. Compiled by R.W. Rumberger (see note 32).

pools that are non-unionized. While this form of employment is undoubtedly critical for low-skilled workers, it is problematic for the long-term. It does not offer income opportunities comparable to those being lost in the older, declining industrial sectors, and therefore provides neither easy transition for displaced workers nor long-term prospects for higher income or career mobility. If anything, it has been argued that the high level of education and technical skill required by the technical/professional part of the labor force tends to decrease prospects that production workers could ever be anything more.[29]

So, while the available empirical evidence does not seem to support the idea of a significant negative impact exercised by information technologies on the aggregate level of employment in the US, there are a number of substantial new trends in the evolution of the occupational structure:

(1) A fast rate of growth of high-technology manufacturing and advanced services-related jobs, yet accounting for only a small propor-

tion of total new jobs, and an even lower share of overall aggregate employment.[30]

(2) A bipolar occupational structure in high-technology manufacturing, as well as in manufacturing industries, fostered by intensive penetration by microelectronics-based process technologies. This bipolar structure is characterized by the juxtaposition of two main groups of workers: professional, engineers, and technicians on the one hand, most of them being white and male; and low-skilled, low-paid direct manufacturing jobs, generally held by women and ethnic minorities.[31]

(3) A massive increase in service jobs, which will account for about 75 percent of all new jobs in the period 1982–95. Most of these jobs will be in low-skill, low-pay occupations, such as building custodians, cashiers, secretaries, waiters, general clerks, etc.[32]

(4) A significant increase in the share of total employment taken by high-level occupations, such as professionals and technicians, from 16.3 percent in 1982 to 17.1 percent in 1995. Meanwhile operatives' share of the total will decline somewhat from 12.8 percent to 12.1 percent.[33]

Along with the proliferation of low-skill service jobs, it appears that the process of bipolarization is not confined to high-technology industries but, on the contrary, increasingly applies across the entire occupational structure. By bipolarization we understand the simultaneous growth of the top and the bottom of the occupational spectrum at a rate such that there is an increase in the relative shares of both extreme positions in the overall population distribution. If these projections are confirmed, and if the characteristics of the growing and declining occupations hold the educational and wage attributes revealed by Levin and Rumberger's analysis, it would seem that the process of restructuring leads to the simultaneous upgrading and downgrading of the occupational structure, although with changing emphasis in different industries and occupations.

Nevertheless, the question arises as to the specific relationship between new technologies and the emerging profile of the occupational structure I have described. In other words, it could be argued that the secular transformation toward the "service economy," and the specific characteristics of a number of service activities, are a more likely source of the new occupational structure than the introduction of new technologies into the work process. A serious attempt to answer this question with recourse to empirical data has been undetaken, for the US, by Ronald Kutscher, Associate Commissioner of the Bureau of Labor Statistics.[34] Kutscher proceeds in two steps. First, he analyzes the specific impact of technological change on employment by industry and by occupation between 1967 and 1978, comparing the actual level of employment to what would have resulted from holding technological input–output coefficients constant at their 1967 level. He then goes on to evaluate the impact of technology on future employment change by calculating a factor analysis of the 1977-95 projections by industry and by occupation, isolating the specific impact of input-output coefficients after having controlled the effect of other factors, in particular GNP growth. It has to be noted that Kutscher's definition of technological change is very broad, and refers to the technical coefficients of the input-output matrix, thus reaching beyond information technologies to include all changes in the goods and services required to produce each industry's goods or services. Nevertheless, his findings still represent a useful approximation for dealing with the question we are analyzing.

Table 4.7 provides Kutscher's estimates of the specific effects of technology on the evolution of employment in the period 1967-78. According to his findings, technology had a significantly negative effect on employment in agriculture and in manufacturing, a positive effect on the construction industry, a slight negative effect on wholesale and retail trade (offsetting the positive effects of the increase in output), and a positive effect on employment in finance, insurance, and real estate, which becomes strongly positive for job creation in "office services." According to data not shown in this table, negative effects on manufacturing employment have been concentrated in textiles, apparel, iron and steel, and motor vehicles. Positive effects have been particularly relevant in "other services," primarily miscellaneous business services. The statistical analysis of occupational change between 1967 and 1978 shows a positive effect on technology on the proportion of professionals

Table 4.7 Employment by Major Sector, % distribution

	Actual 1978	1978 with constant 1967 input-output coefficients	1978 with constant 1967 input-output and employment output coefficients
Agriculture, forestry and fisheries	3.9	3.6	5.5
Mining	0.8	0.8	0.7
Construction	7.0	7.6	5.1
Manufacturing	24.5	24.5	29.6
Durables	14.6	14.7	17.2
Non-durables	9.8	9.6	12.4
Transportation	3.6	3.5	3.0
Communications	1.5	1.3	2.0
Public utilities	1.0	1.1	1.1
Wholesale and retail trade	26.0	27.2	24.2
Finance, insurance and real estate	7.6	7.5	6.8
Other services	20.3	18.2	17.3
Government enterprises	1.8	2.4	2.0
Households	2.2	2.2	1.8

Source: Kutscher (see note 34).

Table 4.8   Largest declines in employment resulting from technological change, as measured by input–output coefficients, 1977–1995

Selected industries	Selected occupations
Iron and ferroalloy mining	Metal-working operatives
Non-ferrous metal ore mining	Factory material repairers
Sugar	Foundry workers
Wooden containers	Metal engineers
	Glassware operators
	Miscellaneous machine operators, binary metals
	Machine operatives, leather and leather goods
	Roadbrake operators
	Automotive engineers
	Road car repairers

Source: Kutscher (see note 34); my selection.

and technicians, a negative effect on operatives and farmers, and a lack of impact on the numbers of clerical workers.

Analysis of future trends is made more complex by the projective nature of the data. Also, because Kutscher kept his database at a high level of disaggregation, to make possible his factor analysis, the trends he shows for 1977–95 are less clear. Still, tables 4.8 and 4.9 provide some hints on the matter by pinpointing those industries and occupations most affected in the decline or increase of their employment by technological factors. It does appear that those most negatively affected by technological progress are the traditional manufacturing industries, and particularly the manual workers in those industries, while clerical work does not appear among the 40 occupations with the largest decline in employment. On the other hand, high technology and advanced services are the industries in which employment is most positively influenced by technological change. Yet the occupations showing the largest increase in employment due to technology are not actually high-technology-related jobs, but service-related occupations. Thus, security-related workers, household repair and maintenance workers, and financial experts outweigh communications mechanics or computer programmers in their rate of increase as a direct effect of technological change. Services are not only the major source of job creation in general, but also the sector whose expansion is most directly related to technological progress, after accounting for the effects of GNP growth, productivity, and staffing patterns. It is worth noting that this overwhelming expansion of service sector employment does not mean the demise of manufacturing. Manufacturing employment grew by 4.5 million jobs between 1959 and 1979, and although it lost 2.2 million jobs in the 1980–2 recession it will, according to BLS projections, gain a further 4.3 million jobs between 1982 and 1995,

Table 4.9   Largest increases in employment resulting from technological change, as measured by input–output coefficients, 1977–1995

Selected industries	Selected occupations
Electronic components	Termite treaters
Communications	Protective signal operators, installers, and repairers
Credit agencies and	Private detectives
financial brokers	Survey workers
Business services	Communications equipment mechanics
	Central office operators and repairers
	Directory assistance operators
	Installers, repairers, section maintainers
	Credit reporters
	Employment interviewers

Source: Kutscher (see note 34): my selection.

maintaining its share of total employment at about the 1982 level, that is, 19 percent. On the other hand, the overwhelming proportion of new job creation (23 million out of 28 million between 1983 and 1995) will take place in the service sector, and particularly in the "other services" category, which includes business services, health, hotels and restaurants, and personal services. This "other services" category will account for about one-third of all new jobs, and will represent in 1995 one-fourth of total US employment.

The interesting point in Kutscher's analysis is that while the general trend toward the increasing share of services in total employment is largely due to GNP growth, it is also attributable in some degree to the specific effect of technological change on the structure of employment, according to the results of his factor analysis. Technology appears to have a two-fold effect on the type of jobs created in the new economy: on the one hand, being a major factor in promoting economic growth, it accelerates the expansion of the service economy; on the other hand, it stimulates employment growth in high-technology manufacturing and in new service activities, as a direct effect of technology itself.

Therefore, on the basis of Kutscher's analysis at least, it seems that there is a statistical relationship between the current process of technological change and the specific profile of the occupational structure emerging in the US. High technology and information processing, in fostering productivity and competitiveness, play a crucial role in creating highly paid new technical and professional jobs. Productivity increases achieved by automation in both factories and offices "frees" labor, which is used by an expansionary service sector whose lower level concentrates most women, minorities, and immigrants in low-skill jobs. These occupations, lacking in organizational strength, become also low-paid, ill-protected jobs.

High technology does not, then, create unemployment by itself, particularly against the background of a declining growth rate of the labor force. On the contrary, when used to foster productivity and economic growth, it contributes to higher demand, investment, and output, ultimately expanding employment, mainly outside the high-technology sector of the economy. Yet high technology does seem to contribute to an occupational structure characterized by polarization and segmentation of the labor force. It probably does so, in spite of the upgrading of much of the labor working in high-technology industries and advanced services, by contributing to the dissolution of the social fabric that for decades protected wage-earners from the unrestrained imposition of the logic of capital. Otherwise it would be difficult to explain why clerical work is less well paid than assembly-line work, or why the wages of electronics production workers do not match those of their counterparts in the automobile industry. It is my hypothesis that the main reason for the current transformation of the occupational structure lies in the dissolution of old industrial forms and activities, and the subsequent creation of new ones, under the powerful impetus of a new, technology-led round of economic growth. It is in this precise sense that high technology appears to exercise a fundamental effect on work and employment: by the role it plays in the broader socio-economic restructuring of the labor process, at the roots of the new social structure.

Information Technology and the Restructuring of the Relationship between Capital and Labor

The introduction of information technology in the work process in factories and offices affects labor deeply. But the specific impact of technological change depends largely on the form in which technology is used and the objectives according to which it is applied. Furthermore, decisions affecting technological diffusion can only be understood within the framework of the restructuring process that has characterized capital–labor relationships in advanced industrial societies since the structural crisis of the 1970s.

The causes and characteristics of the restructuring process that has taken place, under different forms, in most societies, and with special intensity in the US, were presented in chapter 1. The diffusion of information technology in the work process has generally been an instrument, and a powerful one, of restructuring strategy. Therefore, we can only understand the orientations and outcome of technological change in organizations, and its impact on labor, by examining the interaction between the two processes, namely, the restructuring of capital–labor relationships and technological diffusion, under the dominance of the former. However, it should be clearly recognized that the use of information technology is part of a broader set of goals and motivations, and that technology is only one, and not necessarily the most important, of the instruments through which capital reorganizes the labor process.

Capital has had two main goals in pursuing the restructuring of labor in the particular historical circumstances produced by the economic crisis of 1973–4. The first is to change qualitatively the power relationships between management and organized labor in favor of business interests. The second is to enhance substantially the flexibility of labor at all levels, through deregulation, sectoral and geographical mobility, networking and sub-contracting, and constant redefinition of working conditions according to the changing strategies and interests of firms. The two objectives are inter-related, but they remain distinct in terms of their logic as well as of their implementation. The introduction of information technology in the work process plays an instrumental role in fostering both.

The use of information technology enhances capital's bargaining position *vis-à-vis* labor by providing management with a broad range of options: automation of jobs considered to be too expensive or not amenable to management requests; decentralization of production facilities to other regions or other countries, while maintaining links with other productive units and with the markets; sub-contracting of production and distribution to other firms in which labor works under different, generally less favorable conditions. Under these circumstances, capital does not necessarily need to adopt a confrontational strategy. Given its unfavorable position, organized labor will usually be forced to accept wages and working conditions below the historically established standards, just to keep the jobs at their current level. This explains the practice, widespread during the 1980s, of "voluntary" wage cutbacks in union contracts, as well as the two-tier contract system, under which newly hired workers do not benefit from the same wages as senior workers, thus fundamentally splitting the workforce. Also, in many instances, capital has taken a more aggressive stand, and has used technological change as a weapon to automate jobs in those segments of the labor force where organized labor was strongest. As a result of various tactics, backed up by the potential use of the technological medium both as an instrument and as an occasion to change working rules and practices, the position of organized labor has been decisively weakened in the core of manufacturing industries; and it has been unable to organize effectively in the new industries, particularly electronics and in advanced services, the leading sectors of the new economic era.

The second major goal of the restructuring process is to increase labor flexibility. And here also information technology plays a fundamental role, both in intra-firm flexibility and in inter-firm linkages. Within a particular organization, information technology forces a reclassification of job categories to accord with the new tasks, providing for multitask jobs that, while less routinized, are also more open to arbitrary, non-programmed definitions of the performance expected from each particular category. From this follows more direct managerial control, as responsibilities, and related conditions of work, shift with the needs of the company's changing organization of the work process. Flexible manfacturing technologies and microcomputer-based information-processing activities allow for variable volumes of production without increases in production costs. Part-time work, temporary labor contracts, and flexible working schedules become at the same time both possible and convenient for the firm, furthering the trend toward a variable geometry of labor and of labor conditions, able to reflect rapid changes in the market. Organizations certainly become more efficient, leaner, and more productive; but labor loses control over the labor process, and ultimately over its working conditions.

An even more important trend promoted by new technologies is the growing practice of sub-contracting and networking in the production process. The "just in time" system, able to reduce inventories drastically, is the quintessence of this tendency, organizing firms around networks of suppliers that rely on extremely precise information systems. Sub-contracting of entire phases of production to other firms, often in other countries, also allows for a combination of economies of scale and effectively decentralized production and management that increases efficiency and competitiveness. At the same time. labor is made extremely flexible, fitting into the specific conditions required by each unit of the network. Yet this trend also results in the segmentation of labor in a series of distinct organizational situations, while the unity of the production and management processes are largely preserved. Information technologies do not cause the generalized use of networks and sub-contracting in the pursuit of flexible production, or, therefore, the consequent segmentation of labor; but they provide the indispensable material infrastructure for such practices to develop. It is my belief that this trend in the organization of production is irreversible, with mass production being phased out as inefficient, as Piore and Sabel have brilliantly argued.[35] The so-called "Benetton Model" is a prototype of the industrial future of most effective productive organizations.[36] However, the contrast between the networking of capital and the segmentation of labor creates a new historical situation that is clearly undermining the social fabric inherited from earlier stages of industrialization. Considered against the background of organized labor weakened in the restructuring process, these trends clearly have threatening implications for the protection and living conditions of salaried workers, in the absence of a new round of social struggles leading to the formation of a new social contract based on different organizational and technological premises.

A detailed empirical analysis of the themes suggested here clearly exceeds the specific purpose of the research presented in this chapter, namely, to establish the precise connection between the restructuring of labor, information technology, and the new urban social structure. However, a few illustrations, drawn from available empirical studies on the introduction of new technologies in the labor process, will help to clarify the argument.

Watanabe has shown the different uses of new technology by comparing strategies and results in the process of introducing robots into the automobile industry in the US, in Japan, and in western Europe.[37] While in Japan, the much greater introduction of robots resulted in increased employment, in the US fewer robots displaced more workers, with a large total job loss; and in Italy robots displace more workers than in France (see tables 4.10 and 4.11). The obvious reason for the discrepancies is that, both in the US and in Italy (particularly in Fiat) robots were introduced with the specific aim of saving labor, while in Japan quality considerations and flexibility of production were the main motives for the robotization program. In fact, Watanabe argues that to use robots to trim labor is an ill-conceived strategy, since special-purpose machines, less sophisticated and less expensive, are better suited as direct replacements for assembly-line jobs. His analysis also shows that, in the case of Japan, the competitive edge obtained by a productivity-driven, quality-oriented use of technology resulted in work-amplifying effects of the new technology sufficient largely to offset its labor-saving impact, actually increasing overall employment in the automobile industry. In the US on the other hand, a short-sighted strategy aimed at trimming labor to reduce production costs could not shore up the competitiveness of US manufacturers in their own market. The use and effects of technology depend more on management strategies than on technology itself. By ensuring life tenure of employment to their workers, Japanese automobile companies were able to

Table 4.10   Estimates of labor savings made possible by robotization in the automobile industry (two-shift operation)

Country	(1) No. of robots[a]	(2) No. of workers replaced	(3) Change in employment, 1979–84	(2)/(3) (%)
Japan[b]	10,000	7,000	+60,000	–
United States[c]	5,000–7,000	10,000–15,000	−300,000	3.3–5.0
France	800	1,000	−50,000	2.0
Italy (Fiat)	800	2,400	−68,432	3.3

[a]"Robot" is defined broadly in line with the concept used by the Robotic Industries Association
[b]The Japanese figures relate to playback and higher categories of robots only.
[c]Includes robots installed in Canada.
Source: Watanabe, (see note 37).

Table 4.11 The labor-saving effect of robotization in selected countries

Country	% of robots replacing or substituting for labor	Average gross no. of workers[a] replaced by a robot in 2 shifts where introduced to replace labor	Maintenance staff required per robot[b]
Japan	50	1.4	0.2
United States	Almost 100[c]	2	0.1–0.17
West Germany (Hanover VW)	–	2–4	–
France (Renault)	25–30	4	–
Italy	Almost 100[c]	3	–
Brazil	–	4	–
Sweden (Volvo)	–	2	0.5

[a]Not counting new jobs created in maintenance and programming.
[b]Based on only one or a few observations except for the United States.
[c]Implicitly assumed in the calculation of the employment impact.
Source: Watanable (see note 37).

concentrate on the developmental aspects of technological enhancement, regardless of its labor-saving effects. The inability of US firms to cooperate with labor unions in the process of technological change led them to concentrate on labor costs and on means of undermining the position of organized labor, as a pre-condition for flexibility, thus downgrading the productivity potential of new technologies.

The attitude revealed by this case study is consistent with the traditional approach of American management toward labor unions and toward labor in general. David Noble, in his detailed case studies of technical change in manufacturing, particularly in the analysis of the introduction and development of numerical control machines, has documented the deliberate use of technological change to reduce workers' control over the labor process, actually de-skilling the tasks directly performed by the operative, and seriously limiting the productivity potential of new technologies at the shop-floor level.[38] This is also an argument put forward by Harley Shaiken on the basis of his study of the forms and processes of introduction of computer-aided instruments in manufacturing.[39] He shows that while new technologies could allow for greater work autonomy, enabling higher-quality output and higher productivity, the particular way in which they are introduced is biased by the deliberate goal of limiting machinists' autonomy in performing their work, a basic requirement of the Taylorist organizational principle on which most of American management still relies. Under these historical circumstances, what are the specific effects of new information technologies on the restructuring of the labor process? To illustrate what appear to be the general answers to this fundamental question I will turn to two empirical studies, one concerning manufacturing, the other focusing on office work.

Carol Parsons, in her Berkeley PhD dissertation, studied the role of flexible production technology in the industrial restructuring of the metal-working and apparel industries.[40] In the case of metal-working (including machinery, automobiles, appliances, machine tools, and small metal goods), there has been extensive introduction of microelectronics-based technologies during the 1980s. Among the firms surveyed by Parsons, the reduction of direct labor was the purpose for the use of flexible technology most frequently cited in line with the argument presented above. Firms used new technologies within the framework of their existing management practices and production strategies, without taking advantage of them to modify their position in the industrial structure. Large firms continued to rely on mass production, in spite of the potential offered by new, flexible equipment for economical production on a short-run basis. Small firms remained job shops, whose use of new equipment allowed them to become more efficient suppliers.

Yet the introduction of computer numerical control (CNC) machines and computer-aided manufacturing equipment did have some important effects on the labor processes of the metal-working industries. Plants were closed and the new ones that were opened differed in important respects. First, there was a shift from unionized plants to non-unionized plants. According to Hicks, cited by Parsons, 59.6 percent of the oldest plants (established before 1920) were unionized, while 93.8 percent of those established after 1973 were not unionized.[41] Interestingly enough, companies did not change region when opening a new non-union plant; they remained concentrated in the mid-west, as implementation of the new "just-in-time" method required close proximity to an industrial network. Secondly, most companies engaged in extensive sub-contracting, both regionally and internationally, making use of the new communication facilities and the automated standardization of parts. Thirdly, firms reorganized their internal and external labor processes. Internally, new technologies required the reclassification of jobs with a shift to multiskilled positions. In this way, the content of work was enriched. But, as Parsons writes:

At the same time, however, the over-riding motive for multiskilling was to reduce labor costs. One manager explained that "when one person does five jobs the plant gets more flexible without hiring four more people". Moreover, "not only do I save on the wages and benefits of those other workers but the featherbedding goes way down". Traditional demarcations between jobs, that are the hallmark of American job control unionism and create the featherbedding this manager referred to, are largely incompatible with multiskilling.[42]

As a result of the restructuring process, employment fell substantially in all metal-working industries with the exception of office equipment. Yet net job loss owing to plant turnover was 17 times higher than net job loss owing to layoffs within existing plants during the 1980–2 recession. In other words, rather than introducing new equipment in existing working situations, the restructuring took the form of installing the new machines in a new working environment characterized by transformed labor relationships, the absence of unions being the most notorious change. In terms of the transformation of the occupational structure, following the process of organizational and technological restructuring, there was an acceleration of the shift from direct to indirect labor, partly caused by the use of new technology to reduce direct labor inputs. Holding demand constant, professional, managerial, and technical employment grew rapidly, while production employment declined. And for production workers, the occupational structure showed a trend toward bifurcation, as craft work and simple labor both increased and the number of operatives, most of them assemblers, shrank. Thus, overall, Parsons observes the following features: a reduction in metal-working's manufacturing labor force; an upgrading of the occupational structure, through the trimming of numbers of production workers; and an internal polarization of the remaining production workers between craft workers and simple laborers, while traditional assembly-line operatives are squeezed out by automation. However, she insists that these trends do not result inevitably from the use of flexible production technology, but are the outcome of managerial decisions concerning the use of the technologies, for example, refusing to let machinists program CNC machines by themselves, in spite of their knowledge of the production process and the simplicity of the operation. Parsons also cites alternatives examples of Japanese factories where a more recent version of the same technology has enabled machinists to program their own working tools, with the consequence of added productivity. Within the parameters of the vertical management system, the introduction of new information technologies leads to a reduction of the traditional labor force and to increasing internal segregation of the remaining workers, split between indirect and direct labor, and between craftspeople and unskilled workers.

Parsons' analysis of the US apparel industry is also revealing in the sense that most of the process of technological change here concerns the linkages of the firms with their suppliers and markets, rather than automation of the production process itself. It would seem that, with some exceptions, the majority of apparel firms have decided not to compete with the NICs in terms of production, and are actually relying on foreign suppliers to keep their markets. (I would add, although Parsons does not contemplate this hypothesis, that a substantial element in the decentralization of production in apparel is the existence of the sweatshops of the informal economy in large American cities, particularly in New York and Los Angeles.) The basic element in this industry remains the importance of the network as the organizational form of the surviving companies. The key procedure in this regard is the "quick response" (QR) strategy. As Parsons writes:

A Quick Response strategy is the amalgamation of innovations in interrelated but distinct links in the soft goods chain: one is the textile production–apparel production link; another the retailer–apparel marketing link; and a third the retailer–apparel production link. All of these linkages depend on better flows of information and the use of more flexible manufacturing technology. While a variety of technological innovations are involved in QR electronic data exchange is crucial because, in simple form, a QR system begins with and is driven by information collected by the retailer. . . . In principle, this information ripples back to apparel, textile and fiber producers. Thanks to telecommunications advances, textile mills and apparel producers are beginning to forge QR relationships.[43]

The main implication of these technological developments for the labor force in the apparel industry is that direct production workers in the traditional factory are being phased out. These low-paid, low-skilled jobs, generally held by women and minority workers, are rapidly disappearing under the combined impact of technological change, import penetration, and organizational restructuring toward networking and sub-contracting. The industry is rapidly evolving into a dispatching center connecting the demand of the largest market in the world with suppliers that will be increasingly located overseas or established underground in the US. The net result is a complex labor force composed of highly skilled designers, telecommunicated sales managers, and downgraded manufacturing workers either offshore or in domestic sweatshops. Here again technology per se has not determined the fate of the industry and its workers, but it has been a powerful instrument in diffusing apparel factories, symbolic of early industralization, into flows of exchange between hollow firms, their suppliers, and their retailers. In these conditions labor is not only segmented but dispersed and atomized.

A similarly complex web of interaction among technology, restructuring, and labor can be found in current developments in advanced services organizations. The study by Eileen Appelbaum on technology and the redesign of work in the insurance industry provides an interesting insight into the transformations under way in office work.[44]

The insurance industry has led the pace in office automation since the 1970s, in a movement stimulated by the deregulation of financial markets, the need to fight inflation and the wide variation of interest rates. Increasing mobility of capital has been the overarching objective, leading to emphasis on cash-flow management rather than on returns from premiums. Accordingly, versatility becomes crucial for competitiveness in the insurance industry. Instead of the standardized rationalization and mainframe-dependent data entry processes characteristic of the first stages of office automation, insurance companies during the 1980s relied on automation of routine paperwork, greater flexibility and decision-making capacity by a decentralised network of agents, and control and information processing by relatively skilled clerical workers that would handle sales, assess risks, explain procedures to customers, and answer agents' queries, on the basis of the full computerization of underwriting and rating operations.

The impact of these trends on the work force is profound and lasting. On the one hand, unskilled data entry jobs are being massively eliminated through automation. These routine jobs account for the majority of the 22 percent job loss over the next two decades predicted for clerical jobs in the insurance industry.[45] On the other hand, the remaining clerical positions are being re-skilled, by integrating tasks into multidimensional jobs susceptible of greater flexibility and adaptation to the changing needs of an industry that is becoming increasingly diversified. The skills needed for such positions do not necessarily require formal training: high general literacy, verbal communication skills, and an aptitude for arithmetic. On the other hand, professional jobs have been also been differentiated between less skilled tasks, that have been taken on by the upgraded clerical workers, and highly specialized tasks that require formal specialized education, generally on the basis of a college degree.

The resulting configuration of jobs [Appelbaum writes] varies from firm to firm, but in every case job categories have become more abruptly segmented while the avenues of mobility between them have been sharply reduced. . . . As a result of the automation of underwriting and claims estimating for standardized insuranced products, career ladders from skilled clerical to insurance professional positions have been eliminated. The gap between the skills of clerical workers and those of professionals has widened despite the elimination of unskilled clerical work such as coding and sorting mail and much filing, and the reduction of routine keyboarding. Skill requirements for clerical workers have increased at the same time that jobs have become overwhelmingly dead-end. . . . Thus the introduction of microprocessor-based technologies and the dramatic redesign of jobs is altering the distribution of occupations in insurance. Office automation has wiped out thousands of jobs for low skilled clerical workers, created new jobs for skilled clerical workers, and eliminated many professional jobs that comprised the middle of the occupational distribution – and that used to constitute the rungs of a career ladder by which clerical workers could climb up into more highly skilled professional jobs. Declines in unskilled clerical jobs have limited the entry-level job opportunities for minority and working-class women. What is more, the opportunities for advancement by even the more highly skilled clerical workers are being closed. The bottom and the middle of the occupational distribution are both shrinking in the insurance industry.[46]

As in the case of manufacturing, the transformation of the occupational structure in the insurance industry, which could well be indicative of trends in advanced services at large, is not solely the result of office automation: it is the restructuring of the industry and of its labor force that lie behind the process of technological change. Occupational changes are specified by gender, class, and race: while machines are replacing ethnic-minority and uneducated women at the bottom of the scale, white, educated women are in general replacing white men in the upper clerical and lower professional positions –

yet for lower pay and reduced career prospects at a comparable level of skill and responsibility. Multiskilling of jobs and individualization of responsibilities, generally accompanied by ideologically tailored new titles (for example, "assistant manager" instead of "secretary"), also make more difficult the collective grouping of interests in an industry that was never highly unionized and seems unlikely to become so in the near future. The simultaneous re-skilling of job tasks and downgrading of wages and occupational mobility for a given level of responsibility provides a good illustration of the social bias of technological innovation in office work.

The articulation between socio-economic restructuring and the diffusion of information technologies, both in factories and in offices, is transforming labor and the labor process in ways that appear to be consistent when the trends are observed from a macroeconomic as well as from a microsocial perspective. Computer-based automation is not ushering in an era of widespread and indiscriminate unemployment, but a selective redefinition of occupational positions and labor characteristics. While a substantial number of jobs are being upgraded in skills, and sometimes in wages, in the most dynamic sectors an even larger number of jobs are being eliminated in key manufacturing and advanced service industries, and these are generally jobs that are not skilled enough to escape automation but are expensive enough to be worth the investment in technology to replace them. Increasing educational qualifications, either general or specialized, required in the re-skilled positions in the occupational structure further segregate the labor force on the basis of education, itself a highly segregated system because it responds institutionally to a segregated residential structure. Downgraded labor, particularly in the entry positions for a new generation of workers, made up of a majority of women and ethnic minorities, is recycled in the proliferation of low-skill, low-pay activities in the miscellaneous service sector, or integrated in the booming informal economy in both manufacturing and services. The bifurcated and polarized occupational structure reflected in aggregate statistics is not a secular trend linked to the expansion of the service economy. Its profile is socially determined and mangerially designed in the restructuring process taking place at shop-floor level within the framework, and with the help, of fundamental technological change. This restructuring of labor is profoundly affecting the social stratification system, as is shown by recent trends in income distribution. It is to this issue that we now turn.

The Impact of Occupational Change on Wages, Income, and Social Stratification: The Declining Middle

The transformation of the US occupational structure during the 1980s, under the impact of the process of techno-economic restructuring, has had profound consequences on wages and incomes. The polarization of the labor market is reflected in increasingly uneven income distribution, with low-wage jobs expanding much faster than better paid occupations. The job creation capacity of the American economy, which grew by 20 million new jobs in the decade after the 1974 crisis, was attained at the price of lowering the wage rate for the large majority of those new workers. As a consequence of this process, the middle segment of the social stratification system has gradually shrunk, in one of the most debated and politically charged developments of the 1980s.

Bluestone and Harriston have investigated the matter in one of the most important and most controversial studies of recent years, conducted for the Joint Economic Committee of the US Congress.[47] They analyzed the level and distribution of annual real wages earned by American workers for two periods, 1973–9 and 1979–84 (inclusive of 1984). They classified employment in three categories, high-, middle-, or low-wage, and they compared changes in the proportion of workers in each category during the two periods. They also recalculated their findings differentiating the data by industrial sector, region, age, race, gender, education, and working time (part-time versus full-time employment). They found a fundamental change in the wage distribution of new jobs in the second period, 1979–84, which is generally identified as the historical moment of economic restructuring. In that period about 60 percent of all new jobs were created in the low-wage category, paying less than $7,000 per year (in 1984 dollars). In the same period, the number of workers with earnings at least as high as the 1973 median of wage distribution ($14,024 in 1984 dollars) declined by 1.8 million, while workers with wages below the 1973 real median increased by 9.9 million. Overall, 58 percent of all net new employment between 1979 and 1984 paid annual wages less than $7,000. At the same time, there was a decline of 450,000 jobs in the

Table 4.12   Employment levels and employment shares, all US workers (000s)

	Number of Employees			Earnings shares (%)			Shares of net new employment (%)	
	1973	1979	1984	1973	1979	1984	1973–79	1979–84
Low stratum	29,648	32,063	36,750	31.8	30.4	32.4	19.9	58.0
Middle stratum	48,107	55,908	59,745	51.6	53.1	52.7	64.2	47.5
High stratum	15,441	17,374	16,932	16.6	16.5	14.9	15.9	−5.5
Total	93,196	105,345	113,427	100.0	100.0	100.0	100.0	100.0

Source: Uniform CPS (Mare-Winship) data files, calculated by Bluestone and Harrison (see note 47).

high-wage category. Indeed, all of the employment increase between 1979 and 1984 was accounted for by jobs that paid less than the median wage in 1973. The "middle-wage" earnings category did increase, but the growth was concentrated at the bottom end of the category. Table 4.12, and figures 4.1 and 4.2 display the key findings.

Although women and ethnic minorities continued to be concentrated in the low-wage stratum, the biggest losers in relative terms were white men, for whom 97 percent of employment gains were in the low-wage category, in sharp contrast with previous experience. Although young workers were particularly hit by low-wage employment, the trend was also present in workers over 35 years of age, thus contradicting the hypothesis that the expansion of low-wage employment was a temporary phenomenon linked to the entry into the labor market of a large cohort of "baby boomers." Low-wage employment was also the dominant trend throughout all regions of the

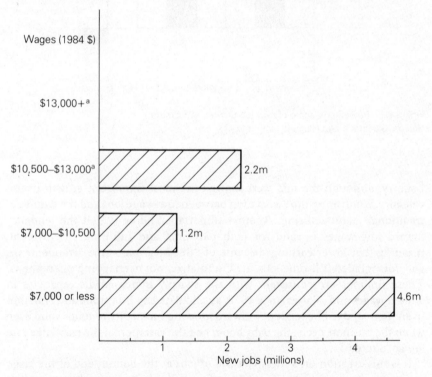

Figure 4.1   Net increase in new jobs, 1979–1984, by annual wage grouping
Source: Bluestone and Harrison (see note 47)

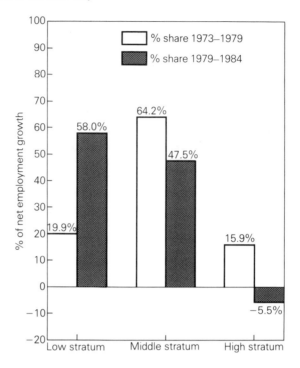

Figure 4.2   Percentage share of new job growth, all workers
Source: Bluestone and Harrison (see note 47)

country, although the mid-west showed the most significant growth in this category, confirming the association between low-wage jobs and the demise of traditional manufacturing. Another important finding is that the tendency toward low wages is valid for both part-time and full-time employment, meaning that lower earnings because of "flexible," part-time arrangements, and downgraded full-time jobs, are cumulative, not overlapping phenomena. These findings are consistent with the sharply increased discrepancies in annual wages and salaries since 1978, as calculated by Bluestone and Harrison in another study. The tendency toward growing inequality remains valid even when the business cycle, the baby boom and the variation of the exchange rate are accounted for.

It is this creation on a massive scale of jobs at the bottom end of the wage spectrum, along with the stagnation of new employment in the upper tier, that underlies the trend towards the "decline of the middle" in the stratification system of American households, as Kuttner pointed out in a notorious and ferociously criticized article in 1983.[48] In fact, the decline of individual wages, as shown by the Bluestone and Harrison study, has been somewhat compensated for in real standards of living by the presence of two wage earners in an increasing proportion of families, particularly in the professional and managerial sector. Yet in terms of the relative distribution of household earnings, the deterioration of wages has resulted in a shrinking proportion of middle-income households in the overall distribution. Thurow calculated that, if percentage income distribution is examined with the age distribution of households kept constant at the 1967 level, the percentage of households with middle-income levels is seen to have declined from 28.2 percent in 1967 to 23.6 percent in 1984.[49] Following the same line of argument, Steven Rose's analysis of the changes in social stratification between 1978 and 1983 showed that while 55 percent of urban families in 1978 fell between the low and high budget lines, in 1983 this figure was down to 40 percent, and the percentage of families below the low budget line had increased from 30 percent to 40 percent.[50]

Given the implications of these analyses, it is not surprising that a host of economists, demographers, and sociologists have made a cottage industry of criticizing the statistical methodology and theoretical assumptions of most of these studies.[51] However, the most standard alternative explanation for the "declining middle" thesis, that is, the suggestion that it is mainly a result of demographic changes in the age structure of the population and in the composition of households, has been refuted by Bradbury in a powerful study. On the whole, as research progresses, there is a growing body of evidence that bears witness to both increasing inequality of income, among both individuals and households, and a tendency toward the decline of the middle-income group, as shown in Nancy Leigh-Preston's doctoral dissertation[52]. It is less clear, however, in empirical terms, what are the causes of the phenomenon. The most solid hypothesis advanced in the literature relates growing inequality and polarization in the stratification system to the changes in industrial and occupational structure as a result of economic restructuring and diffusion of new technologies. Bluestone and Harrison have established an analytical connection between their thesis of the de-industrialization of America and the trends they have observed in income inequality.[53] They have also provided some empirical support for their claim that the sources of employment change are structural, and cannot be explained by the effect of the business cycle.[54] From a different theoretical perspective, Lester Thurow advances a similar hypothetical interpretation when he writes:

Part of the change in income distribution is due to the characteristics of America's new growth industries. High-technology industries such as microelectronics tend to have two levels of income distribution – high and low – as opposed to the smokestack industries, like machine-tools, with their high wage, skilled blue collar workers. There is usually a large group of low-wage assemblers, but not many middle-income jobs. To some extent, the reduced number of middle-income jobs is a product of technology and to some extent it is a product of non-union environment. For what unions did in industries such as autos, steel or machine tools was to convert jobs that probably weren't middle-income jobs. Earnings were redistributed within the industry toward those with least skills.[55]

One could not express better the close connection between high techno-logy, socio-economic restructuring, and the emerging system of social stratification.

A new type of labor demand, then, determined by a new occupational structure, is creating new types of jobs, characterized by a bifurcated distribution in which the bulk of new jobs pay lower wages and enjoy less social protection than in recent historical experience. At the same time, to fill jobs a new supply of workers is also changing the characteristics of labor, generally making workers more vulnerable to management requirements in terms of their social characteristics, along the lines of gender, race, nationality, and age discrimination in society at large. As figure 4.3 shows, the new labor of the 1980s and 1990s contains a large majority of women and ethnic minorities. We should also take into account the hundreds of thousands of immigrants arriving each year in the US labor market, most of them undocumented. The downgrading of the majority of jobs and the transformation of the gender and racial characteristics of the main pool of labor go hand in hand, in a process that can only be reversed by the raising of the consciousness and organization of the new breed of workers entering the transformed labor process.

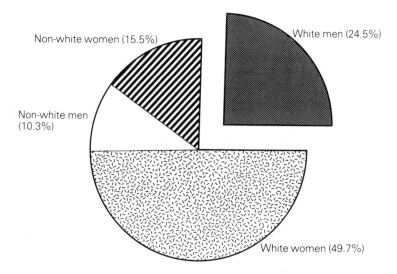

Figure 4.3 Composition of labor force growth, 1984–1995
Source: US Bureau of Labour Statistics

This new, increasingly polarized occupational structure, and the income inequality that results from it, are also territorially specific. As the process of uneven development sees both high-growth activities and downgraded labor concentrated in the largest metropolitan areas, these areas become the spatial expression of the contrasting social conditions into which the effects of the restructuring process are ultimately translated. The trends toward the polarization and segmentation of the social structure underlie the rise of the "dual city."

Toward the Transformation of the Urban Social Structure: The Dual City

Introduction: The Dynamics of Economic Dualism in the Inner City

The polarization and segmentation of the labor force under the impact of the process of techno-economic restructuring has specific spatial manifestations. Although much attention has been given to the regional disparity of the processes of new growth and decline, often simplified under the summary opposition between the sunbelt and the "rustbelt,"[56] probably the most significant spatial expression of the restructuring of labor is taking place within the largest metropolitan areas, and particularly in the dominant world cities, such as New York and Los Angeles.[57] With the exception of some old industrial cities whose fate has been overwhelmingly determined by the old manufacturing industries (Buffalo, NY, for example[58]) processes of sectoral growth and decline, and the reallocation of jobs and labor, are taking place simultaneously within the same metropolitan areas, in a complex pattern that combines the creation of new, highly paid jobs in advanced services and high-technology sectors, the destruction of middle-level jobs in old manufacturing, the gradual shrinkage of protected jobs in the public sector, and the proliferation of new, low-paid jobs both in services and in downgraded manufacturing. At the same time, three inter-related phenomena add complexity to the emerging urban social structure: the explosion of the informal economy, unregulated income-generating activities in a context where similar activities are government-regulated; the reduction of the rate of participation in the labor force, as officially defined, indicative of a growing surplus population in the formal economy; and the proliferation of the criminal economy, particularly in activities related to the drug trade, which becomes the shop floor for a growing proportion of ethnic-minority youth in the largest inner cities.

Interpretations of these trends vary, according to different intellectual traditions. Two predominant theses, nevertheless, formulate a plausible argument, in terms that are largely complementary, in spite of the ideological and theoretical differences between their respective proponents.

One school of thought points to the mismatching of skills between the jobs that are being created and those being destroyed.[59] Advanced services and high-technology industries require a higher level of education than most of the traditional manufacturing and menial jobs that are being phased out, thus substantially changing and upgrading the skills required to obtain employment in the new labor market. With most of the new jobs being created in the advanced services clusters of the large CBDs,[60] and many of the disappearing traditional jobs being concentrated in the old urban industrial cores surrounding these CBDs,[61] it follows that the new expanding labor markets are concentrated in the nodal centers of the large metropolitan areas, as are the pools of obsolete labor, no longer employable, which are made up predominantly of ethnic minorities. John Kasarda, a leading urban scholar forecasting the rise of the dual city,[62] has analyzed the creation of knowledge-intensive jobs and entry-level jobs for nine major US cities between 1970 and 1980 (see table 4.13). His data show the occupational shift in favor of knowledge-intensive jobs, particularly for the largest north-eastern cities. Such a transition could in fact be beneficial for the upgrading of the social structure, were it not for the mismatching of skills determined by inequality in the educational system, itself a result of spatial segregation by class and race. Public schools in the largest inner cities receive proportionally fewer resources than those in the suburbs, and cater to the poorest sectors of the population, with an overwhelming proportion of ethnic minorities with the greatest educational need to overcome a cultural disadvantage in their family background. The majority of the resident population of inner cities, then, cannot match the skill requirements of the new labor market because of the inefficiency and segregated nature of the public school system. In the northeast region in 1982, 42 percent of black males aged 16–64 had not completed high school; the proportion for white males was only 31.4 percent. Adding to this racial discrimination in the labor market, we see that 26.2 percent of those relatively uneducated black males were unemployed in the north-eastern central cities in 1982, against an average of 10.2 percent of white males.[63] For all regions in 1982, 16.5 percent of all black central city residents aged 16–24 were neither in school nor in the labor force, with the same figure increasing to 17.1 percent for the 25–64 age group. The corresponding figures for whites were only 5.4 percent and 9.2 percent. Of these black males not in the labor force and not in school, 40 percent were on welfare, with the proportion increasing to 82 percent for black females. Central cities in the largest metropolitan areas host the majority of the growth in highly paid jobs, while they come to be inhabited mainly by an ethnic-minority population which is increasingly inadequate to fill these jobs. The dual city, manifested in the spatial coexistence of a large sector of professional and managerial middle-class with a growing urban underclass, epitomizes the contradictory development of the new informational economy, and the conflictual appropriation of the inner city by social groups who share the same space while being worlds apart in terms of lifestyle and structural position in society. Yet while the mismatching thesis underlines a fundamental trend of the new urban social structure, it has some serious methodological and theoretical shortcomings, as has been argued by Norman Fainstein.[64] It also fails to explain why there has been substantial growth in job creation in general, including low-paying jobs, in the largest inner cities, particularly during the 1980s. Indeed, after the 1980-2 recession, unemployment has steadily reduced in most inner cities, even for ethnic minorities, although it remains

Table 4.13   Employment changes by industry's average educational requirements, for nine US cities, 1970–1980 (000s)

City and industrial categorization[a]	Number of jobs, 1980	Change, 1970–80	
		Number	%
New York			
Entry-level	763	−472	−38.2
Knowledge-intensive	462	92	24.9
Philadelphia			
Entry-level	208	−102	−32.9
Knowledge-intensive	91	25	37.8
Baltimore			
Entry-level	108	−52	−32.4
Knowledge-intensive	32	5	20.6
Boston (Suffolk County)			
Entry-level	115	−34	−22.6
Knowledge-intensive	75	19	33.3
St Louis			
Entry-level	103	−23	−18.2
Knowledge-intensive	21	−8	−26.3
Atlanta (Fulton County)			
Entry-level	136	−19	−12.1
Knowledge-intensive	41	11	35.6
Houston (Harris County)			
Entry-level	457	194	73.8
Knowledge-intensive	152	83	119.4
Denver			
Entry-level	110	14	14.5
Knowledge-intensive	44	21	91.4
San Franciso			
Entry-level	142	13	10.2
Knowledge-intensive	65	21	46.8

Sources: US Bureau of the Census, Current Population Survey tape, March 1982, and County Business Patterns, 1970, 1980. Figures are rounded. (Compiled and adapted by Kasarda (see note 62).
[a]Entry-level industries are those where mean schooling completed by employees is less than twelve years; knowledge-intensive industries are those where mean schooling completed is more than fourteen years.

very high for the youth of these minorities. Moreover, this increasing employment rate has taken place in a context where hundreds of thousands of new immigrants have arrived in the metropolitan labor markets, attracted in particular to the booming economies of New York and California.

There are in fact four distinct, though inter-related, processes at work here:

(1) The decline of some industries and the increasing obsolescence of a segment of semi-skilled labor that is being expelled from the labor force.
(2) The dynamism of two macro-sectors, one in advanced services and the other in high-technology industries, both of which also include a substantial number of low-paid, low-skill jobs, such as janitors, low-level secretaries, assembly workers.
(3) The growth of new, downgraded manufacturing activities, many of them informal, which recycle some of the surplus labor expelled from the declining sectors, while incorporating some of the new immigrants, particularly women.
(4) The expansion of informal and semi-formal service activities spurred on by the overall economic dynamism. These service activities, many of them in consumer services, provide numerous jobs for immigrants, ethnic minorities and women.

This is the analysis put forward by a number of scholars, most notably by Saskia Sassen, in an interpretation that links the thesis of polarization of the occupational structure with the process of restructuring of capital–labor relationships.[65] In this perspective, the dual city is not simply the urban social structure resulting from the juxtaposition of the rich and the poor, the yuppies and the homeless, but the result of simultaneous and articulated processes of growth and decline. Furthermore, according to Sassen's analysis, growth occurs at the same time in the formal and in the informal sectors of the economy, at the top and at the bottom of the newly dynamic industrial sectors, and affects both skilled and unskilled labor, although in segmented labor markets that cater variously to the specific requirements of each segment of capital invested in the different sectors of the local economy. From this follows a highly differentiated social structure, both polarized and fragmented, with segments divided on the basis of class, gender, race, and national origin. Some of the labor surplus is recycled in the dynamic structure of the new informational economy, while the rest leaves the formal labor force, to be distributed among the recipients of welfare, the informal economy, and the criminal economy. This new social dynamics has profound consequences on the spatial organization and processes of the large metropolitan areas. However, since the complexity of these processes makes the analysis hardly comprehensible at a high level of generality, I will introduce here a summary account of the transformation of the urban social structure of

New York and Los Angeles in order to clarify the precise meaning of the rise of the dual city as the new urban form linked to the overall process of techno-economic restructuring.

New York, New York! Dreams and Nightmares of the Restructuring Process

After its dramatic fiscal crisis in 1975–7, New York City bounced back in one of the most spectacular cases of local economic development in recent history.[66] In the decade 1977–87, the city added 400,000 new jobs in an expansion interrupted only by the nationwide recession of 1981–2.[67] Of these jobs, 342,000 were in the private sector, with finance, insurance, real estate, and business services accounting for about 70 percent of new job creation. These industries employed in 1987 664,000 workers, amounting to about one-fifth of all private jobs. At the same time, the building boom linked to the expansion of advanced services, with their demand for office space and upgraded residences for the professional labor force, generated about 64,000 new construction jobs. In addition, growing local revenues and the political needs of the city's patronage system restored, selectively, public services and service jobs, so that by December 1987 local government employment, including education, had risen to 450,000 jobs. However, this process of growth and job creation went hand in hand with a dramatic restructuring process, both among industries and in the labor market. While 153 industries experienced growth in the city in 1977–86, a greater number, 207, actually declined. Most of this decline took place in manufacturing, which shrank in absolute numbers from 539,000 jobs in 1977 to 396,000 in 1986, representing in the latter year slightly over 11 percent of the total labor force (see figure 4.4). In fact, in the 1980s, New York City lost manufacturing jobs at three times the national rate of decline. Furthermore, in the 1982–7 period, the US economy recovered about half the manufacturing jobs lost during the 1980–2 recession, but New York lost an additional 100,000 factory jobs in these years, with the greatest losses concentrated in apparel, miscellaneous manufacturing and electrical–electronic equipment, and the bulk of them being unskilled and semi-skilled jobs. One the other hand, about half of the new jobs were in professional, managerial, and technical positions. As a result, the overall occupational composition of the labor force in New York City has been upgraded. Executives and managers accounted for 11.7 percent of the labor force in 1983 and 13.3 percent in 1986, while the proportion of professionals also increased from 13.9 percent in 1983 to 15.8 percent in 1986. Including technicians, the upper level of the occupational structure in 1986 accounted for 31.3 percent of the total labor force, establishing as a fundamental presence a large group of professional labor that possesses the purchasing power, the demographic weight, and the educational skills to dominate the city economically, culturally, and politically.

This trend is in direct conflict with the changing composition of the New York City population, characterized by a growing proportion of minimally educated minorities, and recent immigrants whose education is hardly marketable in the US. The overall drop-out rate in the city's high schools reached a staggering 37 percent in 1987, 80 percent of which appears to concern ethnic minorities (if we extrapolate the 1980 data for the 16–19 age group). The mismatching of skills is particularly striking in the case of New York. On the one hand, for the American labor force as a whole, one or two years in college seems increasingly to be the norm for obtaining a job: the proportion of the labor force with some college attendance in 1987 stood at 46

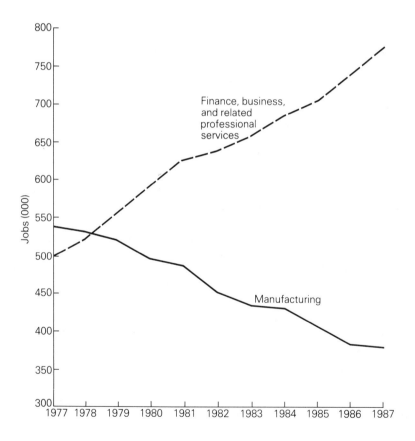

Figure 4.4   Payroll employment in manufacturing and finance, business and related professional services, New York City, 1977–1987
Source: Ehrenhalt (see note 67).

percent, double that of 1970, and it continues to rise. On the other hand, ethnic minorities seem to have accounted for most of net labor force growth in the 1977–87 period and are projected to continue to do so for most of the net increase in New York City's labor force in the 1990s. They accounted in 1987 for 49.5 percent of the total labor force (see figure 4.5); yet ast the same time they exhibit the highest school drop-out rates, and are exposed to the declining quality of the spatially segregated public school system.

Mismatching and racial discrimination in the labor market result in a substantially above-average unemployment level for ethnic minorities, even in the context of sustained economic expansion in the 1980s. In New York in 1987, unemployment levels were 3.1 percent for non-Hispanic whites and 8.5 percent for ethnic minorities. A more important phenomenon, likely to be linked to the inappropriateness of the new labor demand for the urban labor supply, is the low rate of labor-force participation in New York, ten points

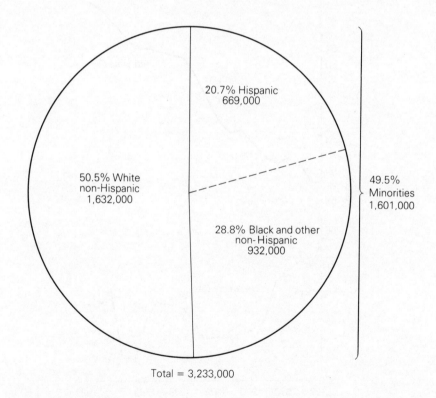

Total = 3,233,000

Figure 4.5   Estimated distribution of the New York City resident labor force by race and Hispanic origin, 1987
Source: Ehrenhalt (see note 67)

below the national average, with the disparity increasing over the past 20 years (see figure 4.6). According to Samuel M. Ehrenhalt, New York Regional Commissioner for the Bureau of Labor Statistics: "It would take something on the order of a half million more New Yorkers in the labor force to lift the New York participation rate to the national average. This points to a considerable job deficit in the local economy and a substantial number of New Yorkers outside the mainstream."[68]

Nevertheless, a great number of jobs have been created, as indicated, showing the strength and the vitality of the new economy. Indeed, most of the ethnic minorities, including recent immigrants, have improved their relative position in the economy.[69] However, this is partly a mere statistical construct: a growing economy, creating a large number of office and service jobs in a

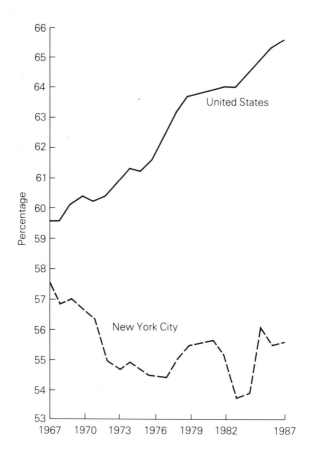

Figure 4.6   Labor force participation rates, United States and New York City, 1967–1987 (total, age 16 years and over)
Source: Ehrenhalt (see note 67).

context of increasing representation of ethnic minorities in the labor market, must necessarily include a higher proportion of minorities in the new service jobs. Yet the tendencies toward polarization described in the preceding sections of this chapter are reflected in an ethnically and gender segregated occupational structure in the new labor force of New York City, as can be seen in the data calculated by John Mollenkopf detailing occupational position by gender and by ethnic group for 1980. As an illustration of these trends, table 4.14 has been constructed on the basis of Mollenkopf's data. Three occupational positions have been selected representative respectively of the top of the occupational scale (managers), of the middle to low position in services (clerical), and of the low-skill manual workers (operatives). For each position, an elementary scale has been built, taking as its zero level the proportion of WASP (white Anglo-Saxon Protestant) males who hold such occupational positions (as a percentage of overall employed WASP males).

Table 4.14   Ethnic composition of occupations in New York City, 1980, by gender (differences in percentage points between proportion of WASPs in each occupational group and proportion of each ethnic group in the same occupation)

Ethnicity	Occupation				
	Managers and professionals	Managers	Clerical	Operatives	% of male/ female population
MALE					
WASP	0.0	0.0	0.0	0.0	2.15
Jewish	+6.0	+1.5	−1.5	−5.9	4.29
Italian	−5.9	−3.1	−1.5	+6.3	16.90
Irish	−5.9	−3.3	+0.9	+2.1	8.18
Black (NY)	−5.9	−4.1	+4.5	+6.1	11.35
Jamaican	−8.4	−4.7	−2.9	+6.5	2.38
Puerto Rican	−10.3	−4.2	−6.5	+14.1	10.46
Dominican	−13.6	−6.2	−10.1	+20.2	3.23
Chinese	−0.6	+0.6	−11.3	−2.6	2.58
FEMALE					
WASP		−2.8	+28.3	−12.3	2.35
Jewish		−3.4	+30.3	−7.7	5.56
Italian		−4.9	+32.4	−14.1	16.14
Irish		−4.2	+33.8	−15.0	9.56
Black (NY)		−5.2	+26.1	−10.0	14.08
Jamaican		−7.7	+9.6	−12.2	3.68
Puerto Rican		−7.7	+7.7	+18.7	8.67
Dominican		−9.5	−6.3	+39.7	3.85
Chinese		−5.4	−6.3	+37.9	2.52

Source: 1980 US Census Public Use Microdata Sample, calculated by John Mollenkopf and elaborated by the author.

The difference has been simply calculated in percentage points between the proportion of WASP males in a given occupational position and the corresponding proportion for each ethnic/gender group. Obviously, positive signs indicative over-representation, while negative signs indicate under-representation. Without going into the details of the table, it can be observed that, for managers, Jewish males and WASP males are over-represented, while all women and ethnic minorities are under-represented, with ethnic-minority women being in the most disadvantaged position.

One apparent anomaly merits explanation: Chinese males are over-represented among the managers, even overtaking WASP males. An analysis of the sectoral distribution of Chinese male workers, provided by Mollen-kopf's database, dissipates the myth of the Chinese male "already making it in corporate business:" 51 percent of Chinese male workers are in "restaurants, hotels, and bars," and thus, they are "managers" of their community-based restaurants. As for employed Chinese women, 67.3 percent are manufacturing workers.

Concerning clerical work, women in general, but particularly Caucasian women, are overwhelmingly over-represented, while recent immigrant, non-English-speaking women are, as one might expect, under-represented. As for operatives, recent immigrants, both male and, even more, female, are concentrated in these jobs, sharing the joys of industrial working-class life in the informational city with the remnants of Italian, Irish, and black workers in the restructured manufacturing sector. Overall, groups privileged by gender and ethnic background (translated into higher education) occupy the top of the hierarchy; women form the bulk of the new white-collar working class of the service economy; and recent immigrants, along with Puerto Ricans, assume the new positions in downgraded manufacturing and low-skill consumer services. To complete our picture of the emerging occupational structure we should add the expansion of new retail commerce (neighbour-hood grocery stores, for example) on the basis of recent immigrants (Koreans, Indians, Chinese), and the growing concentration of blacks in public services: New York blacks in government services (17.1 percent of black males work in public services), and West Indian blacks in health services (11.4 percent of Jamaican males and 29.9 percent of Jamaican females work in health services).

Although the only empirical way of assessing rigorously the polarization of New York City's occupational structure would be to undertake an analysis of income and educational levels for each occupation and industry (which are not available in the published information), the existing data together with most of the specialized research literature on the subject all seem to indicate that the process of growth during the 1980s has generated, at the same time, a significant segment of well paid professionals and technical jobs, a mass of low-paid, semi-skilled clerical jobs for women, and an insufficient but growing number of low-paid jobs for ethnic minorities and immigrants both in downgraded manufacturing and miscellaneous services.[70]

An important element in connecting the new dynamism of the New York economy and the restructuring of labor is the growth of the informal economy. Saskia Sassen has investigated this topic over several years, combining secondary data analysis, ethnographic research, and interviews with key informants.[71] Without being able to estimate the overall size of the phenomenon, in terms of either regional GDP or employment, she has found enough evidence to indicate that it is a sizable economic reality and one that is rapidly expanding to become an indispensable element of the local economy as well as of New Yorkers' way of life. Much of these informal income-generating activities concern manufacturing, particularly in apparel, footwear, toys, sporting goods, and electronic components and accessories. For instance, she reports estimates by labor unions that in 1981 there were in New York about 3,000 sweatshops in the garment industry, employing about 50,000 workers, with a further 10,000 workers doing home work in garments. She also reports, on the basis of data provided by the New York State Labor Department and the Industrial Board of Appeals, considerable informal sub-contracting work in the electronics industry, working out of "garage-shops" and "basement-fronts." She observed that while the furniture industry lost 9 percent of its registered labor between 1982 and 1987, at the same time a number of furniture-making shops were opening in areas that were not zoned for this kind of work, such as Ridgewood Astoria in Queens, and Williams-burg in Brooklyn. In addition, construction work on a small scale is also predominantly informal: Sassen estimates that about 90 percent of all interior remodeling in New York is done without a building permit, by craft workers and contractors who are not registered, most of them recent immigrants. "Gypsy cabs" have taken over the transportation business to the numerous areas of the City where regular cabs refuse to go.[72]

The development of the informal economy is connected to two broader trends of which it is an essential, though certainly not a unique, component. The first of these is the downgrading of manufacturing, with the phasing out or relocation of traditional manufacturing activities, for instance in the garment industry, while low-labour-cost, largely unregulated operations open up in New York to cater to the booming retail market represented by the largest and probably most demanding market in the world. Secondly, there is an explosion in customized services, from gourmet grocery stores to laundry and housekeeping, linked to the new lifestyles of the substantial segment of the population made up of professionals and managers, either single or dual-income households, with little time but high purchasing power and increasingly sophisticated tastes (or, at least, with the idea of being sophistic-ated, and the desire to become so). As Sassen argues, the new consumption pattern, shifting from middle-level suburban families to high-level urbanite professionals, represents a shift from capital-intensive consumer goods to labor-intensive consumer services, thus stimulating a very large labor demand for customized services, both in high-skill occupations (fashion design, *chefs de cuisine,* in-house "artists") and low-skill occupations ("24-hour tailors," waiters, drivers, security guards).[73] While many of these jobs are by no means part of the informal economy, their definition and their working conditions are usually on the border-line, being extremely flexible, and making part-time, overtime, one-time service, and sub-contracting, the working rule rather than the exception. Hence the polarization and segmentation of an increasing pool of activities, and therefore of labor, on the vibrant New York scene.

A largely unexplored segment of New York's economy is linked to booming criminal activities, particularly related to the drug traffic. While these activities do generate income and a kind of employment for some sectors of the ghetto population, particularly for drop-out youths, they are not limited to the underclass. In fact, the money-laundering activities that are a substantial part of the drug economy lie behind the flourishing of many ephemeral businesses, from restaurants to art galleries, that blossom and disappear in the space of a few months, creating and then destroying a number of jobs that are as ephemeral as their source. Ironically, these money-laundering processes epitomize the oft-praised flexibility of the new economy. While the role of the criminal economy must not be exaggerated, it is important to keep in mind its existence, which adds to the complexity of the overall restructuring process.[74]

The informal economy, and more generally the new flexibility of labor relationships, have greatly contributed to the opening up of job opportunities for the new wave of immigration that has hit New York since the late 1970s, ranking it with Los Angeles and Miami as the most ethnically diverse metropolises in the world. In 1980, 24 percent of New Yorkers were foreign-born (excluding of course Puerto Ricans who are US citizens), and this proportion is predicted to rise to about one-third of the resident population by 1990. Most of these foreign-born residents are recent entrants, a substantial proportion of whom are undocumented.[75] It is estimated that there are about 350,000 Asians (Chinese, Koreans, Vietnamese, Cambodians, Indians), at least 400,000 Dominicans (the largest recent group of immigrants to New York), about 500,000 West Indians, about 250,000 non-Puerto Rican Hispanics (from Colombia, Mexico, Ecuador, Peru, etc.) over 200,000 Europeans (most of them Russian Jews and Italians), and a large number of Arabs, particularly from Egypt and the Lebanon. While living conditions are very harsh for most of the immigrants, particularly for those from Latin America and the Caribbean, they have succeeded in integrating themselves into the labor market, generally in the entry-level jobs, although some groups with financial and educational resources have established small businesses in a number of sectors (for example, middle-class Koreans in the grocery business, Indians in the newspaper stands).[76] Bailey and Waldinger have shown how the living conditions of these immigrants improve in the context of an expanding local economy, sometimes exceeding the achievements of local young blacks and New York Puerto Ricans.[77] However, a number of indications point to the fact that racial discrimination and class barriers are likely to prevent these immigrant families attaining social mobility on a similar level to the non-WASP Caucasian immigrants of former generations, with the potential exception of some middle-class groups, particularly among the Koreans and Chinese.[78] In fact, instead of witnessing the expansion of an informal economy, or of flexible manufacturing and customized services, as a consequence of the drive and entrepreneurialism of the new immigrants, we observe the opposite phenomenon: the new economy, with its flexibility and its polarized occupational structure, has been able to integrate an immigrant labor force that because of its greater vulnerability, linked to racial, class, and language discrimination, and often to its uncertain legal status, is ready to accept working conditions that American workers, including native ethnic minorities, do not accept or are not trusted to accede to by their employers. The new immigration provides the labor supply necessary for the restructuring of labor implicit in the polarized occupational structure of the informational economy.

The process of labor restructuring in New York, proceeding along the lines presented, has specified spatial manifestations. As Saskia Sassen writes:

These processes can be seen as distinct modes of economic organization and their corresponding uses of space: the postindustrial city of luxury high-rise office and residential buildings located largely in Manhattan; the old dying industrial city of low-rise buildings and family type houses, located largely in the outer-boroughs; and the Third World city imported via inmigration and located in dense groupings spread all over the city. . . . Each of these three processes can be seen to contain distinct income-occupational structures and concomitant residential and consumption patterns, well captured in the expansion of a new urban gentry alongside expanding immigrant communities.[79]

Richard Harris has proceeded to a systematic analysis of the spatial differentiation of the New York metropolitan area as an expression of the tendencies toward class, race, and gender polarization in the occupational structure.[80] His data show an increasing functional specialization of the area, with advanced services concentrated in Manhattan, the rest of the core specializing in transportation and public administration, and the inner and outer rings absorbing a growing proportion of manufacturing and retailing. In terms of residence, table 4.15 shows the dramatic trend toward the concentration in Manhattan of managers and professionals, while clericals and the lower occupational groups are over-represented in the inner city outside Manhattan, and the inner and outer rings oscillate moderately around the average, with a slight over-representation of managers and of the middle strata, together with an under-representation of the new and old working classes (clerical, operatives, and laborers). This occupational differentiation of residential patterns is reinforced by distinct lifestyles derived from different

Table 4.15 Occupational specialization of the resident labor force in the New York metropolitan region, 1950, 1970 and 1980

Occupation	Specialization index (NYMR = 100)											
	Manhattan			Rest of core			Inner Ring			Outer Ring		
	1950	1970	1980	1950	1970	1980	1950	1970	1980	1950	1970	1980
Managers	93	112	127	93	77	76	122	120	109	84	114	106
Professionals	128	148	163	82	79	74	113	106	99	106	120	107
Clerical	95	94	82	115	117	122	90	90	96	72	74	85
Sales	93	90	94	104	91	87	102	113	109	88	107	106
Crafts	57	50	43	102	101	96	107	107	103	127	128	119
Operatives	94	77	74	104	114	116	92	96	94	109	83	98
Laborers	92	67	57	94	109	117	99	100	100	133	102	94
Service	190	130	105	84	102	116	81	88	90	93	100	94

Source: Hoover and Vernon, *Anatomy of a Metropolis*, 1962, p.148; Kamer, "The Changing Spatial Relationship Between Residence and Workplaces in the New York Metropolitan Region," 1977, pp.448-449; calculated from US Bureau of the Census, *General Social and Economic Characteristics*, Connecticut, New Jersey and New York, table 177 by Richard Harris (see note 80).

household structures. Thus, while the suburbs continue to be based on a typical nuclear family, in Manhattan the average household size (1.7) is lower than in any other country. This single or childless way of life characterizes the consumption patterns and the cultural models of the new professional elite in world cities such as New York.

In terms of income, the core of the city exhibits an interesting bimodal pattern, with the resident population of Manhattan concentrated in the highest and lowest strata of income distribution (see figure 4.7). This stratification pattern is in contrast to that prevailing in the other spatial components of the metropolitan area, as can also be observed from the data displayed in figure 4.7. The outer boroughs of the inner city contain a high concentration of low-income population, while the inner ring is biased toward the upper segments of the distribution, and the outer ring is the closest to the average of the overall income distribution. Thus, there is at the same time intra-metropolitan segregation by income (the suburbs being the privileged space), and intra-urban residential segregation within Manhattan, which hosts both the highest income group and some of the poorest sectors of the population. Ethnic residential segregation closely follows this general pattern, with blacks being the most concentrated and segregated social group, followed by Hispanics. Immigrants of different ethnic groups find their interstitial space either as microcommunities within large segregated areas of other ethnic minorities, or in enclaves inside the predominantly white city, in a symbiotic relationship that is more successful when they provide services to the higher-income resident population.

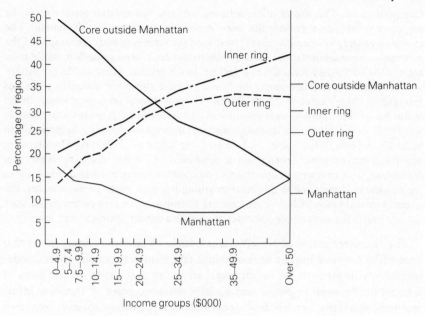

Figure 4.7   Geographic distribution of households by income, New York metropolitan region, 1979
Source: Harris (see note 80)

However, the spatial coexistence of very different social groups in an increasingly valuable space in most of Manhattan is increasingly challenged by the skyrocketing of real estate prices and the increasing functional and social attraction of the central urban space for the professional–managerial segment, representing close to one-third of the employed population. The consequent process of widespread gentrification is gradually, but surely, changing the social characteristics of residential space in the inner city, further segregating social groups and pushing the ethnic minorities into increasingly secluded areas, such as Harlem and the south Bronx. Old white ethnic neighborhoods barricade themselves against both the threat of minorities and their risk of displacement.[81] The urban dynamics resulting from these conflictual processes is characterized both by territorial defensiveness and increasing social and ethnic homogenization of specific neighborhoods. The dual city is a shared space within which the contradictory spheres of the local society are constantly trying to differentiate their territories.

Richard Harris concludes his study on the spatial differentiation of New York with a statement relevant to the present analysis:

The restructuring of New York's economy in the past thirty years has created greater inequality. The contrasts between rich and poor neighborhoods have become greater. Different parts of the metropolitan area have been affected in different ways, and the

City most of all. The loss of manufacturing jobs has had greatest impact upon the boroughs while office growth has been especially important in Manhattan. The changing geography of employment has shaped the emerging social geography of the metropolitan area. Substantial parts of Manhattan have been gentrified, while most areas in the boroughs have suffered a decline. In the process, a new and larger pattern of contrasts between Manhattan, the boroughs, and the outer suburban rings has emerged. . . . Many kinds of informal work have grown up to serve local needs. In the South Bronx this informal work means survival; in the SoHo it means a fashionable way of life; in new ethnic communities scattered throughout the city it helps people to build a home away from home. . . . Life on Long Island or in Fairfield County, as in any American suburbs, depends on a good deal of unpaid domestic labor. But Manhattan, with its towers of apartments and condominiums, more than any place in the continent, is designed to minimize anything but paid work. In this manner, the homes and workplaces of New York together constitute a complex geography of work that embodies the continuing polarities of class and gender, ethnicity and race.[82]

The characterization of New York as a dual city does not simply mean that opposition between executive limousines and homeless people: more fundamentally, it represents an urban social structure that exists on the basis of interaction between opposite and equally dynamic poles of the new informational economy, whose developmental logic polarizes society, segments social groups, isolates cultures, and segregates the uses of a shared space.

The Last Urban Frontier: The Restructuring of Los Angeles

Nowhere is the process of urban restructuring more completely manifested than in Los Angeles, the city where, in the image suggested by its urban analyst, Edward Soja, "it all comes together," as in Borges' Aleph.[83] Like New York, in the past two decades Los Angeles has become a leading financial and business center at the international level, second only to New York in the US, constituting itself the corporate hub for trade and investment in the Pacific Basin.[84] In fact, trans-Pacific trade has surpassed trans-Atlantic trade for the US, and almost half of its volume is concentrated on the LA ports of San Pedro and Long Beach. Around this core of internationally-oriented corporate services, and a still buoyant entertainment and media industry, a number of producer and consumer services have clustered, leading to a spectacular office boom which, together with the residential demand generated by rapid growth in jobs and residents, has fueled one of the largest and most profitable real estate markets in the country.

In addition to this development of advanced services, and in contrast to New York, Los Angeles' manufacturing sector also expanded dramatically during the 1970s and 1980s, to become, in 1984, the largest manufacturing center in the US, in terms of the absolute number of manufacturing jobs in the greater Los Angeles area. This is in sharp contrast with the popular image of Los Angeles as the postindustrial city. Indeed, Los Angeles saw the creation of 250,000 manufacturing jobs in the 1940s, of another 400,000 in the 1950s, of 200,000 in the 1960s, and, in the 1970s, at a moment of slow manufacturing growth in the US, of another 225,000 manufacturing jobs, almost a quarter of total US manufacturing job creation during the decade. The newest manufacturing growth is based on two very different sectors: on the one hand, aerospace and defense-oriented electronics, constituting a booming high-technology sector, concentrated around Los Angeles International Airport and in Orange County, as indicated in chapter 2; and on the other hand, consumer goods, particularly garments and apparel, which account for about 125,000 manufacturing jobs that are low-paid and frequently filled by immigrant women, most of them undocumented. At the same time, as shown by Soja, Morales, and Wolff in their pioneering study on the restructuring of Los Angeles, traditional manufacturing has been phased out. Los Angeles, once boasting the second largest concentration of automobile assembly industries, in the 1980s lost all its automobile factories but one.[85] The city's entire rubber industry, also the second largest US concentration after Akron, also disappeared in the late 1970s. In the 1978–82 period alone 70,000 manufacturing jobs were lost, three-quarters of them in the auto, tire, steel, and civilian aircraft sectors.

The labor force of Los Angeles has altered correspondingly. Unionized labor has been substantially reduced during the 1980s: in Los Angeles County the level of unionization in manufacturing dropped from 30 percent to about 23 percent, and in Orange County from 26.4 percent to 10.5 percent. While the proportion of craft workers and operatives in the labor force substantially decreased, Los Angeles now holds the largest concentration of engineers and scientists anywhere in the US, fueled by its role as the top location, in absolute terms, for defense contracts. At the other end of the employment spectrum, as in New York, corporate services, particularly in finance and law, have created hundreds of thousands of professional and managerial jobs, while low-paid service jobs have increased by about 500,000 in the past twenty years, pushing the region's total to 5.5 million jobs in the mid-1980s.

As in New York, new immigrants to the area have filled many of the jobs in downgraded manufacturing and consumer and personal services, with probably an even greater proportion than in New York of undocumented workers, particularly from Mexico and Central America. Since the late 1960s Los Angeles has received an estimated number of over 1 million Mexicans, 300,000 Salvadoreans, 200,000 Koreans, and several additional hundreds of thousands of Chinese, Indochinese, Filipinos, Thais, Iranians, Arabs, Armenians, Guatemalans, Colombians, and Cubans, among others. Los Angeles blacks have been discriminated against in the labor market, and their levels of unemployment are often above those of the new immigrants, who are considered less threatening by employers in search of flexibility and acquiescence from a socially and politically vulnerable labor force. Soja, Morales, and Wolff report that the ghetto areas of south-central Los Angeles, including Watts, saw their social condition deteriorate during the 1970s, falling below their level of 1965 at the time of the Watts riots.

This process of economic and social restructuring is also spatially specific. While most of the plants closing were concentrated in Los Angeles County and in the Long Beach industrial area, suburban Orange County picked up most of the new, high-technology based manufacturing development. Advanced services organized in a multinuclear urban structure in the downtown area, in the Wilshire Corridor toward the affluent Westside, and are increasingly decentralizing toward Orange County (particularly in the booming Irvine Business Complex[86]), Pasadena, and Glendale–Burbank (see map 4.1). Downgraded manufacturing clustered in whichever spaces could escape administrative controls, generally in low-income areas, such as central and east Los Angeles.

A sharply polarized labor force, with large segments of minority youth excluded from it, has led to a highly segregated residential structure, probably the most ethnically segregated of any major city in the US (only tentatively indicated in map 4.2). Class is also a major factor in residential segregation, as is shown by the clustering of the residences of engineers displayed in map 4.3. An important reason for the high level of spatial segregation in Los Angeles is its extreme administrative fragmentation, for the city of Los Angeles represents a much smaller proportion than New York of its metropolitan area. The fragmentation of a very large, extremely decentralized conurbation (home to over 12 million people) makes possible a strict segregation of public services, in particular of public schools, whose quality, dependent upon local revenue per capita, is a primary factor in determining residential location for concerned middle-class parents. Interestingly enough in such a multi-ethnic local society, class is taking over from ethnicity as the primary criterion for residential segregation, although the large black and Chicano ghettoes (Watts and east Los Angeles respectively) are substantially homogeneous in ethnic terms, largely because class and race reinforce each other as factors leading to the segregation of the overwhelmingly low-income black and Chicano communities.

In these ghettoized communities many youths have no prospect of making it in a an upgraded economy where the low-level jobs are sought after by an increasing pool of downgraded labor coming from all horizons. In the late 1980s, with drop-out rates at an all-time high, these youths often turn to gang formation, most of them simply to build up networks of personal interaction and affirm their identity; too often these gangs also become vehicles for the drug trade, now a multibillion-dollar business. Some of the Los Angeles gangs have won control over national markets for the wholesale distribution of drugs. A surge of violence reminiscent of 1920s Chicago provoked in 1988 a ferocious backlash from public opinion, leading to massive raids by the police, who in several instances arrested hundreds of suspects, detaining them in the Olympic Coliseum Stadium to investigate their gang connections. The police were under instructions to arrest people who could be seen in the streets of some areas (generally in central and south Los Angeles) and who "dressed or

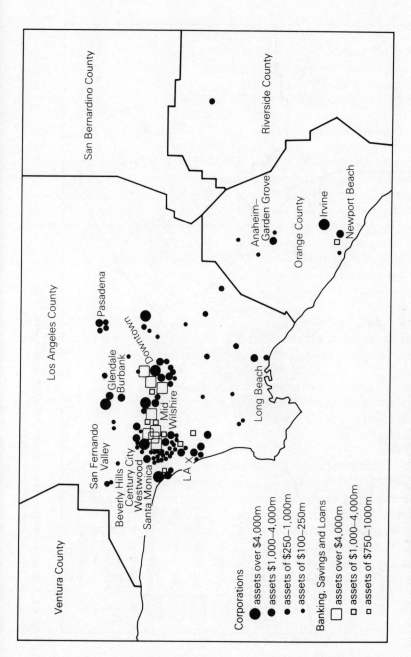

Map 4.1 Corporate and banking headquarters in the Los Angeles region
Source: Soja, Morales, and Wolff (see note 85)

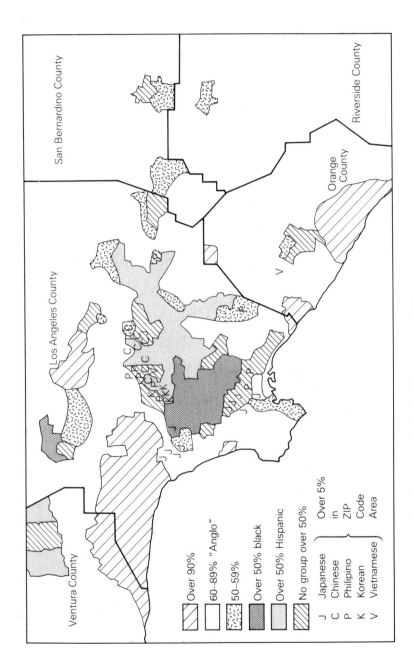

Map 4.2   Distribution of major ethnic groups in the Los Angeles area, 1980
Source: Soja, Morales, and Wolff (see note 85)

Over 90%

60–89% "Anglo"

50–59%

Over 50% black

Over 50% Hispanic

No group over 50%

J   Japanese   Over 5%
C   Chinese   in
P   Philipino   ZIP
K   Korean   Code
V   Vietnamese   Area

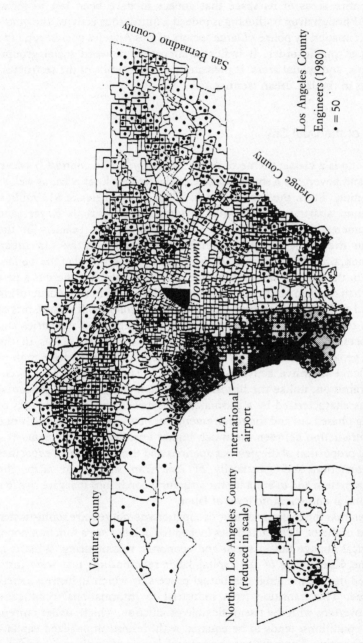

Map 4.3 Residential location of engineers, Los Angeles County, 1980
Source: Soja, Morales, and Wolff (see note 85)

Los Angeles County
Engineers (1980)
● = 50

San Bernardino County

Orange County

Downtown

LA
international
airport

Ventura County

Northern Los Angeles County
(reduced in scale)

acted as gang members."[87] Thus, the boundaries of "normality" and "abnormality" have been traced and enforced. The dual city resorts to policing entire areas of its space that appear to have been lost to social disorder. Although drug trafficking is indeed a murderous activity, the quasimilitary occupation by police of large sectors of Los Angeles goes beyond the protection of public order. It indicates alienation between social groups, social norms, and spatial areas. It indicates the outer limits of the restructuring process in the last urban frontier.

The Rise of the Dual City

The dual city is a classic theme of urban sociology.[88] The contrast between opulence and poverty in a shared space has always struck scholars, as well as public opinion. Thus, the coexistence in 1980s Los Angeles of $11 million condominium apartments, sold with a complimentary Rolls Royce, and 50,000 homeless wandering in the streets and on the beaches of the Californian dream, is but an extreme manifestation of an old urban phenomenon, probably aggravated in the 1980s by the removal of the welfare safety net in the wake of neoconservative public policies. Yet there is a new form of urban dualism on the rise, one specifically linked to the restructuring process and to the expansion of the informational economy. It relates, first of all, to the simultaneous processes of growth and decline of industries and firms, processes taking place most intensely at the nodal points in the economic geography, namely, the largest metropolitan areas where most of the knowledge-intensive activities and jobs are concentrated. This occupational transition, unlike the historical shift from agricultural to industrial societies, is characterized by a mismatching between the characteristics of labor being phased out and the requirements for new labor. This is partly due to the contradiction between the much higher knowledge components of a substantial proportion of the new occupations and the institutional capacities of most societies, and specifically of American society, to adapt the educational system and to enhance the structural conditions that give rise to a higher cultural and scientific level of labor.

Yet given that the majority of new occupations do not require sophisticated skills, most of the new characteristics looked for in labor are a function not of technological change but of social and economic restructuring. What is at stake is the dismantling of the capital–labor relationships that were institutionalized during the long, conflictual process by which industrial society was formed. The transition from industrial to informational production processes overlaps with the rise of flexible production, which, under current historical conditions, tends to be equated with de-institutionalized capital–labor relationships. There follows the general demise of traditional labor, not only in manufacturing, and the conditioning of new labor to new organizational conditions, characterized by its relentless adaptation to the needs of firms and agencies as perceived by management, generally under the rule of market logic. Growth and decline do not compensate each other, as they did during the transition toward the industrial society. Part of the new potential labor force, especially among ethnic minority youth, is not integrated into the new labor market, and becomes surplus population. The majority of labor is restructured, both by the imposition upon it of new working conditions, generally in a different sector of activity, and by changing the characteristics of the labor pool itself, increasing the proportion of women, immigrants, and ethnic minorities in the labor force, taking advantage of the greater social vulnerability of these groups in a social context of gender and racial discrimination. Nevertheless, a significant proportion of labor, recruited from the better educated social groups, is upgraded in skills and social status, and becomes the backbone of the new informational economy, both in advanced services and in high-technology manufacturing. The differential reassignment of labor in the process of simultaneous growth and and decline results in a sharply stratified, segmented social structure that differentiates between upgraded labor, downgraded labor, and excluded people. Dualism refers here both to the contradictory dynamics of growth and decline, and to the polarizing and exclusionary effects of these dynamics.

The new dual city can also be seen as the urban expression of the process of increasing differentiation of labor in two equally dynamic sectors within the growing economy: the information-based formal economy, and the downgraded labor-based informal economy. The latter is a highly dynamic, growth-oriented, and often very profitable sector, whose reality is far distant from the survival activities with which it has generally been associated. The informal economy cannot be equated with urban poverty, and in this sense urban dualism does not pertain to the realm of social stratification but to a new socio-economic structure characterized by the different growth dynamics of two distinct, though articulated, components. What differentiates the two sectors, as argued in chapter 1, is the breakdown of state intermediation between capital and labor, resulting in different production relationships, and ultimately in different characteristics of labor, either because it was molded to the requirements of unregulated relationships or because it was selected (or self-selected) in the first place on the basis of its malleability to new working conditions. The widespread observation concerning the entrepreneurialism of the new immigrants fits this model, but so does the adaptation of clerical women to higher skilled jobs at lower rates of pay and without job security, on a part-time basis and without a contract. The informal economy, being concentrated in the largest and most dynamic metropolitan areas, particularly in the central cities, also contributes to the new urban dualism; two equally dynamic sectors, interconnected by a number of symbiotic relationships, define specific labor markets and labor processes in such a way that the majority of workers are unlikely to move upwardly between them. The economy, and thus society, becomes functionally articulated but organizationally and socially segmented.

A third major process of dualization concerns the polarized occupational structure within the rising sectors of advanced services and high technology, with its impact on a stratification system; because of the shrinkage of its middle levels, the system appears to be less open to occupational mobility than in the recent past. Given the relatively large proportion of labor in the upper levels of the occupational structure, the higher levels of the society are no more a secluded elite inevitably forced to interact with the overwhelming majority of the society, but can be functionally and socially self-contained, while the lower tier loses the attraction of the social role model provided by the higher social strata because the privileges, skills, and values of the upper-level, professional class seem to be unreachable for most of the semi-skilled labor force.

Thus the non-complementary processes of informational growth and industrial decline, the downgrading and upgrading of labor, the differentiation between the formal and the informal sectors, and the polarization of the occupational structure in the new industries, together produce a highly differentiated labor force that crystallizes in very distinct lifestyles in terms of household structure, inter-gender family relationships, and uses of the urban space. In fact, structural dualism, along the series of dimensions we have indicated, does not result in two social worlds, but in a variety of social universes whose fundamental characteristics are their fragmentation, the sharp definition of their boundaries, and the low level of communication with other such universes. The dual city is a multifaceted reality, but structural dualism manifests itself in the transformation of bipolar dialectics into dual dichotomies. It is in this sense, and only in this sense, that we can speak of dualism.

Structural positions in the relationships of production and distribution crystallize in lifestyles that become less and less communicable, as they presuppose radically different financial means and cultural skills, and so lead to the formation of micro-societies through the patterning of space. Residential areas become exclusionary devices where the dynamics of real estate costs tend to impose social homogeneity, both in terms of class and in terms of ethnicity. The adaptation of a desirable space historically occupied by ethnic minorities or working-class families to its new privileged status as residential location for the new urbanites of the informational society takes place through systematic gentrification and displacement that further segregates the city. What results is a spatial structure that combines segregation, diversity, and hierarchy. The upper tier of the society, mostly white, and largely male-dominated, either by single men or through patriarchal relationships, occupies select spaces, both in the inner core and in exclusive suburbs, and maintains them in a separate circuit of lifestyle, services, and leisure, increasingly protected by both public and private security forces. The vast majority of downgraded workers and new laborers share an excluded space that is highly fragmented, mainly in ethnic terms, building defensive communities that fight each other to win a greater share of services, and to preserve the territorial basis of their social networks, a major resource for low-income communities. Downgraded areas of the city serve as refuges for the criminal segment of the informal economy, as well as reservations for displaced labor, barely maintained on welfare. Newcomers to the dual city often pioneer transformations of these areas, increasing the tension between conflicting social interests and values expressed in territorial terms. On the other hand, a large proportion of the population, made up of low-level labor forming the legions of clerical and service workers of the informational economy, insert themselves into micro-spaces, individualizing their relationship to the city, which becomes reduced, in their living experience, to a tenuous connection between home and work, in the vain hope of not being whirled into the changing dynamics of community structuration and destructuration. Structural dualism leads at the same time to spatial segregation and to spatial segmentation, to sharp differentiation between the upper level of the informational society and the rest of the local residents as well as to endless segmentation and frequent opposition among the many components of restructured and destructured labor.

The territorially based institutional fragmentation of local governments and of schools reproduces these cleavages along the lines of spatial segregation. Since educational and cultural capacity are key elements in labor performance in the informational economy, the system is largely self-reproductive, unless modified by social protest and/or deliberate political intervention.

The social universe of these different worlds is also characterized by differential exposure to information flows and communication patterns. The space of the upper tier is usually connected to global communication and to vast networks of exchange, open to messages and experiences that embrace the entire world. At the other end of the spectrum, segmented local networks, often ethnically based, rely on their identity as the most valuable resource to defend their interests, and ultimately their being.[89] So the segregation of space in one case (for the large social elite) does not lead to seclusion, except regarding communication with the other components of the shared urban area; while segregation and segmentation for defensive communities of ethnic minorities, workers, and immigrants do reinforce the tendency to shrink the world to their specific culture and their local experience, penetrated only by standardized television images, and mythically connected, in the case of immigrants, to tales of the homeland. The dual city opposes, in traditional sociological terms, the cosmopolitanism of the new informational producers to the localism of the segmented sectors of restructured labor.

The series of processes I have shown to be linked to the spatial dimension of labor restructuring in the informational economy converge toward a fundamental outcome of the dual city: its role in restructuring and destructuring social class formation. On the one hand, the recycling, downgrading, and conditioning of labor leads to the configuration of a number of territorially segregated, culturally segmented, socially discriminated communities that cannot constitute a class because of their extremely different positions in the new production relationships, reflected and amplified in their territorial differentiation in the city. On the other hand, a large proportion of the population (between one-fourth and one-third in the largest metropolitan areas) hold the strategic position of information producers in the new economy, enjoy a high cultural and educational level, are correspondingly rewarded in income and status within the stratification system, and control the key to political decision-making in terms of their social influence and organizational capacity. This new professional–managerial class, that by and large is white-dominated and male-dominated, is spatially organized, in terms of residence, work, and consumption activities, and tends to appropriate an increasingly exclusive space on the basis of a real estate market that makes location in that space a most valuable asset. This social group is not a ruling class in the traditional sense. It is a hegemonic social class that does not necessarily rule the state but fundamentally shapes civil society. The spatial articulation of its functional role and its cultural values in a very specific space, concentrated in privileged neighborhoods of nodal urban areas, provides both the visibility and the material conditions for its articulation as a hegemonic actor. In contrast, the endless social and spatial fragmentation of the diversified segments of restructured labor at the lower level fixes their cultural and territorial identities in terms irreducible to other experiences, breaking down the pattern of social communication with other communities and among different positions in the work process. And this is probably the essence of the dual city in our society: an urban form that articulates the rise of the new socially dominant category in the informational mode of development, while disarticulating and opposing the fragments of destructured labor as well as the components of the new labor incorporated into the emerging economic structure. The fundamental contemporary meaning of the dual city refers to the process of spatial restructuring through which distinct segments of labor are included in and excluded from the making of new history.

5

High Technology and the Transition From the Urban Welfare State to the Suburban Warfare State

Introduction: From the Welfare State to the Warfare State

The process of economic restructuring underway in the 1980s is challenging one of the cornerstones of post-1945 industrial democracies: the welfare state. By this term is understood, as in most of the literature,[1] a particular type of state in recent history, characterized by the fact that one of its fundamental principles of legitimacy lies in its redistributive role in delivering goods and services through public institutions, outside the rule of the market, to citizens entitled to such delivery simply by being citizens. I share Morris Janowitz's view that:

.the Welfare State and welfare expenditures are not synonymous. The Welfare State rests on the political assumption that the well-being of its citizens is enhanced not only by allocations derived from their occupations and the marketplace but also from grants regulated by the central government. . . . The Welfare State involves at least two additional elements. First, under the Welfare State, the extent and nature of welfare expenditures are conditioned decisively by parlimentary regimes, that is they political demands and consent and not authoritarian decisions. Second, it is accepted as a legitimate goal of the political system to intervene through governmental institutions in order to create the conditions under which its citizens can pursue their individual goals.[2]

This is to say that the welfare state is above all, as is any form of state, a political phenomenon. Yet it has decisive economic consequences, in terms of both the distribution of the product and its impacts on supply and demand. It would be pretentious to attempt here the analysis, that remains to be undertaken, of the origins, development, and crisis of the welfare state in the US.[3] What is crucial for the present specific analytical purpose is that in the 1970s the welfare state reached its peak in America, at a level that business interests were not ready to accept on economic grounds, and under political conditions that made it possible for conservative forces to mobilize important sectors of the American public against it.[4] Table 5.1 shows the rapid growth of social welfare during the 1960s and its stabilization during the 1970s at a level that greatly contributed to the dramatic decrease of capital's net share of GNP

Table 5.1   Labor and capital share of total output, 1984–1980, as % of GNP[a]

Year	Consumption by labor financed by wages and salaries	Social welfare spending	Capital's gross share	Capital depreciation	Non-social welfare spending	Capital's net share
1948	58	8	34	7	11	16
1950	58	8	34	7	12	14
1955	55	8	37	9	15	13
1959	55	10	35	9	15	9
1965	54	11	35	8	15	12
1972	52	19	29	9	14	6
1977	50	19	31	10	14	6
1979	50	18	32	10	14	8
1980	51	19	30	11	14	5

[a] The total labor consumption share equals column 1 plus column 2; capital's gross share equals 100 minus the total labor consumption share. Capital's net share equals capital's gross share minus capital depreciation minus non-social welfare spending. The net share represents that part of GNP available for net domestic and foreign investment and capitalists' consumption.

Sources: 1948–72: Bowles and Gintis, tables 5 and 6 (see note 5); 1977–80: calculations based on Bowles and Gintis' method, using more recent data. Calculated by Carnoy, Shearer, and Rumberger (see note 7)

from 12 percent in 1965 to 5 percent in 1980.[5] Another important observation from these data is the decline during the 1970s of the proportion of consumption by labor financed by wages, which amounts to an increase in the role played by taxes and social security contributions in financing welfare expenditures. This trend was tantamount to a redistributive process from capital to labor and from middle-income workers to low-income families, including the poor and unemployed. The complexity of this trend is explained by three factors: the growing importance of indirect wages over direct wages in labor's consumption; the process of redistribution in favor of non-working households and low-income families; and the skyrocketing cost of public agencies, particularly because of their role as employers of a growing proportion of the workers, offering better opportunities than the private sector to workers, especially from ethnic minorities. This situation laid the economic ground for an alliance between business interests and middle-class taxpayers to launch a decisive attack against the welfare state. Yet this attack, which was incorporated into the mainstream of conservative politics and, as a result, into the national policies labeled "Reaganomics," was successful only because of the existence of a number of economic, ideological, and political conditions underlying the current transformation of the capitalist state.[6]

Economically, the crisis of the 1970s was partly the consequence of the refusal of business to continue investing under the institutional conditions represented by the welfare state and its regulatory policies. As Carnoy, Shearer, and Rumberger put it:

Government management failed because once big business saw that liberal governments could and would give in to wage earners, the poor, and the old at the expense of profits, it gradually made the New Deal solution unworkable. An important fraction of the business community was and is willing to do whatever is necessary – including bringing on a series of severe recessions, as occured in the 1970s and early 1980s – to get the new and satisfactory conditions of low wages, low welfare spending, low corporate taxes, minimal regulations and weak unions consistent with high profit margins and control over capital formation. Far from wanting government off people's back, business in the 1970s was pushing for government intervention in its favor.[7]

Nevertheless, in a democratic society, economic interests, even when they are structurally dominant, cannot impose their logic unless mediated by ideological and political processes.[8] Ideologically, the reality of bureaucratization of state institutions, and the individualistic, almost libertarian tradition of American culture, favored the deregulation of welfare institutions.[9] Nevertheless, as Vicente Navarro has pointed out,[10] most public opinion polls during the past decade show consistent public support for the fundamental institutions of the welfare state, and particularly for the most costly entitlement program, social security, although rejecting transfers made under the "welfare" label. This is to say that the ideology rooted in individualism and the work ethic rejects the notion of a "free lunch" for the "lazy poor," but is certainly comfortable with major social benefits obtained by and for the working people, such as social security, unemployment benefits, health, and education. The deliberate political attack on the welfare state consists precisely in the ideological confusion of general programs of social benefits with specific programs targeted to the poor.

The relative success of the anti-welfare strategy lies in the differing political origins of two kinds of social programs. In other words, the American welfare state is a two-tier institutional system, originating in two different historical periods around different social actors and political conditions, even if in both cases the Democratic Party came to be its political expression.[11] As we know, the major institutional foundations of the welfare state resulted from the mobilization of the labor unions in the 1930s,[12] when a social contract was reached between business, organized labor, and government, in the form of the New Deal, setting up both the basis for post-World War II economic growth and the political framework for the expansion of the welfare state.[13] These social contracts excluded both ethnic minorities and the new social movements that came to the forefront of collective action during the 1960s, most notably the women's movement, community organizations, environmentalists, countercultural protestors, and ethnic liberation movements, often associated in the anti-war movement.[14] Thus, a new, fragile political coalition appeared in most large US cities toward the end of the 1960s, built upon the concessions made to various minorities and communities by the business–labor political alliances that had controlled the local political institutions in the early 1960s, enlarging and destabilizing the political grouping that John Mollenkopf has characterized as the "pro-growth coalition."[15] To remain in power the pro-growth coalition had to broaden the welfare state to cover poor urban communities, in a movement of such depth that it could be challenged only slightly by the Nixon administration.[16] Once the institutions were in place, by 1969, the bureaucratic logic of the entitlement system pushed them forward, in terms of services, payments, and jobs, turning American inner cities into powerful redistributive machines.[17]

The distinctive features of this new round of welfare state activity were its diversity and its pragmatic specificity. Resulting from uneven development of social struggles, and following the variable geometry of local political coalitions and intergovernment relationships, the urban welfare state was a piecemeal construction of programs and agencies that favored groups and areas whose legitimate entitlement became slowly buried with the passage of time, and the fading of collective memory.[18] Furthermore, the new political alliances were not as firm as that which underlay the New Deal, and basically failed to draw in the new, active middle class, living mainly in the suburbs, as well as the new social movements.[19]

In fact, the political context in which most of the "great society" programs came to maturity, namely the Nixon administration, was no small contributory cause of the lack of consistency of the new liberal coalition. As John Mollenkopf writes.

The conservative counterpoint added to the irrationality, internal inconsistency, and lack of political accountability of the federal urban program delivery system. By undercutting Democratic programs, conservatives reduced the delivery system's responsiveness to the beneficiaries for whom it was initially designed. Since conservatives added new programs more easily than they could terminate old ones, programs increasingly worked at cross purposes. During the periods of conservative ascendency, the number of demoralized and crippled programs also increased, subsequently burdening Democrats as well as Republicans. Over time this build-up of bureauratic ineffectiveness and lack of accountability has become one of the system's primary problems and one that, despite considerable rhetoric about efficiency and reorganization, neither liberals nor conservatives have been able to resolve.[20]

Thus, to some extent, while the mobilizations of the 1930s led to a solid coalition that crystallized in the national institutions of the welfare state, the social movements of the 1960s, while they succeeded in reforming the local state, obtaining welfare programs that expanded during the 1970s, were not able to build stable coalitions that could resist a determined offensive by powerful adversaries such as business, the new middle class, or ideological movements in defense of traditional family values.

This analysis is the basis for one fundamental hypothesis that I will try to substantiate in this chapter: the attack against the welfare state, as a key element of the process of economic restructuring, developed first along the weakest line of defense of welfare institutions, namely, the local welfare state, which was barely sustained by co-opted minority bureaucracies and insulated community organizations, while major entitlement programs, such as social security or unemployment insurance, much more significant in budgetary terms, escaped largely unscathed during the heyday of Reaganomics, in spite of the weakness of organized labor. The historic alliance of the New Deal, along with its powerful ramifications in the Democratic Party, was strong enough to hold much of its ground against the storm of neo-conservatism, while the regulatory institutions conquered by environmentalists and the safety net obtained by the urban poor during the 1960s were what suffered in the blundering attempts to dismantle the welfare state. The urban social landscape was thus much more deeply affected by the turnaround of public policies than was the social wage established by labor-supported reformers in the era of responsible capitalism.

The tentative dismantlement of the welfare state in the process of restructuring is taking place simultaneously with the rise of a new "warfare state." Although I use the term, coined originally by Herbert Marcuse,[21] because of its powerful resonance, I give to it quite a different meaning. I would certainly not imply that the American state, or indeed most states in industrial democracies, are now engaging in active warfare. For one thing, they have already done it, regrettably, in the past decades. Neither do I believe they are aiming to trigger off a new world war. In characterizing the new historic trends under the notion of the warfare state I refer to a number of major social processes. In the first place, on purely empirical grounds, in the 1980s the American state undertook the largest ever defense build-up in peacetime, and in absolute dollar value, the largest military program in the history of mankind (see table 5.2 and figure 5.1). Secondly, and at a more analytical level, one of the main issues at stake is the replacement of the state's principle of legitimacy as economic regulator and social redistributor, forged during the Depression era, by a new principle, powerful enough to justify the reinforcement of the state and the growing budget deficit caused by defense spending and pro-business tax cuts,[22] in spite of the libertarian tone of the discourse targeted against the welfare state. The old conservative justification for the strength of the state as the rampart of national security and the guardian of domestic law and order came to be the main motto of the political program of economic restructuring. Thus, to some extent the demise of welfare and the rise of warfare are intertwined as processes of contradictory political legitimation, whose peaceful coexistence in the 1950s and 1960s became socially and economically untenable in the 1980s.

Furthermore, the political crisis suffered by the American state both domestically (Watergate) and internationally (Vietnam; Iran; the erosion of its political control in Africa and Central America; increasing economic and technological competition from new powers, particularly Japan; strategic parity achieved by the Soviet Union in the arms race) called for a state of emergency in which the greatest power on earth would flex its muscles to show, in a responsible yet determined manner, that it was ready and willing to

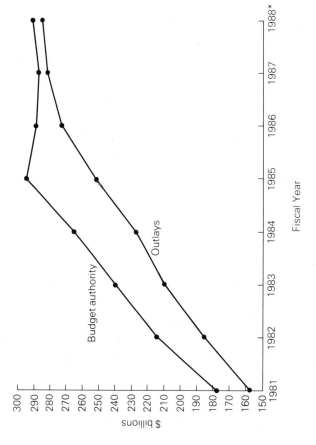

Figure 5.1   The Reagan defense budget, 1981–1988

Table 5.2 Reagan defense budget, 1981–1988

	1981 $bn	annual growth rate (%)	1982 $bn	annual growth rate (%)	1983 $bn	annual growth rate (%)	1984 $bn	annual growth rate (%)	1985 $bn	annual growth rate (%)	1986 $bn	annual growth rate (%)	1987 $bn	annual growth rate (%)	1988[a] $bn	annual growth rate (%)
Budget authority	178.4	–	213.8	19.8	239.5	12.0	265.2	10.7	294.7	11.1	289.1	-1.9	287.4	-0.6	291.4	1.4
Outlays	157.5	–	185.3	17.7	209.9	13.3	227.4	8.3	252.7	11.1	273.4	8.2	282.0	3.1	285.4	1.2

a Projected.

Source: Executive Office of the President, Office of Management and Budget, *Budget of the United States Government*, various years.

engage in sharp confrontations to preserve its status and power. Business interests, both in the US and internationally, redeploying themselves on a planetary scale in the aftermath of the crisis, welcomed this newfound resolution in the leader of the free world, both for its symbolic value and for its global practical consequences.

Together with tax cuts for corporations and upper-income groups, defense spending provided the substitute for the demand and jobs generated by social welfare spending and hence the basis for a new state-led economic policy replacing classical Keynesianism with a "perverted Keynesianism," made up of military expenditures and regressive income redistribution.[23]

To proceed with this new policy, a new power bloc had to be built at the core of the warfare state, able to replace the old liberal coalition which was now deeply in crisis. As Carnoy, Shearer and Rumberger write: "New Deal ideology, fostering an economic development based on a historical compromise among labor, business, and government could not abandon its labor-conscience political base to achieve what business wanted. Neither was it willing to abandon its business ally to strike out in new, imaginative pro-community, pro-labor, pro-consumer directions. It thus collapsed as a viable political ideology."[24]

Business took the initiative in this collapse by breaking the two social contracts achieved during the 1930s and 1940s, and the 1960s, to regain decisive advantages over labor and over the welfare state, and to win a new edge in the international economy. Business enthusiasm for the neo-conservative coalition organized around President Reagan is hardly a mystery. Still, it was not enough decisively to overturn the Democratic majority among the public, and to make them forget so quickly the disturbing tendencies in the Republican administration revealed during the Watergate affair. However, on the basis of the electoral and public opinion data we can hypothesize that the new power bloc was constituted behind the warfare state (without necessarily supporting military action) on the basis of several elements:

(1) The traditional conservative constituency, reinvigorated by the new strength lent by business support and the skills and charisma of a new political leader with good communication skills: Ronald Reagan.

(2) The array of social groups brought together by the backlash against minorities and social movements, particularly among working-class whites reacting against minorities, anti-segregation policies ("busing," for instance) and countercultural movements (feminism, gay liberation, etc.).

(3) Middle-class professionals, reacting against the welfare state because of its benefit of low-income groups at the expense of their tax burden, while supporting the new economy fostered by defense spending and international business, regardless of their ideology as individuals on specific issues.

(4) New regions, benefiting from the new economy in terms of jobs, population, and resources, and emerging as new power-makers outside the traditional alignments generally controlled by the Democratic Party.

Because of the diversity of these interests and their loose socio-political organization, this power bloc had great difficulty in making progress in Congressional and local elections. Yet their social strength was significant enough to coalesce on the national scene around the powerful figure of Ronald Reagan, masterfully dominating the unifying institution of American national politics: the media.

Once in power, the political elite reshaping the Federal government in the direction of the warfare state undertook the task of transforming a conservative current of opinion into a new historic power bloc. However, at least during the 1980s, it failed in this attempt. The causes of this failure are complex and cannot be rigorously examined within the limits of this chapter. It is enough to say here simply that two important factors were the political ineptitude of the President's aides (leading, among other things, to the Iran–Contra affair), and the damaging results of contradictory economic policies that amassed the largest budget deficit and trade deficit in history, prompting demands from business circles for a more rational policy.[25] However, the Reagan administration did set in motion a series of trends that future political leaders will find difficult to reverse: a social and political climate inclined to the deregulation of economic and social activity; the weakening of organized labor, with its corollary in terms of greater freedom on the part of government and business to renounce social programs; a more conservative judiciary, which will be likely to slow down major social changes at the institutional level; an anti-inflationary attitude that will lay the ground for fiscal austerity, once the flow of foreign financing of the deficit decreases; and, above all, a new emphasis on strong defense on the basis of a technological renewal of the armed forces that is likely to be pursued by subsequent administrations, in the form of both strategic policy and industrial policy, in spite of the ups and downs of defense spending.

The process of economic restructuring then, developed on the basis of a socio-political transformation that laid the ground for the transition from the welfare state to the emerging warfare state. Much of this realignment translated into decisive urban and regional restructuring, as a later part of this chapter will go on to analyze. To focus once more on the specific research interest of this work, what was the actual role played by technological change in a process that we have analyzed primarily in economic and political terms?

As in other dimensions of the restructuring process, high technology in fact played a very important role in the transition from the welfare to the warfare state. This is, first of all, because of the technological obsolesence of military equipment brought about by dramatic changes in electronics, communications, and special materials. Certainly, such obsolesence is significant because of the *political* decision to strengthen US defense; once that decision was taken, for reasons that will be discussed briefly in the third section of this chapter, technological modernization of the military became the key instrument for achieving strategic superiority and modifying conventional forces to meet the new international conditions of modern warfare.[26] Although the defense build-up *per se* is independent of technological change, the pace of such change shaped the new defense policy, magnified and accelerated the replacement component of military procurement, and engaged the nation in a number of costly programs aimed at a new generation of sophisticated weapons.[27] Because this rejuvenation of the defense system was given political priority in a period of intended fiscal austerity, it also determined to a large extent the size and characteristics of budget cuts in welfare expenditures. Indeed, it was the combination of tax reductions and defense spending which created the largest federal budget deficit in history, in a paradoxical expression of the internal contradictions of the restructuring process. The obvious complementary policy would have been a dramatic shrinkage of welfare expenditures, as Budget Director David Stockman actually attempted.[28] Yet, as Stockman himself pointed out, many of the institutionalized welfare state programs from the 1930s–1940s legislation, particularly social security entitled payments, by far the largest item in the welfare state, became untouchable, and cuts were concentrated instead on the more recent and politically weaker urban welfare programs. There is, therefore, a systemic connection linking technological modernization of the military, increased defense spending, and selective dismantlement of some institutions of the welfare state.

Also, high-technology-led economic development favors, as has been observed in preceding chapters, the rise of new occupations and new regions to positions of greater wealth and power, undermining the social basis of the New Deal coalition, and fostering the formation of a new power bloc politically more likely to support both the warfare state and the downgrading of the welfare system. This does not mean that new social groups, for instance engineers and upper-level professionals, are warmongers. In fact, many of them were active in the anti-movement, and are often quite liberal in their personal ideology, as the political behavior of "yuppies" seems to indicate.[29] Yet they tend to be distrustful of unions, and scared of minorities, particularly when it comes to sharing public services for their children, and thus they distance themselves from the socio-political coalitions representative of the welfare state. The new model of development based upon high technology and advanced services creates the social conditions for a political realignment of the American public, offering the chance for new policies, such as the strategic project of the warfare state, to find new constituencies. This explains the apparent paradox of seeing one and the same social group, for example middle-class professionals, simultaneously supporting the nuclear freeze and voting for President Reagan, notwithstanding his pro-defense policy. We will see below how technology is used for political ends in the attempt to solve this ideological contradiction in the new power bloc by aiming, at least symbolically, at a non-nuclear, yet strategically superior, new defense system.

This ambiguous combination of liberal ideals and political neo-conservatism disappears in the case of the new regional elites, clearly supportive of the warfare state on the basis of a model of growth that associates closely high technology, the military–industrial complex, and free-wheeling capitalism competing in the international economy.[30] California, Texas, Florida, Arizona, and much of the west, are clearly setting the pace, although New England's liberal stand should sound a note of caution about making a mechanistic association between military industries and political neo-conservatism. All in all, high-technology-led economic restructuring is stimulating the transition from welfare to warfare, through its influence on the transformation of the occupational and regional structures of American society.

There is a third major technological factor that is likely to play an important role in the restructuring of the welfare state. This is the potential of office automation and on-line information systems in the public services.[31] This perspective, still very much undeveloped, could provide the technological basis for reducing public employment while maintaining the level of services, breaking union power, and generalizing the practice of subcontracting to private firms, on the basis of a lean, highly sophisticated public-service sector. Although at present political obstacles and bureaucratic routine to a great extent block the organizational restructuring of the public sector, should the new state prevail and consolidate, such restructuring would certainly be in the logic of the new administrative apparatuses; new information technologies would be a decisive tool in increasing the bureaucratic efficiency of government while insulating it further from citizens' control.

Overall, it is my hypothesis that high technology is an indispensable tool for the fundamental political–economic restructuring taking place in the state institutions of industrial democracies, and particularly in the US, in the last two decades of the twentieth century. This restructuring has roots that go deeper than the ideological preferences of a particular administration. It relates to the emergence of a new power bloc and to the reorganization of economy and society to cope with both new sources of social change and the technological revolution. Given the historical openness of the process, it is impossible to assess the actual extent of its lasting effects. Nevertheless, in about a decade the transition from the welfare to the warfare state will have taken place, producing a substantial, maybe irreversible, impact on the social and spatial structures.

The Rise and Fall of the Urban Welfare State

As stated above, the development of the welfare state in the US results from two major social trends originating in two key historical periods:[32] first, the

1930s, when the economic crisis and labor struggles led to the New Deal and its broad stream of Federal income-transfer programs, ushered in by the 1935 Social Security Act; [33] secondly, the 1960s, when the urban crisis and community struggles forced a realignment of local politics and fostered a new series of collective entitlement programs whose scope went far beyond the Democratic Party's "great society" programs, expanding throughout the 1970s during the conservative Nixon administrations. [34] What characterized this second tier of the welfare state was, on the one hand, its emphasis on the inner cities of large metropolitan areas; and on the other, its decisive role in the dynamics of local governments and in the local political arena. [35] The reversal of historic trends in the orientation of the state in the US, namely, the curtailment of its redistributive functions during the 1980s, is in large part concerned particularly with this urban dimension of the welfare state. [36] This is why the rise and fall of urban social programs are decisive in the shaping of American cities and regions.

In the period extending, approximately, from the mid-1960s to the late 1970s, three parallel trends deeply transformed the urban fabric of the US.[37] First, a substantial increase occurred in the share of total government spending taken by social welfare expenditure, with health, social insurance, and public aid showing the greatest increases. Overall, government domestic expenditures grew from 20.3 percent of GNP in 1969 to 25.9 percent of GNP in 1977. Even more significant, the ratio of domestic to defense spending changed from 2:1 to 4:1, while for much of this period the US was still engaged in the Vietnam War. [38] Social welfare spending as a proportion of total government spending increased from 37 percent in 1948 to 41.1 percent in 1966, 52.8 percent in 1973, and 56.8 percent in 1980. Within social welfare, social insurance increased its share of total social welfare spending from 21 percent in 1950 to 46.5 percent in 1980, while health and medical spending increased over the same period from 13 percent to over 20 percent.

Secondly, a growing flow of funds took place from the Federal government to state and local governments, which became major agents of social redistribution: Federal aid as a percentage of state and local expenditures increased from 18 percent in 1969 to 28 percent in 1977. For every dollar raised locally in 1978 cities received almost 50 cents from the Federal government.[39] In 1972, the Revenue Sharing Act established new financial ties among federal, state, and local governments, reversing the pro-state bias of US federalism in favor of a greater role for local governments.[40] In 1977 total Federal aid to state and local governments was about $70 billion, representing a five-fold increase in one decade. [41] Thirdly, in one of the most original trends of the new urban welfare state, Federal urban programs were developed that were funded and organized for specific localities, constituting what Gelfand calls a "fourth branch of government" [42] in which professionals, community activists, and Federal bureaucrats come together in a unique blend to shape a powerful current of social reform and citizen participation, accused by its conservative critics of causing "maximum feasible misunderstanding." [43] "War on poverty," "Model cities," and a number of categorical programs, targeted particularly on depressed urban areas and ethnic minorities, created a rich and complex geography of social welfare that even after its consolidation in fewer programs during the Nixon administration (particularly under the Community Development Block Programs or CDBG) continued to grow during the 1970s, providing some safety net to those social groups sufficiently deprived to be entitled to and sufficiently well mobilized to win their demands. [44]

To be sure, the budgetary size of most of these programs was (and is) much smaller than major items of the budget, such as defense, social security, or interest payments. Yet, their symbolic value, as a public commitment to people's needs independent of market forces, made these programs the focus of a social debate aimed at restoring social discipline and enhancing the individual work ethic. [45] Furthermore, their targeted distribution made these programs actually significant , in material terms, for their recipients and for the spatial areas they inhabited. [46] Similarly, Federal aid per capita favored bigger cities, that is, generally speaking, cities where social problems tend to more acute. It is true that small cities in depressed regions tend to be poorer than large cities, but research has established that social problems, and thus social welfare, are linked less to the actual level of poverty than to the social visibility of such problems, which is as much as to say, to the capacity for social mobilization of those concerned. [47]

In other words, a fundamental characteristic of the new welfare state that developed during the 1960s and the 1970s in a highly chaotic way, under the variable influence of socio-political factors, was its close association to specific spatial settings. George Vernez provides empirical proof of this hypothesis in one of the few systematic analyses of the spatial impact of Federal spending differentiated by specific programs. [48] His findings are shown in table 5.3. Vernez examined the distribution of Federal outlays by budget function for fiscal year 1976, as well as the evolution over 1970–6, in different spatial areas categorized in terms of income, economic growth, index of social hardship, size, and ecological position within the metropolitan area. He also calculated the distribution of these Federal outlays per region, although I have omitted here the presentation of these details, concentrating on his findings. The reader is referred to Vernez' article for a presentation of his methodology, which follows standard, generally accepted, procedures. A review of the main findings throws up the following points:

In a summary view of the main findings, we observe the following:

(1) Total Federal outlays, Federal outlays by major functions of the Federal budget, and the major individual grant-in-aid programs directed more funds per capita to central cities rather than to the suburbs, with one major exception, namely defense (primarily, according to Vernez, because of a higher concentration of top defense suppliers in suburban areas than in central cities).

Table 5.3 City concentration ratios of Federal outlays by budget function and type of city, fiscal 1976 (values over 1 indicate greater concentration)

(a)

Function	Per capita income, 1970		Population growth, 1970–5			Unemployment rate, 1976	
	Low-income cities (≤$3304)	High-income cities (>$3304)	Declining cities (≤0)	Slow-growth cities (0–15.0)	Rapid-growth cities (>15.0)	Low unemployment cities (<8.9)	High unemployment cities (≥8.9)
Development							
Area and regional development	1.32	0.68	1.00	1.01	0.90	1.52	0.69
Community development	1.30	0.70	1.05	0.89	0.87	1.03	0.98
Other advancement and regulation of commerce	0.94	1.05	1.10	0.75	0.89	0.92	1.04
Total 1976	1.26	0.75	1.05	0.89	0.87	1.08	0.95
(1970)	(1.19)	(0.80)	(1.08)	(0.82)	(0.77)	(0.98)	(1.00)
Access infrastructure							
Air transport	1.20	0.80	0.96	1.14	0.82	1.49	0.71
Water transport	0.70	1.28	1.24	0.46	0.56	0.75	1.14
Ground transport	0.85	1.14	1.31	0.38	0.27	0.40	1.34
Other transport	0.39	1.57	0.49	2.58	0.03	0.31	1.39
Total 1976	0.92	1.07	1.17	0.66	0.50	0.81	1.10
(1970)	(0.93)	(1.05)	(1.17)	(0.62)	(0.64)	(0.90)	(1.05)

Human capital							
Manpower training	1.20	0.80	0.98	0.97	1.17	1.13	0.92
Education and social services	0.30	1.66	1.29	0.42	0.23	1.90	0.47
Vocational education	1.08	0.91	0.88	0.99	2.14	1.47	0.72
Higher education, research, and general education aid	1.14	0.86	0.96	0.99	1.34	1.19	0.88
Health	0.48	1.49	1.30	0.36	0.37	0.51	1.27
Total 1976	0.85	1.14	1.12	0.70	0.92	0.89	1.06
(1970)	(1.08)	(0.91)	(1.03)	(0.87)	(1.13)	(1.20)	(0.87)
Relief							
Social services	1.03	0.96	0.97	0.84	1.85	1.49	0.71
Retirement and disability insurance	1.10	0.89	1.03	0.97	0.76	0.89	1.06
Unemployment insurance	1.00	1.00	1.13	0.74	0.57	0.69	1.17
Public assistance and other income supplements	0.87	1.12	1.05	0.81	1.10	0.79	1.11
General revenue sharing and fiscal assistance	1.08	0.92	1.04	0.87	0.99	0.90	1.05
Disaster relief and insurance	0.90	1.09	1.03	1.09	0.25	0.94	1.03
Total 1976	1.07	0.92	1.03	0.95	0.82	0.89	1.06
(1970)	(1.16)	(0.83)	(1.02)	(0.98)	(0.75)	(0.88)	(1.06)
Defense							
Construction	0.61	1.62	0.38	1.42	5.44	1.96	0.44
Supply price contracts	0.80	1.19	0.86	1.32	1.05	1.06	0.96
Payrolls	1.23	0.78	0.63	1.68	1.98	1.39	0.77

Table 5.3 Continued

(a)

Function	Per capita income, 1970		Population growth, 1970–5			Unemployment rate, 1976	
	Low-income cities (≤$3304)	High-income cities (>$3304)	Declining cities (≤0)	Slow-growth cities (0-15.0)	Rapid-growth cities (>15.0)	Low-unemployment cities (<8.9)	High-unemployment cities (≥8.9)
Total 1976	0.95	1.04	0.78	1.45	1.42	1.18	0.89
(1970)	(1.03)	(0.96)	(0.89)	(1.17)	(1.34)	(1.28)	(0.83)
Other							
Atomic energy defense	1.48	0.54	0.72	1.76	0.81	0.89	1.06
General science, space, and technology	0.68	1.30	0.96	1.17	0.70	0.81	1.10
Water resources and power	1.20	0.80	0.88	1.25	1.16	1.33	0.80
Pollution control and abatement	0.99	1.00	1.03	0.81	1.30	1.05	0.96
Energy	0.93	1.06	0.82	1.37	1.30	1.06	0.96
Recreation	1.00	0.99	0.90	0.80	2.70	1.24	0.85
Law enforcement and justice	1.03	0.96	1.04	0.83	1.14	0.83	1.09
Postal service	1.03	0.96	1.10	0.81	0.68	0.84	1.09
Veterans benefits	1.09	0.91	0.92	1.20	0.98	1.15	0.91
All Federal expenditure (except national debt interest)							
1976	0.98	1.01	0.98	1.04	0.99	1.01	0.98
(1970)	(0.98)	(1.01)	(1.02)	(0.95)	(0.87)	(1.03)	(0.97)

Table 5.3 Continued

(b)

Function	Hardship Index		Size (000s)			Central cities	Suburban cities
	Low-hardship cities (<100)	High-hardship cities (≥100)	Small cities (<100)	Medium-sized cities (100–300)	Large cities (>300)		
Development							
Area and regional development	0.86	1.03	0.83	1.67	0.77	1.18	0.18
Community development	0.81	1.15	0.75	1.33	0.95	1.08	0.63
Other advancement and regulation of commerce	0.75	1.20	0.44	0.79	1.30	1.13	0.38
Total 1976	0.81	1.14	0.72	1.31	0.87	1.10	0.54
(1970)	(0.74)	(1.20)	(0.73)	(1.32)	(0.95)	(1.10)	(0.49)
Access infrastructure							
Air transport	1.22	0.81	0.54	0.74	1.28	1.14	0.35
Water transport	0.32	1.57	0.31	0.29	1.56	1.14	0.37
Ground transport	0.32	1.49	0.17	0.74	1.42	1.18	0.18
Other transport	0.20	1.66	0.18	2.94	0.48	0.40	3.62
Total 1976	0.60	1.30	0.31	0.67	1.39	1.15	0.32
(1976)	(0.66)	(1.26)	(0.41)	(0.50)	(1.43)	(1.14)	(0.34)
Human capital							
Manpower training	0.95	1.02	0.72	1.62	0.83	1.13	0.38
Education and social services	0.38	1.50	0.38	0.61	1.39	1.14	0.37
Vocational education	1.14	0.82	0.81	1.78	0.73	1.16	0.25

Table 5.3 Continued

(b)

Function	Hardship Index		Size (000s)			Central cities	Suburban cities
	Low-hardship cities (<100)	High-hardship cities (≥100)	Small cities (<100)	Medium-sized cities (100–300)	Large cities (>300)		
Higher education, research, and general educational aid	0.91	1.05	0.82	1.38	0.90	1.12	0.45
Health	0.36	1.52	0.19	0.58	1.48	1.17	0.23
Total 1976	0.69	1.23	0.50	1.13	1.13	1.15	0.31
(1970)	(0.88)	(1.05)	(0.66)	(1.39)	(0.95)	(1.09)	(0.55)
Relief							
Social services	1.03	0.95	0.73	1.67	0.81	1.19	0.12
Retirement and disability insurance	0.84	1.12	0.99	1.12	0.95	1.02	0.88
Unemployment insurance	0.70	1.24	0.79	0.93	1.10	1.06	0.71
Public assistance and other income supplements	0.75	1.20	0.69	0.82	1.19	1.10	0.51
General revenue sharing and fiscal assistance	0.79	1.17	–	0.96	1.10	1.08	0.63
Disaster relief and insurance	0.82	1.05	–	1.00	1.17	1.11	0.47
Total 1976	0.83	1.13	–	1.09	0.98	1.04	0.81
(1970)	(0.85)	(1.11)	–	(1.22)	(0.89)	(1.01)	(0.93)

Defense							
Construction	1.72	0.40	—	0.70	1.21	1.15	0.33
Supply price contracts	1.34	0.71	—	1.26	0.78	0.78	1.93
Payrolls	1.31	0.73	—	1.31	0.91	1.06	0.70
Total 1976	1.33	0.72	—	1.27	0.83	0.88	1.48
(1970)	(1.24)	(0.80)	—	(1.28)	(0.90)	(0.94)	(1.24)
Other							
Atomic energy defense	1.12	0.89	—	1.93	0.39	0.82	1.76
General science, space, and technology	0.86	0.90	—	1.95	0.73	0.79	1.90
Water resources and power	0.78	1.18	—	1.35	1.18	1.21	0.07
Pollution control and abatement	0.76	1.19	—	1.41	0.85	1.03	0.84
Energy	1.14	0.81	—	1.80	0.83	1.02	0.88
Recreation	0.92	1.06	—	1.45	0.97	1.02	0.86
Law enforcement and justice	0.76	1.20	—	0.62	1.38	1.08	0.11
Postal service	0.75	1.20	—	0.96	1.13	1.08	0.61
Veterans benefits	1.05	0.95	—	1.04	1.00	1.03	0.85
All Federal expenditure (except national debt interest) 1976	0.96	1.03		1.12	0.99	1.01	0.91
(1970)	(0.93)	(1.04)		(1.13)	(1.00)	(1.01)	(0.92)

Source: Vernez (see note 48).

(2) Federal outlays in aggregate and for each major function favor medium-sized cities (population between 100,000 and 300,000) over both large and small cities, with the exception of outlays on transportation infrastruture. However, this trend became weaker between 1970 and 1976, in favor of the large cities rather than the smaller cities. Here again, defense spending has a different pattern: defense oulays *per capita* increased in small cities by 23 percent in 1970-6, while decreasing in large cities by 8 percent.

(3) Outlays in all major categories, again with the exception of defense, favored declining cities over rapidly growing cities, on a per capita basis.

(4) Concerning the distribution between high-income cities and low-income cities, the pattern of Federal outlays is somewhat more diversified by function: more was spent *per capita* on relief expenditures, development outlays, and most individual Federal grant-in-aid programs in low-income cities, while transportation infrastructure, human capital investment, and defense outlays went more than proportionately to high-income cities.

(5) Also diversified are the concentration ratios of Federal outlays regarding cities with high unemployment rates as compared to those with low unemployment rates. The former attract more than their proportional share of outlays for relief, transportation, and human capital, while the latter have a greater concentration of expenditure in defense, development, and most of the largest grant-in-aid programs.

(6) In terms of the regional distribution of Federal spending (not shown in these tables) there is a pro-southern, pro-Pacific bias, related to defense and relief outlays, although Vernez remarks on the broad variation of spending patterns within regions, making almost impossible any serious interpretation of policy orientations on the basis of such an aggregate level of analysis.

Overall, the concentration ratios of Federal spending in the 1970s by type of spatial area appear to support the predominance of a redistributive orientation in Federal policy, with the systematic exception of defense outlays which work at cross-purposes to other budgetary items. Central cities in declining, high-hardship areas received a disproportionately large share of most Federal programs. Other classifications indicate a more complex pattern of resource allocation, as one might expect in a politically determined process. Yet many of the trends point toward defining the role of most Federal urban programs as welfare-related programs, in the broad meaning here given to this concept, fundamentally targeted to the urban areas suffering greater social stress. The decade 1966-76 did witness the rise of an urban welfare state in the US.

Both the critics and the advocates of these developments relate them to the urban fiscal crisis that shook many central cities of the large metropolitan areas in the 1970s, triggering in a policy debate that eventually led to the reversal of the trend toward social redistribution and the prevalence of public interest in urban policy. So much has been written on the "urban fiscal crisis" of American inner cities that it seems unnecessary to reopen a debate both outdated and inconclusive.[49] But for the present analytical purpose, it is important to stress that, whatever the structural causes of the fiscal crisis (suburbanization of affluent populations and of jobs, deindustrialization, uneven regional development, general economic crisis, etc.)[50] the way it developed was determined by policy decisions at various local levels and at national level, as a result of a political process.[51] In other words, one of the reasons for the expansion of the urban welfare state during the 1960s and 1970s was precisely to respond to the structural urban crisis by means of redistributive public policy, either Federally initiated or Federally funded.[52] This accounts for the increasing role of state and local governments in the US economy and in the production and management of the means of collective consumption.

Between 1960 and 1975, while US GNP rose by 200 percent, municipal expenditures increased by 350 percent. Over the same period, city expenditures increased 4.6 times while Federal aid to cities increased 18 times, jumping from a total of $592 million to $10.9 *billion*. Most of these expenses were financed through debt, thus contributing to inflationary pressures, and outstanding municipal debt grew from $23.2 billion in 1960 to $68.8 billion in 1975.[53] There was clearly an economic need, as well as social pressure, to bring public spending under control, particularly at the local level. Middle-class constituencies revolted against tax increases perceived as means to support social programs for the urban poor and to provide for the jobs and benefits of the public sector unions. To reinforce the fiscal protectionism fostered by institutional segregation within metropolitan areas, voters revolted at the state level to avoid both further taxation, and redistribution through state or municipal legislation.[54] 1978 was a turning point, with the passage of California's Proposition 13, establishing by referendum mandatory limits to the increase in local taxes. Other local measures, such as Massachusetts' Proposition 2 1/2 added political pressure to the grassroots resistance to urban social programs in the following years.[55] In the late 1970s, similar votes took place in many cities and states.

Nevertheless, the key element in turning the tide was the adoption of a new social policy at the Federal level that downplayed the emphasis on the wellbeing of inner cities, by now largely under control, once most of their political leaders had been integrated into the new local political coalitions. Then, as Tomaskovic-Devey and Miller write:

In the late seventies . . . the urban fiscal crisis, national recapitalization, and the social and economic contradictions produced by structural changes in economic activity led to political attacks on urban governments and on the federal government as incompetent, bloated, and a drag on the private sector. High taxes to finance state payrolls and social services, not the movement of private capital, were identified by business, the media, and some academics as the cause of dangerous fiscal gaps in the budgetary process.[56]

The same authors concluded that:

New York City served as the Hiroshima of the welfare state, demonstrating the bankruptcy threat that faced a city profligate enough to provide services to the poor and to have decent salaries.[57]

The fiscal crisis of New York City in the 1975–81 period was indeed exemplary of the attempted dismantlement of the urban welfare state. William Tabb has described it in a powerful, though admittedly controversial, book.[58] New York City was at the forefront of welfare spending, public services delivery, and favorable working conditions for city employees,[59] largely because of the politicization and level of organization of New York citizens. At the same time, the burden of providing municipal services for a business complex as large as the one located in Manhattan put tremendous pressure on the city that had experienced a massive exodus of virtually its entire middle-class population to the suburbs, along with an equally massive influx of minority populations in search of jobs and welfare benefits. The city had to rely increasingly on state and Federal aid, which in 1959 represented 28 percent of its revenues, jumping to 47 percent in 1969. During the 1960s, to cope with New York's aggravated social problems, state aid increased by 250 percent and Federal aid by 706 percent. With taxes already too high, and its political leverage to obtain additional public aid exhausted, New York City turned more and more to borrowing money from New York banks, as indeed it had often done throughout its history. In 1960, tax-exempt municipal bonds accounted for 21.6 percent of bank portfolios; by 1979, that proportion was 50 percent. In June 1975, the city's debt was $12.3 billion, about 40 percent of which was in notes payable within a year.

New York's financial elite came to be increasingly anxious about the city's prospects, both in terms of its solvency, and in terms of the quality of services that could be provided to the essential business quarters of Manhattan, and to its exclusive neighborhoods. Furthermore, the city was blamed for its demagoguery, let alone its corruption and inefficiency, for having given too much attention to its poor population, and for having made excessive concessions to its buoyant public-sector labor unions. As financial expert Roger Starr put it, business saw a growing contradiction between the political city, providing services for which people were unable or unwilling to pay directly, and the economic city, made up of productive citizens, on which the political bureaucracies and their clienteles were living as parasites;[60] a contradiction that had become impossible to sustain. Thus, when in February 1975 the city attempted to issue new securities, the Bankers Trust refused to underwrite the issue, and stopped all new lending. Chase Manhattan refused to form an alternative syndicate. With New York City bound for a default that could trigger a major financial crisis, and the Federal government refusing to provide additional help, the banks designed a rescue plan that included major budgetary and political conditions. The plan developed in three stages. First, in June 1975, a Municipal Assistance Operation was created as a State of New York agency, able to issue bonds to finance the city, backing these bonds with city revenues and the "moral obligation" of the state. Secondly, an Emergency Financial Control Board was created in September 1975 to step up local financial policy in the face of the resistance from municipal workers' unions and to overcome the reluctance of Mayor Beame to the new policy. The Board was made up of the Governor of New York, the Mayor, the State and City Comptrollers, and three representatives from the business world, selected by the Governor. Its function was to control the city's budget and finances. As a symbol of the business community's new political control over the city, in September 1975 a prominent member of that community was appointed as Deputy Mayor in charge of Finance: Mr Kenneth Axelson, from Lazard Freres and J. C. Penney. The Board urged the city to implement an austerity budget, emphasizing major cuts in social programs and the public employees payroll. Still, and thirdly, the Federal government had to be called upon. After tense negotiations, and with the warranty of New York's Governor and the business community, a "New York City Seasonal Financing Act of 1975" provided loans for three years, under a number of financial conditions supervised by the Secretary of the Treasury.

When a new Mayor, Edward Koch, was elected after a campaign that basically espoused the goals and means of the austerity program, new institutional and financial conditions were in place for a dramatic restructuring of New York City policy. In 1978, at a public ceremony, President Carter signed the "New York City Loan Guarantee Act of 1978," signaling the continuity of effort across party lines. For several years, New York City trimmed its social programs while providing tax abatements and business subsidies. Welfare payments decreased, about 25 percent of municipal jobs were eliminated, including 20 percent of the police force, 19,000 teachers, and 2,000 street sweepers, Public workers' unions, after an initial reaction of protest that was rapidly repressed by the city, not only resigned themselves to the measures but contributed about one-third of their pension funds to back the city's finances. Hospitals, schools, transportation, garbage collection, parks and recreation services all suffered drastic reductions in staff and services, while increasing their fees. By 1981-2, Mayor Koch was able to claim a balanced budget, restoring much of the city's financial credibility, albeit at a high social cost.[61]

On the basis of this fiscal and political restructuring the economy of New York City took off during the 1980s, taking advantage of the internationalization of capital flows, the development of advanced services, and the real estate boom triggered off by the new demand for office space and upmarket urban residences (see chapters 4 and 6). Furthermore, with city revenues increasing as a result of the economic bonanza, the Koch administration was able to restore almost all lost public jobs by 1987,[62] and to distribute public funds and support to some community organizations in a reconstruction of the networks of patronage politics.[63] However, the process of new economic growth in New York was highly polarized, and led to an increasingly unbalanced social structure (see chapter 4); and the new public sector did not expand fast enough to meet the new needs generated by this model of growth. The emphasis in city policies was on support for downtown business services (such as the Teleport project), and on improving the living conditions of the professional elite (for example, stepped-up police patrolling in Manhattan). Efforts were more often devoted to cosmetic image-making than to tackling fundamental social problems. Millions of dollars were spent on cleaning graffiti off subway cars, but New York bridges rapidly deteriorated for lack of maintenance: as a result, Williamsburg bridge closed in 1988, causing traffic nightmares. In another illustration of the same logic, the city set up a program to paint the facades of abandoned buildings to disguise dereliction for the benefit of suburban travellers; yet little was done to tackle the problem of the homeless, which went out of control in New York in the second half of the 1980s. In sum, the restoration of the quantitative level of the public sector, in terms both of jobs and of spending, to that of the mid-1970s, was biased socially and functionally toward business interests and middle-class groups. In the face of the mounting needs of the lower segments of the population, the retrenchment of the local welfare state deepened the trends toward the urban–social form that I have called the dual city.[64]

The most important change in the local state in the case of New York was the transformation of the political agenda, as revealed by the treatment of the fiscal crisis of the 1970s. It became clear that, beyond the ups and downs of social spending and clientelistic policies, the city was committed, first and foremost, to the well-being of the professional groups and to fulfilling the needs of the business interests on which the city's health relied, regardless of the social costs involved in the satisfaction of such interests. It is in this precise sense that the politics surrounding the welfare state involve power above everything else, and not just economic redistribution. The welfare state that was particularly present in the expansion of New York social programs in the 1960s and 1970s, was fundamentally a social contract, redistributing power among different social actors, including the organized poor communities. It was this pact that was renounced during the fiscal crisis and never restored during the 1980s, in spite of the excellent condition then of the local economy. The Koch administration played on ethnic divisions to implement class-oriented policies, thus downgrading the status of the local welfare state to pork-barrel politics.[65]

Similar processes, although less well publicized and in some cases more limited, took place at the turn of the decade in several large central cities in America, including among others Cleveland, Detroit, Buffalo, St Louis, Chicago and Philadelphia.[66] However, the restructuring of New York is particularly significant for the present analytical purpose, for two reasons.

First, it took place as early as the mid-1970s, thus signaling that socio-economic restructuring was a structural need of the system, delayed until the 1980s only because of political factors. Secondly, it was implemented, and with the harshest determination, by a Democratic Mayor in a predominantly Democratic city, actually demonstrating that some aspects of the restructuring process are not linked to Reaganism as such, or even to a Republican administration, but to the defense of class interests when threatened by economic crises and social conflicts. However, it took a new Republication President, fully committed to the defense of such interests, and with exceptional ability to build public support on the basis of political image-making, to undertake the assault on the welfare state, with particular focus on its urban dimension.[67]

The different treatment of the various departments in the Federal government by the Reagan administration was indicative not of government restraint, but of selective retrenchment and expansion. If we use a direct indicator of the expansion of government services, namely the number of employees in each department, between 1980 and 1987 we see the Justice Department *increasing* its labor force by 20 percent, the State Department by 5.4 percent, and the military by 5.2 percent. On the other hand, Health and Human Services experienced personnel *cuts* of 12.4 percent, and Education's work force was cut by 22.4 percent.[68] Beyond the Federal government departments, there was during the Reagan years a reduction in total Federal aid to state and local governments, both in constant dollars, and as a proportion of total Federal spending: the total of such aid fell substantially from 15.5 percent of Federal spending in 1980 to 10 percent in 1987 (see figure 5.2).

The most important issue in the present context, however, is the selective orientation of federal programs toward cities and regions according to the different items in Federal government financing. Norman Glickman has undertaken the most extensive empirical analysis of the restructuring of urban policies under the first Reagan administration (1981-4), with particular emphasis on the urban effects of economic and defense policies – what Glickman calls "Reagan's real urban policy."[69] I will examine his findings in some detail, as they are crucial for my argument concerning the crisis of the urban welfare state.

First of all, Glickman combined all urban-related expenditures in the Federal budget, in some itemized detail, and traced their evolution from 1977 to 1984, as shown in table 5.4. From these figures one can observe the generally rapid and consistent increase of the share of urban-related outlays in the Federal budget between 1967 and 1978, in line with the analysis above. Since 1978, on the contrary, we observe a decrease in that proportion, a decrease that accelerates as the trend proceeds. Furthermore, a reading of table 5.4 shows an actual *decrease* in real urban outlays as a whole (-1.24 percent in 1984 over 1980; -9.0 percent in 1982 over 1981: -4.53 percent in

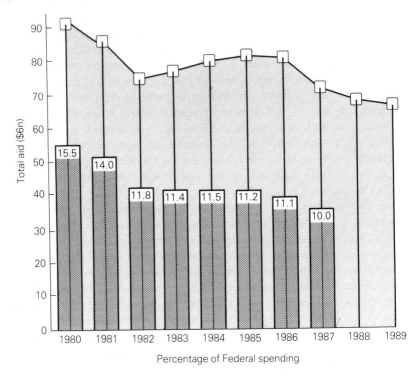

Figure 5.2   Total Federal aid to state and local governments, $bn (constant 1980 $), and aid as percentage of total Federal spending, for fiscal years 1980–1989. Figures for 1988 and 1989 are estimated
Source: Office of Management and Budget and the Brookings Institution

1983 over 1982; −9.36 percent in 1984 over 1983). This trend actually began in 1978, under the last period of the Carter administration, another sign that we are not simply observing a change in the political framework. By the early 1980s at least, a reversal is apparent in the trends concerning the urban welfare state, shifting from its expansion to its decline in absolute terms, as well as in terms of its proportion of the Federal budget.[70] A deepening of these trends during the second Reagan administration has also been observed, although in a less systematic analysis.[71] In addition, the policy of "New Federalism" has transferred a number of programs and responsibilities to state and local governments without allocating corresponding budgetary resources, thus actually reducing the capacity of local governments to meet urban social needs.

The new implicit urban policy has been to stimulate economic growth by creating incentives for private investment, assuming that such growth will solve urban problems. Tax cuts for corporations and upper-income groups

Department and program	1977	1978	1979	1980	1981	1982	1983	1984
Housing and urban development								
Community development block grants	2089	2458	3161	3902	4013	3791	3525	3526
Urban development action grants	–[a]	–	73	225	371	388	488	512
Rehabilitation loan fund	41	47	100	165	60	–23	1	–
Planning assistance	77	67	62	52	39	20	4	–
New communities assistance grants	2	1	*[b]	*	1	1	1	–
Subsidized housing programs	2443	2920	3559	4529	5747	6880	7774	8532
Housing for elderly/handicapped	4	176	459	752	817	742	255	51
Operating payments: low-income housing	506	691	654	824	929	1008	1582	1558
Emergency mortgage purchase assistance	–224	360	271	1039	–74	–37	–227	–
Urban renewal	850	376	281	212	144	90	70	50
Neighborhood self-help development program	–	–	–	2	9	–	–	–
Urban homesteading	–	–	–	–	–	12	20	12
Miscellaneous Appropriations[c]	19	11	15	2	5	1	2	–
Troubled projects operating subsidy	–	–	–12	23	53	29	23	13
Congregate services	–	–	–	*	1	3	5	6
Housing counseling assistance	*	4	5	8	5	3	3	3
FHA fund	492	357	193	151	182	–237	–329	–1546
Low-rent public housing loans and other expenses	–32	11	–3	34	77	–21	102	136
Non-profit sponsor assistance	*	1	1	1	*	*	*	*
Rental housing assistance fund	–7	–12	66	*	3	*	2	–
New communities fund	87	97	31	45	49	16	37	–
Fair housing assistance	–	–	–	–	1	2	11	6
GNMA: Special assistance functions fund	–805	–55	58	396	1303	1666	1433	–
GNMA: Guarantee of mortgage-backed securities	–22	–41	–55	–74	–92	–119	–156	–182
GNMA: Participation sales fund	–4	–21	–12	34	59	–20	–63	–75
Urban-related, HUD	5516	7446	8907	12322	13702	14195	14563	12602
Total HUD Outlays	5838	7589	9213	12576	14033	14491	14853	13737
% Percent Urban-related	94.5	98.1	96.7	98.0	97.6	98.0	98.0	91.7

Table 5.4 Continued

Department and program	1977	1978	1979	1980	1981	1982	1983	1984
Commerce								
Local public works program	585	3057	1741	416	83	40	30	30
Business development loans:								
Econ. Dev. Revolv. Fund	−20	−33	−33	45	−5	46	24	−24
Financial and technical assistance	1	*	–	*	*	*	–	–
Job opportunities program	98	12	2	5	*	1	–	–
Minority business development	54	54	54	56	49	50	57	57
Economic dev. assistance programs	297	330	436	546	502	337	270	207
Urban-related commerce	1015	3420	2200	1068	629	474	381	270
Total commerce outlays	2606	5239	4072	3755	11484	2045	1969	1699
% urban-related	38.9	65.3	54.0	28.4	5.5	23.2	19.3	15.9
Environmental, Protection Agency								
Construction Grants	3530	3187	3756	4343	3881	3756	3100	2800
Urban-related, EPA	3530	3185	3756	4343	3881	3756	3100	2800
Total EPA outlays	4365	4071	4800	5602	5241	5080	4370	4075
% urban-related	80.9	78.3	78.3	77.5	74.1	73.9	70.9	68.7
Transportation								
Federal highway administration (urbanized areas)[d]	861	988	1135	932	808	732	800	800
Urban mass transportation fund	1709	2028	2458	3207	3855	3864	3818	3488
Urban-related, DOT	2570	3016	3593	4139	4663	4596	4818	4288
Total DOT outlays	12514	13452	15486	18963	22509	19917	21157	24370
% DOT-related	20.5	22.4	23.2	21.8	20.7	23.1	21.8	17.6
Small Business Administration								
Business loan and investment fund	464	458	471	721	574	704	270	263
Urban-related, SBA	464	458	471	721	574	704	270	263

Total SBA outlays	700	2766	1631	1899	1913	631	577	262
% SBA-related[e]	66.3	16.6	28.9	38.0	30.0	111.6	46.8	100.4
Community Services Administration								
Community services programs[f]	640	768	780	2170	664	133	39	–
Urban-related CSA	640	768	780	2170	664	133	39	0
Total CSA outlays	640	768	780	2170	664	133	39	–
% CSA-related	100.0	100.0	100.0	100.0	100.0	100.0	100.0	0
Department of Health And Human Services and Education								
Education[g]	2593	3047	3450	1512	4262	3872	3686	3813
Health services administration[h]	1029	1079	1183	1311	1298	1924	1573	786
Grants to states for Medicaid[h]	9713	10680	12407	13957	16833	17391	19326	20799
Assistance payments program[h]	6293	6639	6610	7306	8503	7990	7766	7094
Grants for social and child welfare services[h]	2518	2809	3091	2763	2646	2567	2571	2500
Urban-related, HHS	22146	24254	26741	26851	33542	33744	34922	34922
Total HHS and education outlays	147455	162856	181182	207815	228115	265347	288844	302283
% HHS-related	15.0	14.9	14.8	12.9	14.7	12.7	12.1	11.6
Department of The Treasury								
State and local fiscal assistance trust fund	6760	6823	6848	6829	5137	4569	4567	4567
Anti-recession fiscal assistance fund	1699	1329	*	–	–	–	–	–
Urban-related Treasury	8459	8152	6848	6829	5137	4569	4567	4567
Total Treasury outlays	49560	56355	56044	76691	93372	110521	118025	134997
% Treasury outlays	17.1	14.5	10.5	8.9	5.5	4.1	3.9	3.4
Department of Labor								
Employment and training assistance[i]	3291	4764	6158	7065	6848	4110	3724	3595
Urban-related, DOL	3291	4764	6158	7065	6848	4110	3724	3595
Total DOL outlays	22374	22890	22649	29724	30084	30736	42995	34268
% DOL outlays	14.7	20.8	27.2	23.8	22.8	13.4	8.7	10.5

Table 5.4 Continued.

Department and program	1977	1978	1979	1980	1981	1982	1983	1984
Total urban-related outlays	47631	55465	59454	65508	69640	66281	66184	63377
Urban-related outlays (without Medicaid)	37918	44785	47047	51551	52807	48890	46858	42578
Total Federal outlays	400506	448368	490997	576674	657204	728375	805202	848483
Urban outlays as % of Federal outlays	11.9	12.4	12.1	11.4	10.6	9.1	8.2	7.5
% change urban-related spending	22.94	16.45	7.19	10.18	6.31	−4.82	−0.15	−4.24
% change urban spending (without Medicaid)	25.66	18.11	5.05	9.57	2.44	−7.42	−4.16	−9.13
Real urban outlays (1972 $)	32795	35346	34762	35016	34583	31469	30043	27230
% change urban outlays	7.13	7.78	−1.65	0.73	−1.24	−9.00	−4.53	−9.36
Real urban outlays (without Medicare)	26107	28540	27508	27556	26224	23212	21270	18293
% change real urban outlays (without Medicaid)	17.83	9.32	−3.62	0.17	−4.83	−11.49	−8.37	−14.00

aNo outlays

bLess than $500,000.

cMiscellaneous appropriations represent the remaining outlays of the model cities program and the community development training and urban fellowship programs. Model cities was terminated in 1975 and the others in 1973.

dDollar amounts for the Federal highway administration's urbanized areas program represent obligations rather than outlays. The *Budget Appendix* does not supply information on outlays at that level of the program.

eUrban-related outlays may exceed total outlays for an agency due to additional revenue from other sources. In 1982 and 1984, loan repayments from the disaster loan fund created additional revenue which reduced total outlays.

fThe increase in 1980 CSA spending results from the energy assistance program which represented $1,160,000 in obligations.

gEducation outlays are combined in order to simplify the many organizational changes which took place between the Departments of Health, Education and Welfare and Education. Two programs were included in FY 1977 to 1980: elementary and secondary education and emergency school aid. Emergency school aid became the equal educational opportunities program in 1980. The program structure changed in FY 1981 and three new programs replaced the two existing ones. From FY1981 to 1984, compensatory education for the disadvantaged, special programs and populations, and bilingual education have been included in the education category.

hThe dollar amounts for the health services administration, grants to the states for Medicaid, assistance payments program, and grants for social and child welfare services represent obligations rather than outlays.

iYouth programs are included in employment and training assistance.

Source: US *Budget Appendix* (annual). Calculated and elaborated by Glickman (see note 69)

seem to be the cornerstone of this policy, thus favoring social groups and localities that benefit from selective affluence, in a context in which income inequality in the US is increasing substantially, as shown in chapter 4.

Glickman has tried to apply to the 1981–4 data a methodology similar to that used by Vernez to analyze the spatial impact of Federal spending in the 1970–6 period. Table 5.5 shows some limited calculations for concentration ratios of Federal spending by ecological characteristics in 1981–4.

We can easily appreciate that practically all urban-welfare-related expenses, with the exception of the Small Business Administration, are much more heavily concentrated in central cities than in suburbs; and we have seen that these programs are the ones that have been cut. Central cities, then, have suffered proportionally more than suburbs from the shrinkage of the urban welfare state. Also, although the trends here are somewhat less clear, small cities have generally higher concentration ratios for most programs, implying that medium-sized and large cities with their greater social problems have suffered more also from the cutbacks. Finally, although we do not have concentration ratios for 1981–84 for the remaining variables, it may be assumed that the general trends are probably very similar to those calculated by Vernez for 1970–6. If this were the case, we could observe the relationship between the variation of Federal spending by program in 1981–4 and the concentration rate of each program in each type of locality, as presented in table 5.5.

From these observations we can conclude, in general terms, that programs having suffered substantial cutbacks in 1981–4 are concentrated more than proportionally in low-income cities (with the exception of mass transit), in high-hardship cities (with the exception of vocational education and work-incentive programs) and in declining cities (with the same exceptions). The shrinkage of the welfare state tends to be spatially specific: the harder-hit a type of locality, the more likely it is to receive the burden of budget cuts. On the contrary, booming defense spending in 1981–4, and particularly procurement, is associated with suburbs rather than with central cities; with small and medium-sized cities; with high-income, rapidly growing, low-unemployment, low-hardship localities.

There is undoubtedly a process of spatial polarization that stems from the crisis of the urban welfare state and is being spearheaded by the rise of the new warfare state. Is this a short-term trend or the beginning of a broader development? To answer this question it will be necessary first to examine the spatial consequences of defense policy, under the conditions generated by technological change.

High Technology, Industrial Policy, and the Warfare State

The current technological revolution poses a fundamental challenge to the warfare state. If it fails to master the formidable discoveries occurring at an

Table 5.5 Concentration ratios for selected programs by city type

Program	Real % outlay change, 1981–4	All cities	Low-income	High-income	Declining	Slow-growing	Rapidly growing
State and local fiscal assistance	−11.5	1.00	1.08	0.92	1.04	0.87	0.99
Employment and training (CETA)	−47.6	2.41	1.22	0.78	0.99	0.94	1.18
Community development block grants	−24.8	1.91	1.41	0.60	1.03	0.92	0.94
Urban mass transit assistance	−21.9	2.24	0.75	1.23	1.35	0.31	0.13
Vocational education	−7.4	2.39	1.19	0.81	0.84	1.04	2.32
Work incentive program (WIN)	−93.9	1.82	1.08	0.91	0.98	1.01	1.04
Small business administration	−88.2	1.50	1.06	0.93	0.96	1.04	1.18
Defense	+37.0		0.95	1.04	0.78	1.45	1.42
Construction	+53.9	0.58	0.61	1.62	0.38	1.42	5.44
Payroll	+11.4	–	1.23	0.78	0.63	1.68	1.98
Procurement	+61.7	–	0.80	1.19	0.86	1.32	1.05

Explanatory note: Columns 1 and 2 represent per capita income in 1970. Low-income cities are defined by per capita income less than or equal to $3.304; high-income cities have per capita income greater than $3,304. Columns 3, 4, and 5 are defined by population growth between 1970 and 1975; declining cities exhibited negative growth, slow growth cities grew by less than 15% over the period, and rapid growth cities grew by greater than 15%. Columns 6 and 7 define 'low' and 'high' unemployment by a 1976 unemployment rate of less than, or greater than or equal to 8.9%, respectively. Columns 8 and 9 are based on a hardship index of 100. Finally, city size is defined by cities with populations of less than 100,000 for small cities. 100,000–300,000 for medium cities, and greater than 300,000 for large cities.
Calculated and elaborated by Glickman (see note 69)

Low-unem-ployment	High-unem-ployment	Low-hardship	High hardship	Small	Medium	Large	Central	Suburbs
0.90	1.05	0.79	1.17	0.76	0.96	1.10	1.08	0.63
1.10	0.93	0.97	1.01	0.65	1.59	0.87	1.13	0.42
1.01	0.99	0.81	1.14	0.89	1.45	0.84	1.04	0.80
0.28	1.41	0.26	1.53	0.09	0.60	1.51	1.18	0.17
1.76	0.56	1.26	0.72	0.87	2.19	0.54	1.19	0.13
1.51	0.70	0.99	0.94	0.68	2.07	0.66	1.19	0.13
1.02	0.98	0.91	1.07	0.69	1.11		1.06	1.07
1.18	0.89	1.33	0.72	1.12	1.27	0.83	0.80	1.48
1.96	0.44	1.72	0.40	0.78	0.70	1.21	1.15	0.33
1.39	0.77	1.31	0.73	0.87	1.31	0.91	1.06	0.70
1.06	0.96	1.34	0.71	1.26	1.26	0.78	0.78	1.93

Source: Concentration ratios from Vernez (see footnote 48). Changes in budget outlays are computed from *Special Analyses, the Budget of the United States Government.* Fiscal Years 1983 and 1984. Defense outlays are computed from *The Budget of the United States Government,* fiscal years 1983 and 1984. Calculated and elaborated by Glickman (see note 69)

ever-accelerating pace, its weaponry will become obsolete. As a result, political and diplomatic means would gain the preference as the predominant form of managing international crises, thus undermining the main rationale supporting the institutions of the warfare state. On the contrary, if the state succeeds in finding and utilizing new information technologies, it could dramatically improve its power by gaining a performance edge over its rivals, and by making possible flexible uses of military force adapted to a diversity of geopolitical situations. In sum, its global reach could be decentralized and specifically targeted. The power of technology could substantially enhance the technology of power.[72]

To be sure, the military use of technology has generally been a driving force in the development and application of scientific discoveries, although the case of Japan in the past twenty years shows that there is no universal rule in this matter.[73] In the US, World War II brought together a number of scientific breakthroughs that developed into major applications in such areas as aircraft design, jet propulsion, electronics, communications, and nuclear power. The global arms race triggered off by the cold war stimulated the frantic search for a technological lead that would enable military supremacy to be attained.[74] Given the national priority accorded to such programs, resources were mobilized toward this goal with relative ease, transforming the US into what Daniel Bell calls a "mobilized polity," that is, "a society in which the major resources of the country are concentrated on a few specific objectives defined by the Government."[75] In Bell's words: "In one sense . . . military technology has supplanted the 'mode of production' in Marx's use of the term, as a major determinant of social structure."[76] Between 1945 and 1990, the US will have spent on defense about $3.7 trillion (in constant 1972 dollars),[77] that is, enough to buy everything in America, with the exception of land. Defense spending averaged about 7 percent of US GNP per year.[78] To some extent, "military Keynesianism" has been repeatedly used to stimulate the market during the downturn of the business cycle, particularly during the Reagan administration: defense spending is credited *directly* with at least 0.5 percent of GNP growth and 20 percent of employment gains during the 1982–4 recovery.[79]

Between 1981 and 1985 defense outlays increased by 60 percent and Defense Department spending more than doubled in real terms, the annual increase jumping from 2.8 percent during the Carter administration to an average of about 7.5 percent under the Reagan administration.[80] In the mid-1980s, Defense accounted for, on average, about one-third of the annual Federal budget, a total in excess of $300 billion. In addition to its role in boosting the economy, defense spending is particularly stimulating for US manufacturing in the short term, because, as Ann Markusen has pointed out, the Defense Department requires most of the production to take place in the US, slowing down the tendency toward offshoring by US companies.[81]

The role of defense is particularly important in research, with an emphasis on information technologies. In the mid-1980s, the Department of Defense accounted for about 60 percent of the total research budget of the Federal government. This proportion increased to 90 percent of Federal spending for applied research in electrical engineering, and to 88 percent of applied research in computer sciences.[82] The role of the Defense Department has continued to expand during the 1980s, particularly strongly in the field of research and technological development as a result of the priority accorded to the SDI Program, so that by 1988 the Defense Department accounted for over 70 percent of the Federal R&D Budget.[83] This emphasis on the connection between defense and high technology has already had dramatic effects in the labor market for engineers and scientists. In 1986, estimates from the Congressional Budget Office indicated that the Department of Defense or defense-related industries employed 47 percent of all aeronautical engineers in the US, 30.3 percent of the mathematicians, 24.4 percent of the physicists, 18.3 percent of the electrical engineers, 15.7 percent of the industrial and mechanical technicians, and 28 percent of the total number of science and engineering graduates. However, in 1987–8 defense appropriations were slowed down by political opposition and budgetary constraints, making it unlikely that such dramatic rates of growth in defense spending would continue in the post-Reagan era. Nevertheless, the strong link between high-technology-induced growth and defense policy will remain. The relative containment of defense spending (at a level of about 30 percent of the Federal budget) will feed back into the restructuring of the defense budget itself. There will be lower allocations of funds to personnel, administration, and traditional military procurement, while investment in the design, production, and maintenance of technologically sophisticated weapons systems will be stepped up. Thus, in all likelihood, the new warfare state, with its core in high-technology warfare systems – both strategic and tactical – will continue to expand even in a period of fiscal austerity that will slow down defense spending.

We should not conclude that defense spending and military-oriented research are the result of policies designed to favor economic growth. In fact, most of the existing evidence points to the opposite conclusion: that the predominance of defense interests in economic policies and research programs actually undermines American economic competitiveness and leads technological innovation into commercial dead-ends, contributing to America's economic decline.[84] Leontieff and Duchin have shown that military expenditures are less expansionary than other public expenditures;[85] Gold, Paine, and Shields argue that military expenditures create fewer jobs that other forms of investment;[86] Robert Reich thinks that excessive emphasis on defense spending is at the root of the increasing trade gap with Japan and western Europe;[87] Ann Markusen, while acknowledging the short-term stimulant effect of defense spending, insists on its slow diffusion in the economy and, above all, opposes its racist, sexist biases, and its distorting impacts on regional development;[88] Lloyd J. Dumas shows the limits and deformations inherent in university research on Pentagon-related contracts;[89] David Noble argues that excessive military specification has hampered US technological development, citing as an example the case of numerical machine tools, a key new technology in which the Japanese took over most of the commercial market because of the narrow definition of objectives when the technology was first developed in the US under contract with the Defense Department;[90] Mary Kaldor even objects to the military effectiveness of the "baroque arsenal" produced under the new technological conditions, with "overdeveloped" and unnecessarily sophisticated new weapons.[91] In a more balanced analysis, Jay Stowsky[92] examines different key examples of inter-actions between defense and industry in developing new technologies, to conclude that

the creation of military–industrial firms, of a military-dependent and uncompetitive industry structure, is aided by military programs that focus on the development of specific military product applications instead of promoting the general technological state-of-the-art; that draw the attention of commercial producers away from the development of technological applications consistent with the commercial market requirements of the involved industry toward esoteric, over-sophisticated military applications; that rely on sole-source contracts and cost-plus, weapons-competitive production technologies instead of promoting competitive product development and efficient, generalizable production technologies; that promote small-batch, "one-of-a-kind" custom production instead of mass production or flexible sophistication aimed at creating economies of scale and scope; that disrupt established technological trajectories and investment patterns in mature industries or that skew the techno-logical development trajectory of brand-new industries by pointing them in a single, defense-oriented direction; that routinely reward established suppliers over small, innovative start-ups; that restrict the diffusion of military-sponsored advances through technological oversophistication or direct export and publication controls; and that do all or most of these things in the face of parallel, commercially-oriented R&D projects sponsored by foreign competitors and aimed explicitly at advancing the commercial state-of-the-art over the same time span as the military program.

The problem, then, is how to explain the decisive role of the Defense Department in Federal spending and research policy in spite of its poor contribution to economic performance.[93] The most popular explanation of this trend is the influence of the military–industrial complex,[94] a hypothesis to which President Eisenhower himself contributed when he stated in his 1961 farewell address that "The Military Establishment, not productive of itself, necessarily must feed on the energy, productivity and brain power of the country, and if it takes too much, our total strength declines."[95] Some more sophisticated analyses add to the direct influence of the defense industry the political influence of the defense lobby, that is the several dozen Congressmen and Senators whose constituencies are major recipients of defense spending.[96] Both arguments are true, but neither is sufficient as an explanation. Both implicitly assume a very primitive, almost conspiratorial, theory of the state. State policies and decisions result from the interplay of contradictory social, cultural, and economic interests. But, above all, they result from political decisions, that is, strategies aimed at holding power, either as a means or as a goal. This is particularly true for the state of a major nation with global responsibilities. Thus, the fundamental goal of defense policy, regardless of its economic impact, is the strengthening of US national security, as perceived by its elected leaders. As former Secretary of Defense Caspar Weinberger has said: "Even if achieving the security needed for [peace with freedom] meant some dislocation in the economy – and it does not today – who would suggest any other course?"[97] All other elements in the formation of defense policy, including economic growth and job creation, political clientelism toward some regions, concessions to the defense lobby, the reinforcement of military bureaucracy – all are important, yet all remain subordinate to the primary objective of achieving global supremacy. In pursuit of such supremacy, the Pentagon has been a major force in technology planning, and through the combined effect of spending and shaping technology, has constituted the only systemic industrial policy in the US, as a by-product of its political goals.[98] The evidence and analyses on the relationship between defense, technology, and economic growth may be summarized as follows:

(1) Defense capabilities depend upon technological excellence. Therefore, the Defense Department has concentrated its efforts in R&D in a number of key areas, particularly in aerospace and information technologies.
(2) In so doing, the Pentagon has guided and stimulated technological development, and created huge markets on which hundreds of companies have prospered, some of them among the biggest and most successful in US industry. At the same time, a military–industrial complex, personally and politically linked to the defense-related industrial bonanza, has flourished, creating powerful vested interests in the continuation of such policies.
(3) Nevertheless, the Defense Department's goals are fundamentally to ensure military performance and to reinforce its own bureaucratic power within the state. Personal rewards, economic success, or commercial spin-offs are only by-products of a fundamental political strategy to develop technology in the first instance for its military use.

It is true, then, that defense policy is the major, if implicit, industrial policy in the US; that its core lies in its connection with high-technology industries; that this industrial policy is not the best possible policy, given the short-sightedness of its perspective, its socially undesirable effects, and its poor performance in promoting commercial applications of key technologies; yet that, because the ultimate goals of defense policy are not economic or scientific, but political, defense-oriented industrial technological growth has been, and will most likely continue to be, a fundamental line of development for the US economy, actually constituting the core of high-technology research and manufacturing in the US.

The relationship between defense and the electronics industry was particularly close in the first stage of development of the industry, during the 1950s.[99] Around 1960, government markets represented 90 percent of the US semiconductors market.[100] However, once commercial development of electronic products had taken place, with the entry into the market of new, innovative companies, the proportion plummetted down to about 10 percent in the late 1970s. Indeed, some major discoveries, such as that of the microprocessor by Ted Hoff at Intel in 1971, were totally independent of military support. The trend, however, was once more reversed during the 1980s, and this is what is qualitatively new about the Reagan administration's defense build-up. In quantitative terms, this administration's policy did not depart dramatically from former levels of defense spending when calculated as a percentage of GNP. Even compared with the two previous build-ups, during the Korean and Vietnam wars (see table 5.6), Reagan's defense spending was not significantly higher in relative terms. What was really fundamentally different about policy under Reagan was the concentration of defense spending in military procurement, and its emphasis on new technologies and new weapons systems. In her analysis of the relationship between defense and high-technology industries, whose data are shown in table 5.7, Ann Markusen found that "of the top twenty defense manufacturing sectors, only ship-building and non-ferrous foundries were not high tech. In addition, the military oriented sectors in table [5.7] accounted for 47 percent of all high-tech manufacturing jobs in the 1977 Census of Manufacturers, or approximately 2.25 million jobs. By 1984, given the recent build-up, they undoubtedly account for an even higher percentage."[101]

Table 5.7 shows that the projected defense output growth for computers in the 1982–7 period was 141 percent, well above the average for other defense sectors. Also, the Pentagon has involved itself more deeply in the planning of research on strategic technologies. The Defense Advanced Research Project Agency (DARPA), famed for its managerial flexibility and its bold understanding of scientific research,[102] has launched a number of ambitious programs, connecting leading universities and high-technology companies in defense-targeted research programs, among them, the "Very High Speed Integrated Circuits" program (VHSIC), and the Strategic Computing Initiative (SCI). VHSIC aims at developing advanced custom chips of 1.25 micron and then sub-micron size, through cooperation between researchers and companies coordinated by DARPA.[103] Although Brueckner and Borrus have questioned the commercial value of this program,[104] it does represent a major breakthrough in technological planning in the US. Similarly, the Strategic Computing Initiative aims to achieve a quantum leap in artificial intelligence and development of parallel computer architectures, by distributing research funds and potential markets among different firms and research organizations.[105] In this case, DARPA plays two roles simultaneously: that of the venture capitalist and that of the client setting up product specifications. Here too, criticisms have been levelled against the excessively specialized character of the technologies being developed.[106] Yet, the initiative represents a further step in computer software research and in the guidance of such research by military programs. Finally, in 1987 the Defense Department mobilized its political and financial resources to help major electronics corporations set up a large research facility concentrating on manufacturing technology for semiconductors, a critical area in which the Japanese have taken the lead over the US. Because of the national security implications of this, with the possibility of the US becoming dependent upon Japanese chips in the near future, the Defense Department sponsored the creation of an applied research consortium, SEMATECH, to be located in Austin, Texas. Semiconductors manufacturers supported the initiative enthusiastically despite the significant departure it represented from their libertarian ideas about the undesirability of government interference.[107]

It is clear, then, that the acceleration of the technological revolution, and its particular emphasis on information technologies, represents a qualitatively different stage in the close interaction among the military, technological change, and industrial development. The defense policy of the Reagan administration had in fact three different components: first, and most publicized, a particularly strong defense commitment, linked to Reagan's conservative ideology and explicitly presented to the American public; secondly, a turnaround in US foreign policy toward a more assertive role in the world after the relative decline of US hegemony in the 1970s; thirdly, and perhaps the most lasting element, a renewed effort to use technology as a decisive tool to translate the scientific leadership of the US in the field of information technologies into military superiority. This defense policy is not confined to the ideology and politics of the Reagan administration: in its

Table 5.6 Three US military build-ups: Korean War, Vietnam War, and Reagan

	Change in national defense budget share (%)	Change in military burden (% GNP)	Increase in defense budget outlays ($ bn; 1972 $)
Korean War (1950–3)	29.1–65.6	4.7–13.8	29.7–96.6
Vietnam War (1965–8)	40.1–44.0	7.2– 9.5	69.3–101.7
Reagan (1981–7)	23.2–32.6	5.2– 7.4	71.3–118.9

Source: Office of the Assistant Secretary of Defense (Comptroller), National Defense Budget Estimates for Fiscal Year 1983, tables 7.8 and 7.2. Reagan projections from Executive Office of the President, Office of Management and Budget, Budget of the United States Government, Fiscal Year 1985, pp. 2–11, 9–61. Defense spending is equivalent to national defense function budget outlays. Compiled by Mosley (see note 23).

Table 5.7 Major Defense Industrial Base Sectors, Employment and Defense Shares

SIC	Industry	Employment (000)		% change 1977–82	Defense 1982 BIE[a]	Defense share 1983 DEIMS[a]	Output growth[b]
		1977	1982				
3721	Aircraft	222.8	286.6	+29	270	65	+59
3761	Missiles	93.9	99.6	+6	68	65	+64
3724	Aircraft engine	106.3	128.6	+21	54	64	+33
3764	Missile propulsion	17.0	25.2	+48	54	64	+33
3728	Aircraft parts	101.9	146.1	+43	41	57	+35
3769	Missile parts	10.9	20.5	+88	41	57	+35
3662	Radio, TV, communications equipment	333.0	471.3	+42	58	61	+54
3811	Engineering and scientific institutions	42.2	43.1	+2	34	49	+60
3674	Semiconductors	114.0	164.5	+44	13	23	+51
3675–9	Other electronic devices	228.0	315.8	+39	17	29	+49
3822	Measuring devices	197.0	246.0	+20	n.a	35	n.a
3883	Optical instruments	29.9	50.6	+69	28	17	+38
3489	Ordnance	19.0	27.4	+44	78	100	+35
3731	Shipbuilding	176.4	168.5	−5	62	75	+24
3483	Ammunition (excl. small arms)	20.6	23.3	+13	91	98	+56
2892	Explosives	11.5	11.9	+3	34	44	+59
3795	Tanks	12.1	18.0	+49	94	99	+47
3484	Small arms	17.5	17.5	0	14	66	−43
3482	Small arms ammunition	12.2	10.1	−17	25	n.a.	+130
3573	Computers	193.7	339.6	+75	7	n.a.	+141

Sources:

[a] Shutt, 1984. From the Department of Defense. DEIMS (Defense Economic Impact Monitoring System), using an input-output model from DRI.

[b] Henry, 1983. From Bureau of Industrial Economics, Department of Commerce, input-output model. These appear to be lower than the following column because of different methods of incorporating foreign sales. Both chart indirect as well as direct demand impacts. Complied by Markusen (see note 81).

essential aspects it represents the emergence of the new warfare state, reassessing its technological foundations. The Strategic Defense Initiative (SDI) appears to be the most ambitious development along these lines, and the clearest example of the close and politically determined relationship between new technologies and the warfare state. Because of the importance of this program in the present analysis, it will be examined here in some detail. By using "Star Wars" as a case study, we will try to gain a better understanding of the social logic of the new defense policy, its relationship to high technology, and its implications for the economic and spatial restructuring of the United States.

The New Technological Frontier of the Warfare State: The "Star Wars" Program. A Case Study

Introduction

Much has been written, and even more speculated, on the importance of the Strategic Defense Initiative (SDI – popularly known as "Star Wars"), the military–technological program undertaken by the Reagan administration in 1983.[108] Its significance can hardly be overestimated. However impossible it is to achieve its explicit goal (an efficient shield against attacking ICBMs), it is likely to alter the military–political balance of power in the world; if pursued, it would constitute one of the most formidable technological programs in humankind's history, surpassing the ambitions and dimensions of the Manhattan project or the Apollo program. Furthermore, I would argue that it represents a qualitatively new relationship between the dynamics of the state, technological innovation, and economic growth. Thus, its significance goes well beyond its actual implementation. It could well happen that the new administration would limit the scope of SDI as a specific program; but if my analysis is correct, what will probably last for the forseeable future is an increasingly close relationship between the warfare state and the cutting edge of technological development. Advances in information technology, laser, and new materials, and their application to military strategy will be decisive in world power relationships in years to come. Given the political priority of military-oriented technological policies, what SDI truly represents is not so much a strategic doctrine (which could prove unfeasible) as a new organizational–technological formula aimed at harnessing technology and high-technology industry for the assertion of American power in the world against growing challenges to it.

Many of the technologies targeted by SDI were already under development in different sectors of the American defense research complex. What SDI did was to organize these technologies into a system, and to provide political support and greater budgetary resources for their development, within a co-ordinated program directed and implemented by a new, specialized unit within the Pentagon: the SDI Office (SDIO), more flexible and more autonomous than any other bureaucratic unit of the defense establishment. Such a concerted effort is indeed producing significant changes in the defense industry and in research policy in the United States. It also contributes to the emerging shape of the new urban and regional structure, in ways that will be explored in the next section of this chapter.

By focusing on the origins, development, and implications of SDI, and trying to understand its spatial dimension, we are in fact addressing a broader issue: the political determination of the uses to which new technologies are being put in the production of a new socio-economic organization. To present this analysis in a systematic form, I will proceed step by step: first, I will try to substantiate my hypothesis according to which, SDI is, above anything else, a political strategy: secondly, I will examine its actual military and organizational content as it relates to basic technological choices; thirdly, I will examine the industrial policy component of SDI, and its likely impact on the economy; and finally, I will elaborate on the urban and regional dimension of the political–military–technological–economic processes spearheaded and articulated by SDI. (This last analysis will be presented in the next section of this chapter.)

SDI and the State

When, on 23 March 1983, President Reagan wished upon a star, aiming at the obsolescence of strategic nuclear weapons through revolutionary technologies, he may have surprised observers, and even many in the Pentagon; yet he was giving voice to a deliberate, well grounded political strategy that responded to at least six layers of factors, all of them fundamental elements in the dynamics of the modern global state.[109]

First of all, the major technological revolution through which we are living was to become the key factor in determining world power. Of course, technology has always been closely connected to the state and to the military. Yet with the exception of the short period when the US had the monopoly on the A-bomb, this is the first time in recent history in which technological superiority becomes the central factor in achieving military, and thus political, supremacy. The US is aiming at a quantum leap in its warfare capabilities, taking on the Soviet Union in the one area in which the latter's ability to compete is seriously undermined by the very characteristics of its social system: the development of information technologies. By rendering strategic weapons less effective, and by ensuring a technological edge in greatly strengthened armed forces, the US could succeed in stalling the deterioration of its power in the aftermath of the Vietnam War and as a consequence of the Soviet achievement of parity in strategic nuclear terms.[110] New technologies, with all their implications in terms of human, institutional, and economic capabilities to sustain a scientific arms race, became the corner-stone of state power in an increasingly interdependent planet.

Secondly, the array of new technologies envisaged by SDI are not confined to strategic nuclear weapons; they will have a substantial impact on conventional weapons. It is debatable whether SDI, as programmed, is indeed a non-nuclear program (or a 90 percent nuclear-free program) as its advocates claim. But it does represent a shift away from a nuclear-based, strategically oriented military strategy to technologically advanced "smart weapons," susceptible of being used in conventional, non-nuclear warfare. In this sense, it represents the development of the new line of military thinking that emerged after the Vietnam War,[111] when the greatest military power in the world found its ability to react to perceived aggressions or encroachment on its sphere of influence paralyzed because of the combination of two factors: on the one hand, Soviet nuclear power would deter any crisis of major proportions that could risk world peace (the reciprocal argument is, of course, also true); and on the other hand, direct American involvement in military conflicts had become too costly, and generally unacceptable to the American public after the unforgettable tragedy of Vietnam, as demonstrated by strong opposition to direct intervention in Central America. Under these circum-stances, new options were sought to enable American power to exercise itself. Symbolic actions, such as that in Grenada, were effective, but limited. Covert operations, and open support for counter-insurgency (in El Salvador), or to insurgency (the Contras in Nicaragua; Unita in Angola) could be instru-mental in the application of pressure, but could not by themselves deal with major regional military conflicts. US forces still needed the means to intervene "surgically" in any area of the world that might be required; if for no other reason, then to be able to make credible threats that could reinforce the US position in the lower levels of conflict, without necessarily leading to escalation. It is within this perspective that new technologies, and particularly communications, electronics, and a new generation of aircraft armed with precision guided weapons, play a decisive role. To some extent, new technologies are making conventional warfare possible again, at low cost for the holder of superior technology. Advances in microelectronics and computing are required not only to counter Soviet ICBMs, but to overcome the threat posed by Soviet SA-7s or French Exocets in the hands of a hostile Third World army. By assuring its technological superiority, the US military would once more be able to protect the interests of the western world, at a cost politically acceptable to the American public. A striking illustration of this new, "surgical" strategy for military intervention on the basis of advanced conventional weapons was the bombing of Qadhafi's residence in Tripoli, in retaliation for his support of international terrorism. Several observers have pointed to the fact that the actual objective of the raid was to kill the Libyan leader with a high-precision guided bomb fired from a speeding jet. The strategy worked only approximately: the bomb hit the children's room.

The main fact to retain from this analysis is that SDI-induced military technologies are not confined to this illusion of an anti-ballistic shield. They represent a fundamental breakthrough in warfare, mainly because of the precision with which they can be applied, as well as their flexibility in handling. These new military technologies could allow for a greater adaptation of the use of force to the specific conditions under which a global power has to operate at different moments and in different areas, thus linking the military instrument to the new political–military strategy of restrained, but continuous, intervention in the global arena. In this sense, we can use the term of the warfare state literally, because current technological programs are aimed, fundamentally, at returning to the state its warfare capabilities.

In the third place, the political dimension of SDI is not limited to the military expression of state power; it also refers to the search for legitimacy, in one of the most paradoxical twists of world politics in the last decade. SDI was, at least in its origins, a political response from the Reagan administration to the growing strength of the peace movement worldwide, and in the US in particular.[112] Accepting the ideals of eternal peace and of permanent banning of nuclear weapons, it provided a technological solution to the problem that, unlike political negotiations between two sides, relied solely on America's ingenuity and resources. The utopian tone of the White House's proclamations was in quest of new legitimacy among the peace-conscious, anti-nuclear "yuppie" voters, who are becoming the new political mainstream in US elections. Both Reagan himself and the Pentagon insisted on the non-nuclear character of the program, going as far as not to adopt some of the technical proposals made by Edward Teller so as visibly not to comply with his pro-nuclear bias. In spite of later developments that seem to accept a "minor" nuclear component in the program, SDI's officials have systematically emphasized its defensive and non-nuclear characteristics, thus giving in, at least apparently, to the universal demands for peace and nuclear disarmament. The strategy seemed to work, at least initially in the US: public opinion polls in 1984–6 showed *simultaneously* support for SDI and a majority opinion for nuclear disarmament.[113]

Aside from the real purpose of the program, SDI's ideological appeal consists in playing on a very old and deep-rooted American utopian faith in the solution of all problems through a technological fix. Belief in science and technology is the religion of the informational age. Playing powerful roles in terms of both the coercive capacity and the ideological legitimacy of the state, "Star Wars" reveals itself as an attempt at establishing political hegemony on new historical ground.

In 1987 the Reagan administration seized the opportunity offered by greater openness in Soviet policy under Gorbachev and, in spite of all its rhetoric, engaged in nuclear arms reductions agreements with the Soviet Union of historic significance. At the same time, it maintained its commitment to SDI, a commitment that became non-negotiable in the summit meetings. The logic underlying this position is that the nuclear arms race does not allow the US to gain the strategic advantage over the Soviet Union, is militarily risky and politically unpopular; while on the other hand, American technological superiority could gain the upper hand over the USSR's military power in the long term through a gradual process of reducing to obsolescence Soviet military equipment.This is precisely why the Soviet Union is so fearful of "Star Wars," and is also why Pentagon strategists will continue to give the highest priority to the technological weapons race.

The analysis of SDI presented up to this point has focused on the long-term, structurally determined tendencies of the American state, as they express the interests of the social system in which it is rooted. Yet state policies are also the result of the strategies of individual actors defending their own specific interests on the basis of their influence in the power networks to which they have access. It is this interplay between the historical interests of the system and the particular interests of powerful individual actors that generates the complexity of any particular political process, such as that leading to the formulation and implementation of SDI. The fourth factor to be taken into consideration, then, is the influence of the defense lobby, or the military–industrial complex, as it is labeled, in US politics.[114] It is unquestionable that defense contracts, which looked like running out of steam once the last programs (the MX missile, the Midgetman missile, the B-1 bomber) were wound up or cancelled, found in SDI a new driving force with the political strength to foster the defense build-up and, following on down the line, to renew the entire military hardware through induced technological obsolescence. As the spearhead of the new advance in defense procurement, "Star Wars" propels some of the most powerful companies into hyperactivity. According to Seymour Melman, by 1980, for every $100 of capital investment in the civilian economy, the US put $38 into the military. In 1988 the same ratio could be 100:87.[115] Many of the defense contracts are concentrated in only a few companies, with long-established ties to the navy, army, and air force, and this pattern seems to be reproduced in the case of "Star Wars." While the first $2 billion in research contracts for "Star Wars" was spread among 1,500 companies, the top ten "Star Wars" contracts accounted for 60 percent of the funds distribution up to 1985.[116] In 1987, as table 5.8 shows, it is generally the same large companies who specialize in the production of missiles, aircraft, and related electronic equipment, with the addition of the major national laboratories. True, the research money involved is relatively small by Pentagon standards: about $10 billion in 1984–7, maybe $39 billion in 1988–92 (see table 5.9);[117] but should the system come to be deployed, it would be the most expensive military program in history (and, therefore, the largest market ever); estimates widely vary for figures between $400 billion and $1.6 trillion, since no one really knows what such a system would involve. In any event, what is certain is the gigantic scale of such military markets, and their potential spin-offs in a wide range of industries: electronics, materials,

Table 5.8   Top 20 SDI contractors (March 1987)

Rank	Organization	Contracts awarded ($m)
1	Lockheed	1,024
2	General Motors (Hughes Aircraft)	734
3	TRW	567
4	Lawrence Livermore Lab	552
5	McDonnell Douglas	485
6	Boeing	475
7	EG&G	468
8	Los Alamos Lab	458
9	General Electric	420
10	Rockwell International	369
11	Massachusetts Institute of Technology (MIT)	353
12	Raytheon	248
13	LTV	227
14	Fluor	198
15	Grumman	193
16	Gencorp	191
17	Teledyne	189
18	Honeywell	151
19	Martin Marietta	134
20	Textron	118

Source: Federation of American Scientists; reprinted in High Technology Business (December 1987). Compiled by Jay Stowsky.

nuclear reactors, weapons procurement and ordnance, etc. This is the reason why companies seek from the outset to position themselves in the research stage of the program: companies with inside knowledge of the technological options adopted for each part of the system will have a decisive advantage in securing future contracts. Given the high business stakes involved, it is not surprising that these interests have been fully mobilized to assure the success of the "Star Wars" policy. A particularly crucial effect is the influence exerted on numerous representatives whose constituencies grow ever more dependent on military-induced funding to shift from traditional manufacturing to high-technology industries. Yet, though this factor is important, it is not the only one, or even the predominant one, that explains the rise of "Star Wars." This is because the defense lobby is a permanent feature of the American political system.[118] Given the opportunity, its influence greatly expands, and it becomes a driving force in obtaining a substantial share of the Federal budget; but this opportunity is itself generated by forces and considerations that go far beyond the defense lobby, as we already stated. True, it is likely that during the Reagan administration a new political elite, with Western and Southern roots, has consolidated its position, and reinforced the access of the defense-related businesses to the higher circles of power. Yet the military-industrial complex is an old feature of the system, and there is no evidence

Table 5.9 Strategic defense Initiative budget authority ($), by types of weapons and services

	Actual				Total	Requested					Total
	1984	1985	1986	1987	1984–7	1988	1989	1990	1991	1992	1988–92
Surveillance, acquisition, and tracking	367	546	847	911	2,671	1,493	1,859	–	–	–	–
Directed energy	323	377	803	844	2,347	1,104	1,246	–	–	–	–
Kinetic energy	196	256	596	729	1,777	1,075	1,200	–	–	–	–
Systems analysis and battle management	83	100	211	387	781	627	787	–	–	–	–
Support	23	118	230	358	729	922	1,190	–	–	–	–
DoD total	992	1,397	2,687	3,229	8,305	5,221	6,282	7,400	8,400	9,800	37,103
DoE total	118	224	285	514	1,141	569	390	390	390	390	2,129
SDI total	1,110	1,621	2,972	3,743	9,446	5,790	6,672	7,790	8,790	10,190	39,232

Sources: RDT&E Programs (R-1), Department of Defense Budget for Fiscal Year 1988 and 1989, January 5, 1987. Data for FY 1989–92 from SDIO budget break-down released February 25, 1987, and Congressional Budget office, *Selected Weapons Costs From the President's 1988/1989 Program*, 2 April 1987. (Reproduced from Council on Economic Priorities, *Star Wars: The Economic Fallout* (Cambridge, Mass.., Ballinger, 1988), pp. 28–9.

that defense-oriented pork-barrel politics vary very much according to the geographic or social origin of the governing elite: political decision-making is a somewhat more subtle process.

Some analysts, in fact, would argue that in this case a more important factor has been the influence of the scientific and research lobby.[119] By this, I understand an informal network of scientists and research managers that connects leading US universities, national Federal laboratories (these include 775 facilities, with total expenditures of over $15 billion per year), research branches of large companies, specialized private research firms, and Federal government agencies, particularly, though not only, the Pentagon. The most prominent institutions in this complex network are MIT's Lincoln Laboratory in Lexington, Massachusetts, the national laboratories in Livermore, California and Los Alamos, New Mexico, operated by the University of California, and the weapons-development research facility Sandia Laboratory in Albuquerque, New Mexico, initially operated also by the University of California and transferred in 1948 to ATT's management. Together these institutions probably concentrate some of the best scientific potential in the US in terms of a co-ordinated, targeted effort. DARPA, the prospective research agency of the Pentagon, has been crucial in creating bridges among the most advanced research and defense applications through generous funding, flexible procedures, and a generally good understanding of the specific dynamics of basic research.[120]

This scientific network holds tremendous power in an age in which science and technology hold the key to both military and economic superiority. It also has specific interests, namely, the enhancement of the means and resources provided by government to their ever more ambitious scientific programs, which accelerate in scope and scale with the exponential expansion of knowledge during the current technological revolution. Of course, cozy living conditions, special privileges and honors and, sometimes, participation in successful companies, are also among the rewards of the defense-connected, scientific elite. (This elite by no means encompasses the majority of the US scientific community, as widespread scientific and scholarly opposition to "Star Wars" research shows. Indeed, the majority of leading scientists in the US are opposed to "Star Wars.") The most fundamental interest of the scientific lobby, however, is to increase the organization itself, namely, to obtain indefinitely the vast resources they need to engage in activity on the new frontiers of science, in a self-reinforcing spiral of scientific discovery and military power. In the context of priorities, "Star Wars" is the dream program for the scientific lobby. Not that it represents the best way to promote research, as we have already discussed,[121] but what matters for this analysis is that development of "Star Wars" was an effective strategy to win over the US state to a renewed, massive effort in cutting-edge research in key fields of science and technology, very much in the same way that the first Soviet "Sputnik" triggered off the massive expansion of research and higher education in the US during the 1960s. Moreover, when we speak of the "scientific lobby" we are referring, mainly, to those scientists and institutions which have already been engaged in military-related research for many years, a connection that for the most prominent of them can be traced back to the Manhattan project and to work in Los Alamos, the most remarkable spin-off of which was the Lawrence Livermore Laboratory, probably the world's leading center in the design of advanced weapons.

In fact, the day-to-day story of the genesis of "Stars Wars" provides some convincing evidence on the role of the scientific lobby in inspiring the program and urging a favorable Presidential decision on it.[122] A key figure in helping to convince the President was Dr George A. Keyworth, appointed as the President's science adviser in May 1981, a post in which he served until 1985. Dr Keyworth was a nuclear physicist, closely associated with Edward Teller, the father of the H-bomb, and the founder and main supporter of the Livermore National Laboratory. Dr Teller himself appears to have played a major role in conceiving the program in its initial version, and in successfully arguing for it. As the story goes, in 1981 a group of influential scientists, industrialists, military men, and aerospace executives began to meet in Washington DC at the Heritage Foundation, a consevative "think tank." Their goal was to formulate a plan for creating a national system of defense. Among them were Dr Teller, Dr Wood, and such members of the President's "kitchen cabinet" as Joseph Coors, a beer executive; Justin Dart, a wealthy businessman, and Jacqueline Hume, an industrialist. The group's top officer was Karl R. Bendetsen, once Under Secretary of the Army, later chairman of the board of the Champion International Corporation, and a long-term member of the Hoover Institution on War, Revolution, and Peace. He had known Dr Teller, who in addition to his weapons work also held a post at Hoover, since the 1940s. The group's second-in-command was General Daniel O. Graham, now retired from the army and a former head of the Defense Intelligence Agency. All group members received security clearance enabling them to learn about and discuss secret details of new technologies and weapons.

By late 1981, dissension began to arise within the group over differing visions of how to carry out the task of space-based defense. Mr Bendetsen, Dr Teller, and the Reagan "kitchen cabinet" split off into a small group to investigate sophisticated proposals that would require much more research before being ready to apply, while General Graham and his group, known formally as High Frontier, emphasized systems that could be built primarily "off the shelf." Another factor in the split, according to General Graham, was that Dr Teller insisted on the inclusion of third-generation weapons powered by nuclear bombs. "He wanted very much to leave in the nuclear options," the General said. The split had vast implications in terms of Presidential access: Mr Bendetsen and his friends visited the White House with ease; General Graham did not.

This division went to the heart of a dispute that today haunts the Pentagon's search for a defensive shield – the rivalry between pure and applied scientists. On one side are the national laboratories and universities that carry out basic research on such directed-energy weapons as lasers and particle beams. Systems based on their results might be decades away. On the other side are contractors who want to turn dollars into demonstration projects without delay and are pushing for quick deployment of prototypes. The winners have tended to be the barons of basic research. An example can be seen at the Sandia National Laboratory, one of three facilities in the nation for the design and development of nuclear weapons. Based in Albuquerque, in 1986 it invested in a $70 million center to investigate "Star Wars" technologies. About 10 percent of the Strategic Defense Initiative's budget is devoted to the development of nuclear weapons.

The recommendation taken to the President by Mr Bendetsen, Dr Teller and their group was to start a stepped-up program of advanced research rather than trying to create a defense with "off the shelf" technology. Beyond the Teller group's role in the decision-making process, "Star Wars" largely relied on a series of research programs already underway in various laboratories, for instance, radars and computer software at the Lincoln Laboratory, lasers and supercomputers (S-1) at Livermore. The first X-ray laser, powered by a nuclear explosion, was tested as early as 14 November 1980, in the Nevada desert. "Star Wars" was the symbolic and political device that brought together a number of military research programs already underway.[123] By giving them a focus, and by linking all these military technologies to a new, articulate political strategy, it greatly expanded the resources of all the constituent programs and the power of the brains (and bodies) behind them.

At this point the key actor in the "Star Wars" saga enters: President Reagan himself. Reagan's deep personal conviction of both the need for military superiority and the route to its achievement through American-grown technology, are fundamental elements in understanding the scope, the direction, and the resources of the program.[124] In the same way that one cannot understand the French nuclear power policy, with its military dimension, without taking De Gaulle personally into account, so we need to consider Ronald Reagan's role as crucial in the formulation and development of SDI. Not only were the political elements of such a program explicitly contained in the Republican Party Electoral Platform of July 1980; Reagan's commitment to technologically based military development dates back to his period as Governor of California, and to his personal interest in the work conducted at Livermore, and especially in Teller's ideas, as early as 1967. As soon as the opportunity arose he explored the feasibility of concepts that had been hovering over the California military research establishment for many years.[125] In 1981, under the President's instruction, Caspar Weinberger asked the Pentagon's Defense Science Board to study the possibilities of anti-ICBM defense. In January 1982, Edward Teller held the first of four personal meetings with the President to advise him on the feasibility of such a program; and when Reagan announced his decision to propose research aimed at SDI, his call was aimed primarily at American scientists. The circle was closed. This time, the "great communicator" had something of historic relevance to communicate: the dream of eternal peace in a US-dominated world won over by American ingenuity that would also provide markets, jobs, and technology for the nation's industries, as well as substantial rewards for their powerful lobbies. The new warfare state would emerge as the reconstructed coalition of new social groups and old economic interests on the basis of its mastery of technology at the dawn of the informational society.

The Technological Search for a Military El Dorado

SDI is, above all, a military program. Given the media attention that has been lavished on its specific content and its evolution, it is not necessary to recall its characteristics, except when relevant to an understanding of its technological implications. We do, however, need to consider the subject that has dominated public debate concerning "Star Wars:" its feasibility.

Scientists, political leaders, and the media have battled with fury in the arguments for or against the possibility of building a non-nuclear shield.[126] The debate generally has oversimplified extremely complex technical matters that I am not competent to assess. Moreover, each time SDI scientists are forced on to the defensive, they hide behind the classified nature of the technological answers they claim to hold to the gigantic problems faced by an effective space-based defensive system. In fact, informed opinion on both sides of the debate tends to converge toward a realistic assessment of SDI possibilities in the following terms:[127]

(1) The concept of a leak-proof shield seems to be out of the question, particularly because of the difficulty in constructing the software necessary to such a system, and the impossibility of testing it. Nevertheless, taking as read the success of the program, a reasonably effective anti-ICBM system could be deployed, capable of destroying a significant proportion of attacking missiles, increasing uncertainty about the fate of their intended targets, and therefore of enhancing deterrence by achieving strategic superiority.

(2) Consequently, since defense could not completely disregard deterrence, offensive capabilities should be maintained at a significant level, and SDI would be not a defensive system, but a fundamental addition to an offensive system.

(3) Although nuclear weapons would not necessarily be an integral part of the system, a nuclear component would still be present in it, with space-based nuclear reactors as energy sources; possibly, nuclear bombs able to

generate X-ray lasers; and certainly, nuclear warheads in the case of a re-
taliatory attack.

Reformulated in these terms, the feasibility of SDI is a much more open
technical question. And, given the support for it existing among the defense
establishment, the odds are that it will probably be pursued, in a scaled-down
form, by the post-Reagan administration.

To some extent, the feasibility question that has taken the forefront of the
debate about SDI in its initial stage is largely irrelevant. It was important at
the outset because it mobilized public support, or at least non-hostile
curiosity, around an apparently peaceful technological utopia. Once the
program was underway, however, its proponents and participants became less
concerned with the fulfillment of the stated ultimate goal than with the
technological breakthroughs to be attained in the pursuit of it, particularly
because most of these technological advances have an outstanding importance for conventional warfare. For instance, predominance was given to
surveillance equipment, especially sophisticated sensors, satellites, and
communications, in the first round of funding for SDI. These technologies
are fundamental in rapid, precisely targeted strikes carried out by planes or
ships in modern warfare; and this is the type of action for which US armed
forces are being prepared. Thus, while most of the attention is being focused
on the strategic defensive capabilities of "Star Wars," work toward the actual
military objectives of the program (strategic offensive superiority, technological edge in conventional warfare) is well in hand. Witnessing this dynamism
are the organizational strength of the program, its growing independence of
established administrative channels, its priority in the defense budget, and the
flexibility in its management procedures. The management of the SDI
program is centralized in one special office within the Department of
Defense with large discretionary powers in the use of its $4 billion annual
budget. James Abrahamson, an air force general with recognized public
relations skills, was appointed as program chief in an effort targeted at
winning political support for the program. The SDI office initiates research
contracts with universities, national laboratories, and private companies, on
the basis of objectives and problems determined by SDI's own technical staff.
Additional research for the program is convened and operated by the
Department of Energy. To add to this flexibility, in 1986–7 a new SDI
Institute was created in Washington, under contract from the Defense
Department, to co-ordinate and plan all research and testing activities being
performed in literally hundreds of technological units. A very important
feature of the SDI program is its systematic effort to enlist the support of foreign governments and foreign companies, particularly in Japan and in
western Europe, offering funding, potential markets, and access to US
technology in exchange for the possibility of utilizing for the purposes of SDI
some of the best technological teams in each particular field.[128] SDI could be

the first step in setting up a comprehensive military-oriented plan for technological development, not only in the US, but on a worldwide scale, by far surpassing the role of Japan's MITI as planner and guide of strategic research programs.

This perspective is particularly relevant when one considers the kind of technologies SDI is trying to advance. The core of the program, in the long term, concerns the development of supercomputers able to process all information at great speed, as well as the writing of adequate software, leading to major progress in artificial intelligence. In this sense, SDI could overwhelm, in both resources and scope, Japan's much-publicized "fifth generation" computing plan. A second major group of technologies centers around communication and sensor satellites, with direct implications for radar and new forms of detection and navigation. A third series of technologies aims at creating new weapons (free-electron lasers, particle-beam weapons, "smart chips," etc.) that represent qualitative breakthroughs in lasers, energy generation, and, most importantly, microelectronics. Advanced materials are also an essential component of the strategy.[129] Including space-related manufacturing and the use of solar energy to power space-based activities, SDI involves all key technologies that matter for future industrial and economic development, with the major exception of genetic engineering (and even in this field, there are also a number of little-known, classified research programs).[130] For instance optical sensors, that are crucial to SDI, are the key element in pushing robotization beyond its current primitive stage in manufacturing. The cost of global communications could be lowered by the technological spin-offs of the program; industrial applications of new forms of lasers are likely to revolutionize precision manufacturing; a new generation of "smart power chips" is in the making; and the breakthrough in artificial intelligence could finally open the era of widespread computer literacy. In sum, SDI brings together *in one system* the the most important new technologies and provides the economic and institutional support for their cumulative development. In this sense, SDI is a major technological program. I am not implying that this is the only or indeed the best way to mobilize research in all these key areas. In fact, a number of leading scientists argue that much talent is being wasted in dead-end research initiatives that are of only marginal interest for the advancement of knowledge, because of their specific military purpose.[131] Yet the fact that an alternative research program could yield better results does not change the basic fact that SDI, regardless of its morality, and in spite of its shortcomings, is a technological program on the grand scale. As the Spanish conquerors explored and colonized the entire American continent in their futile search for the treasures of El Dorado, "Star Wars" scientists and planners are dramatically expanding technological innovation, and framing it into specific applications, while pursuing the military Grail set up for them as a mobilizing goal.

SDI as Industrial Policy

Because of the decisive role of high technology in economic development, SDI as a technological program could become one of the agenda-setting instruments for America's industrial policy.[132] Projected funding for SDI-related R&D is estimated to be about $70 billion for the period 1984–93.[133] But, as stated above, the really important matter concerns the capacity of the first contractors to position themselves favorably for the huge potential offered by the contracts that will follow the research stage, either to deploy an ABM system or to develop the new generation of conventional weapons, or both.

The main beneficiaries of SDI contracts are the major traditional defense contractors in aerospace, missiles, communications, and electronics, as shown in table 5.8. Thus, SDI reforged the close links between high-technology industries and military programs, after their gradual disassociation during the 1970s. There is, however, a fundamental difference from the situation of the 1950s and early 1960s, when high technology was closer than ever to defense markets: namely, that while in the earlier period high-technology industries constituted a very small proportion of total manufacturing, they now represent its most significant component, and the element which determines the overall competitiveness of the US economy. SDI is therefore in a position to guide and frame industrial policy overall.

The influence of SDI has extended far beyond the traditional defense procurement activities. The program has created a large market for information-processing and research firms, which represent the cutting edge of a new form of industrial production in the informational economy.[134] These companies specialize in computer simulations, system analyses, weapons performance assessment, and so on, and include Kaman Corp. (Bloomfield, Connecticut), Rand (Santa Monica, California), SRI (Stanford, California), Mission Research and General Research (both at Santa Barbara, California), Sparta, Inc., and the most prominent in this category, Science Applications International (SAIC), of La Jolla, California. SAIC is an example of the new type of military informational industry fostered by SDI. Its 5,700 workers produce only technical and strategic studies, for an annual revenue of $420 million in 1984, of which 90 percent came from US government contracts. In fact, SAIC was itself very much involved in formulating some of the initial concepts of SDI, beginning in 1981. Its board of directors is an embodiment of the intimate connections among the defense establishment, the defense industry, the scientific community, and the intelligence agencies. It includes former Defense Secretary Melvin R. Laird; former chief of the National Security Agency Admiral Robert R. Inman; former Under Secretary of State Lucy W. Benson; MIT's Provost John M. Deutch; General Welch, formerly with the National Security Agency; and Donald A. Hicks, from Northrop's Corporation, who subsequently resigned from SAIC to become the Pentagon's research director. This company, boasting some of the most sophisticated experts both in technology and in security analysis, is representative of the new breed of defense industry that is being bred by SDI.

Another major new development in information industries directly linked to SDI is the Pentagon's growing role in generating new software.[135] Particularly important here is the creation and diffusion of the ADA language, that allows different software systems to communicate. Tens of thousands of advanced software companies are now being directly funded by the SDI office. In addition, the Defense Department established a new office to provide venture capital for high-technology start-up firms prepared to work in areas of interest to SDI. It is estimated that such SDI funding will account for about 20 percent of all high-tech venture capital in the period 1986–90.[136]

The extent of SDI-inspired activity, then, goes way beyond the traditional realm of the defense industry, to embrace the most advanced research fields, including basic analytical programs. As a result, the personnel employed by SDI-related investment will be in the upper tier of the technical ladder. According to a study by the Council of Economic Priorities, SDI-related production will employ six times as many scientists and engineers as the average industry.[137] This is a development that will affect the high-tech labor market dramatically, creating a shortage of skilled professionals in the civilian markets, and concentrating some of the best talent in the military–industrial sector by paying higher salaries, offering better equipment, and providing better working conditions. From this will follow a gradual technological advantage on the part of the defense industry.[138] These trends are arousing serious concern among economic experts and leading industrialists. It is argued, rightly, that the secrecy surrounding much of the research will inhibit its diffusion, restricting the commercial and civilian spin-offs of the program.[139] Given the slowness of diffusion from military-related innovation, critics argue that increasing dependency on defense-inspired technological change will considerably hamper US economic competitiveness. The analysis by Stowsky already cited[140] on the shortcomings of defense spending as a technological–industrial policy applies also to SDI-related initiatives. The channeling of so large a proportion of technological resources into the defense field will be likely to slow down the rate of innovation and to decrease productive efficiency, to the benefit, for instance, of commercially-oriented Japanese competition.

The response of the Defense Department to this challenge is, of course, to try to universalize SDI, reaching out to foreign companies and opening huge potential markets that could lure into the realm of US defense spending much of the foreign technological potential. Yet it remains most likely that foreign companies, and particularly Japanese firms, will continue to target most of their production to civilian applications, and this offers the prospect of a global bifurcation of high-technology industries, with the US electronics companies being overwhelmed in many areas by Japan, Korea, and western

Europe, while the hard core of US high technology takes refuge in the growing military market. This development could trigger off a new round of economic restructuring within the high-technology industries, as well as a recomposition of the international division of labor.

In sum, SDI has become the core of high-technology defense policy, and could also become an indication of the future industrial policy of the US, both because of its capacity for defining the goals of technological innovation, and because of its potential in creating markets and attracting the most skilled scientific labor force.[141] On the other hand, because of the inherent shortcomings of defense production in relation to civilian industrial development, SDI could trigger off a profound restructuring of the international and national economies from which the US would probably emerge with a shrunk industrial structure, yet with a superior technological edge confined to its own military, statist logic. SDI could choke off the market-driven entrepreneurialism that accompanied the expansion of the American high-tech industries, ushering in a new stage in which economic growth would take second place to the technological exercise of global power. While the warfare state might have important economic consequences and motivations, its ultimate logic is fundamentally political.

Down to Earth: The Urban and Regional Effects of High-technology-based Defense Policy

Technology-driven defense policy is having significant effects on the urban and regional structure of the US. To analyze the resulting spatial forms and processes, it is necessary first to understand the process by which defense industries are geographically located in the US, since much of the current impact is dependent on the established spatial pattern. Special attention will be given here to the role played by technological change in this process, in order to assess the relative likelihood of historical continuity or modification of the existing spatial structure. We will then examine the particular spatial effects of recent defense policies and analyze the specific influence of the new technological factor introduced in these policies.

Much has been written on the regional impact of defense spending in the US,[142] although considerably less is known about the intra-metropolitan and urban effects of military activities or of defense industries. Yet even at the regional level, few studies have approached the issue from the angle that is now crucial according to my hypothesis, namely, the relationship between defense spending and high-technology industries in the formation of a new regional structure.[143] Fortunately, we can rely on the preliminary findings of a major study on this subject, conducted at the University of California by Peter Hall, Ann Markusen, Scott Campbell, and Sabina Dietrick.[144] I am indebted to this study for much of the information underlying the analysis that follows.

The main finding of the study concerns the historical continuity of the location of defense industries since the 1930s, with California (particularly Los Angeles), New England, the north-east, and Texas the main areas of concentration of defense-related industrial jobs. Table 5.10 provides some information on the matter at a very aggregate level. Although a certain degree of regional domination does appear, particularly in the New England and Pacific regions, it is important to analyze the processes of formation of the military–industrial sphere, since spatial continuity may actually disguise the existence of a succession of different processes, whose dynamics could be very distinct, carrying the potential for reversing the spatial patterns over time. This hypothesis seems to be confirmed by the fact that, although most of the sites of the defense industry were already in place in the late 1930s, their relative importance has changed greatly during the past 40 years, with the old manufacturing belt in the mid-west losing out to the west and the south-east, and New England transforming its old industrial base into a new one, definitely connected to defense-related production. Three major factors seem to have accounted for this evolution, and it is my hypothesis that these same factors are the main forces in shaping the regional structure of the US during the current defense build-up. The three factors are:

(1) rapid technological change, organized around new technologies in aerospace and electronics;
(2) the specific nature of the production process in the defense industry; and
(3) the political and institutional process surrounding defense policy and the allocation of defense resources.

It is the interaction among these three specific factors that has redrawn the manufacturing map of America in the past 40 years, on the basis of the critical role played by defense in what is left of manufacturing in the US. Let us examine the specific influence of these factors on spatial processes, one after the other.

Technology entirely transformed military equipment after World War II with the shift of strategic importance to aircraft, then to missiles, as potential vehicles for nuclear weapons (see table 5.11).[145]

Thus, while traditional ordnance (artillery, tanks, mechanized personnel carriers, battleships) was incrementally improved, and was still produced in the mid-western and north-eastern manufacturing belt, the new defense industry expanded around the aircraft industry, itself divided between engine constructors and airframe manufacturers. Production of engines was (and still largely is) located in the New England area, following the tradition of precision engineering in the region since the nineteenth century.[146]

Table 5.10 Distribution of defense procurement, by state and region, 1982

| State | Number of employees | | Value of shipments | |
	Total (000s)	As % of US total	Total ($m)	As % of US total
Pacific	281.4	29.70	25,386	29.03
California	267.2	28.20	23,923	27.35
Oregon	3.7	0.39	268	0.31
Washington	9.9	1.04	944	1.08
Alaska	d		d	
Hawaii	d		d	
New England	135.6	14.31	12,405	14.18
Maine	6.2	0.87	545	0.62
New Hampshire	14.1	1.49	911	1.04
Vermont	4.9	0.52	354	0.40
Massachusetts	46.4	5.11	5,058	5.78
Rhode Island	6.1	0.85	706	0.81
Connecticut	51.9	5.48	4,831	5.52
Middle Atlantic	129.3	13.64	11,569	13.23
New York	69.6	7.34	6,261	7.16
New Jersey	25.9	2.73	2,199	2.51
Pennsylvania	33.8	3.57	3,109	3.55
South Atlantic	121.7	12.84	9,060	10.36
Delaware	0.1	0.01	136	0.16
Maryland	26.1	2.75	2,123	2.43
D. of Columbia	D		D	
Virginia	40.0	4.22	2,758	3.15
West Virginia	A		11	0.01
North Carolina	3.5	0.37	245	0.28
South Carolina	1.6	0.17	132	0.15
Georgia	10.9	1.15	1,053	1.20
Florida	39.4	4.16	2,603	2.98
East-North-Central	81.6	8.61	8,331	9.53
Ohio	26.7	2.82	2,848	3.26
Indiana	19.2	2.03	1,907	2.18
Illinois	12.7	1.34	1,125	1.29
Michigan	15.4	1.63	1,819	2.08
Wisconsin	7.6	0.80	632	0.72
West-North-Central	67.3	7.10	8,193	9.37
Minnesota	17.0	1.79	1,603	1.83
Iowa	4.0	0.42	328	0.38
Missouri	31.6	3.33	4,707	5.38
North Dakota	D		D	
South Dakota	D		D	
Nebraska	0.9	0.09	53	0.06

Table 5.10 Continued

State	Number of employees Total (000s)	As % of US total	Value of shipments Total ($m)	As % of US total
Kansas	13.8	1.46	1,497	1.71
East-South-Central	26.0	2.74	2,020	2.31
Kentuky	0.4	0.04	110	0.13
Tennessee	8.0	0.84	620	0.71
Alabama	7.0	0.74	385	0.44
Mississippi	10.6	1.12	905	1.03
West-South-Central	68.6	7.24	6,857	7.84
Arkansas	1.1	0.12	64	0.07
Louisiana	2.6	0.27	468	0.54
Oklahoma	5.6	0.61	499	0.51
Texas	59.1	6.24	5,876	6.72
Mountain	36.2	3.82	3,637	4.16
Montana	A		23	0.03
Idaho	0.1	0.01	13	0.01
Wyoming	A		8	0.01
Colorado	11.0	1.16	1,050	1.20
New Mexico	1.1	0.12	140	0.16
Arizona	16.2	1.71	1,583	1.81
Utah	7.8	0.82	820	0.94
Nevada	A		0	0.00
US total	947.6	100.0	87,458	100.0

Source: US Bureau of Census; US Bureau of Labor Statistics.

Table 5.11 Changes in the composition of military hard goods, 1942–1944 to 1980

Type of military goods	Fiscal year			
	1942–4[a]	1953[a]	1962[b]	1980[b]
Aircraft	27.3	31.5	25.7	31.9
Missiles	0.0	0.5	33.7	19.6
Ships	26.2	6.8	7.4	13.1
Electronics and communication equipment	6.6	11.2	16.6	22.4
Tank-automotive, weapons, ammunition and other	39.9	50.0	16.5	12.9

[a] Composition (%) based on value of deliveries.
[b] Composition (%) based on value of prime contracts.

Source: Malecki (see note 143).

Airframe manufacturers grew up in California, with two major exceptions, which became the two biggest companies, located for accidental reasons, in Seattle (Boeing) and St Louis (McDonnell-Douglas).[147] Southern California saw a flurry of pioneer entrepreneurial activity in aviation as early as the 1920s:[148] Lockheed started in a Hollywood garage moving to Burbank in 1929; Douglas started in an abandoned studio in Santa Monica in 1920; Jack Northrop, after working for both Lockheed and Douglas, set up his own company in Hawthorne in 1939; and in the mid-1930s, Consolidated started operations in Glendale, Convair in San Diego, and North American in Inglewood. All these firms were to become major companies fueled by military contracts during World War II.

Why southern California? Physical conditions have often been cited: large expanses of undeveloped flat land; a sunny, mild climate, favoring flight testing and outdoor industrial work;[149] and a large supply of skilled labor. Yet, Peter Hall and his colleagues[150] argue that the decisive factor was the quality of technical education, particularly for aeronautical engineers, with Cal Tech, in Pasadena, and Stanford being among the only five universities to offer such programs in the 1920s (the others being MIT, University of Washington, and the University of Michigan). Yet in spite of that early start in California, other airframe manufacturers were still located in the old industrial belt: in Buffalo, New York; in Baltimore; in Bridgeport, Connecticut: in Long Island, New York; and, of course, there was the McDonnell plant in St Louis. To explain the continuity of the expansion of the aviation industry in the west and in New England along with its discontinuity in the oldest industrial belt, it is necessary to introduce the factors proposed as explanatory of the defense industry's locational patterns: in particular, the shift to missile technology, which represented both a challenge and an opportunity for the airframe manufacturers.[151] Electronics became a crucial component of the new aerospace industry, particularly after the shock of Sputnik in 1957 launched the race to the moon. Electronics companies positioned themselves strongly in the defense sector, with 90 percent of semiconductors being produced for the government in the 1950s. As we know,[152] major advanced electronics areas were, in temporal sequence, New England, California (particularly northern California), and Texas. Those airframe manufacturers that were able to team up with the new electronics companies, or that developed around them their own electronics suppliers, were able to jump into avionics and missiles, entering the aerospace age as the nucleus of the new defense industry.[153] Southern California was particularly successful in organizing aerospace production around the electronics industry. Texas followed along the same path. New England maintained its position in aircraft engines production and combined this with its strong electronics industry to become the region which, in proportion to its size, most heavily specialized in defense production, in spite of all the ideological discourse about the west;[154] Silicon Valley concentrated mainly on electronics, although it did also become a major missile producer, with the

Lockheed facility in Sunnyvale. The important factor was that by the mid-1960s a fundamental connection had been created between the defense industry (centered around aerospace) and high-technology manufacturing (centered around electronics) that was going to favor decisively the development of those regions able to bring together these two terms of the new techno-military equation, under the dominance of one term or the other (aerospace defense in southern California and Texas, electronics in Silicon Valley, a combination of both in New England).

But why were these particular areas able to maintain their head start in the trade (or even to initiate it, as Texas did), while the mid-west or the north-east (except New England) by and large dropped out of the race? Here two additional factors come into play that will at the same time also help in explaining some other locational developments of the advanced military and space industry, particularly in the south-east.

As stated above, the second major factor determining the location of the defense industry is the specific nature of the industrial organization itself. Defense production is characterized by a close, tight network of day-to-day interaction among companies, their clients (military institutions and government agencies), and the companies' sub-contractors and auxiliary services.[155] Production itself, in the aircraft industry, is largely free of assembly-line operations; instead, it is characterized by batch fabrication, and involves considerable interaction with the researchers and designers of the technological product, as well as with the client, to satisfy detailed specifications.[156] All these elements converge toward the creation of an *industrial milieu* that, once in place, perpetuates itself, reinforcing its prominence and undertaking new initiatives in the new fields of defense as soon as they are opened up by technological innovation. The existence of a tightly knit industrial milieu is also favored by the the fact that the defense industry is characterized by a high level of concentration and dominated by a handful of firms. The top 100 companies control 70 percent of total value of contracts, the top 50 control 50 percent of the market, and the top five, 20 percent.[157] Large defense companies typically obtain multi-million-dollar orders from the Pentagon which they then contract out to many sub-contractors of different sizes and specialties, from metal-work shops to software engineers.[158] It is widely believed that such contracting and sub-contracting involves a great deal of personal contact and face-to-face interaction; the defense industry is a *social* milieu as much as an industrial milieu. High-ranking officers often retire from the military to take up jobs in defense companies, while remaining close to their long-standing friends. A sort of cultural empathy pervades the whole system, sustaining a tight network of values, interests, feelings, and ideas around which major strategic decisions are nurtured, and substantial business deals are agreed upon.[159] Sometimes, critics argue, bribery and pay-offs are almost necessary practices in the sub-contracting business, the famous Lockheed foreign government briberies being of course the most notorious case of what is said to be a structural element of the industry's workings. Whatever the reality, it is quite clear that the defense industry operates as a milieu, requiring spatial clustering of its core activities, regardless of the widespread decentralization of its sub-contracting operations. The existence locally of military installations greatly contributes to the formation of such milieux, particularly when other key elements occur in the same location, such as the presence of aircraft and electronics industries, and the existence of high-level research and technical education institutions. California, of course, and particularly southern California, is also favored in terms of proximity to military bases; and Lockheed's location in Sunnyvale (Silicon Valley) seems to be in direct relationship with Moffit Air Naval Base. Texas also has a comparative advantage on these grounds, particularly because of the army's installations around San Antonio, potentially connecting with the future Austin–San Antonio high-tech corridor.

Nevertheless, the social and industrial milieu of defense activity seems to be all-important by itself, regardless of any spatial connection with military facilities, as demonstrated by the strong defense orientation of New England, in spite of a much less conspicuous military presence there. Once the ingredients of a military–industrial milieu are in place they expand, reinforcing themselves with their technological, commercial, and social externalities; yet the coming together of these elements in a particular area is largely a function of the political and institutional dynamics of the defense establishment, in which ultimately lies the power to decide on particular production lines, and the ability to obtain and allocate the necessary *public* resources.

A vast literature has documented the consistent bias of defense spending toward some regions. For instance, the major study on the subject by Roger Bolton for the period 1952–62 found that defense demand accounted for 21 percent of personal income growth in the Pacific region, while contributing a *negative* 21 percent to that growth in the east-north-central regions. He also showed that defense purchases accounted for 34 percent of current personal income in the Pacific, 23 percent in the Mountain, 23 percent in the south Atlantic region, and 22 percent in New England, while all other regions had shares below 20 percent.[160] Ann Markusen, reviewing the evidence on the regional distribution of defense outlays, states that

especially remarkable has been the regional shift of prime contract awards away from the northeastern and north central states (which, in 1951, received the highest aggregate and per capita amount of such awards and the largest proportion of the national total) toward the southern and western states (which by 1976 received the highest amount and the highest proportion). In addition, the largest number and greatest proportion of installations continued to be located in the southern and western regions up through the mid 1970s.[161]

Table 5.12 presents the top ten states in terms of benefit from direct defense spending in 1959–60 and 1980, showing the continuity of the pattern.

Table 5.12   Top states in receipt of prime defense contracts. 1959–80

Fiscal year 1959–60		Fiscal year 1980	
State	% of US total	State	% of US total
California	24.0	California	20.4
New York	11.4	New York	8.3
Texas	5.8	Texas	8.0
Massachusetts	5.3	Connecticut	5.7
New Jersey	5.0	Massachusetts	5.5
Ohio	4.4	Virginia	4.9
Connecticut	4.2	Missouri	4.8
Washington	4.0	Washington	3.4
Michigan	3.3	Pennsylvania	3.3
Pennsylvania	3.2	Florida	3.0

Source: Malecki (see note 143).

The direction of defense spending to certain regions is obviously, then, a powerful factor in influencing the location of defense industries. But what are the reasons for these regional preferences on the part of the Pentagon? It has been argued that the shift to the west and the south as the home ground of Presidents, and the coming into power of a new Californian and Texan political elite, have played an important role in both reinforcing defense policy, and tying it to the geographic origins of political support for the defense build-up.[162] Markusen and Block have also introduced the argument of political culture, according to which the old manufacturing belt with its strong union tradition and its liberal political climate was not suited to accommodate the national security priorities of the military and of the defense establishment.[163] It is undeniable that local support for military installations, and for related defense expenditures, is an important consideration for any defense agency to feel comfortable setting up in the regions; and that the development of a network of relationships among regional political leaders, public opinion, defense companies, and military settlements creates a strong, sustained basis for defense production in a particular area. Nevertheless, such factors are not overriding, as the case of New England again demonstrates – not exactly a south-western, conservative region, yet one of the most heavily defense-oriented regional economies. There is often a confusion between the location of military bases and test sites (which critically favor the west and the south-west because of their natural conditions: open spaces, depopulated areas, fair weather, sunny skies), and the location of the defense industry. While proximity to military installations is important, it is even more important to have access to the industrial milieu to which I have referred; and this milieu is conditioned largely by the development of high-technology industries and research facilities. It is the combination of a political environment, a technological base, and an industrial milieu which accounts for the development of major defense production in California and Texas, while New England's technological might was sufficient of itself to override the supposed military reluctance to rely on the old industrial regions for building their new productive base.[164]

In fact, it seems that the internal political rivalries of military bureaucracies have been more important than external political factors; namely, the competition among the army, the air force, and the navy to control the technological transition to the new warfare system. Peter Hall and his colleagues have described in some detail what they call "the most extraordinary saga of inter-service rivalry in which the Army and Air Force, in particular, behaved liked competitive capitalist corporations" in trying to secure control of the new missile program between 1953 and 1960.[165] The army had the original mandate for it, and the additional technological advantage of Von Braun and his team. On the other hand, the air force had its strong connection to the aircraft industry and its early lead in electronics equipment. The three services developed in parallel the three first major missile programs: the air force, Atlas, from 1954; the army, Titan and Jupiter, from 1955; and the navy, Polaris, from 1956. Two different organizational logics led to different spatial location patterns. The army favored in-house production of its own equipment, following both the traditional logic of the weapons arsenal, and Von Braun's own experience with the German army. Accordingly, the army organized a major aerospace research and production center in Huntsville, Alabama, connected to the test site at Cape Canaveral, Florida. The air force was more inclined to rely on the private sector, and turned naturally to the Los Angeles complex, and to the research resources of Cal Tech's Jet Propulsion Laboratory. The navy also followed its west coast connection, so that Polaris was developed by Lockheed in Sunnyvale, while Convair built Titan (in Los Angeles), North American (also in LA), built Hounddog, and Boeing, in Seattle, took charge of the Minuteman program, with electronics support from Texas Instruments. To put a halt to waste and inefficiency in the wake of the Sputnik syndrome, the Federal government stepped in, put the air force in charge of most missile programs, quashed the army's stubborn opposition, and in 1958 created NASA around the Alabama–Florida pole of activities, to which were attached some research facilities on the west coast, most notably the Jet Propulsion Laboratory. A number of defense, electronic, and aerospace firms took up locations in Florida and the south-east around the market represented by the Apollo program: most notably Martin Marietta in Orlando and United Technologies in Palm Beach, constituting a new high-tech–defense oriented industrial pole. Yet the real winner of the competition was once again California, and particularly Los Angeles, whose business circles and political influence had been skilfully mobilized by the air force in support of its own programs.

Thus, the location of aerospace and electronic industries, the characteristics of the industrial organization of defense production, and the internal and external politics of military bureaucracies explain most of the location patterns of a defense industry driven and transformed by rapid technological change in the past 30 years.

Only two exceptions remain outside the main preferred locations resulting from the dynamics described above: production of atomic warheads, that for obvious safety reasons is concentrated in remote areas, fundamentally in Oak Ridge, Tennessee, and Amarillo, Texas; and Seattle, which remained a major aerospace production center around the company founded in 1915 by William E. Boeing, a Seattle timberman with a vision of the future, and Conrad Westervelt, a naval officer who, once returned to active duty, may have been crucial in obtaining for Boeing some of its first plane orders from the navy.[166] St Louis also remained at the forefront of aircraft production on the basis of the company founded in 1938 by James Smith McDonnell, an MIT graduate in aeronautical engineering and an air force officer.[167] St Louis' McDonnell-Douglas (as it became after Douglas was absorbed into the business) is the only significant remnant of the early dominance of the mid-west in airframe manufacture, an anomaly attributable to the dynamism of the company and its ability to team up with electronics companies on the west coast and in New England.

From this complex process of development of a powerful defense industry emerged a new economic landscape in the US. Its most extraordinary feature is the formation of the Los Angeles military–industrial complex, probably the largest and most advanced in the world. According to a study by Tiebout in 1966, in the 1960s 7.7 percent of employment in the Los Angeles–Long Beach SMSA was directly tied to defense and space production, a proportion which rose to 43.5 percent when all indirect and induced effects were incorporated. Estimates by the same study for the entire state of California were of 8 percent of employment directly related to defense, and 40 percent with all indirect effects taken into consideration.[168] Since this type of study often relies on arbitrary assumptions about multiplier effects, it is probably inadvisable to take the data too literally. Yet it is unquestionable that the defense industry, and its role in stimulating aircraft production and elec-tronics, had a decisive effect on the growth of the Californian economy, as well as, according to a study by Sabina Dietrick, on the migration of population to California;[169] and it continues to be a major factor in the state's economic prosperity, as borne out by Michael Teitz's analysis of the period 1982–6.[170]

Similarly, the ability of New England, and particularly of Massachusetts, to shift its economy away from its old manufacturing basis in textiles and machine tools to its new high-technology manufacturing and advanced services complex, was and is highly dependent upon the military markets that seem to account for about one-third of the manufacturing work force in the Route 128 area.[171] If we add Texas, Arizona, and Florida to the group of affluent states, and, a later development, the defense-induced industry in Colorado at Denver and Colorado Springs, it is clear that the defense industry's pattern of location is responsible for much of the new uneven regional development in the US. Nevertheless, the dynamics and content of this uneven development are *not* the direct consequence of defense spending, but of the combination of defense policy and high-technology industry,[172] itself resulting from the changes introduced by technological advance in the realm of warfare. The defense industry is driven, as Malecki has put it,[173] by a "technological push" which, by connecting state policy and economic dynamism, becomes a crucial factor in shaping the spatial structure of the nation.

The first major spatial impact of a defense policy driven by global technological competition, then, is the restructuring of regional dominance, accelerating the process of uneven development but revising some of the traditional locational patterns. This regional restructuring does not take place along the simplistic dichotomy between the sunbelt and the snowbelt, but follows, fundamentally, the technological industrial capacity concentrated in each region. The combination of high-tech manufacturing, advanced research, and defense spending seems to be one of the major factors in explaining the new regional dynamics of the US. The result is the displacement of economic and political power to California, Florida, Texas, New England, and, to some extent, certain areas in the west. While New York retains its dominance on the basis of its advanced services complex, much of the urban industrial complex in the north-central and north-eastern regions is suffering a dramatic decline, while the new industrial south appears unable to stand up to international competition.[174] Defense-driven high-technology industries, and technology-driven defense-related industries, are now the core of manufacturing in the US; and because of their spin-off and multiplier effects, they have become a fundamental force underlying the new regional structure.[175]

Within any given metropolitan area, the expansion of the defense industry has taken place in the new suburbs, thus powerfully contributing to the process of suburbanization of manufacturing, and to the economic dynamism of suburbs, as opposed to the central city.[176] The reasons for this trend should be clear as a result of the preceding analysis of the characteristics of the defense industry. The need for large expanses of undeveloped land and easy access to a network of subsidiaries in the area favor a strip-shaped suburban development along the freeway. Proximity to military bases, which are generally located on the outskirts of metropolitan areas, reinforces the pattern. It has also been proposed, by Ann Markusen and Robin Bloch, that the cultural preference of the military, and their related industries, is for seclusion in a separate world, both for security reasons and because of their anti-big-city, anti-cosmopolitan bias.[177] If such a preference exists, it would certainly be reinforced by the co-existence of residence and workplaces within the same suburban world, often through housing procured by the company, or obtained through arrangements with military agencies.

Nevertheless, it is crucial to distinguish between strictly defense industries (for instance, a weapons production facility), and defense-*related* industries (such as aircraft and electronics companies). In the former case, spatial segregation seems to be the tendency; in the latter instance, spatial and social structures are much more diversified, and tend to mingle with the overall social system of the host area. What seems to apply to both is the suburban character of the defense industry, as well as of most of its labor force. But this is also an attribute of high-technology manufacturing and R&D in general. What we are observing is not so much a defense space as the generalization of a new industrial space, with large batch production facilities combined with automated subsidiary plants, in the vicinity of test sites and relatively close to the research and design centers. Access to a large, resource-ful area by means of the freeway system seems to be the main spatial requirement. This is why the defense industry (as with high-technology industry) tends to be peripherally located in large metropolitan areas which are able to provide sufficient diversity and density of interaction to constitute the industrial milieu which is the essential ingredient of the whole process. In fact, the study by a group of Berkeley graduate students on the characteristics of defense-related industries in California[178] shows a great diversity of situations, with, again, the only common factor being their suburban, or even ex-urban, location. The blue-collar community of Vallejo, adjacent to a naval base in the San Francisco area, is in striking contrast to the campus-like community of Livermore, site of the Lawrence National Laboratory. The Los Angeles area complex and Silicon Valley have, of course, highly diversified social and spatial structures that hardly allow for specific social subsets related to defense activity, in contrast to the situation in military–industrial company towns such as, for example, Amarillo, Texas.

The defense industry also presents major differences in occupational structure and its residential manifestation, according to the type of activity involved. Large airframe manufacturers in Los Angeles have a significant proportion of blue-collar workers and a higher share of black workers than manufacturing as a whole in the area. By contrast, Hispanics are underrepresented in the defense industry, and non-US citizens are barred from employment by DoD regulations. Women are particularly under-represented in the industry: as manual workers because these are generally male-dominated occupations, and as engineers, in accordance with the general situation throughout the entire realm of high-technology industries. When industrial location and residential areas coincide spatially, the result is a traditional nuclear family suburb, with men at work and women at home, in higher proportion than in the rest of the area.

In fact, there are two clearly distinct patterns of residence associated with defense industry work. On the one hand are the traditional ordnance and ammunition facilities that, both for safety reasons and by cultural choice on the part of their managers, tend to locate in medium-sized cities in predominantly rural areas, very much following the model of military bases.[179] On the other hand, as table 5.13 shows, in 1983 defense industrial employment was highly concentrated in major urban industrial centers. An observation of the areas included reveals three outstanding features: the overwhelming dominance of the two metropolitan areas of Los Angeles and Anaheim (in fact the same spatial unit) that, together, have 161,800 defense-related jobs, accounting for about one-quarter of all defense-related jobs, at least in the restrictive definition used by Mosely; the extraordinary role played by Boston in the military–industrial complex, in proportion to the size of its work force; and the quantitative importance retained by some old industrial

Table 5.13　Concentration of Department of Defense procurement: top ten metropolitan areas by employment involved and value of shipments, 1983

(a)

Top ten metropolitian areas by employment	No. of employees in establishments involved in DoD procurement (000s)
1　Los Angeles–Anaheim–Riverside, CA	161.8
2　New York–Northern New Jersey–Long Island, NY–NJ	71.9
3　Dallas–Fort Worth, TX	52.0
4　San Francisco–Oakland–San Jose, CA	48.2
5　Boston–Lawrence–Salem, MA–NH	43.9
6　Norfolk–Virginia Beach–Newport News, VA	27.8
7　San Diego, CA	24.3
8　Seattle–Tacoma, WA	22.1
9　Baltimore, MD	20.2
10　Hartford–New Britain–Middletown, CT	20.1

(b)

Top ten metropolitian areas by value of shipments	Value of shipments to DoD ($ m)
1　Los Angeles–Anaheim–Riverside, CA	15,896.3
2　New York–Northern New Jersey–Long Island, NY–NJ	6,541.6
3　San Francisco–Oakland–San Jose, CA	5,465.7
4　Dallas–Fort Worth, TX	4,698.5
5　Boston–Lawrence–Salem, MA–NH	4,540.0
6　Hartford–New Britain–Middletown, CT	2,334.5
7　Philadelphia–Wilmington Trenton, PA–NJ–DE–MD	2,021.2
8　San Diego, CA	1,925.9
9　Norfolk–Virginia Beach–Newport News, VA	1,713.2
10　Baltimore, MD	1,668.7

Source: Department of Commerce, Current Industrial Reports.

areas, such as New York–New Jersey, in the defense industry. For defense workers living in such large, complex areas, it is difficult to imagine much specificity in residential pattern. What is significant is that the overwhelming majority of them work and live in the suburbs, and, increasingly, in the newest, most far-flung suburban areas. Therefore, the spatial trend to be associated with the defense build-up is the growth of suburbs, as the location for manufacturing, for related services and for the workers' residences. This trend explains why Glickman's calculations, as cited,[180] show a high concentration of defense spending in suburbs, that is, where the defense procurement industries are located, and where their employees tend to live. This is, of course, hardly a specific spatial behavior; yet the orientation of government policy toward defense greatly encourages the suburbanization process characterizing metropolitan America.

How did recent defense policy, biased toward high technology as represented by the SDI program, fit into this spatial pattern? It is my hypothesis that the industrial dynamics generated by a politically determined defense policy of the SDI type produce specific urban and regional effects that will become increasingly significant with the ever-increasing emphasis on technologically-led defense R&D and manufacturing. To examine this hypothesis I turn to the preliminary findings of a study conducted at Berkeley by Rebecca Skinner on the spatial distribution of SDI contracts, on the basis of information files provided directly by SDIO.[181] At the time of writing, her data refer mainly to all contracts issued by SDIO in 1987, when the program enjoyed full support from the administration and had come to maturity. We must keep in mind that at this stage of SDI, all contracts concern research and development, although it is fair to assume, on the basis of past experience in the defense industry, that research contractors will have a competitive edge when it comes to manufacturing contracts, so that the current pattern of spatial distribution of research by and large foreshadows the future pattern of defense manufacturing production.

Skinner calculated the spatial distribution of SDI contracts using the amount of funds contracted as the accounting unit. Let us first observe the pattern of regional distribution, and try to understand what distinguishes SDI contracts from defense contracts in general, and from all defense contracts concerning "research, development, test, and evaluation" (RDTE). Table 5.14 compares the distribution of SDI contracts for the top ten states in 1987 to that of the other two categories of contracts in 1985 (the last year for which Skinner could construct a complete data set). It appears that there is a very high concentration in a few states, and that this concentration increases with the research component of the program: the top ten states account for 65.2 percent of the value of all defense contracts, 80.6 percent of the RDTE contracts, and 92.9 percent of SDIO contracts. California dominates all three categories, but its leadership increases, in absolute terms, with the research component: California accounts for 20.8 percent of all contracts, 38.8 percent of RDTE contracts, and 40.6 percent of SDIO contracts. States appear in the

Table 5.14   Ranking of top ten states according to the value of defense contracts (SDIO; research (RDTE); prime contracts), 1985 and 1987

(a) Top ten SDI states

State	SDIO 1987 value, $ m	% Total SDIO	% Total top ten
California	553.965	40.60	42.90
Alabama	170.676	12.00	13.22
New Mexico	142.566	10.10	11.04
Washington	121.928	8.60	9.44
Massachusetts	113.397	8.00	8.78
New York	72.902	5.20	5.65
Colorado	38.079	3.00	2.95
Virginia	29.21	2.00	2.26
Texas	25.654	1.80	1.99
Maryland	23	1.60	1.78
Sum top 10	1291.377	92.90	
Sum other	123.531	8.73	
Sum USA	1414.908	100.00	
Sum, 1st five	1102.532	79.3	85.3
Sum, 2nd five	188.845	20.7	14.6

(b) Top ten DoD states

State	DoD 1985 value, $ m	% Total DoD	% Total top ten
California	29114.5	20.80	31.90
Texas	10561.5	7.50	11.57
New York	10032.7	7.20	10.99
Massachusetts	7713.54	5.50	8.45
Missouri	7612.71	5.40	8.34
Virginia	6166.76	4.40	6.76
Connecticut	5543.44	4.00	6.07
Florida	5271.23	3.80	5.78
Ohio	4648.32	3.30	5.09
Maryland	4608.10	3.30	5.05
Sum top 10	91272.9	65.20	100.00
Sum other	48823.3	34.80	
Sum USA	140096.0	100.00	
Sum, 1st five	65035.0	46.40	71.25
Sum, 2nd five	26237.8	18.80	28.75

(c) Top ten RDTE states

State	RDTE 1985 value, $ m	% Total DoD	% Total top ten
California	5835.949	31.30	38.82
Massachusetts	2125.93	11.40	14.14
New York	1594.241	8.60	10.61
Maryland	995.193	5.30	6.62
Washington	969.504	5.20	6.45
Texas	915.753	4.90	6.09
Virginia	755.163	4.10	5.02
Colorado	691.588	3.70	4.60
New Jersey	640.589	3.40	4.26
Florida	508.754	2.70	3.38
Sum top 10	15032.66	80.60	1
Sum other	3593.74	19.40	
Sum, USA	18626.40	100.00	
Sum, 1st five	11520.81	61.80	76.64
Sum, 2nd five	3511.847	18.80	23.36

Source: Skinner (see note 181).

SDIO top ten list that are not included in the other categories: Alabama, because of the army's Space Center Research and Testing Center at Huntsville; New Mexico, because of the importance of Los Alamos and Sandia National Laboratories; and Washington because of Boeing. On the other hand, states of the old manufacturing belt that are important in terms of general contracts received, such as Missouri and Ohio, are neither in the RDTE top ten nor the SDIO top ten, although Missouri still ranks reasonably high overall because of the continuing significance of McDonnell-Douglas. Table 5.15 presents the location quotients for the three categories of contract and provides a clearer picture of the regional profile of SDIO contracts. Five states stand out in a class by themselves: New Mexico, Alabama, Washington, California, and Massachusetts. These five in fact represent three different types of defense-oriented industrial R&D location, that further specify the logic introduced by SDI-like defense policy. New Mexico and Alabama represent the new secluded, exclusively defense-oriented, RDTE space, isolated from any major metropolitan area; Washington exemplifies the industrial enclave linked to a major corporation, in this case Boeing. California and Massachusetts offer the most significant illustrations of what could be the future defense-oriented industrial space. It is these two areas (Massachusetts should in fact in this context be extended to include most of New England, particularly Connecticut) that we are witnessing the merger between high-technology industries and defense design and manufacturing in the backbone of the US production system. This merger is taking place under the impact of a "technology push"

Table 5.15 Comparison between spatial distribution of SDIO contracts, defense research contracts (RTDE) and DoD prime contracts, 1987 and 1985

Location quotient

Greater than 2.0		*1.0–2.0*		*0.5–1.0*		*0.25–0.5*		*Less than 0.25*	
DoD prime contracts									
Connecticut	2.97	Alaska	1.8	Alabama	0.60	Iowa	0.34		
DC	3.00	Arizona	1.0	Arkansas	0.58	Oklahoma	0.31		
Massachusetts	2.25	California	1.88	Colorado	0.82	Tennessee	0.28		
Missouri	2.57	Georgia	1.0	Delaware	0.71	Wisconsin	0.37		
		Hawaii	1.01	Florida	0.79	Wyoming	0.41		
		Kansas	1.69	Indiana	0.98				
		Maine	1.40	Louisiana	0.82				
		Maryland	1.78	Michigan	0.52				
		New Hampshire	1.15	Minnesota	0.93				
		Texas	1.09	New Jersey	0.87				
		Virginia	1.84	New Mexico	0.57				
		Washington	1.37	New York	0.96				
				North Carolina	0.53				
				North Dakota	0.51				
				Ohio	0.73				
				Pennsylvania	0.62				
				Rhode Island	0.75				
				Utah	0.81				
				Vermont	0.52				
SDIO contracts, 1987									
Alabama	7.16	Colorado	1.98	Maryland	0.88	Indiana	0.44	Alaska	0.13
California	3.545	Connecticut	1.15	New York	0.69	New Jersey	0.32	Arizona	0.04
Massachusetts	3.28	DC	1.16	Virginia	0.86	Minnesota	0.38	Arkansas	0
New Mexico	16.58					Missouri	0.49	Delaware	0
Washington	4.66					Tennessee	0.25	Florida	0.12
						Texas	0.26	Georgia	0.02

Hawaii	0
Idaho	0
Illinois	0.07
Iowa	0
Kansas	0
Kentucky	0
Louisiana	0
Maine	0
Michigan	0
Mississippi	0
Montana	0
Nebraska	0.01
Nevada	0
New Hampshire	0
N. Carolina	0.23
N. Dakota	0

RTDE contracts, 1985

California	2.837	Missouri	1.186	Alabama	0.600	Michigan	0.264	Alaska	0.010
Colorado	2.743	New Jersey	1.085	Arizona	0.911	N. Carolina	0.321	Arkansas	0.020
Maryland	2.904	New Mexico	1.267	Connecticut	0.944	Ohio	0.447	Delaware	0.167
Massachusetts	4.680	New York	1.148	DC	0.788	Pennsylvania	0.473	Georgia	0.137
Washington	2.818	Utah	1.798	Florida	0.573	Rhode Island	0.450	Hawaii	0.130
		Virginia	1.696	Kansas	0.680	Tennessee	0.279	Idaho	0
				Minnesota	0.884			Illinois	0.134
				New Hampshire	0.648			Indiana	0.189
				Texas	0.717			Iowa	0.236
								Kentucky	0.015
								Louisiana	0.008
								Maine	0.059
								Mississippi	0.011

Source: Skinner (see note 181).

from the Pentagon, of which SDI has been the first formal expression, but whose strategic and institutional logic is likely to survive the political avatars of the "Star Wars" mythology.

These new high-technology, defense-oriented industrial milieux are also specific in their urban forms and in their appearance in certain areas. Skinner has analyzed the spatial distribution of SDI contracts within California for 1987 and has found that southern California accounted for 76.7 percent of all funds contracted, with the largest concentration by far in the Los Angeles–Orange County area. She also found that SDI contracts were overwhelming concentrated in the suburbs: 87 percent of them were situated in the suburbs of a large metropolitan area, predominantly Los Angeles. With 84.3 percent of the top twelve defense corporation receiving SDI funds located in suburbs, the destination of SDI contracts fully reflects the metropolitan suburban world of high-technology defense industries. Greater Los Angeles (particularly around Los Angeles International Airport, and in the El Segundo and Redondo Beach areas) and Orange County (around Anaheim) have become the largest, technologically most advanced defense industrial complex in the world, specializing increasingly in manufacturing the material basis of the warfare state on the basis of self-expanding research capabilities in information technologies and aerospace. Similar patterns, although on a much smaller scale, are to be seen along Route 128 in Boston (concentrated on systems design and manufacturing), in Santa Clara County (Silicon Valley), in the Denver area (location of Martin Marietta), in McLean, Virginia (location of BDM), and in Melbourne, Florida (location of Harris) – among others.

The suburban character of SDI-related industrial development also applies to the residential pattern of these industries' labor force. SDI has markedly upgraded the already high level of skills in this particular labor market. SDI-employed scientists and engineers are well paid enough still to be able to afford, as many of the young middle-class professionals cannot, the American dream of the large suburban house in a green suburb. Enjoying relative proximity to their work locations, and the necessary easy access to the freeway, the new high-tech defense workers live very differently from the industrial workers of the large defense procurement plants, who often live in company towns reminiscent of the first industrial cities. Affluent suburbs, secluded communities, and a spatial landscape made up of distinct functional locations around a freeway system are the basic elements of the urban structure associated with a technologically advanced defense industry fostered by SDI.

SDI brings an additional, and more distinctive, urban expression of the new social logic to industrial development: the *space of secrecy*. Perhaps the most distinctive character of the new defense industry organized around SDI is the high level of classified activity it involves.[182] In accordance with its ultimate goal of achieving technological military supremacy, the Defense Department is stepping up its controls to make sure that the Soviet bloc does not receive any technology transfer on time, that is, before the technology has already been rendered obsolete by new discoveries, in an endless race in which the US is intended to enjoy a cumulative lead.[183] This secrecy is perhaps the major obstacle to the industrial and commercial diffusion of results of SDI-inspired technology policy, and is the basis for its critics' most powerful argument. It also has a number of important spatial consequences. Areas where the most advanced high-tech industries are concentrated are likely to become increasingly secluded and kept under surveillance. Each company tends to be isolated from the outside world, both because of the DoD's requirements and because of its own interest in keeping ahead of the competition. The spatial layouts of the companies follow this logic, with discrete buildings scattered along the freeway, isolated from their immediate surroundings. This spatial arrangement does not contradict the tendency toward the formation of a new industrial milieu: it further defines it. On the one hand, each major technological center tends to have its own network of auxiliary enterprises and sub-contractors, most of them in the same spatial area, so that clusters of activities co-exist without necessarily intermixing; on the other hand, the requirement for secrecy leads to a very hierarchical spatial organization within the companies themselves, with the top research centers being segregated from other activities in areas of higher status, provided with better facilities, and more easily isolated and protected. At the very top of the research hierarchy of the SDI-related organizations, major national laboratories constitute their own spaces, in campus-like locations removed from the vicinity of major urban areas, so that social influences can be limited and the physical and cultural distance maintained: such is the case of the Lawrence Laboratory in Livermore, northern California, of Los Alamos and Sandia in New Mexico, and, to a certain extent only, of Lincoln Laboratory in Lexington, Massachusetts.[184] The secrecy of military-related scientific activities fosters the spatial diffusion of the new industrial milieux, emphasizes the importance of the inner world of the company and its network, reinforces the need for face-to-face contact *within* this restricted technical and managerial class, and tends to create a new world of secluded communities that remove themselves both socially and spatially from the context of pre-existing urban organizations.

When SDI's scientific warriors go down to Earth they create a new landscape of specialized, hierarchical, secluded locations, further distinguishing themselves within the already distinct spatial organization of the defense industry.

Conclusion

The transformation of the state in advanced capitalist societies exercises fundamental effects on the shaping of urban and regional processes. The crisis of the urban welfare state and rise of the new warfare state are dramatically altering the structure of cities and regions in different countries, and very especially in the United States. This transformation is a political phenomenon in its origins, characterized by the demise of the New Deal coalition and the emergence of new regional elites and of a new power bloc, based upon the alliance of multinational business and the technical-managerial middle class. In addition, growing challenges to American power and competitiveness on the international scene have called for a more assertive role on the part of the US government in the exercise of its global responsibilities. Altogether, a historical trend has developed in the past decade toward the formation of a specific political dynamic whose essence I have tried to capture under the notion of the transition from the welfare state to the warfare state, in spite of the risks of ideological oversimplification of this formulation. The matter in question is that the primary principle of legitimacy of the new state has shifted from its redistributive role to its power-building function. I believe this to be a fundamental tendency and not limited to a given administration (Reagan) or party (GOP). It is in fact a profound social realignment that has found its expression, and been politically reinforced, in the 1980s under Reagan. Certainly, as in all political processes, the development of the new state is open-ended, and could involve alternative political orientations that would eventually affect again the structure of the state itself. Nevertheless, such conflictive evolution is unlikely to restore the previous situation. We are entering a new political era that in its initial stages is dominated by what I call the warfare state, albeit its future development will be shaped, and may be transformed, by new social movements and political actors yet to enter upon the scene.

As we have seen, new technologies are an important factor in this transformation of the state, although they are by no means at its origin. The technological challenge posed to the institutions of the warfare state has been met with a massive appropriation of scientific and economic resources to the building of a new defense system that would leapfrog over the existing stalemate to achieve military superiority, both strategically and in conventional regional warfare. Budgetary constraints, political priorities, and changing social constituencies all determine the necessary connection between the technology-driven defense build-up and the dismantlement of the urban welfare state. New political coalitions regroup around the ideas of national security, world power, technological progress, and individual well-being, achieved through hard-working entrepreneurship and superior education. The new state is socially exclusive, but ideologically inclusive, with the government's role being reduced to the mediation between the great Americans and the Great America. High technology is presented as the instrument through which both ends meet, economically and functionally. Thus, economic competition in the world arena becomes successful through technological modernization at home and controlled leasing of know-how abroad. Military superiority, and therefore political supremacy, are achieved by the obsolescence of rival armies imposed by leadership in the technological race. And, most importantly, individual well-being is obtained by profound re-tooling of the economy, and by massive reskilling of new workers. This scenario is *not* an ideological artifact; it corresponds to a positive, feasible development policy. What is ideological in this respect is to offer as a general perspective for the whole of society a process that, in reality, will be highly selective, restricted to some social groups, to specific occupations and industries, and to some regions and cities. In this sense, the transformation of the state, which is inherent in the technological revolution, is closely intertwined with the overall process of socio-economic restructuring that has been analyzed in preceding chapters. Changing the principles of political legitimacy, and thus the workings of state institutions, is only possible because of the transformation of the social structure, strongly linked to the new social relationships of production. In turn, the new policies implemented by the state, in particular the technology-driven defense priority, deepen and reinforce the new economic and social organization. The process of restructuring is both multidimensional and interconnected.

The main theme of this chapter has been the impact of such a process of restructuring, and particularly of the transformation of the state, on the urban and regional process. I have also shown how information technologies have played an important role both in the restructuring itself, and in the mediation between the modification of the state and the organization of cities and regions.

First of all, the regional bias of the crisis of the welfare state, damaging further already depressed regions, and the general preference of the warfare state for booming, high-tech-prone areas, have exacerbated uneven regional development. At the same time, some of the traditionally dominant economic regions (for instance the mid-west as opposed to the south-west or the south-east) have been unable to prevail in the new process of growth. So, although the process of uneven development is intensified, the overall spatial pattern does not lead to greater regional disparity, since some of the historical unevenness is now to an extent corrected. What emerges is a much more complex regional structure, with processes of alternate growth and decline, producing an economic space of variable geometry, with acute processes of social dislocation.

Secondly, the demise of the urban welfare state removes the safety net for the large proportion of inner-city residents that fall down the cracks of the new informational economy. In so doing, the new state policies contribute to the process of dualization that characterizes both the labor market and the residential space of large metropolitan areas. The dual city, as an essential part of the informational city, is institutionalized by the state which abandons the spaces of destitution to their own decline, while concentrating resources in and targeting policies on the preserved spaces of functional management and upgraded consumption. Urbanism and the state continue to be tightly linked in the socio-spatial process, although in a direction historically opposite to that which emerged, with the welfare state, during the 1960s.

Thirdly, the rise of a technologically-oriented warfare state has a definite suburban form on the fringe of the large metropolitan areas in expanding regions, for the reasons presented in this chapter on the basis of available empirical evidence. Militarization, high-technology development, and suburbanization seem to be closely related processes, in the specific conditions of the US, and as a consequence of the policies associated with the rise of the warfare state. Given the impetus of this process, the suburban landscape will increasingly be the predominant spatial form of American cities, in spite of all the images of revival of the city cores, a real but limited phenomenon. The suburbanization of residence, of manufacturing, and of services, is now reinforced by the suburbanization of leading industries, associated with defense and high technology, as well as of their relatively affluent workers. It is likely to result in a new type of suburb, more dense, yet extending over a much greater area, in an endless strip served by secondary axes connecting exurban dwellings.

The transformation of the state in the informational age deeply affects spatial organization, by exacerbating uneven regional development, reinforcing intra-metropolitan social dualism, and fostering a new breed of suburbanization. In addition, it also influences two key processes at the roots of urban regional dynamics.

On the one hand, the attack on the urban welfare state provokes strong resistance among politically conscious minorities, which organize new local political coalitions in which neighborhoods and minorities have a greater say than in the former pro-growth coalition, in order to retrench themselves in the local state against the predominance of the warfare state logic at Federal and state government level. The example of a large US central city with a populist government, such as Chicago, Washington DC, San Francisco, or Boston, could become general if the demise of the welfare institutions on which patronage resources were based continues, laying the ground for more militant coalitions in which business interests would be secondary to the interests of defending and expanding collective consumption.

On the other hand, the rise of the warfare state is connected to the extension of the logic of military secrecy to the places of work and residence of a substantial proportion of the technological elite. There follows a greater social distance between these exclusive suburban spaces and their surrounding local societies. Cities become more internally segregated, not only socially, but culturally and functionally. Spaces of exclusion, tightly closed communities, co-exist with spatial sprawl of meaningless places structured around their functional activity.

The welfare state was born in the furnaces of life of large inner cities. The warfare state expands over an open space of distance and silence.

6

The Internationalization of the Economy, New Technologies, and the Variable Geometry of the Spatial Structure

Introduction

The internationalization of the economy at an accelerating pace is a fundamental element of the process of economic restructuring now under way. Although the process of internationalization represents a secular trend of capitalism, it has since the 1970s taken on much greater proportions, and has embraced new dimensions, in the attempt by corporations to overcome the contradictions revealed by the structural crisis of the world economy, by increasing the rate at which capital circulates and by constantly searching for the most advantageous location for investment, production, and markets the planet has to offer. National economies have become increasingly inter-dependent through the relentless expansion of world trade and the growing volume of exchange of multidirectional capital flows. While all countries are being drawn into this global network, the internationalization of the US economy is particularly significant because for a long time, while the reach of its companies extended throughout the world, its domestic market had been by virtue of its size and self-sufficiency, relatively insulated from international movements. This process of internationalization proceeds simultaneously on all fundamental dimensions of the economy: markets, investment, means of production, labor, and capital flows. The proportion of exports of goods and services in US GNP was only 5.0 percent in 1950; it increased to 6.78 percent in 1970, then to 12.54 percent in 1981, only to decline subsequently to 8.86 percent in 1986, because of the loss of competitiveness of American industry. Imports' share of GNP increased faster, from 4.26 percent in 1950 to 5.96 percent in 1970, again to 11.42 percent in 1981, and remaining around that level in 1986 (11.37 percent). The importance of foreign trade in goods production and consumption has grown at an even higher rate. In 1970, only 9 percent of goods produced in the US were exported; by 1980, the proportion had climbed to 17 percent. In 1970, 9 percent of goods sold in the US were imported: in 1980 the corresponding figure was 21 percent. About 25 percent of the increase in US consumption of goods during the 1970s was taken up by imports, while 75 percent of American-produced goods must, in the 1980s, face competition in the international market.[1]

Investment and production by American firms have also become increasingly internationalized. Investment overseas by American firms tripled in value between 1970 and 1984. By 1982, US-based multinationals had total assets of about $3.5 billion and employed 20 million workers. Their foreign affiliates had assets of $751 million and employed 6.8 million workers. As early as 1977, American multinationals produced the equivalent of one-third of the US GNP in their offshore facilities. In 1985, the 150 largest US multinationals earned 34 percent of their pre-tax profits abroad, on sales of $415 billion. While the share of world markets for US firms operating in America declined, the exports share of overseas US affiliates increased from 9 percent to 13.4 percent of world exports between 1966 and 1977, indicating a widening gap between the performance of American companies and that of the US economy.[2] Total US direct foreign investment abroad has increased by a factor of five from $51,792 million in 1965 to $259,890 million in 1986 (current dollars), with manufacturing accounting for 40 percent of the total in 1965 and 41.3 percent in 1986. Map 6.1 shows the spatial distribution of employment linked to manufacturing exports in the US.

Offshoring of manufacturing has become an increasingly important feature of US companies in key industries, particularly in electronics, automobiles, textiles, and garments: in 1982, offshore employment accounted for about one-quarter of US manufacturing workers. A particularly important development has been the expansion of offshore production for American companies in northern Mexico, under the protection of Sections 806 and 807 of the US Tariff Code, which permit the export of American components and their re-import after processing in Mexico, with duties to be paid only on the value added. The "maquiladora" plants working in Mexico under such arrangements have increased in number from 300 in 1978 to 760 in 1985, with employment in them growing from 80,000 workers to 300,000. Investments by US firms in these plants and sub-contracting arrangements amounted to $2 billion in 1985 and are still expanding.[3]

Simultaneously, an unprecedented wave of foreign direct investment has swept the US, in all sectors, leading to further interpenetration of the most advanced economies. The value of foreign direct investment in the US in 1985 was $183 billion: 14 times the 1970 level. Between 1979 and 1985 there occurred over seven thousand acquisitions, mergers, and investments in new plants by foreign firms, particularly from the United Kingdom, the Netherlands, Canada, Japan, West Germany, and France. In 1984, foreign firms had $596 billion of total assets, owned 13 million acres of land, and employed 2.7 million workers in the US, including 1.4 million workers in manufacturing, equivalent to 7 percent of total manufacturing employment. Foreign

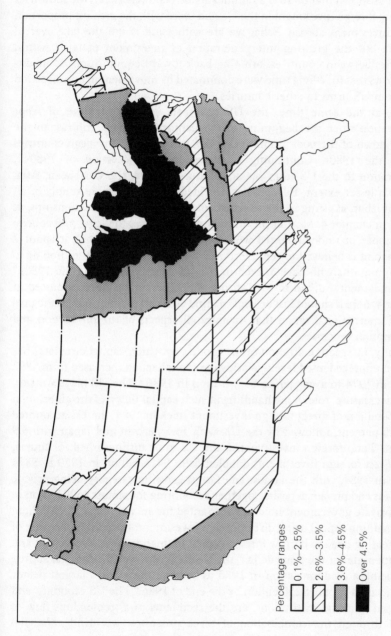

Map 6.1 Employment related to manufacturing exports as a percentage of total civilian employment by state, 1976
Source: Business America, 19 November 1974; compiled by Agnew (see note 1)

Percentage ranges
0.1%–2.5%
2.6%–3.5%
3.6%–4.5%
Over 4.5%

manufacturers further internationalized the patterns of trade, accounting for
one-quarter of total exports and one-third of total imports in 1984.[4] In fact,
Little[5] has shown that there is a significant correlation between the industries
receiving foreign investment in the US and those with the greatest proportion
of US investment abroad. What we are witnessing is not the take-over of
America but the growing interpenetration of investment patterns within
industries between countries, bringing back toward equilibrium the investment flows that for a long time were dominated by movement in one direction
only from US firms to other countries.

Also, at the same time, the US has seen its greatest wave of labor
immigration since the beginning of the century, in sharp contrast to the
scaling down of the pool of immigrant labor in western European countries
during the 1980s. Continuing unabated by the recession of 1980–2,
immigration to the US from Mexico, Latin America, the Caribbean, Asia,
and, to a lesser extent, Europe, has provided an inexhaustible supply of all
kinds of labor, assisting in the restructuring of capital–labor relationships, as
argued in chapter 4. Most of this immigration bypasses the legal procedures:
the number of undocumented workers in the US is estimated at about 7
million, and is believed to represent over three-quarters of the million or so
new immigrants who have arrived in the US every year during the 1980s.[6]
The fundamental urban impact of this phenomenon has been discussed in
chapter 4; here it should just be kept in mind as another dimension of the process of internationalization that includes all aspects of the production and
consumption processes.

Finally, internationalization of the process by which capital circulates has
reached unprecedented levels. Worldwide capitalization increased from $892
billion in 1974 to a staggering $5.2 trillion in 1986.[7] The US plays a major,
albeit decreasing, role in the handling of such capital flows: of the global total
of $549 billion of direct foreign investment stock in 1984, the US accounted
for 42.5 percent, followed by the UK with 15.5 percent and Japan with 6.9
percent. Total foreign investment in the US to be distinguished, of course,
from *direct* foreign investment) doubled from $416 billion in 1979 to $874
billion in 1984, with the largest and fastest-growing category being private
portfolios and private deposits, together accounting for almost $500 billion in
1984; private government holdings accounted for an additional $196 billion,
the remaining capital being direct foreign investment. In addition, because of
its increasing need to borrow foreign capital to finance the budget deficit and
to compensate for the trade deficit, the US, as is now well known, has shifted
from being a creditor nation in 1980 to become the world's largest debtor
nation, with a debt of $250 billion by the end of 1986.[8] The US economy, and
US-based financial institutions, are the recipients of a tremendous flow of
capital through the combination of three processes: worldwide financial
investments handled from the US; massive inflows of foreign investment into
the US; and increasing lending from foreign capital to US firms and the US

government. Altogether, the American financial system has become entirely interdependent in a global network of capital flows of which the US is indeed a major center, but no longer a dominant one in terms of control over the extent and direction of capital flows. The linkage between capital flows and the balance of trade through the dollar's exchange rate has further constrained domestic fiscal policy, and tied the US inextricably to the interdependent evolution of the world economy.

This multidimensional process of internationalization and growing interdependence has been made possible by widespread utilization of new information technologies.[9] In the same way that the railroads were the indispensable infrastructure for the formation of a national market in the US in the nineteenth century, so the expansion of information systems, based on telecommunications and computers, has provided the technological medium for the formation of a world economy functioning in real time on a day-to-day basis. Without such information systems it would have been impossible to maintain the unity of management while decentralizing worldwide the production and markets of any given firm, at the same time as firms stepped up their interaction in every market. Without information systems, capital mobility could never have reached the volume and velocity illustrated by the data presented above. And without information systems, international trade could hardly constitute the dominant feature of advanced economies.

Furthermore, competitiveness in the new international economy is increasingly determined by the ability to develop and assimilate new technologies in the processes of production and management. Mastery of the technological medium becomes an indispensable requirement to win a competitive edge in a merciless worldwide competition, with new actors entering every day, struggling for survival, searching for domination. Access to technological sources, and ability to use them, adapt them, and improve them, becomes one of the most important forces in shaping the competition and its outcome, that is, the new economic structure. Production of new information-technology devices becomes one of the biggest world markets, whose control largely conditions the performance of firms and countries in all industries. Being the most internationalized industry, the manufacturing of information technologies, and their use, become the backbone of the new international economy, both as a market and as an instrument of competition. The more the economy is internationalized, the more crucial a role information technologies play in its shape and evolution. The technological medium conditions the fate and outcome of economic restructuring by its decisive impact on the process of internationalization, the fundamental feature of the new economy.

From this follows a transformation of spatial processes in all countries, and specifically in the US, whose contours we will examine by focusing in turn on each one of the dimensions of the internationalization process: trade, offshore production, foreign investment, and global financial flows.

International Trade, Competitiveness, and the Rise and Fall of American Regions

The growing integration of the US economy in international trade has far-reaching, and somewhat unsuspected, implications for both the US itself and the world economy at large.[10] Since the mid 1970s manufacturing exports have been growing steadily, as has the share of exports in manufacturing for almost all industries. However, the confrontation of US manufacturers with foreign competition in the world marketplace has proved disastrous for America. In spite of their growing relative importance in US terms, American exports of manufactured goods have declined in proportion to those of other countries, as America's share of world markets in value terms has declined from 26 percent in 1960 to 18 percent in 1980, before the overvaluation of the dollar; and it continued to slip during the 1980s.[11] On the other hand, imports skyrocketed, particularly in consumer electronics, automobiles, textiles, clothing, footwear, and machine tools. The merchandise trade balance, which was positive from 1893 to 1970, turned negative in 1971, and, with the exception of 1973 and 1975, continued negative, with the deficit reaching catastrophic proportions in the 1980s: from a deficit of $38.4 billions in 1982, the negative trade balance set a new record every year, reaching the figure of $171.2 billion in 1987. The extremity of the situation of American trade can be judged by recalling that the trade deficit figures for December 1987 were considered good news, because they showed only a $12.2 billion deficit in just one month!

For some time, losses in manufacturing trade were partially offset by surpluses in agriculture, in services, and in high-technology balances. However, after being stimulated by government policies in the early 1970s, agricultural exports were also exposed to foreign competition, and the surplus was reduced from $30 billion in 1979–80 to just $4 billion in 1986. As for services, the surplus gradually declined as US earnings abroad diminished, and revenues from foreign capital lent to the US increased, until 1985, when the US also posted a deficit in its service account.[12] While the technology chapter of the service account was still positive (but represented only $5 billion), the manufacturing–technology balance deteriorated rapidly over the 1980s.[13] And in 1985 the US imported $463 billion worth of goods and services.

The reasons for this startling loss in competitiveness are rooted in the structure of the American economy. It is true that other factors have to be taken into consideration, in particular the exchange rate: when in 1987 the value of the dollar against the main international currencies plummeted, falling as much as 40 percent from its February 1985 peak, some of the economy's competitiveness was restored and exports started to improve, merchandise exports rising 15 percent in 1987. However, the losses in foreign trade show up during phases when the dollar has been undervalued as well as when it has been overvalued in the last 15 years; and the shares of the US market won by imports have been largely preserved by foreign competitors slashing profit margins to retain their market position. More important in explaining the decline in trade is the role played by the Reagan administration's macroeconomic policy in creating fiscal and monetary conditions that undermined US competitiveness. By artificially stimulating the economy through a runaway budget deficit, Reaganomics stimulated consumer demand for imports by consumers; and by borrowing foreign capital on an unprecedented scale to finance the deficit, it drove the dollar up, which attracted more capital, but made exports more expensive and imports cheaper.[14] Consequently, the *de facto* devaluation of the dollar in 1987 could not be pursued indefinitely because to do so would dry up the sources of capital needed to finance the budget deficit (in this sense the two mega-deficits are interwined). Restoration of competitiveness, then, cannot be achieved by the sole means of manipulating the exchange rate.

The roots of the crisis in competitivness seem to go deeper, and to reach beyond the entry of new economic actors catching up with the US on the international scene. Cohen and Zysman, in a powerful and well informed book,[15] have argued that the decline of American competitiveness lies in a combination of external factors and internal weaknesses. On the one hand, the structure of costs in newly industrializing countries, the state support granted to many foreign firms, and the closing of some major markets, most notably Japan, to American products, certainly placed US firms at a disadvantage. However, the domestic factors seem to be more important. By forgetting the crucial linkage between manufacturing and services, and by concentrating too exclusively on high-technology innovation and services, instead of rooting both in the rejuvenation of industrial production, American companies have created a "hollow economy," dominated by "paper capitalism," that cannot resist the assault of new competitors (Japan, West Germany, and the Asian NICs), who systematically upgrade their production technologies, and concentrate on keeping manufacturing quality up and manufacturing costs down to outpace their competitors in the international market. On this competitive basis they accumulate capital, which ultimately puts them in the position where they control the process of circulation itself. By emigrating to low-cost locations or sub-contracting production internationally, instead of automating and upgrading the production process in the US, American companies have created the conditions of their own demise. Finally, the inability to overhaul the educational system to provide on a sufficiently large scale the new skills required in the informational processes of production and management also places the US behind its competitors, who also do not have to sustain the burden of unproductive, technology-draining military expenditures. Overall, the US is too expensive as a location from which to operate, and too unsophisticated to be worth the investment of staying in the country. Only the attraction of the market remains; but this increasingly has to be shared with foreign investors, and will not last indefinitely, given the precipitous decline in American living standards. While the process is reversible, its unfolding logic shows the contradictions introduced in the economic structure by the processes of internationalization and technological change when, instead of being harnessed within a long-term view, they are approached with a short-term, individualistic strategy aimed at maximizing immediate profits.

The erosion of American competitiveness has had profound effects on the country's economic and occupational structure. Traditional manufacturing, most heavily struck by competition, and by runaway shops trying to reproduce the competitors' cost structure in offshore locations, experienced a substantial decline during the 1976–86 decade. According to the Bureau of Labor Statistics, between 1979 and January 1987, there was a loss of 1.9 million manufacturing jobs, although not all of them can be related to the trade deficit. These losses included 500,000 jobs in primary metals, 450,000 in machinery, 350,000 in textiles and apparel, and 300,000 in fabricated metals. Other sectors that suffered job losses were stone, transportation, leather, chemicals, petroleum, and food.[16] In another study by the Urban Institute, it was estimated that about 2 million jobs were lost because of rising imports between 1979 and 1984, particularly in steel, automobiles, and apparel.[17] High-technology industries were not immune to competition: electronics went into a major slump in 1984–5, with computers being particularly severely hurt. An econometric study by John Lederer relates loss of jobs in California's electronics industry to foreign competition, and more specifically to lower labor costs in the Japanese companies.[18] The more an industry is exposed to competition, the more it is vulnerable to lower production costs, and the more its share of both domestic and international markets will decline. As early as 1979, the US imported 21 percent of its cars, 16 percent of its steel, 50 percent of its televisions, radios, tape recorders, and VCRs, and 90 percent of its knives and forks.[19] Lester Thurow's calculations attribute the loss of 3 million jobs to loss of international competitiveness in overseas markets.[20] An OTA study indicates that half of all workers displaced between 1979 and 1984 worked in manufacturing industries, particularly in those hard hit by foreign competition, such as steel, automobiles, industrial equipment, textiles, and apparel.[21] The effects of loss of competitiveness are not limited to the core manufacturing areas themselves, but, as Cohen and Zysman have argued, are also apparent in related manufacturing and services activities. According to *Business Week*,[22] the total impact on the economy for each billion dollars' worth of imported cars was $2.43 billion, including $1.3 billion lost in auto production, $778 million in manufacturing suppliers, and $387 million in related service industries.

These effects are territorially specific. Since manufacturing, and particularly traditional manufacturing, is unevenly distributed among regions, those areas with industries specially vulnerable to foreign competition will be most hurt by the loss of market share. Map 6.1 shows the concentration of manufacturing exports in 1976, in the early stages of the loss of competitiveness, and table 6.1 exhibits the relative importance of manufacturing exports

Table 6.1 Manufacturing exports by state in the United States. 1976–1984

	Total manufacturing export ($m)			Export as % of total shipments		
	1976	1984	Average annual rate of growth (%)	1976	1984	Average annual rate of growth (%)
Alabama	832	4,198	22.4	4.6	11.6	12.3
Alaska	233	643	13.5	23.5	27.2	1.8
Arizona	639	2,481	18.5	10.3	15.6	5.3
Arkansas	651	2,405	17.7	6.1	10.5	7.0
California	8,072	28,764	17.2	7.9	13.0	6.4
Colorado	616	2,790	20.8	6.5	13.1	9.2
Connecticut	1,598	5,436	16.5	10.7	15.6	4.8
Delaware	188	1,132	25.1	3.7	11.7	15.5
District of Columbia	7	72	33.9	0.7	4.2	25.1
Florida	1,363	5,975	20.3	7.5	12.5	6.6
Georgia	1,364	5,061	17.8	4.8	8.2	6.9
Hawaii	183	414	10.7	9.9	12.1	2.5
Idaho	169	666	18.7	4.9	10.7	10.3
Illinois	6,660	13,332	9.1	8.1	10.6	3.4
Indiana	2,828	9,380	16.2	6.3	12.2	8.6
Iowa	1,500	3,296	10.3	7.2	9.8	3.9
Kansas	635	2,630	19.4	4.3	8.6	9.1
Kentucky	1,137	4,077	17.3	5.6	10.9	8.7
Louisiana	1,383	6,990	22.4	5.5	12.7	11.0
Maine	255	1,215	21.6	5.8	12.2	9.7
Maryland	641	2,328	17.5	4.3	9.9	11.0
Massachusetts	2,502	8,768	17.0	9.3	15.0	6.2
Michigan	6,888	16,662	11.7	8.6	12.8	5.1
Minnesota	1,567	5,294	16.4	7.7	12.4	6.1
Mississippi	698	2,237	15.7	6.4	10.0	5.7

Table 6.1 Continued

Missouri	1,622	5,375	16.2	5.9	10.2	7.1
Montana	44	319	28.2	1.7	8.4	22.1
Nebraska	309	1,328	19.9	3.5	8.7	12.1
Nevada	27	183	26.9	3.8	10.3	13.3
New Hampshire	291	1,129	18.5	8.3	12.9	5.7
New Jersey	2,660	8,024	14.8	5.8	10.3	7.4
New Mexico	69	330	21.6	4.5	8.4	8.1
New York	5,320	15,993	14.7	7.0	11.9	6.9
North Carolina	2,020	8,477	18.4	6.1	10.8	7.4
North Dakota	85	290	16.7	6.8	11.2	6.4
Ohio	5,794	17,381	14.7	6.9	12.3	7.5
Ohlahoma	579	2,288	18.7	5.7	9.3	6.3
Oregon	824	2,709	16.0	6.7	12.9	8.5
Pennsylvania	4,706	12,827	13.4	6.5	11.4	7.3
Rhode Island	269	946	17.1	5.9	11.1	8.2
South Carolina	935	3,982	19.8	5.6	11.7	9.6
South Dakota	68	245	17.3	4.2	7.0	6.6
Tennessee	1,253	5,008	18.9	5.1	10.1	8.9
Texas	5,201	22,093	19.8	6.7	12.6	8.2
Utah	224	1,298	24.6	4.8	12.6	12.8
Vermont	200	617	15.1	9.7	16.2	6.6
Virginia	1,545	4,781	15.2	7.5	10.9	4.8
Washington	3,235	8,632	13.1	17.2	22.4	3.4
West Virginia	447	1,853	19.4	5.6	17.2	15.1
Wisconsin	2,209	5,785	12.8	6.2	9.3	5.2
Wyoming	10	152	40.0	1.2	6.3	23.0
United States, total	83,098	268,278	15.8	7.0	11.9	6.9

Source: US Department of Commerce, *Annual Survey of Manufactures*, 1976, 1984.

by state. If we relate these data to the statistics on job displacement presented in tables 6.2 and 6.3, elaborated by Candee Harris[23] we observe a general correspondence between the regions with a strong trend in manufacturing export-related jobs and those with low replacement ratios for jobs lost and created. Overall, the old manufacturing belt underwent a massive contraction in employment between 1967 and 1980: 24.8 percent down for New York, 11.1 percent for New Jersey, 14.3 percent for Pennsylvania, 11.2 percent for Michigan, 12.5 percent for Illinois, 9.2 percent for Ohio, and 7.3 percent for Indiana.[24]

However, not all these manufacturing jobs disappeared: some moved offshore, and some relocated to other areas, particularly the south and the

Table 6.2   Employment loss in dissolutions of manufacturing establishments by region (%)

Region	1972–4	1974–6	1978–80	1980–2
New England	8.0	8.1	7.4	11.4
Mid-Atlantic	7.9	11.0	7.1	11.5
East-north-central	5.4	8.9	6.4	10.8
West-north-central	7.0	9.9	5.6	10.5
South Atlantic	8.1	11.6	7.3	13.7
East-south-central	7.6	10.3	6.0	13.7
West-south-central	7.8	11.1	7.3	12.6
Mountain	9.2	14.1	7.1	14.7
Pacific	8.6	10.9	9.0	14.0

Sources: 1972–4, 1974–6, David Birch, The Job Generation Process (final report to the Economic Development Administration, US Department of Commerce, grant no. OER-608-G78-7, June 1979); 1978–80, 1980–2, unpublished tabulations, US Establishment and Enterprise Microdata Base. Calculated by Harris (see note 23)

Table 6.3   Manufacturing job replacement ratios for all establishments by region

Region	1972–4	1974–6	1978–80	1980–2
New England	1.42	0.45	1.58	0.52
Mid-Atlantic	1.06	0.28	1.45	0.52
East-north-central	1.85	0.57	1.33	0.22
West-north-central	2.15	0.65	2.21	0.57
South Atlantic	1.65	0.61	2.16	0.69
East-south-central	1.97	0.71	1.83	0.32
West-south-central	1.86	1.16	2.94	1.05
Mountain	1.70	1.01	3.01	0.88
Pacific	1.60	1.47	2.10	0.86
US total	1.60	0.67	1.85	0.57

Sources: 1972–4, 1974–6, David Birch The Job Generation Process; 1978–80, 1980–2, unpublished tabulations, US Establishment and Enterprise Microdata Base. Calculated by Harris (see note 23).

south-west, trying to find there better conditions with which to fight foreign competition, most notably lower wages and less stringent labor laws. In 1967–80, Texas showed the largest increase in manufacturing employment of any state, in absolute numbers, with particularly high increases in chemicals, petroleum, and primary metals. According to Bluestone and Harrison, for the period 1969–76 the balance between jobs created and jobs destroyed was a positive 8,851,900 million for the whole of the US, of which 6,624,000 were in the sunbelt.[25] Nevertheless, the majority of losses as a result of declining international competitiveness took place after 1976, and Peter Hall's calculations for the 1975–85 period are therefore more relevant.[26] Two sub-periods must be differentiated. In 1975–80, the US economy generated 15.7 million new jobs, of which only 13 percent were in manufacturing, and only 27 percent in the manufacturing belt. Of every five of these new jobs, three were located in the sunbelt, and two-thirds of them in what Hall labels the "new perimeter," meaning the sunbelt and New England together. In fact, 70 percent of new manufacturing jobs in this half-decade were created in the sunbelt, and only an additional 11 percent in New England. In the second half of the decade, 1980–5, only 4.2 million new jobs were created. Of these, 87 percent were in the sunbelt, and 96 percent in the sunbelt plus New England. If New England were to be omitted from the traditional manufacturing belt, this manufacturing belt would be shown to have suffered a net loss of 400,000 manufacturing jobs, although they were more than compensated for numerically by the creation of service jobs. In this sense, the manufacturing belt may be divided into two areas: the mid-Atlantic, which had the worst performance in manufacturing jobs, losing 276,000 of them, but which performed well in terms of creating compensatory numbers of service jobs; and the east-north-central states, which lost fewer manufacturing jobs (138,000) but could not create enough service jobs to compensate for the loss, resulting in a net decline in employment.

Four processes, then, appear to be at work simultaneously: loss of traditional manufacturing, partially linked to foreign competition, both abroad and in the domestic market; relocation of manufacturing jobs in the south, south-west, and west, in search of a labor and regulatory environment that makes competition easier; growth of manufacturing jobs in new industries, as in the case of New England and California, both established manufacturing regions (although only New England is regionally integrated in the old manufacturing belt); and a capacity of generation of new service jobs, through linkages either with the new expanding regional economy (the sunbelt) or with the nodal metropolitan centers in the international economy (in the north-east and the west). In addition, it must be noted that traditional manufacturing is vulnerable to the new conditions of the international economy wherever it may be located. The automobile industry has been hurt in California as much as it has in the Great Lakes; and the textile and garment industries in the south were devastated by foreign competition, before engineering a comeback on the basis of new technologies.[27]

Regional fortunes have also been linked to the sharp variations in commodity prices on the world markets. When the price of oil in the 1970s appeared to have no limit but the sky, Texas rode on the crest of a spending wave that has left its mark on Houston's architectural monument to self-infatuation. When the administration's policies geared toward offsetting the manufacturing deficit by means of increasing agricultural exports pushed up farm prices in the early 1970s, and encouraged farmers to borrow and expand, the mid-western farm belt believed in the permanence of the earth's bounty. And when one state, such as Oklahoma, was blessed with both agricultural endowments and oil resources, everything seemed possible. But then came the glut of oil and the fall of energy prices, along with fiercer competition in the grain markets from the EEC; and by the mid-1980s there had come into being what has been called a "deflation belt" throughout middle America.[28]

The basic phenomenon, therefore, is not the irreversible demise of certain regions, linked to forms of production that were becoming technologically obsolete in the world economy. Silicon Valley went into a recession in 1984–6, much as Iowa did in the mid-1980s. And while electronics was doing well in 1987, so was agro-business in California. New England taught the world a lesson about how to operate the transition from deindustrialization of old manufacturing to reindustrialization of high technology. Michigan combined depressed areas in Detroit with booming business around Flint and Ann Arbor's "robot alley." The new industrialized south was also losing jobs in textiles, as foreign competition showed its resistance to tariffs by modifying its price structure. All over America's industrial landscape there was a diversity of reactions and adjustments to the new conditions of international competition. Some strategies emphasized upgrading of manufacturing through technology and re-skilling. Others imitated Third World over-exploitation and reinvented the sweatshop. Others still relied on foreign supplies or on Mexican border operations to combine the best of both worlds from a business perspective. The fundamental transformation, common to all industries and to all regions, was the tight linkage between world dynamics and regional dynamics. Never again would the US be able to take refuge in its own land, or to live by its own habits. The law of internationalization, imposed upon the world on an unprecedented scale by American capitalism, was now coming home to roost. Among the corollaries of this process are extreme volatility of production and consumption, and therefore of income and everyday life, according to the state of play in the competition of capital between and within regions. The rise and fall of American regions no longer follows the script written by American capital or the American state. It just happens, in complex interaction among world economic processes, individual firms' strategies, and confused policies from local, state, and Federal governments. The internationalization of the American economy has led to the fragmentation of its regions and to the constant realignment of its processes of regional development; and its reaction, in the attempt to recover autonomy through protectionism at different levels, has triggered the ultimate response from economic competitors worldwide: to penetrate deeply the US economy with foreign investment, some of it dating from the good period of successful exports to the largest market in the world, a time when American companies moved a significant proportion of their own production offshore to enable them to compete in their own market.

Restructuring, Internationalization of Production, and Technological Change: The Case of the American Automobile Industry

The internationalization of the production process itself is one of the dimensions of the process of restructuring. New technologies of telecommunication, transportation, and automation allow firms to separate their different manufacturing operations across boundaries, while reintegrating them into a unified system under the control of the company's management. The resulting locational pattern modifies profoundly the characteristics of the industrial space and its impact on urban and regional development.

In chapter 2 the internationalization of electronics production was analyzed, the pioneer industry in offshoring assembly operations. This section will focus on the automobile industry, a major industrial sector in the American economy, whose direct and indirect employment accounted in 1977 for about 21 percent of the total labor force.[29] Particular attention will be concentrated on the dialectics between offshoring of production and more recent tendencies toward reconcentration in the core, stimulated by newer and more sophisticated automation technologies in manufacturing.

The automobile industry exemplifies the complex interplay between economic and technological restructuring and the internationalization of production and investment. The oil shock of 1973–4 plunged into a worldwide crisis an industry that had been the leading sector in the industrialization process based on mass-production that took place between the 1920s and the 1960s.[30] The effects of that crisis were exacerbated for the US by increased foreign competition from cheaper, better-quality, more fuel-efficient cars. US production represented over 75 percent of total world production of automobiles in 1950, but the proportion was only 29 percent in 1974, and continued to slide down to 19.3 percent in 1982, although it re-covered slightly after that date. Foreign imports' share of passenger cars in the US market rose from 15 percent in 1950 to 28 percent in 1982. The combined impact of oil prices, economic slump, and product obsolescence drove Chrysler to the edge of bankruptcy (from which it was pulled back by the US government), seriously damaged Ford's profitability, and even put the giant

General Motors on the defensive. The industry responded with one of the boldest restructuring processes in recent economic history, focusing at the same time on new products and new processes.[31] New technologies were massively introduced both in factories and in the cars themselves. In the factory, robotization, CAD/CAM, and flexible manufacturing systems rapidly transformed the assembly lines, while computers were introduced in all processes of design and testing.[32] New materials changed the basic characteristics of cars and new electronic systems their operations. The evolution of the automobile from the electrical–mechanical complex to the electronic–plastic product accelerated.[33] At the same time, advances in telecommunications, air transportation, and bulk cargo technologies increased the mobility of parts and vehicles between sites of production, and between production sites and the markets. Altogether, the industry was once again a pioneer in experimenting with new production techniques and, to some extent, with new methods of management. Fifteen years later, it is, by and large, a new industry, whose geographic distribution at the world level has been modified by the scale of its transformation.

The restructuring process went through different stages and revealed different emphases in various countries and firms. In the US the first move, for all companies, was purely defensive. It amounted to retrenchment, with plant closures, massive lay-offs, sales of assets, and reductions in investment. Chrysler liquidated its foreign subsidiaries. The launching of new models, adapted to the new energy circumstances and more highly discriminating consumer tastes, helped to absorb some of the initial shock of the crisis, particularly for GM, which, shielded by its size and financial resources, actually benefited from the catastrophic performance of its US competitors. In the late 1970s, the more positive strategy aimed at surviving the crisis and arriving on more stable ground, came into being along two different lines: stepped-up internationalization of production and distribution; and automation and computerization of the industry, both to save labor and to improve quality, thus enhacing productivity. The two strategies were used simultaneously by all firms, but, as will be explained below, with different emphases from company to company and within different time-frames. They also led to different locational consequences.

The process of internationalization took place on the basis of the decentralization that US companies, and particularly Ford, had effected since the 1950s in Europe, and since the 1960s in Latin America. By 1980, 37.2 percent of the total motor vehicle production of the four leading US manufacturers was located abroad. Indeed, in 1980, the US share of world car production was down to 21.7 percent, but US *manufacturers'* share of world production was still 33.4 percent.[34] The restructuring process initiated in the 1970s saw some additional steps taken along the path toward internationalization of production. The most direct expression of this trend was increased offshoring of sourcing, first of parts, but later of major mechanical elements, including engines. In 1980–3 US imports of engines grew by a factor of about four, from 544,020 units to 2,183,842. Most of these came from Brazil, France, joint-venture operations in Japan, and, particularly, from Mexico. In 1982, all American manufacturers had major engine plants in Mexico: Ford in Chihuahua, producing 400,000 engines (90 percent of them for export to the US and Canada); Chrysler in Ramos Arizpe, with 220,000 engines, equivalent to half of the four-cylinder engines used in Aries and Reliant cars; American Motors in Torreon, producing 300,000 engines for the R-9 built in Kenosha, Wisconsin; and GM in Ramos Arizpe, turning out 360,000 V-6 engines for the "8" and "X" models.[35] In 1984, Mexico exported to the US 700,000 automobile engines. Overall, by 1985, according to UNIDO, agreements to supply engines from offshore sources to US-located manufacturers included 1.5 million engines for Ford, over 1 million for GM, and 1.1 million for Chrysler.[36] The trends are similar for transmissions, cylinder heads, electronic control devices, power train items, and more.[37] Automobile imports, of both vehicles and parts, contributed $40.4 billion to the trade deficit in 1985.[38]

There are basically three reasons for this wholesale move offshore, which increased dramatically from the late 1970s onwards, to Mexico in particular: lower costs of production, mainly because of cheaper labor; government subsidies (in the case of Mexico and Brazil); and better quality (particularly for Japan). The net result is the hollowing out of a substantial part of automobile manufacturing in the US, which comes to be focused on assembling and marketing for the domestic market engines and parts that increasingly have been produced abroad.

The ultimate expression of the internationalization strategy is the "world car" concept, put forward mainly by Ford in the 1970s.[39] It refers to the design of cars that, with some minor modifications, can be sold in many different markets, if not in all countries. Their production takes place in different countries, following the competitive advantages of each location, and the components are assembled close to or in the final markets. The Ford Fiesta was the first example of such a car, with engines made in Valencia, Spain, and components and major parts in England and France, to be assembled in Spain, England, and Germany, and sold in the EC and North America. The strategy avoids duplication of effort in engineering and design, and takes advantage of the best possible location for each phase of the production process, putting into practice the concept of the "global factory." Harley Shaiken[40] has shown the decisive role played by new information technologies in the feasibility of this strategy. On the one hand, computerization of design and sophisticated telecommunications facilities linking engineering centers allow for interaction among research centers in different countries, as well as for the reintegration of the management process despite the multiplicity of production sites and markets. On the other hand, automation of production allows for precision and exact specification of components that can be assembled without being tested in the same plant.

However, the most important element in the "world car" strategy is, in the words of Ford's Chairman, "more common brains than common parts."[41] Ford's Erika Project, according to the company, saved 15,000 engineering/man years and $150 million, by implementing the "world car" strategy.

The spatial implications of the internationalization process center on decentralization of production and interrelationships both among plants and between plants and markets. Offshoring of component manufacture eliminates jobs in the US and diversifies the location of the industry. Global reintegration through communication channels enables this locational diversity to grow while maintaining the unity of the process. In terms of the regional impacts in the US, Ross and Trachte[42] have shown the dramatic effects of both automation and internationalization on employment in automobile manufacturing. Overall, total US employment in automobile manufacturing reached a peak of 1,004,900 jobs in 1978, to decline by 1983 to 704,800, below its 1951 level. In 1980–1, the industry went into full recession. The three major companies suffered combined losses of $3.5 billion; they laid off 250,000 workers, and an additional 400,000 workers in the supplier companies also lost their jobs.[43] The regions and cities that were the traditional centers of the industry, such as the Great Lakes and the Detroit area, were particularly badly hurt. Total motor vehicle employment in Michigan declined from 411,000 jobs in 1956 to 287,000 in 1982; in Detroit, over the same period, it fell from 252,000 jobs to 167,000. The impact of automobile retrenchment on Detroit was devastating. By 1981, one in every three residents in Detroit was receiving some form of public assistance. Central city infant mortality rates were at the level of Peru or Guyana, standing at four times higher than those of Detroit's suburbs. As Agnew writes:

The history of Detroit captures in one place the history of the American manufacturing belt. From 1870 until 1910 Detroit was one of several multipurpose cities of the industrial belt. From 1910 until the late 1960s the automobile industry and war production made Detroit a major national industrial center. But the country's sixth largest city has now become enmeshed in a web of uneven development spun first by the flow of industrial and commercial capital to the suburbs, and then to the Sunbelt and, more recently, by the reorganization and decentralization of the auto industry on a global scale. . . . Detroit is a victim of the world car.[44]

The impact of restructuring in the automobile industry was by no means limited to the Great Lakes area. In fact, Los Angeles held, after Detroit, the second largest agglomeration of automobile manufacturing in the US. Between 1975 and 1983, California lost 21,835 jobs through the closing of auto-related plants, most of them in northern California. The ratio of production to sales of cars in California went from 0.78 in 1968 to 0.12 in 1983.[45]

Looking beyond the decline of certain regions, what is really significant is the international mobility of capital, which determines the fate of industrial sectors, labor market segments, spatial areas, and local communities.

The global integration process, epitomized by the "world car" strategy, was not the only line pursued by US companies in the restructuring of the automobile industry. As the MIT study on the future of the automobile revealed,[46] a number of alternative options could be, and indeed were, explored. Paramount among them was better use of the possibilities offered by information technologies. Flexible manufacturing technologies make possible short production runs without lower productivity, enabling swift responses to market demand through constant redesign of the product, as well as by reprogramming the production process. The most important development in this transformation of both technology and production techniques is the adoption of the Japanese Kanban or "just in time" system, which enables drastic reduction of inventories by precisely tracking needs for parts and components, so that suppliers can provide those components only when and as they are needed. Besides making for considerable savings by avoiding tying up capital in inventory, the system also makes it possible to define a precise relationship to the market in terms of both time and quality, thus establishing flexible and continuous links between suppliers, assemblers, and markets. Fullest use of the Kanban system became possible only with the introduction of CAD/CAM and FIM (Flexible Integrated Manufacturing) techniques. In addition, automation of routine tasks saves labor costs and enhances quality; and computer design develops engineering capability and marketing adaptability to worldwide demand. An alternative to offshoring production to low-cost location is, following the Japanese example, to concentrate production in core areas of mature industrialization, to automate and upgrade substantially the technological level of manufacturing equipment, and to renovate labor practices through introducing team-work and involving workers in quality control of production, through a re-skilling of their professional capacities. According to this strategy, decentralization to low-skilled areas or countries is self-defeating in the long term, since higher quality and productivity through technological enhancement can only be achieved on the basis of a developed industrial infrastructure and a highly educated and motivated labor force. Moreover, location of manufacturing plants close to the core markets, where the overwhelming proportion of demand will be concentrated for a long time, enables the firm to be responsive to the changing demands of increasingly sophisticated customers in the face of stiff competition from highly flexible and well informed foreign manufacturers. These were the conclusions of the MIT study, in line with observed developments in the industry. Womack, one of the authors of that study, concluded in his analysis of Mexico that the main incentive for US auto makers to locate in the neighboring country would increasingly be the expansion of Mexico's domestic market rather than the off-shoring of production, which would decline as the advantages of flexible automation in the US unfolded.[47] A reconcentration of the industry around core markets and technology-endowed industrial regions is thus foreseen.

GM's strategy since 1979 clearly followed this line of argument, with the whole company adapting to what was perceived to be the secret of Japanese competitiveness: high-technology manufacturing and better management from the home-country platforms. Of course, GM still continued to produce worldwide, particularly in Europe, and still relied on considerable sourcing from foreign countries, mainly Japan, Korea, and Mexico. Nevertheless, the emphasis was on re-equipping the entire company with full use of new technologies and the design of a new generation of cars. In 1979 a new strategy was launched aimed at building complete new plants, and at introducing computerized equipment in all GM factories. By 1987, $60 billion had been spent on this ambitious program – more than one-third over the originally planned $40 billion.[48] The most spectacular example of the new strategy was the project to build a new, small, front-wheel-drive car able to outpace the competition on the basis of its technological advancement, both as a product and in its production process. The "Saturn Project," announced in 1982, contemplated the building of the most advanced automobile factory in the world, at a cost of $5 billion, reducing by $2,000 the production cost of a sub-compact car. The initial production target was 400,000 cars per year, with 1990 as the starting year of production. The site selected for the factory, after major competition among many soliciting cities and states, was a rural southern locality: Spring Hill, Tennessee (close to a Nissan plant). The project was pursued in cooperation with the United Auto Workers labor union, and included relocation from the Detroit area of the majority of the workers to ensure reliance from the onset on an experienced, skilled labor force.

In parallel with production developments, GM also pursued a strategy of innovative management procedures, setting up a joint venture with Toyota to produce under the label of the new company (NUMMI) the US version of the Toyota Corolla. In this case, too, the plant, located in Fremont, a San Franciso suburb, rehired in 1985 most of the unionized auto workers of the GM plant who had been laid off on the closing of the former GM plant in 1982. GM's response to foreign competition was to learn from the successes of its competitors, and to adopt, and adapt for its own purposes, twin measures of better working procedures and better equipment.[49] In addition, an audacious technological program, introducing the most advanced microelectronics technology, was intended to provide the company with a technological edge, based on superior American ingenuity.

The spatial implications of this new, more innovative strategy, are quite different from those of the offshoring process, as shown by Erica Schoenberger in her excellent analysis of the subject.[50] Instead of worldwide decentralization, the new production sites tend toward spatial reconcentration, since linkages within the company and between the company and its quality suppliers are crucial to the functioning of such a complex system. Proximity does not necessarily mean immediate spatial contiguity with the traditional manufacturing regions, as the location of the Saturn factory indicates; but the linkage imperative does require a high degree of accessibility, and therefore good transportation and relative proximity to the main manufacturing complexes and final markets. On the other hand, these new manufacturing complexes are fairly footloose, given that the internal relationships of the company, and its connections with its suppliers, are more important than specific location factors, as exemplifed by the massive relocation of the labor required for the Saturn project. In fact, the location of GM's most advanced production facilities in the US show the diverse geographical expressions that can result from the one spatial logic: in contrast to the examples cited in Spring Hill and in Fremont, the fully automated Orion facility near Detroit, and the Buick–City complex around Flint, Michigan (the company's headquarters), show the persistence of some attachment to the industrial heartland. Yet what is really important is that in all instances the spatial logic remains the same: locational constraints are internalized within the company's own dynamics, in the spatial model that Richard Hill has characterized as typical of the new "company town," best represented by Toyota in Nagoya.[51] Thus, Spring Hill, Fremont, Detroit, Flint, are all GM, and it is around these individual sites that the new production complexes are woven, with relationships between these units and their markets following the lines of corporate organization. In this sense, GM's strategy calls for core-based but spatially diversified reconcentration of production, rather than for decentralization and peripheral offshoring, although internationalization remains a support system in the company's global strategy.

It would appear, as the MIT study and Schoenberger's analysis (among other works)[52] suggest, that the process of internationalization of production is being reversed, and decentralization substantially slowed down. However, the process is somewhat more complex than this, for the impact of new technologies on restructuring, and on its spatial consequences, can never be directly inferred from the characteristics of the technology.[53] Several facts challenge the assumption of an irreversible substitution of the flexible automation/spatial reconcentration strategy for the offshore production/ "world car"/decentralization approach that has characterized the strategic debate in the automobile industry during the past decade.

The first fact is that GM's technological restructuring strategy must at the moment be reckoned a failure, while Ford's profits have soared.[54] It should be noticed that the two leading American manufacturers, while combining both strategies, have opted for different emphases. While GM's proportion of production conducted overseas declined from 32.8 percent in 1970 to 28.9 percent in 1980, Ford's jumped from 45.6 percent in 1970 to 57.6 percent in 1980.[55] The net result of these divergent strategies was an increasing productivity advantage by Ford over GM, which translated into a reversal of their relative positions in terms of profits, with Ford overtaking GM in net profits in 1986 for the first time since the 1920s. GM's market share dropped from 48 percent in 1978, at the beginning of its restructuring process, to 41 percent in 1986, yielding ground both to imports and to Ford and Chrysler, in spite of the much greater size and resources of GM (in 1979, when GM launched its technological modernization plan, the $40 billion it invested was equivalent to 14 times Ford's annual pre-tax earnings in that year). Various arguments have been put forward to explain the initial failure of the all-out automation strategy: cheaper gasoline prices, undermining the advantage of fuel-efficient new models; greater foreign competition, particularly from South Korea and Europe, in addition to Japan; organizational mistakes; inability to proceed in parallel with a reform of working processes adapted to the new technological environment; and errors and difficulties in implementing on such a large scale the introduction of information technologies from top to bottom. Whatever the reasons, setting the technological rationality of GM against the business rationality of Ford, it seems that the latter prevails for the moment. Not that the "world car" strategy has been fully implemented to its logical extreme; but the depth of the crisis in Ford forced the company to find, as its first priority, ways of lowering costs and penetrating markets, using information technologies in the service of a short-term survival strategy. On the other hand, GM's long-term view of taking the high technological ground to undermine the competition by using its financial and technological power, has backfired in the short term, actually jeopardizing the long-term strategy. The Saturn project has been scaled down, and some experts foresee its merger in other GM divisions.

The second fact at variance with the assumed predominance of the spatial reconcentration/flexible automation trend is the growing importance of Mexico as a supplier of parts, including engines, and, in the near future, fully assembled cars for US manufacturers, as demonstrated in the thorough study by Hinojosa and Morales. GM itself is the main firm involved in this trade, with about 30 "maquiladora" plants in the border zone in 1987.[56] Between 1979 and 1985 the number of maquiladoras producing transportation equipment in the Mexican border zone rose from 38 to 49, increasing employment from 5,000 to about 34,000. Table 6.4 provides an estimate of the growing importance of production of engines for export for the whole of Mexico. Ford has developed further its strategy in the area since these data were collected by building an advanced plant in Hermosillo, northern Mexico, which started operations in 1988. Ninety percent of the parts to be assembled there will be imported from around the Pacific, and 90 percent of the plant's output will be exported to the US. Three thousand workers will be employed, making about 100,000 cars a year, in a new version of the "world car" strategy; and this in spite of Ford's self-proclaimed abandonment of the term, judged too unpopular with American public opinion.[57]

The third element to be considered in evaluating the balance between the two conflicting tendencies concerns the possibility of increasing the sophistication of offshore production by introducing automated equipment into plants decentralized abroad, including those in developing countries such as Mexico. There is an implicit fallacy in equating the use of flexible automation technologies with US location, consisting in the assumption that neither the

Table 6.4   Principal Mexican export engine plants, 1987

Company	Site	Projected volume	% Export
Chrysler	Saltillo	300,000[a]	85
General Motors	Ramos Arizpe	450,000	95
Ford	Chihuahua	500,000[b]	90
Volkswagen	Puebla	300,000[c]	
Renault	Gomez Palacio	80,000[d]	100
Nissan	Aguascalientes	100,000[e]	

Approximate 1987 total engine exports: 1,600,000

[a]This production is above the plant's capacity of 270,000 annually. The plant has exceeded its rated capacity every year since 1984.
[b]This production is above the plant's capacity of 440,000 annually.
[c]This is the projected 1987 export volume for the plant. An expansion is currently under way to boost capacity to 500,000 annually.
[d]This volume is well under the plant's capacity.
[e]This is entirely an export figure.
Source: Compiled from trade press sources by Shaiken and Herzenberg (see note 58).

industrial infrastructure nor the skills of the labor force would be able to sustain advanced manufacturing processes. Shaiken and Herzenberg, in a remarkable piece of work, have put this assumption to the test of empirical research, analyzing three automobile plants of the same company, each with exactly the same advanced, automated equipment and the same product, but situated respectively in the US, Canada, and Mexico. (Confidentiality forbids identification of the company.)[58] Their results are startling. In spite of a young, inexperienced work force, the Mexican plant achieved, within 18 months, 80 percent of the machine efficiency of the US plant, 75 percent of its labor producitivity, and a level of quality between that of the Canadian and that of the US plant. Figure 6.1 shows the learning curve that brought Mexican workers on a par with their American and Canadian counterparts. They explain the performance by three factors: first, the work force, although inexperienced, was highly educated and highly motivated; secondly, teamwork and control groups were introduced, in line with Ford's Alfa Project on managerial techniques, emphasizing the importance of work procedures if best use is to be made of advanced technology; and thirdly, managers and engineers were brought into the plant from around the world to act as on-site supervisors, training the workers and forming teams with them, so as to avoid a long period of non-supervised, spontaneous learning. Efficient training of an educated labor force accounted for the rapid productivity gains which combined with major savings in labor costs (one-tenth of the equivalent costs in the US) to make the Mexican plant the most profitable of the three, while

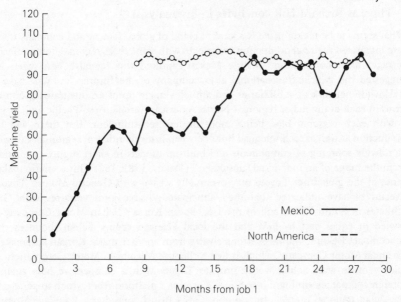

Figure 6.1   Machine yield on the Mexican and North American Block lines, as percentage of 1985 machine yield on North American block line.
Source: Company data complied and elaborated by Shaiken and Herzenberg (see note 58)

still allowing for the introduction of advanced, microelectronics-based equipment. Although these results still leave open the general questions of whether industrial infrastructure is adequate and whether a sufficient pool of educated labor can often be found in such locations, it appears that in principle advanced automation production lines can be moved offshore without a substantial loss of quality. A combination of offshoring and automation strategies thus becomes feasible, and this indeed seems to be Ford's option.

In addition, increasing collaboration among firms of different countries on a world level is blurring the distinction, giving new depth and meaning to the "world car" strategy.[59] American firms, as well as their European and Asian counterparts, have entered into a number of agreements covering co-production, global sourcing, and marketing under another firm's label. Japan and South Korea are the main partners for firms, and these two countries, along with Taiwan, Mexico, and Brazil, are US firms' foremost suppliers in "captive imports," that is, cars produced offshore to be sold under US brand names in the North American market. These captive imports are rapidly increasing, from 6 percent of total auto imports in 1984 to 20 percent in 1988.[60]

Thus, as Richard Hill concludes in his analysis:

What seems to be taking place is a kind of blend of global factory and company town into integrated regional production complexes with some cross-regional, international linkages and coordination. George Maxcy captured this scenario best when he suggested the typical transnational auto company of the future: "... Will have a worldwide network of subsidiaries and affiliates made up of an integrated group of firms in each of the major regions – North America, Europe, Asia–Pacific and Africa – with each regional bloc being more or less self-sufficient. But there will be production as well as technological links between firms in different regions because of worldwide sourcing of components and built-up models in short supply or missing from the range of an individual subsidiary." (Maxcy, 1981: 162) This scenario makes sense of the global net Toyota may eventually weave with General Motors. Toyota executives have indicated that they anticipate possible joint ventures with GM affiliates in South Korea and in the UK. South Korea's Sehan Motor Company is owned in equal part by GM and the local Daewoo group. Sehan produces the subcompact Rekord, and faces strong rivalry from another major Korean automaker, Hyundai Motor Company, which is tied to Japan's Mitsubishi Motor Corporation. A joint venture with Sehan would provide Toyota with a competitive base against foreign companies aiming to use South Korea as a platform from which to penetrate the Asian regional market. In addition, GM's British subsidiary, Vauxhall Motors, which has suffered from continuous deficits over the past few years and is attempting to revitalize its management, would provide Toyota with tariff-free access to the market of the EEC.[61]

The spatial implications of this techno-economic restructuring are, therefore, more complex than is implied by any of the simplified versions of the alternative strategies presented above. Neither generalized decentralization nor general spatial reconcentration is taking place, but rather a global networking of self-sufficient "company towns," that generate around themselves vertically integrated clusters. Because of the different production costs in various specific locations, there will be a hierarchy of relationships among these primary locations, reinforced at the highest level by the technological level of a few engineering centers. Yet the need to relate closely to the markets will disperse these primary places around the main markets of the globe, certainly bypassing most of the Third World. On the other hand, since market penetration will only be achieved on the condition of successful flexible specialization, the importance of the connections among different production centers, following strategic inter-firm alliances, will prevail over any given locational advantage. The net result for the spatial location of the US automobile industry *in the US* will be increasing interdependence with both foreign partners and offshore sources, in order to preserve the command and control functions of primary locations. Flexibility of production will allow independence of specific areas, favoring a process of decentralization from the industrial heartland. This, however, will only be possible to the extent that each firm maintains close relationships with the other units of the firm and with the target markets. Spatial reconcentration and international decentralization are both superseded by their integration, as subsidiary processes, in global networks of design, production, and markets, made possible by information technologies, and constantly restructured by business strategies.

Reverse Flow: Locational Patterns of Foreign Direct Investment in US Manufacturing

At the same time as American manufacturers are locating a significant proportion of their production offshore, foreign direct investment is pouring into the US.[62] In 1984, total assets owned by foreign firms in the US reached $596 billion. In 1985, the value of direct foreign investment for the year was $183 billion, up from $135 billion in 1983. The proportion of this investment that went into manufacturing was about 35 percent in 1983; but a starker picture emerges if one looks at the proportion of employment generated by foreign direct investment accounted for by manufacturing: 52 percent. The expansion of investment in manufacturing has been spectacular, from $2.9 billion in 1962 to $47.8 billion by the end of 1983.[63] The growth rate of direct foreign investment in the US accelerated from an average annual increase of 6.7 percent in real terms in 1962–73, to 9.5 percent in 1973–80, and recent trends show an even greater rate of increase. In 1983, about 33 percent of foreign direct investment in manufacturing was in chemicals, with about 15 percent in food and kindred products, almost 18 percent in machinery, 11.4 percent in primary fabricated metals, and 22 percent in other industries.[64] This major inflow, 77.4 percent of it coming from Europe, 3.5 percent from Japan, and 12.1 percent from other areas, gives rise to an apparent paradox, for simultaneously US firms have been decentralizing production abroad to escape high production costs and a relatively constrained regulatory environment. It certainly shows the complexity of the locational logic in the new international economy, hardly reducible to any single factor, certainly not to labor costs alone.

The major argument for direct foreign investment in US manufacturing is, of course, to assure a presence in the US market, the largest unified market in the world, to pre-empt the potential impact of protectionist measures. But, as Erica Schoenberger argues, a presence in the US market does not necessarily imply actually manufacturing in America.[65] Foreign firms could also decentralize production from the US to lower-cost locations, while still marketing the final assembled products in America. In fact, some Japanese firms are doing just that, locating over the Mexican border to serve the US market from marketing offices headquartered within the US. Yet the bulk of foreign manufacturing firms in the US are setting up complete production lines, sometimes with the exception of the research and development functions that are kept at the home base. Erica Schoenberger, in her doctoral dissertation, investigated the reasons behind this choice of location on the basis of in-depth interviews with a sample of foreign manufacturing firms' executives.[66] Her analysis confirms the widespread view that market considerations are the common concern underlying the decisions to locate, at high cost, in the US. But what is more important is the idea that physical presence of production facilities in the market is crucial to penetrating it and to gaining market share. The notion of linkages seems to be essential: linkages among information on market conditions and technologies, the marketing strategy of the firm, and the characteristics of production. Increasingly customized production targeted on specific markets requires a degree of spatial proximity and social affinity that cannot be obtained unless the firm is rooted in the market it wants to conquer. Also, knowledge obtained through manufacturing in the US is also extremely useful to a firm's efforts to succeed in exports from other locations. Export penetration and direct investment are complementary rather than alternative strategies.

The increasingly important impact of foreign manufacturing investment on the American regional structure has been analyzed by Glickman and Woodward,[67] in the most complete study on the subject to date. Relying on data from the Bureau of Economic Analysis from 1979 to 1983, augmented by data sources from the International Trade Administration, and from Japan's Economic Institute, between 1979 and 1985, Glickman and Woodward provide a detailed account of the spatial pattern of foreign manufacturing investment in the US. The complexity of the trends they observed, and the importance of the subject, require a careful synthesis of their findings, on the basis of which some substantial hypotheses may be proposed.

The regional distribution of foreign employment and foreign manufacturing employment for 1974 and 1983 is laid out in tables 6.5 and 6.6. These data show the south-east to be the favored recipient of such investment, followed by the mid-east and by the Great Lakes. Again, the old and new concentrations of manufacturing employment act as the magnets for new investment from abroad, although the declining share of the old manufacturing belt shows the adaptation of foreign capital to the new industrial space. In terms of emerging trends, the south-west appears to be increasing its attraction much faster than other regions. The west has a relatively modest share of total investment, although this picture changes if Japanese investment alone is examined: 29.5 percent of Japanese-controlled US employment is located in California. Given the likelihood of increased Japanese investment in the second half of the 1980s, it is probable that the west will become substantially more prominent as a home for foreign investment.

Overall, foreign investors created 700,000 new factory jobs in 1974–83, while domestic producers eliminated 2.4 million manufacturing jobs, 93 percent of them in the mid-east and Great Lakes regions. In this sense it contributed toward slowing down the process of deindustrialization in the US. But the regional distribution of this new employment could not reverse the

Table 6.5 Regional distribution of total foreign employment, 1974 and 1983

	1974		1983		Average annual growth
Region	Employment	Share (%)	Employment	Share (%)	rate (%)
New England	67,141	6.0	159,924	6.4	10.1
Mid-east	333,867	29.7	561,955	22.6	6.0
Great Lakes	232,179	20.6	425,286	17.1	7.0
Plains	45,351	4.0	111,758	4.5	10.5
South-east	235,588	20.9	615,150	24.8	11.3
South-west	66,725	5.9	255,650	10.3	16.1
Rocky Mountains	17,022	1.5	54,975	2.2	13.9
Far west	128,091	11.4	301,049	12.1	10.0
Total	1,125,964	100.0[a]	2,485,747	100.0	9.2

[a]Because the figures are rounded, regional shares will not add up precisely to 100%.
Source: Coleman (1985), compiled by Glickman and Woodward (see note 67).

Table 6.6 Regional breakdown of foreign manufacturing employment, 1974 and 1983

	1974		1983		Average annual growth
Region	Employment	Share (%)	Employment	Share (%)	rate (%)
New England	41,955	7.2	86,901	6.7	8.4
Mid-east	149,480	25.6	298,313	23.2	8.0
Great Lakes	121,249	20.7	242,105	18.8	8.0
Plains	21,812	3.7	61,486	4.8	12.2
South-east	167,330	28.6	335,424	26.0	8.0
South-west	19,080	3.3	103,037	8.0	20.6
Rocky Mountains	6,682	1.1	24,392	1.9	15.5
Far west	57,574	9.8	137,769	10.7	10.2
Total	585,162	100.0[a]	1,289,427	100.0	9.2

[a]Because the figures are rounded, regional shares will not add up precisely to 100%.
Source: Coleman (1985), calculated by Glickman and Woodward (see note 67).

decline of the Great Lakes area: there is a similar movement toward industrial decentralization to the south-east on the part of both domestic and foreign capital. In the case of foreign capital this is true in terms of both new employment and capital investment, where the south-east ranked first among the recipient regions. In order to enable an assessment of the trends in foreign and domestic investment on a comparative basis, table 6.7 calculates a location quotient that indicates the over- or under-representation of foreign capital for each region. The south-east and the south-west stand up well to

Table 6.7   Regional breakdown of domestic manufacturing employment, 1974 and 1983, and 1983 foreign/domestic location quotients

Region	1974 Employment	Share (%)	1983 Employment	Share (%)	1983 Location quotient
New England	1,196.4	7.2	1,323.2	7.8	0.859
Mid-east	4,041.0	20.8	3,087.3	18.1	1.282
Great Lakes	5,037.8	25.9	3,716.6	21.8	0.862
Plains	1,318.6	6.8	1,173.4	6.9	0.696
South-east	4,116.2	21.4	3,910.4	23.0	1.130
South-west	1,111.5	5.7	1,214.4	7.1	1.127
Rocky Mountains	291.2	1.5	320.6	1.8	1.056
Far west	2,099.2	10.8	2,272.1	13.3	0.805
Total	19,461.9	100.0[a]	17,018.0	100.0	

[a]Employment in thousands. Because the figures are rounded, regional shares will not add up precisely to 100%.
Source: US Department of Labor, Bureau of Labor Statistics, 1985, calculated by Glickman and Woodward (see note 67).

this examination, but the mid-east emerges as foreign capital's preferred location in relative terms. This result emerges from the combination of the steep decline in domestic manufacturing in the mid-east (954,000 manufacturing jobs lost in 1974–83) with the number of acquisitions of factories and property in the region by foreign firms exploiting the crisis of American manufacturing to establish their presence in the market.

Nevertheless, in absolute terms, the bulk of foreign investment is increasingly being directed toward the southern states, with the west and New England together in second position, as shown in map 6.2. Higher location indexes are registered in the Carolinas, Tennessee, Virginia, and Texas, but here again Japanese investors present a different pattern, being concentrated on the west coast. An important distinction to be made in investment patterns is that between new plants and acquisitions, the former type of investment generally contributing more to regional development. Overall, 63 percent of the plants are new, but the proportion varies between regions. The south-east dominates in terms of new plants, but New England also exhibits a pattern of new industrialization, confirming the claim that New England's reindustrialization is taking place on a basis quite different from that of traditional industry. On the other hand, as one would expect, the Great Lakes and the mid-east show a greater proportion of acquisitions. Foreign manufacturing is at the same time both participating in the new industrial expansion toward the southern US, and replacing (though only to a limited extent) some of the manufacturing operations in the old industrial belt. Interestingly enough, Japanese investors tend to concentrate more on acquisitions (53 percent of all plants) than do European investors.

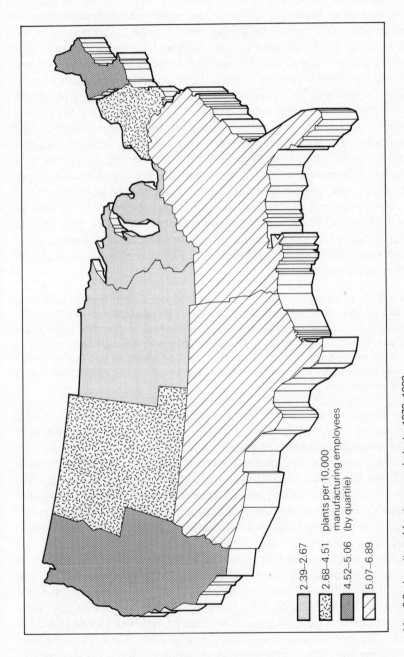

Map 6.2 Location of foreign-owned plants, 1979–1983
Source: Glickmand and Woodward (see note 67)

plants per 10,000
manufacturing employees
(by quartile)

2.39–2.67

2.68–4.51

4.52–5.06

5.07–6.89

The sectoral composition of foreign manufacturing investment shows a great diversity of investment patterns; however, there is a certain concentration on high-technology industries. This high-technology investment is spread among many states, with greater than average concentrations in the south-east, the Rocky Mountains, the mid-east, and the south-west. The important fact to note is that foreign high-technology companies do not follow the locational pattern of domestic high-technology manufacturers. In fact, the far west and New England come bottom of the ranking of foreign high-technology investment shares. This finding runs contrary to the general perception of foreign companies locating in the US to assimilate new technologies. Although this is probably true for a few research facilities located in Silicon Valley or on Route 128, most of the employment generated by foreign firms seems to be geared toward the growing high-technology *markets* in the US, the only ones sufficiently large to make it possible for a foreign firm to expand its markets at a rate corresponding to its rate of innovation. So, while the innovative centers of most of these firms tend to remain on native soil, their manufacturing operations in the US assure them direct contact with the most sophisticated market in the world. As Glickman and Woodward write:

While technology transfer from the US back to the source country is conceivable, so is a transfer flowing in the opposite direction. The high proportion of new high-tech plants relative to acquisitions indicates that multinational corporations (MNCs) are drawing on ownership advantages to directly compete with domestic high technology firms in the national and regional markets of the US. It is likely that foreign-owned firms add to the technological base of regions as much as they imitate and exploit existing technologies.[68]

The locational pattern of foreign manufacturing in general is also characterized by an "urban bias." Fifty-six percent of the new plants were built in the 10 percent of counties that are highly urbanized, while only 12.5 percent were built in rural counties. Even in the south, where the location pattern was less urban, most plants remained concentrated in the corridors adjacent to large metropolitan areas. The predominant market orientation of this type of investment requires spatial proximity and social affinity to the final destination of its products. Thus, while the pattern of location tends to be regionally scattered, it is also concentrated on metropolitan centers.

Glickman and Woodward have also conducted an econometric analysis of the factors determining location of foreign manufacturing investment, and have compared their results with those of a similar analysis for foreign direct investment. Their findings are revealing. Market location is the most important criterion for both types of investment, followed by rate of market growth. The repositioning of manufacturing in the US is at the same time spearheading and following the opening up of new economically vital regions in the south, south-west, and west. Foreign investment also seems to be willing to take risks in new regions that are less developed, for instance the Rocky Mountains, betting on their potential as new frontiers for further decentralization. It is repelled by the threat of unitary tax legislation, emphasizing the important for multinationals of escaping fiscal controls by diversifying location, but it is not particularly shy of other forms of taxation. On the other hand, foreign investment does not seem to be sensitive to labor costs, or to the presence of unions, in sharp contrast to the priorities of domestic manufacturing investment. Several factors may explain this finding, which runs counter to the usual perception of foreign firms moving south to escape unions and reduce labor costs. Many of them, particularly in Europe, are already used to working in an union environment, and indeed one that is usually more militant than the one they find in the US. Investments in the 1980s have often taken place, as mentioned, through acquisitions (37 percent), many of them in the old industrial belt, under conditons that have saved jobs and helped cities, with the result that wage demands and union pressure have been moderate, even in regions traditionally ranking toward the top of the wage scale. And finally, the apparent lack of concern with labor costs and social environment once more highlights the priority target of foreign investment: market presence. Whatever it takes to consolidate a position in the US market, both through local manufacturing activity, and through the flow of information and contacts that such activity will generate, will be worthwhile, as the American economy continues to be the expansionary segment of the world economy. Another surprising finding, that is nevertheless consistent with the hypothesis concerning the dominance of the market strategy, is the fact that domestic investment is positively correlated with the level of state spending on infrastructure, while foreign capital seems to be indifferent to this attraction. In fact, while American firms are relocating to lower costs, foreign firms put a premium in "being there," namely, locating in the most rapidly expanding areas of the American market, in a bold strategy in which maximizing profit in the long run replaces the short-term view of most American businesses.

In sum, a market-driven flow of direct foreign investment is reviving a substantial share of American manufacturing. Its territorial reach is spreading from its early location on the north-eastern seaboard (the western seaboard for Japanese investors), and moving southward and inland. Being scattered all over the US, including those regions that are not yet developed, foreign investment contributes to the reduction of regional disparity. Foreign investors are also contributing to the slowing down of the process of deindustrialization, particularly in the old industrial belt, by acquiring companies and re-opening formerly closed plants. Overall, foreign capital not only reindustrializes, it also re-equilibrates the US regional structure by concentrating most of its impact on the south. On the other hand, it reinforces metropolitan concentration by investing in the most highly urbanized areas, where it will find the most rapidly expanding markets.

In contrast with the locational pattern of US multinationals abroad, generally to be found clustered in the dominant areas of the already industrialized regions, foreign manufacturing capital in the US is contributing to the decentralization of the American productive structure, revitalizing to some extent the declining regions, and spreading industralization into new areas, away from the traditional manufacturing belt. Yet the price of this dynamic, re-equilibrating effect is the increasingly tight linkage between the evolution of American regions and cities and the movements of capital controlled from a foreign base and deployed on a worldwide strategy. The mobility of capital has now embraced in its uncontrollable spiral the heartland of America. An increasing proportion of manufacturing jobs in the US will be located, as they are in most of the world, at a borrowed place, and will live on borrowed time. The interpenetration of markets and production processes has redefined the meaning of regions at the intersection of flows of capital and labor with the memory of their history and the heritage of their geography.

Global Capital, Global Cities

Capital has always moved throughout the world. But only in the most recent period of our history have individual amounts of capital been able to operate daily on a global scale. This is a fundamental change in our socio-economic organization, and it has been the major contributing force in the formation and consolidation of the new urban entities that Saskia Sassen has labeled "global cities,"[69] in similar vein to the "world city" concept proposed by Friedmann and Wolff a few years ago.[70] Capital mobility has increased dramatically in both volume and velocity in the past decade, as a result of two main interacting processes: the mismatching between capital accumulation and investment opportunities within the same national market; and the restructuring of financial institutions and financial markets, in the context of the broader economic restructuring.

A number of new centers of accumulation have appeared since the mid-1970s. The first and most important was the Eurodollar market which attracted and organized floating capital from around the world. The second, and most publicized, was the concentration of petro-dollars in OPEC countries during the golden period for oil producers of 1974–81, a considerable volume of capital that, to a large extent, was recycled in markets and countries outside OPEC. The third, and the one most likely to have far-reaching consequences, was the emergence of Japan as the major world financial power as a consequence of the capital accumulated in its financial corporations after a quarter of a century of exceptional performance by Japanese companies in the international economy. Along with these three major sources of capital accumulation, other less obvious sources also played a role in generating an unprecedented flow of capital constantly shifting around the world's financial markets. For instance, capital generated by money-laundering operations from drug traffic in Latin America and elsewhere, or government-originated payments resulting from shadow weapons markets, are increasingly important elements in the international cash flow. Altogether, worldwide capitalization in 1986 amounted to $5.2 trillion, up from $892 billion (in constant dollars) in 1974.[71] However, working against this expansionary trend, investment opportunities rapidly declined during the 1970s as core economies implemented austerity policies to fight inflation. As Sassen reports,[72] in the early 1980s most advanced countries saw reduced investment levels and experienced declines in investment inflows. In this general context of restraint, only two markets were open to and potentially profitable for to the massive amount of capital searching for the opportunity to fructify. The first of these was the United States, as the economy came to be artificially stimulated, and the US Treasury sought capital from sources all over the world to finance an increasing budget deficit. The US Treasury market has become the single largest capital market in the world, with $2 trillion in outstanding debt bonds; and about one-third of the bonds issued in the 1980s were purchased by Japanese investors. Also, in 1984, the US received 47 percent of global direct foreign investment, while Japan was the leading lender and the leading foreign investor, worldwide. The second possibility for capital seeking a destination was the international financial markets themselves, increasingly working in their own sphere according to a logic distinct from that of any national economy. In addition to stepped-up capital mobility, we are also witnessing the globalization of capital as a separate entity, with the universe of international finance generating its own investment opportunities by scanning all national economies and, more importantly, by taking advantage of financial transactions and monetary trends, on a rationale increasingly separate from the processes of production and consumption.

However, the transformation of the movements of capital into an interconnected global system depended on a number of key institutional and material conditions, without whose existence the world was at risk of suffering an over-accumulation crisis. These conditions were of three kinds: the restructuring of the financial markets and institutions; the provision of the indispensable technological infrastructure; and the formation of organizational complexes functioning as the material bases for the processing of information and decision-making on the capital flows.

All the major world financial centers went through a period of institutional adjustment during the 1980s, under the guiding principle of deregulation.[73] London went the furthest of any major market and won a competitive edge, consolidating its position as the world's largest financial market. Tokyo was the last, actually waiting until 1987 to organize its offshore investment market. Singapore and Hong Kong had always been more flexible and it was this flexibility that attracted to them an increasing share of global financial flows, although they remained in a secondary position as international centers. Paris, Frankfurt, and Zurich also introduced changes but they needed fewer improvements in terms of flexibility because of their traditional formula of linkage between commercial banks and investment banks. In the US, the need for more flexible instruments, able to enter the global competition, combined with developments in the financial industry, prompted by the need to escape the threat of inflationary pressures through deregulation and disintermediation.[74] Large corporations and institutional investors increasingly bypassed commercial banks and started to sell security-type promissory notes to investors. In 1985, the outstanding value of commercial paper in the US, that hardly existed ten years previously, amounted to $350 billion, that is, about one-quarter of all non-financial corporate debt. Bond markets, investment banks, mutual funds, all entered markets traditionally reserved to the commercial banks. As a result, the commercial banks themselves pushed for deregulation of capital markets and started to offer new financial services. Simultaneously, financial firms exerted pressure to obtain the deregulation of security markets, that took place gradually during the 1980s, including the facility for US commercial banks to serve as dealers in US Treasury bonds. As soon as institutional opportunities were created, the securities trade skyrocketed, spearheading a bull market period on the New York Stock Exchange. Between the mid-1970s and the early 1980s, the number of shares traded in Wall Street leapt from 10 million to 100 million.

This volume of transactions, and the global reach of the restructured financial markets, could not have been attained without the massive introduction of information technologies in the financial industry. Telecommunications and computers, functioning in integrated networks, are the indipensable working tools of global capital. A sophisticated telecommunications and air transportation infrastructure are the precondition for any city to become a production site of the new financial institutions, as argued in chapter 3 when analyzing the impact of technology on information-processing location. But the centers of operation of worldwide financial flows cannot be flows themselves. They have very specific location requirements, that are not reducible to a good telecommunications infrastructure. While the emergence of Hong Kong and Singapore as second-tier financial centers bears witness to the possibility for new locations to emerge on the basis of a deliberate policy to organize a market in a given location, the high-level financial centers, commanding operations on a global scale, have historical and geographical roots, linked to their role in the national and international economies. The major centers, and the ones that are truly global cities, are three:[75] London, as the major financial market in terms of number of transactions; New York, as the major recipient of capital flows and exporter of related services; and Tokyo, as the major lender of capital and headquarters of the largest banks in the world. In 1986, New York, London, and Tokyo together accounted for 80 percent of the world market capitalization, up from 73 percent in 1974, in a process of growing concentration and dominance by the top tier of financial centers. New York alone controlled 44 percent of world capital.

Within the US, New York stands in a class of its own as the dominant global city, followed by Los Angeles as a distant second.[76] The role of New York in international financial networks has its roots in its pre-eminence as host to leading corporate headquarters of the American economy, its Stock Exchange, the concentration in the city of the major commercial banks and security firms, and the network of advanced corporate services required to support and execute the decisions made in the command and control centers of these corporations. Some figures are indicative of the concentration of corporate power in New York City:[77] 454 Manhattan-located headquarters are listed on the US stock exchanges, accounting for one-thirteenth of the publicly owned corporations. In 1986, New York banks' assets were $612 billion, equivalent to 34 percent of cumulated bank assets in the US. It is also the leading foreign banking center, with 405 offices, 60 percent of foreign bank assets, and 56 percent of foreign loan activity in the US. In international terms, New York banks and security firms combined concentrate the highest level of earnings in the world ($5.4 billion in 1985, far ahead of Tokyo and London), and ranks second in cumulated assets behind Tokyo. New York is also the prime location for the world's largest insurers and pension funds, one of the most important sources of capital investment as the deregulation of financial markets progresses. US pension funds accounted in 1985 for $1.5 trillion, compared with $225 million for the UK and $210 million for Japan. Mutual funds in the US accounted for an additional $380 billion. Most of the transactions connecting these pools of capital to the financial markets are conducted in New York. In sum, as the Regional Plan Association of New York writes:

With the growth and transformation of global capital markets, the fields of commercial and investment banking are merging, and the all-important function of intermediation is becoming increasingly dominated by a small band of 25 to 30 financial instituitions. Included in this group are: the twelve major New York commercial banks and investment banks, a small number of UK merchant banks, the four big Japanese securities houses, with Nomura in the lead, and the few European universal banks, including Swiss and German.[78]

The key development in the relationship between the restructuring of the financial system and the location of its information-processing activities is the fact that it has shifted from being corporate-centered to being market-centered. It is the circulation process rather than the investment process that dominates. Increasingly, securities firms have overtaken commercial banks as the nerve centers of the accumulation process. Therefore, the emphasis is less on the internal workings of the financial corporations than on the milieu of exchanges weaved around the financial markets, with its core at the Stock

Exchange. This milieu works on the basis of personal acquaintance and face-to-face interaction, often relying on inside information. It has also given rise to a very large network of ancillary services: financial analysts, management consultants, law firms, at the top level; word-processing pools, computer programming, copy and printing shops, and personal services, at the lower level. The dynamism of this finance-led economy has attracted a vast pool of labor, generating its own labor market with highly specialized segments, whose presence in the city becomes an additional locational factor for the development of the high-level capital management functions.

On the basis of its directional functions and its intermediary role between world capital flows and access to capital and investment in the world's largest economy, New York has fundamentally restructured its regional economy and its local society. While dismantling most of its manufacturing, the New York region gained in 1978–86 about 118,000 new jobs in financial services, about one-third of all new jobs in the area, with brokerage and investment houses experiencing the highest rate of growth of all categories of firms. Employment in the securities industry in New York City rose from 90,000 in 1980 to 138,400 in 1986. Table 6.8 shows the rise in financial services, with spectacular rates of growth in securities and legal services. However, the dependence of this economic dynamism on a highly volatile financial market, sensitive to all variations in the world economy and in world politics, also creates a source of instability for the local economy. After the Wall Street crash of October 1987, the ensuing decline of financial activity led to massive lay-offs in securities and brokerage: the city lost about 50,000 jobs in the three months after the crisis. On the other hand, as argued in chapter 4, the development of high-level information processing is inter-related with the incorporation of low-paid, often immigrant, service labor that caters to the demand in low-skill jobs, and in consumer and personal services. Together

Table 6.8   Employment growth rates, producer services: New York City and Chicago, 1977–1984

SIC	Industry	New York City (%)	Chicago (%)
60	Banking	20.98	18.27
61	Credit agencies	36.62	17.99
62	Securities	71.49	73.17
63	Insurance carriers	−11.24	−11.91
64	Insurance agents	16.15	14.89
65	Real estate	1.57	1.70
73	Business services	36.92	53.01
81	Legal services	50.34	65.79
86	Membership organizations	7.04	0.41
89	Miscellaneous services	28.15	19.39

Source: US Bureau of Census, County Business Patterns, Illinois, 1977, 1984; New York 1977, 1984. Compiled by Sassen (see note 69).

with the simultaneous downgrading of manufacturing activities, the two processes create, in the same space of the global city, a highly polarized and segregated social structure. The global city is also the dual city.

The high-level operations of co-ordination and control of world capital flows are performed from a very small area that further specifies the core space of the global city. The Manhattan CBD concentrates 60 percent of New York jobs in 600 million square feet of built space, between 60th Street and the southern tip of the island. The 454 headquarters located in that area control $770 billion in worldwide sales (in 1982 dollars), including 38 financial and securities firms with $100 billion in sales. The same area is also home to half of the foreign branch finance employment of the US which performs 75 percent of all foreign bank business in the country. As Sassen writes: "In brief, much of what constitutes the leading international center for finance multinational headquarters and specialized servicing, is situated in a rather small area in an era of global telecommunications. Since we see this pattern repeated in London and Tokyo it may be indicative of the new forms of centralization required by the new forms of decentralization."[79]

What explains this striking paradox of the increasing concentration of global flows of information, controlling global flows of capital, in a few congested blocks of one particular city? Several elements seem to be at work. The first is the concentration there of high-level directional corporate activity in the US economy, a phenomenon whose logic was analyzed in chapter 3. It is because Manhattan is the CBD of New York, and New York is the corporate center of the largest economy in the world, holding what is still the most important international currency, that capital flows tend to converge on the location of the leading American financial institutions.

Secondly, it is precisely the dependence upon telecommunication networks that requires the concentration of command and control centers in spaces that are provided with the most advanced information systems. And the economies of scale required for the necessary gigantic investments in telecommunications infrastructure are dependent upon a pre-existing concentration of high-level business functions. While terminal points of the telecommunication networks, those required by back offices, can be scattered spatially, the nodal points, requiring the most sophisticated equipment together with round-the-clock repair, maintenance, and reprogramming systems, are concentrated in key locations, where a multiplicity of communication systems complement and reinforce one another. The level of computerization of financial markets can only function on the basis of a technologically highly advanced back-up system.

In the third-place, high-level decision making in an industry entirely dependent upon proper information handling requires access to micro-flows of information, that is to occasional exchanges and to non-public information that translates into a competitive edge in an industry where time is literally money, in billions of dollars. Access to inside information, and speed in gaining and using that information, are crucial characteristics in shaping the macro-flows on the basis of micro-flows. And in the fourth place, around the concentration of high-level functions develops a vast network of suppliers, intermediaries, and implementers in a symbiotic relationship in which they become indispensable to the functioning of the system as a whole.

Once the milieu is consolidated it reproduces its own space; and New York has been the dominant trade and economic center of the US for the past century. However, areas of the city that were well regarded decades ago have since been devastated by social decay and the transformation of its economic base; it is the persistence of the *economically vital* activities in a given space that enhances its value.[80] But when that space affirms itself as a leading corporate center, as is the case for most of Manhattan today, it triggers off a process of continuing re-evaluation, with capital from all over the world investing in its real estate, driving up prices, selecting functions and residents, and transforming the whole area into a highly privileged location. Around such privileges, high-level services develop to provide the global city with the attributes of its power and wealth. Designers come from Europe, imports from anywhere in the world offer the best of everything, and artists perform, compose, paint, sculpt, write, and, above all, sell, for the enjoyment of an elite with increasingly little time to enjoy anything. Ultimately, symbols are attached to location in that space, making the physical presence there of corporate headquarters and high-class residence necessary to credibility as being part of the corporate world or of the high-class population: the functional milieu crystallizes in a social milieu. While New York City has always combined both, its current status as a global city commanding much of the world economy has accentuated the trends toward symbolic recognition of its economic and social dominance, beyond the actual use value of ill-maintained urban services and mediocre French restaurants.

The global city epitomizes the contradictory logic of the space of flows. While reaching out to the whole planet second by second and round the clock, it relies on the spatial proximity of its different command centers, and on the face-to-face interaction of its anonymous masters. Based on telecommunications and information systems that overcome time and distance, it needs a technological infrastructure that can only be provided by agglomeration economies and access to scarce skilled labor. And while determining the destiny of countries and people by spread points in interest rates, it lives in fear of the uncontrolled society generated in its own territory. The global city collapses information flows into social matter.

Conclusion

The growing internationalization of the American economy reshapes cities and regions following the logic of the space of flows. The increasing role played by foreign trade, in a context characterized by loss of competitiveness by US manufacturers, has contributed decisively to the process of deindustrialization in the old manufacturing belt. Faced with decreasing shares of world markets, and loss of domestic markets to foreign imports, American companies have adjusted by relocating a substantial part of their production offshore, as well as in lower-cost areas of the US, particularly in the south. Four phenomena have resulted from this relocation process: an even greater industrial decline in the traditional manufacturing belt; the growing internalization of industrial and commercial flows within corporations, operating across national boundaries; the growth of a border economy along the US–Mexican border, exemplifying the new international division of labor and the close connections among its elements; and the industrialization of the south, that has emerged as the largest manufacturing region in the US, although most of its workers depend upon corporations based in the older industrial cities.

At the same time, other competitive strategies have emphasized the role of automation and upgrading of onshore production, in high-technology manufacturing, and in the automobile and textile industries, among others. Although this movement has contributed toward maintaining some production in the manufacturing belt, most of the automation and modernization of industries is taking place in what Peter Hall calls "the new perimeter," namely the sunbelt and New England.

The threat of massive US protectionism, to halt a trade deficit that has run out of control, and the increasing capital demands of American government and corporations, have caused a massive inflow of foreign direct investment, over one-third of it in manufacturing. Foreign investors have acquired some plants and equipment in the mid-east and Great Lakes regions, helping to slow down the decline of old industries; however, the bulk of new investment has taken place in the southern states, with the addition of the west coast in the case of Japanese capital. Foreign investment has favored high technology, but as a supplier as much as a buyer, actually upgrading the technological level of some southern states. Oriented toward market penetration, foreign firms are reindustrializing America, with emphasis on the "new south."

The combined effects of relocation by US firms and investment by foreign capital is re-equilibrating the economic and demographic balance between regions in the US by reversing the historical dominance of the north-eastern and north-central areas. Although pockets of poverty and underdevelopment still characterize many southern states, for example Mississippi, the overall trend appears to be toward a historic convergence of regions in terms of income and jobs. This is a major trend running against the general assumption that polarized economic growth translates into an acceleration of uneven territorial development. Although there is still great disparity among regions, intra-regional differences seem now to be more important, as the mobility of capital disperses investment, jobs, and income across the American landscape in search of better production locations and newer, more promising markets. While the dislocation of communities in declining regions adds a major social cost to the restructuring process, the new development of formerly depressed areas tends to homogenize America's economic geography.

On the other hand, worldwide capital flows concentrate the operations required for their processing in the directional centers of the higher-level metropolitan areas. New York stands out as the archetypal global city resulting from the formation of a global capital market, but other major cities too are increasingly specializing in financial and international trade activities, as the center of the US economy shifts to advanced corporate services. Los Angeles, with its connection to the Pacific region, and its strong basis in manufacturing, defense , and information industries, stands out clearly as the second global city in the US. Chicago and San Francisco, too, still hold some of their former share of financial power, while Miami (linked to Latin American flows and, to some extent, to the huge but disguised money-laundering operations of the drug trade), Atlanta (financial hub of the new south), Houston, Dallas, and Denver (still relying on the wealth accumulated from oil revenues) are building up their economies and organizing their local societies as regional international capital centers. The more America evolves in the direction of a finance and corporate services economy, the more inter-metropolitan differences supersede regional differentiation. New York suffered a major industrial decline during the 1970s, but emerged during the 1980s wealthier and more powerful than ever on the basis of its international dominance in financial markets and advanced services;[81] on the other hand, most of the Great Lakes region lost industrial competitiveness without being able to connect to the new dominant flows of capital. The process of uneven restructuring within regions and cities also increases disparity within areas rather than among areas. One of the most paradoxical characteristics of the new spatial logic consequent on the internationalization of the economy is the combination of growing regional homogenization with increasing intra-metropolitan inequality. The popular opposition between the frostbelt and the sunbelt is meaningless: the polarization of social dynamics takes place between mid-town Manhattan and the Bronx, or between Westwood and East Los Angeles, rather than between north and south, or east and west. International capital flows segment regional spaces by incorporating them in different ways into the changing geometry of their worldwide logic.

What emerges as the most important characteristic of all cities and regions, regardless of their relative position in the new international division of labor, is the instability of their economic structure and social dynamics, as a consequence of the volatility of movements in the international economy. From Volkswagen's decision to close its plant in Pennsylvania in order to export to the US market from Brazil and Mexico, to the October 1987 Wall Street crash that devastated New York's securities industry, the one feature common to all places in the space of flows is their uncertain fate.

This trend deepens the crisis, while enhacing the importance, of state and local governments. Confronted with worldwide competition and capital mobility, state and local governments in the US have mobilized in the past decade to attract both domestic and foreign capital to their localities, transforming themselves into what, in a perceptive analysis years ago, Robert Goodman labeled "the last entrepreneurs."[82] In order to succeed in this race, they adapted their policies to the perceived needs of business, and re-oriented resources to fostering local economic development, often at the expense of public services and social programs.[83] Even when the strategy succeeded and business-led economic development followed, the benefits of growth, biased toward sustaining a favorable business environment, were not redistributed equally among the population. Thus, local government's entrepreneurship tended to accentuate the polarizing tendencies of the new model of growth, contributing to the extension of the dual city phenomenon. The internationalization of the economy also segments local governments by forcing them to split their constituency between their local voters and their global investors.

A growing social schizophrenia has resulted between, on the one hand, regional societies and local institution and, on the other hand, the rules and operations of the economic system at the international level. The more the economy becomes interdependent on a global scale, the less can regional and local governments, as they exist today, act upon the basic mechanisms that condition the daily existence of their citizens. The traditional structures of social and political control over development, work, and distribution, have been subverted by the placeless logic of an internationalized economy enacted by means of information flows. The ultimate challenge of this fundamental dimension of the restructuring process is the possibility that the local state, and therefore people's control over their lives, will fade away, unless democracy is reinvented to match the space of flows with the power of places.

Conclusion: The Reconstruction of Social Meaning in the Space of Flows

At the end of this analytical journey, we can see a major social trend standing out from all our observations: the historical emergence of the space of flows, superseding the meaning of the space of places. By this we understand the deployment of the functional logic of power-holding organizations in asymmetrical networks of exchanges which do not depend on the characteristics of any specific locale for the fulfillment of their fundamental goals. The new industrial space and the new service economy organize their operations around the dynamics of their information-generating units, while connecting their different functions to disparate spaces assigned to each task to be performed; the overall process is then reintegrated through communication systems. The new professional–managerial class colonizes exclusive spatial segments that connect with one another across the city, the country, and the world; they isolate themselves from the fragments of local societies, which in consequence become destructured in the process of selective reorganization of work and residence. The new state, asserting its sources of power in the control and strategic guidance of knowledge, fosters the development of an advanced technological infrastructure that scatters its elements across undifferentiated locations and interconnected secretive spaces. The new international economy creates a variable geometry of production and consumption, labor and capital, management and information – a geometry that denies the specific productive meaning of any place outside its position in a network whose shape changes relentlessly in response to the messages of unseen signals and unknown codes.

New information technologies are not in themselves the source of the organizational logic that is transforming the social meaning of space: they are, however, the fundamental instrument that allows this logic to embody itself in historical actuality. Information technologies could be used, and can be used, in the pursuit of different social and functional goals, because what they offer, fundamentally, is flexibility. However, their use currently is determined by the process of the socio-economic restructuring of capitalism, and they constitute the indispensable material basis for the fulfillment of this process.

The supersession of places by a network of information flows is a fundamental goal of the restructuring process that has been analyzed. This is because the ultimate logic of restructuring is based on the avoidance of historically established mechanisms of social, economic, and political control by the power-holding organizations. Since most of these mechanisms of control depend upon territorially-based institutions of society, escaping from the social logic embedded in any particular locale becomes the means of achieving freedom in a space of flows connected only to other power-holders, who share the social logic, the values, and the criteria for performance institutionalized in the programs of the information systems that constitute the architecture of the space of flows. The emergence of the space of flows actually expresses the disarticulation of place-based societies and cultures from the organizations of power and production that continue to dominate society without submitting to its control. In the end, even democracies become powerless confronted with the ability of capital to circulate globally, of information to be transferred secretly, of markets to be penetrated or neglected, of planetary strategies of political–military power to be decided without the knowledge of nations, and of cultural messages to be marketed, packaged, recorded, and beamed in and out of people's minds.

What emerges from this restructuring process manifested in the space of flows is not the Orwellian prophecy of a totalitarian universe controlled by Big Brother on the basis of information technologies. It is a much more subtle, and to some extent potentially more destructive, form of social disintegration and reintegration. There is no tangible oppression, no identifiable enemy, no center of power that can be held responsible for specific social issues. Even the issues themselves become unclear, or paradoxically so explicit that they cannot be treated because they constantly refer to a higher level of social causality which cannot be grasped. The fundamental fact is that social meaning evaporates from places, and therefore from society, and becomes diluted and diffused in the reconstructed logic of a space of flows whose profile, origin, and ultimate purpose are unknown, even for many of the entities integrated in the network of exchanges. The flows of power generate the power of flows, whose material reality imposes itself as a natural phenomenon that cannot be controlled or predicted, only accepted and managed. This is the real significance of the current restructuring process, implemented on the basis of new information technologies, and materially expressed in the separation between functional flows and historically determined places as two disjointed spheres of the human experience. People live in places, power rules through flows.

Nevertheless, societies are not made up of passive subjects resigned to structural domination. The meaninglessness of places, the powerlessness of political institutions are resented and resisted, individually and collectively, by a variety of social actors. People have affirmed their cultural identity, often in territorial terms, mobilizing to achieve their demands, organizing their communities, and staking out their places to preserve meaning, to restore whatever limited control they can over work and residence, to reinvent love and laughter in the midst of the abstraction of the new historical landscape. But, as I have shown elsewhere in my cross-cultural investigation of urban social movements, these are more often reactive symptoms of structural contradictions than conscious actions in pursuit of social change. Faced with the variable geometry of the space of flows, grassroots mobilizations tend to be defensive, protective, territorially bounded, or so culturally specific that their codes of self-recognizing identity become non-communicable, with societies tending to fragment themselves into tribes, easily prone to a fundamentalist affirmation of their identity. While power constitutes an articulated functional space of flows, societies deconstruct their historical culture into localized identities that recover the meaning of places only at the price of breaking down communication among different cultures and different places. Between ahistorical flows and irreducible identities of local communities, cities and regions disappear as socially meaningful places. The historical outcome of this process could be the ushering in of an era characterized by the uneasy coexistence of extraordinary human achievements and the disintegration of large segments of society, along with the widespread prevalence of senseless violence – for the impossibility of communication transforms other communities into "aliens," and thus into potential enemies. The globalization of power flows and the tribalization of local comunities are part of the same fundamental process of historical restructuring: the growing dissociation between techno-economic development and the corresponding mechanisms of social control of such development.

These trends are not ineluctable. They can be reversed, and should be reversed, by a series of political, economic, and technological strategies that could contribute to the reconstruction of social meaning in the new historical reality characterized by the formation of the space of flows as the space of power and functional organizations. While the focus of this book has been primarily analytical, outside normative debate about policies, I believe it is important, in concluding, to explore possible ways out of the destructive dynamics identified by this research.

The new techno-economic paradigm imposes the space of flows as the irreversible spatial logic of economic and functional organizations. The issue then becomes how to articulate the meaning of places to this new functional space. The reconstruction of place-based social meaning requires the simultaneous articulation of alternative social and spatial projects at three levels: cultural, economic, and political.

At the cultural level, local societies, territorially defined, must preserve their identities, and build upon their historical roots, regardless of their economic and functional dependence upon the space of flows. The symbolic marking of places, the preservation of symbols of recognition, the expression of collective memory in actual practices of communication, are fundamental means by which places may continue to exist as such, without having to justify their existence by the fulfillment of their functional performance. However, to avert the danger of over-affirmation of a local identity without reference to any broader social framework of reference at least two additional strategies are required: on the one hand, they must build communication codes with other identities, codes that require the definition of communities as sub-cultures able to recognize and to communicate with higher-order cultures; and on the other they must link the affirmation and symbolic practice of cultural identity to economic policy and political practice. They may thereby overcome the dangers of tribalism and fundamentalism.

Localities – cities and regions – must also be able to find their specific role in the new informational economy. This is possibly the most difficult dimension to integrate into a new strategy of place-based social control, since a precise and major characteristic of the new economy is its functional articulation in the space of flows. However, localities can become indispensable elements in the new economic geography because of the specific nature of the informational economy. In such an economy, the main source of productivity is the capacity to generate and process new information, itself dependent upon the symbolic manipulating ability of labor. This informational potential of labor is a function of its general living conditions, not only in terms of education, but in terms of the overall social milieu that constantly produces and stimulates its intellectual development. In a fundamental sense, social reproduction becomes a direct productive force. Production in the informational economy becomes organized in the space of flows, but social reproduction continues to be locally specific. While the overall logic of the production and management system still operates at the level of flows, the connection between production and reproduction – a key element of the new productive forces – requires an adequate linkage to the place-based system of formation and development of labor. This linkage must be explicitly recognized by each locality, so that locally-based labor will be able to provide the skills required in the production system at the precise point of its connection in the network of productive exchanges. Labor – and indeed, individual citizens – must develop an awareness of the precise role of their place-based activities in the functional space of flows. On the basis of such an awareness they will be better placed to bargain for the control of the overall production system as it relates to their interests. Yet this economic bargaining power on the part of the informational labor force is highly vulnerable if it is not backed up by the social strength provided by cultural identity, and if it is not articulated and implemented by renewed political power from local governments.

Local governments must develop a central role in organizing the social control of places over the functional logic of the space of flows. It is only through the reinforcement of this role that localities will be able to put pressure on economic and political organizations to restore the meaning of the local society in the new functional logic. This statement runs counter to the widespread opinion that the role for local governments will diminish in an internationalized economy and within the functional space of flows. I believe that it is precisely because we live in such a world that local governments can and must play a more decisive role as representatives of civil societies. National governments are frequently as powerless as local to handle unidentifiable flows. Furthermore, since the origin and destination of the flows cannot be controlled, the key issue has become flexibility and adaptability to the potential and requirements of the network of flows in each specific situation as it relates to a given locality. Because local governments defend specific interests, linked to a local society, they can identify such interests and respond flexibly to the requirements of the flows of power, so identifying the best bargaining position in each case. In other words, in a situation of generalized lack of control, the more specific the bargaining agenda, and the more flexible the capacity of response, both positive and negative, to the network of flows, the greater will be the chances of restoring some level of social control. It may be instructive to recall that the formation of the world economy in the fourteenth to sixteenth centuries led to the emergence of city-states as flexible political institutions able to engage in worldwide strategies of negotiation and conflictive articulation with transnational economic powers. The current process of total internationalization of the economy may also lead to the renaissance of the local state, as an alternative to the functionally powerless and institutionally bureaucratized nation-states.

Nevertheless, for local governments to assume such a fundamental role they must extend their organizational capacity and reinforce their power in at least two directions. Firstly, by fostering citizen participation they should mobilize local civil societies to support a collective strategy toward the reconstruction of the meaning of the locality in a conflictive dynamics with the placeless powers. Community organization and widespread, active citizen participation are indispensable elements for the revitalization of local governments as dynamic agents of economic development and social control. Secondly, and in so doing, they must connect with other organized, self-identified communities engaged in collective endeavor, taking care to avoid tribalism and acting on the material basis of work and power. Local governments will be unable to control the logic of the space of flows if they remain confined to their locality, while flows-based organizations select their locations at their convenience, playing localized social and political actors one against the other. Local governments attempting to restore social control of the development process need to establish their own networks of information, decision making, and strategic alliances, in order to match the mobility of power-holding organizations. In other words, they must reconstruct an alternative space of flows on the basis of the space of places. In this way they can avoid the deconstruction of their locales by the placeless logic of flows-based organizations.

Interestingly enough both these strategies – active citizen participation and a nation-wide or worldwide network of local governments – could be implemented most effectively on the basis of new information technologies. Citizens' data banks, interactive communication systems, community-based multimedia centers, are powerful tools to enhance citizen participation on the basis of grassroots organizations and local governments' political will. On-line information systems linking local governments across the world could provide a fundamental tool in countering the strategies of flows-based organizations, which would then lose the advantage, deriving from their control of asymmetrical information flows. Information technologies could provide the flexible instrument to reverse the logic of domination of the space of flows built by the process of socio-economic restructuring. However, the technological medium alone will not be able to transform this process in the absence of social mobilization, political decisions, and institutional strategies that would enable local governments to challenge collectively the power of flows and to reinstate the counterpower of places.

These reflections are not intended to provide a specific policy agenda for political action and social change, given the generality of the analysis presented in this book. They aim simply at opening a debate, in both scholarly and political circles, that could begin to address the fundamental challenge posed by the emergence of the space of flows to the meaning of our cities and to the welfare of our societies. The policy orientations I have suggested may appear utopian. But sometimes, a utopian vision is needed to shake the institutions from shortsightedness and stasis and to enable people to think the unthinkable, thus enhancing their awareness and their control of the inevitable social transformation. What we must prevent at all costs is the development of the one-sided logic of the space of flows while we keep up a pretence that the social balance of our cities has been maintained. Unless alternative, realistic policies, fostered by new social movements, can be found to reconstruct the social meaning of localities within the space of flows, our societies will fracture into non-communicative segments whose reciprocal alienation will lead to destructive violence and to a process of historical decline.

However, if innovative social projects, represented and implemented by renewed local governments, are able to master the formidable forces unleashed by the revolution in information technologies, then a new socio-spatial structure could emerge made up of a network of local communes controlling and shaping a network of productive flows. Maybe then our historic time and our social space would converge towards the reintegration of knowledge and meaning into a new Informational City.

Notes

Chapter 1

[1]The social theory underlying this analysis cannot be fully presented in the context of this book, which addresses a specific research topic. However, it is intellectually important to relate this study to the overall theoretical framework that informs it. The elaboration of this theory has built upon several classical traditions: Marx for the analysis of class relationships; Freud and Reich for the understanding of personality on the basis of sexual and family relationships; Weber for the analysis of the state. A number of contemporary social scientists have been crucial to my understanding of links and developments not covered in the classical writings: Nicos Poulantzas, for the recasting of the theory of social classes and the state; Alain Touraine for his analysis on post-industrialism; Nancy Chodorow for the intellectual connection between feminist theory and the psychoanalytical tradition; Agnes Heller, for the understanding of the historical creation of social needs; and Michel Foucault and Richard Sennett for the connection between power and culture. In making explicitly known my theoretical sources, I hope to help place this brief summary of my underlying theoretical framework in the ongoing intellectual debates in social sciences.

[2]Under the term "human-modified matter" I would include what could be called at the risk of paradox, "immaterial matter," that is, the set of symbols and communication codes that are generated by the human mind and which, while they are intangible, are a fundamental part of matter, since they are indeed a material force. One way to understand the informational mode of development, that I will not explore at present, could be the shift from physical matter to mental matter in the process of expansion of nature.

[3]The definition is from Harvey Brooks, cited in Daniel Bell, *The Coming of Post-Industrial Society* (New York, Basic Books, 1973) p. 29 of the 1976 edition.

[4]Ibid.

[5]Alain Touraine, *La Société post-industrielle* (Paris, Denoel, 1969); Radovan Richta, *La Civilisation au carrefour* (Paris, Anthropos, 1969); Bell, *Post-industrial Society*.

[6]For a summary, informed presentation of the rise and implications of information technology see, for instance, Tom Forester, *High Tech Society: The Story of the Information Technology Revolution* (Oxford, Blackwell, 1987); also Bruce R. Guile (ed.), *Information Technologies and Social Transformation* (Washington DC, National Academy Press, 1985).

[7]See E. Braun and S. MacDonald, *Revolution in Miniature* (Cambridge, Cambridge University Press, 1982).

[8]See Edward J. Sylvester and Lynn C. Klotz, *The Gene Age: Genetic Engineering and the Next Industrial Revolution* (New York, Scribner, 1983).

[9]See John S. Mayo, *The Evolution of Information Technologies* in Guile, *Information Technologies*, pp. 7–33.

[10]Nathan Rosenberg, "The Impact of Historical Innovation: A Historical View," in Ralph Landau and Nathan Rosenberg (eds), *The Positive Sum Strategy: Harnessing Technology for Economic Growth* (Washington DC, National Academy Press, 1986).

[11]See Melvin Kranzberg, "The Information Age: Evolution or Revolution," in Guile, *Information Technologies*, pp. 35–55.

[12]See Melvin Kranzberg and Carroll W. Pursell, Jr (eds), *Technology in Western Civilization* (New York, Oxford University Press, 1967), 2 vols.

[13]I. Mackintosh, *Sunrise Europe: The Dynamics of Information Technology* (Oxford, Blackwell, 1986).

[14]Nathan Rosenberg, *Perspectives on Technology* (Cambridge, Cambridge University Press, 1976).

[15]See Eugene S. Ferguson, "The Steam Engine Before 1830," John R. Brae, "Energy Conversion," and Harold I. Sharlin, "Applications of Electricity," in Kranzberg and Pursell, *Technology in Western Civilization*.

[16]For the notion of "technical paradigm" see the analysis in Carlota Perez, "Structural Change and the Assimilation of New Technologies in the Economic and Social Systems," *Futures*, 15 (1983), pp. 357–75.

[17]Marx developed his most far-reaching analysis of the social implications of technology in the *Grundrisse*.

[18]See Robert Boyer and Benjamin Coriat, *Technical Flexibility and Macro Stabilisation*, paper presented at the Venice Conference on Innovation Diffusion, 17–21 March 1986 (Paris, CEPREMAP, 1986).

[19]For an analysis of "Fordism" see Robert Boyer, *Technical Change and the Theory of Regulation* (Paris, CEPREMAP, 1987).

[20]Michael Piore and Charles Sabel, *The Second Industrial Divide* (New York, Basic Books, 1984).

[21]See the fundamental work on the whole series of issues discussed in this chapter, Peter Hall and Paschal Preston, *The Carrier Wave: New Information Technology and the Geography of Innovation, 1846–2003* (London, Unwin Hyman, 1988).

[22]For a discussion of post-industralism, see Manuel Castells, *The Economic Crisis and American Society* (Oxford, Blackwell, 1980), pp. 164–78.

[23]Alfred D. Chandler, *The Visible Hand* (Cambridge, Cambridge University Press, 1977).

[24]Robert Solow, "Technical Changes and the Aggregate Production Function," in *Review of Economics and Statistics*, August 1957. For a summary of the debate on the sources of productivity, see Richard R. Nelson, "Research on Productivity Growth and Productivity Differences: Dead Ends and New Departures," in *Journal of Economic Literature*, XIX (September 1981), pp. 1029–64.

[25]I have relied for this analysis on Nicole Woolsey-Biggart, "Direct Sales and Flexible Market Strategies," forthcoming.

[26]Manuel Castells, "Collective Consumption and Urban Contradictions in Advanced Capitalism," in Leo Lindberg et al. (eds) *Stress and Contradiction in Modern Capitalism* (Lexington, Mass., Heath, 1974).

[27]Morris Janowitz, *Social Control of the Welfare State* (Chicago, University of Chicago Press, 1976).

[28]Michel Aglietta, *Une Théorie de la regulation économique: le cas des Etats-Unis* (Paris, Calmann-Levy, 1976).

[29]Alain Touraine, *La Voix et Le Regard* (Paris, Seuil, 1978).

[30]Philippe Schmitter *Interest Conflict and Political Change in Brazil* (Stanford, Stanford University Press, 1981).

[31]Gordon Clark and Michael Dear, *State Apparatus* (Boston, Allen & Unwin, 1984).

[32]Nicos Poulantzas, *L'Etat, le pouvoir, le socialisme* (Paris, Presses Universitaires de France, 1978), p. 226 (my translation).

[33]See James O' Connor, *Accumulation Crisis* (Oxford, Blackwell, 1984).

[34]Post-depression capitalism did not actually follow the policies proposed by Keynes: the state acted on supply as much as on demand. It would be more appropriate to refer to this form of capitalism as state-regulated capitalism.

[35]See Michel Aglietta, *Regulation et crises du capitalisme* (Paris, Calmann-Levy, 1976).

[36]For the analysis of the causes of the economic crisis of the 1970s and of the potential way out of it through the restructuring process, see Castells, *The Economic Crisis and American Society*.

[37]Samuel Bowles et al., *Beyond the Wasteland* (New York, Doubleday, 1983).

[38]See James O'Connor's classic, *The Fiscal Crisis of the State* (New York, St Martin's, 1973).

[39]See Manuel Castells and Alejandro Portes, "World Underneath: The Origins, Dynamics, and Consequences of the Informal Economy," in Alejandro Portes, Manuel Castells, and Lauren Benton (eds), *The Informal Economy* (Baltimore, Johns Hopkins University Press, 1989).

[40]Michael Reich, *Discrimination in Labor Markets* (Princeton, Princeton University Press, 1982).

[41]Manuel Castells, "Immigrant Workers and Class Struggle in Western Europe," *Politics and Society*, 2 (1975).

[42]Joel Krieger, *Reagan, Thatcher and the Politics of Decline* (New York, Oxford University Press, 1986).

[43]I rely here on an analysis of the state, adapted from Nicos Poulantzas' work, that sees the state's relatively autonomous actions taking place within a dialectical process of ensuring domination and accumulation on the one hand, while trying to maintain legitimation and redistribution on the other. For an attempt at using these concepts in empirical research, see Manuel Castells and Francis Godard, *Monopolville* (Paris, Mouton, 1974).

[44]Fernand Braudel, *Capitalisme et civilisation materielle* (Paris, Armand Colin, 1979); Immanuel Wallerstein, *The Modern World System* (New York, Academic Press, 1974).

[45]By the "creative destruction" of capitalism I refer, of course, to the notion proposed by Schumpeter in his *Business Cycles*.

[46]Robert Boyer (ed.), *Capitalismes fin de siècle* (Paris, Presses Universitaires de France, 1986).

[47]See our analysis of "Reaganomics" in Martin Carnoy and Manuel Castells, "After the Crisis?," in *World Policy Journal*, May 1984.

[48]On the role of flexibility see Boyer and Coriat, *Technical Flexibility*.

[49]The notion of the "recapitalization" of the state has been proposed by S. M. Miller.

[50]For an analysis of flexibility in enhancing competitiveness in the international economy, see Manuel Castells, "Small Business in the World Economy: The Hong Kong Model of Economic Development", Berkeley Roundtable on the International Economy (Berkeley, University of California, forthcoming).

[51]On the analysis of networks see Piore and Sabel, *The Second Industrial Divide* and Woolsey-Biggart, "Direct Sales."

[52]For evidence on the fundamental role of networks in the informal economy, see Portes, Castells, and Benton, *The Informal Economy.*

[53]See Peter Schulze, "Shifts in the World Economy and the Restructuring of Economic Sectors: Increasing Competition and Strategic Alliances in Information Technologies" (Berkeley, University of California, Institute of International Studies, 1987).

Chapter 2

[1]A. J. Scott and M. Storper (eds), *Production Work, Territory: The Geographical Anatomy of Industrial Capitalism* (Boston, London, Allen and Unwin, 1986); Manuel Castells (ed.), *High Technology, Space, and Society* (Beverly Hills, Ca., Sage, 1985); US Congress, Office of Technology Assessment, *Technology, Innovation, and Regional Economic Development* (Washington, DC, Government Printing Office, 1984, OTA-STI-238; Philippe Aydalot (ed.), *Milieux innovateurs en Europe* (Paris, GREMI, 1986); R. Oakey, *High Technology Small Firms: Regional Development in Britain and the United States* (London, Pinter, 1984); Bert Van der Knapp and Egbert Wever (eds), *New Technology and Regional Development* (London, Croom Helm, 1987); M. Storper, *The Spatial Division of Labor: Technology, the Labor Process, and the Location of Industries,* PhD dissertation (Berkeley, University of California, 1982).

[2]See especially Ann Markusen, Peter Hall, and Amy Glasmeier, *High Tech America: The What, How, Where, and Why of the Sunrise Industries* (Boston, London, Allen and Unwin, 1986); M. Breheny, P. Hall, D. Hart, and R. McQuaid, *Western Sunrise: The Genesis and Growth of Britain's High Tech Corridor* (London, Allen and Unwin, 1986); John F. Brotchie, Peter Hall, and Peter W. Newton, *The Spatial Impact of Technological Change* (London, Groom Helm, 1987).

[3]A. J. Scott and M. Storper, "High Technology Industry and Regional Development: A Theoretical Critique and Reconstruction," *International Social Science Journal* (1987); M.D. Thomas, "The Innovation Factor in the Process of Microeconomic Industrial Change: Conceptual Explorations," in Van der Knapp and Wever (eds), pp. 21–44; R. Walker, "Technological Determination and Determinism: Industrial Growth and Location," in Castells, *High Technology, Space, and Society,* pp. 226–64; R. Gordon and L. Kimball, "Industrial Structure and the Changing Global Dynamics of Location in High Technology Industry," in J. Brotchie, P. Hall, and P. W. Newton (eds), *The Spatial Impact of Technological Change* (London, Croom Helm, 1987).

[4]Ann Markusen, *Profit Cycles, Oligopoly, and Regional Development* (Cambridge, Mass., MIT, 1985).

[5]For instance, Edward J. Malecki, "High Technology and Local Economic Development," *Journal of the American Planning Association,* Summer 1984, pp. 262–9; A. J. Scott, "Location Processes, Urbanization, and Territorial Development: An Exploratory Essay," in *Environment and Planning A,* 17, pp. 479–501; M. Taylor,

"Enterprise and the Product-Cycle Model: Conceptual Ambiguities," in Van der Knapp and Wever, *New Technology and Regional Development*, pp. 75-93; Allen Scott, *New Industrial Spaces* (London, Pion, 1988).

[6]See Jeff Henderson and Manuel Castells (eds), *Global Restructuring and Territorial Development* (London, Sage, 1987).

[7]Markusen, Hall, and Glasmeier, *High Tech America*.

[8]A. Glasmeier, *The Structure, Location, and Role of High Technology Industries in U.S. Regional Development*, unpublished PhD dissertation (Berkeley, University of California, 1986).

[9]See John Rees, "Industrial Innovation," in *Economic Development Commentary*, 10, 1 (Spring 1987), pp. 17-21.

[10]See Markusen, Hall, and Glasmeier, *High Tech America*, table 9.1., p. 155.

[11]Storper, *Spatial Division of Labor*.

[12]A. J. Scott and D. P. Angel, *The U.S. Semiconductor Industry: A Locational Analysis*, Department of Geography Research Monograph (Los Angeles, UCLA, 1986).

[13]Servet Mutlu, *Inter-regional and International Mobility of Industrial Capital: The Case of American Automobile and Electronics Companies*, unpublished PhD dissertation (Berkeley, University of California, 1979). Mutlu's work is, to my knowledge, the earliest comprehensive, thorough, and empirical analysis of the spatial implications of high-technology manufacturing in the US.

[14]See Amy Glasmeier, *The Making of High Tech Regions*, forthcoming, ch. 2.

[15]See Glasmeier, *High Technology Industries in U.S. Regional Development*; The Fantus Company, *Local High Technology Initiatives Study* (Washington, DC, US Congress, Office of Technology Assessment, 1983); S. Goodman and V. L. Arnold, "High Technology in Texas," in *Texas Business Review*, Nov.-Dec. 1983.

[16]Glasmeier, *High Technology Industries in U.S. Regional Development*, pp. 316-29.

[17]Mutlu, *Mobility of Industrial Capital*, p. 129.

[18]The major research effort to date on these analytical perspectives is the work conducted by Anna Lee Saxenian since 1980. See, for instance, A. L. Saxenian, "The Genesis of Silicon Valley," in P. Hall and A. Markusen (eds), *Silicon Landscapes* (Winchester, Mass., Allen and Unwin, 1985); A. L. Saxenian, "Silicon Valley and Route 128: Regional Prototypes or Historic Exceptions," in M. Castells, *High Technology, Space, and Society*, pp. 81-105. Mutlu has also analyzed in depth the origins of the two major industrial centers of high technology in *Mobility of Industrial Capital*.

[19]This major fact was brought to my attention by Lenny Siegel, the director of the Pacific Studies Center in Mountain View, Ca. (personal correspondence, 1985).

[20]Anna Lee Saxenian, *In Search of Power: The Organization of Business Interests in Silicon Valley and Route 128*, Department of Political Science Working Paper, (Cambridge, Mass, MIT, 1986).

[21]See Storper, *Spatial Division of Labor*; also J. Henderson and A. J. Scott, "The Growth and Internationalization of the American Semiconductor Industry: Labour Processes and the Changing Spatial Organisation of Production," in M. Breheny and R. McQuaid (eds), *The Development of High Technology Industries* (London, Croom Helm, 1986); A. Sayer, "Industrial Location on a World Scale: The Case of the Semiconductor Industry" in Scott and Storper (eds), *Production Work, Territory*, pp. 107-23.

[22]Scott and Angel, *The U.S. Semiconductor Industry*.

[23]D. Ernst, *The Global Race in Microelectronics* (Frankfurt: Campus, 1983); K. Flamm, "Internationalization in the Semiconductor Industry," in J. Grunwald and K. Flamm (eds), *The Global Factory* (Washington, DC: Brookings Institution, 1985), pp. 38–136.

[24]For data and sources on this section, see Mutlu, *Mobility of Industrial Capital.*

[25]Personal correspondence from Amy Glasmeier, 3 February 1988.

[26]See Markusen, *Profit Cycles*, ch. 9.

[27]See Sarah Kuhn, *Computer Manufacturing in New England: Structure, Location and Labor in a Growing Industry* (Cambridge, Harvard-MIT Joint Center for Urban Studies, 1981).

[28]E. Sciberras, *Multinational Electronics Companies and National Economic Policies* (Greenwich, Conn.: JAI, 1977).

[29]P. Hall, A. Markusen, R. Osborn, and B. Wachsman, *The Computer Software Industry: Prospects and Policy Issues*, Institute of Urban and Regional Development (IURD) Working Paper No. 410 (Berkeley, University of California, 1983).

[30]Ibid., p. 55.

[31]See Edward J. Sylvester and Lynn C. Klotz, *The Gene Age: Genetic Engineering and the Next Industrial Revolution* (New York, Scribner, 1983).

[32]A. Hacking, *Economic Aspects of Biotechnology* (Cambridge, Cambridge University Press, 1986).

[33]N. Simmons, "Biotechnology Industry Offers Specialists a Flurry of Jobs," *New York Times*, 25 March 1984.

[34]Edward J. Blakely, *Developing the Biotechnology Industry: A Case Study of Regional Industrial Planning in the San Francisco Bay Area*, Institute of Urban and Regional Development, Biotech Industry Research Group (Berkeley, University of California, 1988).

[35]M. Kenney, *Biotechnology: The University–Industrial Complex* (New Haven, Yale University Press, 1986).

[36]Peter Hall, Lisa Bornstein, Reed Grier, and Melvin Webber, *Biotechnology: The Next Industrial Frontier*, Institute of Urban and Regional Development, Biotech Industry Research Group (Berkeley, University of California, 1988).

[37]Kenney, *Biotechnology.*

[38]See "Biotech Comes of Age," *Business Week*, 23 January 1984, pp. 84–94.

[39]Hall, Bornstein, Grier, and Webber, *Biotechnology*, p. 14.

[40]Hall, Bornstein, Grier, and Webber, *Biotechnology.*

[41]Kenney, *Biotechnology.*

[42]Edward Blakely with Suzanne Scotchmer and Jonathan Levine, *The Locational and Economic Patterns of California's Biotech Industry: A Preliminary Report*, Institute of Urban and Regional Development, Biotech Industry Research Group (Berkeley, University of California, 1988).

[43]"Biotech Comes of Age."

[44]See Michael Borrus and James Millstein, *Technological Innovation and Industrial Growth: A Comparative Assessment of Biotechnology and Semiconductors*, Research Report prepared for the US Congress, Office of Technology Assessment (Washington, DC, 1982).

[45]See Bruce R. Guile (ed.) *Information Technologies and Social Transformation* (Washington, DC, National Academy Press, 1985).

[46]See US Congress, Office of Technology Assessment, *Information Technology R&D:*

Critical Trends and Issues (Washington, DC, 1985), particularly pp. 139–200.

[47]Ann F. Friedlander, "Macroeconomics and Microeconomics of Innovation: the Role of the Technological Environment," in Ralph Landau and Nathan Rosenberg (eds), *The Positive Sum Strategy: Harnessing Technology for Economic Growth*, (Washington, DC, National Academy Press, 1986), pp. 327–32.

[48]An interesting approach to the analysis of innovative milieux has been proposed by Philippe Aydalot, *L'Aptitude des milieux locaux a promouvoir innovation technologique*, paper delivered at the Symposium on New Technologies and Regions in Crisis, French Language Association of Regional Science, Brussels, 22–3 April 1985. A formal analysis of the notion of innovative technological milieux has been elaborated by W. Brian Arthur, *Industry Location Patterns and the Importance of History*, Food Research Institute Research Paper (Stanford: Stanford University, 1986).

[49]Melvin Kranzberg, "The Information Age: Evolution or Revolution?" in Guile, *Information Technologies*, pp. 35–54.

[50]J. Rees and H. Stafford, *A Review of Regional Growth and Industrial Location Theory: Towards Understanding the Development of High Technology Complexes in the US* (US Congress, Office of Technology Assessment, Washington DC, 1983).

[51]Gordon and Kimball, "Industrial Structure."

[52]This analysis builds on my own contribution to the analysis of the relationship between technology and industrial location in my University of Paris doctoral dissertation (1967). For elaboration on that research, see Manuel Castells, *Sociologie de l'espace industriel* (Paris, Anthropos, 1975).

[53]See M. Carnoy and M. Castells, *Technology and Economy in the U.S.*, paper delivered at the UNESCO Conference on Science and Technology, Athens, September 1985.

[54]See E. Braun and S. MacDonald, *Revolution in Miniature* (Cambridge, Cambridge University Press, 1982).

[55]R. U. Ayres, *The Next Industrial Revolution: Reviving Industry Through Innovation* (Cambridge, Mass., Ballinger, 1984).

[56]Jeff Henderson, "The New International Division of Labour and American Semiconductor Production in South-East Asia," in D. Watts, C. Dixon, and D. Drakakis-Smith (eds), *Multinational Companies and the Third World* (London, Croom Helm, 1986).

[57]Ian Benson and John Lloyd, *New Technology and Industrial Change: The Impact of the Scientific-Technical Revolution on Labour and Industry* (New York, Nichols, 1983); Lionel Nicol, *Communications, Economic Development, and Spatial Structure: A Review of Research*, Institute of Urban and Regional Development, Working Paper No. 404 (Berkeley, University of California, 1983).

[58]The general theme of the spatial division of labor in economic geography has been theorized in masterly fashion by Doreen Massey in *Spatial Divisions of Labour: Social Structures and the Geography of Production* (London, Macmillan, 1984). My own work on this topic is much indebted to Massey's analysis.

[59]R. Gordon and L. Kimball, *High Technology, Employment, and the Challenges to Education*, Silicon Valley Research Group, Working Paper No. 1 (Santa Cruz: University of California, 1985).

[60]M. Carnoy, *The Labor Market in Silicon Valley and its Implications for Education* (Stanford, Ca, Stanford University Institute for Research on Educational Finance and Governance, 1985).

[61]See Scott and Angel, *The US Semiconductor Industry*; Henderson, "New International Division of Labor"; Henderson and Scott, "Growth and Internationalization of the American Semiconductor Industry"; Mutlu, *Mobility of Industrial Capital*; Storper, *Spatial Division of Labor*; Glasmeier, *High Technology Industries in US Regional Development*.

[62]A. K. Glasmeier, "High Tech Industries and the Regional Division of Labor," in *Industrial Relations*, 25, 2 (Spring 1986), pp. 197–211.

[63]Ibid., pp. 202–4.

[64]See Scott and Angel, *The US Semiconductor Industry*.

[65]Ibid., p. 29 of typescript.

[66]See Anna Lee Saxenian, *Silicon Chips and Spatial Structure: The Industrial Basis of Urbanization in Santa Clara County, California*, Institute of Urban and Regional Development, working paper 345 (Berkeley, University of California, 1981); Storper, *Spatial Division of Labor*; Mutlu, *Mobility of Industrial Capital*.

[67]See Henderson and Scott, "Growth and Internationalization of the American Semiconductor Industry."

[68]For a discussion of the evidence on the impact of automation on productive decentralization at the international level, refuting the thesis of "relocation back North," see Manuel Castells, "High Technology and the New International Division of Labor," in *International Labour Review*, October 1988.

[69]Saxenian, *Silicon Chips and Spatial Structure*.

[70]J. Keller, *The Production Worker in Electronics: Industrialization and Labor Development in California's Santa Clara Valley*, PhD dissertation (Ann Arbor, University of Michigan, 1981).

[71]Storper, *Spatial Division of Labor*.

[72]For some key formal and theoretical analyses of milieux of innovation see: W. B. Arthur, *Industry Location and the Economics of Agglomeration: Why a Silicon Valley?* (Stanford, Stanford University Center for Economic Policy Research, 1985); Walter B. Stohr, "Territorial Innovation Complexes," in Aydalot, *L'Aptitude des milieux locaux*, pp. 29–56; A. E. Anderson, *Creativity and Regional Development*, working paper 85-14 (Laxenburg, Austria, International Institute for Applied Systems Analysis, 1985); P. Aydalot, "Trajectoires Technologiques et Milieux Innovateurs," in Aydalot, *L'Aptitude des milieux locaux*, pp. 345–61.

[73]See E. J. Malecki, "Technology and Regional Development: A Survey," *International Regional Science Review*, 8, 2, pp. 89–125.

[74]See George Young, *Venture Capital in High-tech Companies* (London, Pinter, 1985).

[75]E. J. Malecki, "Corporate Organization of R&D and the Location of Technological Activities," in *Regional Studies*, 14 (1980), pp. 219–34.

[76]E. J. Malecki, "Government Funded R&D: Some Regional Economic Implications," in *Professional Geographer*, 33, 1 (1981), pp. 72–82.

[77]Mutlu, *Mobility of Industrial Capital*; John W. Wilson, *The New Ventures: Inside the High-stakes World of Venture Capital* (Reading, Mass., Addison-Wesley, 1985).

[78]Saxenian, *Silicon Chips and Spatial Structure*; Saxenian, *The Political Economy of High Technology Growth Centers: Silicon Valley, Route 128, and Cambridge, England*, PhD dissertation (Cambridge, Mass., MIT, 1988); E. Rogers and J. Larsen, *Silicon Valley Fever* (New York, Basic Books, 1984); Cynthia Kroll and Linda Kimball, *The Santa Clara Valley R&D Dilemma: The Real Estate Industry and High tech Growth*,

Center for Real Estate and Urban Economics, Working Paper (Berkeley, University of California, 1986); Tim Sturgeon, *Industrial Location of the Semiconductor Industry: A Critique*, Honors thesis (Berkeley, University of California, 1987).

[79]See G. A. Van der Knapp, G. J. R. Linge, and E. Wever, "Technology and Industrial Change: An Overview," in Van der Knapp and Wever, *New Technology and Regional Development*, pp. 1–21.

[80]Cf. the analysis by Jay S. Stowsky, *Cultural Industries in the United States*, Department of City and Regional Planning research report (Berkeley, University of California, 1987).

[81]P. Hall, "Innovation: Key to Regional Growth," *Transaction/Society*, 19, 5 (1982).

[82]J. Rees and H. Stafford, *A Review of Regional Growth and Industrial Location Theory: Towards Understanding the Development of High-Technology Complexes in the United States*, Report for the US Congress, Office of Technology Assessment, April 1983.

[83]Saxenian, *Political Economy of High Technology Growth Centers*.

[84]E. J. Malecki, "Dimensions of R&D Location in the United States," in *Research Policy*, 9 (1980), pp. 2–22.

[85]*High Hopes for High Tech* (collective author), (Chapel Hill, University of North Carolina Press, 1985).

[86]See E. J. Malecki, "Corporate Organization of R and D," pp. 227–9.

[87]See Saxenian, "Silicon Valley and Route 128"; Saxenian, "The Genesis of Silicon Valley," in *Built Environment*, 9, 1, pp. 7–17; Lenny Siegel and John Markoff, *The High Cost of High Tech* (New York, Harper and Row, 1985); N. Dorfman, *Massachusetts High Technology Boom in Perspective* (Cambridge, Mass., MIT Center for Policy Alternatives, 1982); Pierre Fischer, Richard Carlson, Jean-Pierre Boespflug, and Pierre Lamond, *Silicon Valley, Anatomie d'Une Reussite* (Paris, Centre de Prospective et d'Evaluation, 1984); Michael Malone, *The Big Score* (New York, Doubleday, 1985).

[88]A. J. Scott, "High Technology Industry and Territorial Development: The Rise of the Orange County Complex, 1955–1984," in *Urban Geography*, 7, 1–43; D. A. Hicks and W. H. Stolberg, *The High-Technology Sectors: Growth and Development in the Dallas–Fort Worth Regional Economy, 1964–84*, Center for Policy Studies Research Report (Dallas, University of Texas, 1985).

[89]F. G. Rodgers, *The IBM Way* (New York, Harper and Row, 1986); Franklin M. Fisher, *IBM and the US Data Processing Industry* (New York, Praeger, 1983); Sonny Kleinfield, *The Biggest Company on Earth: A Profile of AT&T* (New York, Holt, Rinehart, and Winston, 1981).

[90]See Glasmeier, *High Technology Industries in US Regional Development*, pp. 292ff.

[91]A. Glasmeier, *Survey of High Technology Firms in Austin*, unpublished report, Graduate Program in Community and Regional Planning (Austin, University of Texas, 1987).

[92]See Mutlu, *Mobility of Industrial Capital*.

[93]See The City of Pittsburgh, *Strategy 21: Pittsburgh/Allegheny Economic Development Strategy to begin the 21st century*, 1985; Donald S. Shanis, *Transportation Planning for a High-tech Corridor in Suburban Philadelphia*, Delaware Valley Regional Planning Commission, 1985; Ayden Kutay, *Prospects of the Growth of Innovation-based High Technology Clusters in Old Industrial Regions: Pittsburgh as a Case Study*, unpublished research report (Pittsburgh, University of Pittsburgh, 1988).

[94]Henderson and Scott, "Growth and Internationalization of the American Semi-

conductor Industry"; R. P. Oakey, *High Technology Industry and Industrial Location* (Aldershot, Gower, 1981); R. Premus, *Location of High-technology Firms and Regional Economic Development* (Washington, DC, US Congress Joint Economic Committee, 1982).

[95]Storper, *Spatial Division of Labor*.

[96]*International Economic Restructuring and the Territorial Community* (Vienna, UNIDO, 1985).

[97]See Michael Borrus et al., *Telecommunications Development in Comparative Perspective: the New Telecommunications in Europe, Japan, and the US*, BRIE Working Paper (Berkeley, University of California, 1985); U.S. Congress, Office of Technology Assessment, *Computerized Manufacturing: Employment, Education, and the Workplace* (Washington, DC, Government Printing Office, 1984).

[98]See Ernst, *Global Race in Microelectronics*; R. Kaplinsky, *Microelectronics and Employment Revisited: A Review*, A Report for I.L.D. (Brighton, University of Sussex Institute of Development Studies, 1986).

[99]Cf. research in progress by Peter Hall, Ann Markusen, Sabina Dietrick, and Scott Campbell at the Institute of Urban and Regional Development, University of California, Berkeley, supported by the National Science Foundation.

[100]See A. Gillespie (ed.), *Technological Change and Regional Development* (London, Pion, 1983); R. Schmenner, *Making Business Location Decisions* (Englewood Cliffs, NJ, Prentice-Hall, 1982).

[101]Cf. Glasmeier, *High Technology Industries in U.S. Regional Development*.

[102]Jeffrey Henderson, *Semiconductors, Scotland, and the International Division of Labour*, Research Report (Hong Kong, University of Hong Kong Centre of Urban Studies, 1986).

[103]See Saxenian, "The Genesis of Silicon Valley."

[104]On working women in electronics in Asia, see Françoise Sabbah, *Tecnologia Electronica y Trabajo de la Mujer: Una Perspectiva Internacional* (Madrid, Instituto de la Mujer, 1988).

[105]A. J. Scott, "The Semiconductor Industry in South-east Asia: Organization, Location, and the International Division of Labor," in *Regional Studies*, 21 (1987).

[106]Peter W. Schulze, *The Struggle for Future Markets: Sectoral Adaptation and the Internationalization of Production*, discussion paper (Berkeley, Institute of International Studies, 1986).

[107]Juan Rada, *Structure and Behavior of the Semiconductors Industry* (New York, United Nations Center for the Study of Transnational Corporations, 1982).

[108]Manuel Castells and Laura Tyson, "High Technology Choices Ahead: Restructuring Interdependence," in John Sewell (ed.), *Growth, Jobs, and Markets in the International Economy* (Washington DC, Overseas Development Council, 1988).

[109]See Scott, "Semiconductor Industry in South-east Asia"; Dieter Ernst, "Crisis, Technology and the Dynamics of Global Restructuring: The Case of the Electronics Industry," in Henderson and Castells, *Global Restructuring*.

[110]Dieter Ernst, *Micro-electronics and Global Restructuring: The Social Implications of High Tech Neo-Mercantilism*, Discussion Paper (The Hague, Institute of Social Studies, 1986).

[111]J. Northcott, P. Rogers, W. Knetsch, and B. de Lestapis, *Microelectronics in Industry: An International Comparison. Britain, France, and Germany* (London, Policy Studies Institute, 1985).

[112]Scott, "Semiconductor Industry in South-east Asia."

[113]Ibid.

[114]Breheny and McQuaid, *Development of High Technology Industries.*

[115]See Saxenian, *Silicon Chips and Spatial Structure.*

[116]See Storper, *Spatial Division of Labor.*

[117]Markusen, Hall, and Glasmeier, *High Tech America.*

[118]See A. Markusen, *Profit Cycles*, pp. 101-17.

[119]See A. Glasmeier, *High Technology Industries in U.S. Regional Development.*

[120]Amy Glasmeier, personal communication to author of work in progress; see also Glasmeier, *The Making of High Tech Regions.*

[121]See Markusen, Hall, and Glasmeier, *High Tech America*, pp. 80-93.

[122]R. Gordon and L. M. Kimball, *Small Town High Technology: The Industrialization of Santa Cruz County*, (Santa Cruz, University of California Silicon Valley Research Group, forthcoming).

[123]Glasmeier, *High Technology Industries in U.S. Regional Development*, pp. 135-6.

[124]See Norman Glickman, *MCC comes to Austin*, Lyndon B. Johnson School of Public Affairs Working Paper (Austin, University of Texas, 1985).

[125]Amy Glasmeier, *Survey of High Technology Firms in Austin.*

[126]See Gordon and Kimball, "Industrial Structure," pp. 24-5.

[127]See Oakey, *High Technology Small Firms.*

[128]Stephen Cohen and John Zysman, *Manufacturing Matters* (New York, Basic Books, 1987).

[129]See Yasno Miyakawa, "Evolution of the Regional System and Change of Industrial Policy in Japan," in UN Centre for Regional Development, *Regional Development Alternatives* (Tokyo, Maliuze Asia, 1982); Kuniko Fujita, "The Technopolis: High Technology and Regional Development in Japan," in *International Journal of Urban and Regional Research*, 12, 4 (1988), pp. 566-94.

[130]Chalmers Johnson, *MITI and the Japanese Miracle* (Stanford: Stanford University Press, 1982).

[131]M. Borrus et al., *Responses to the Japanese Challenge in High Technology: Innovation, Maturity, and U.S.-Japanese Competition in Microelectronics*, BRIE Working Paper (Berkeley, University of California, 1983).

[132]W. Stohr, "Regional Technological and Institutional Innovation: The Case of the Japanese Technopolis Policy," in J. Federwish and H. Zoller (eds), *Technologie et region, politiques en mutation* (Paris, Economica, 1986).

[133]T. Toda, "The Location of High Technology Industry and the Technopolis Plan in Japan," in Brotchie, Hall, and Newton, *The Spatial Impact of Technological Change*, pp. 271-83.

[134]Ministry of International Trade and Industry (MITI), Japan, *The Technopolis Project in Japan* (Tokyo, MITI, 1981).

[135]Sheridan Tatsuno, *The Technopolis Strategy: Japan, High Technology and the Control of the 21st Century* (Englewood Cliffs, NJ, Prentice Hall, 1986).

[136]See the analysis presented in R. Gordon and L. M. Kimball (eds), *The Future of Silicon Valley*, (Boston, Allen and Unwin, forthcoming).

[137]Dieter Ernst, *U.S.-Japanese Competition and the Worldwide Restructuring of the Electronics Industry: A European View*, Institute of International Studies, Policy Papers, Fall (Berkeley, University of California, 1986).

[138]This is a trend observed and analyzed by key experts on the topic, particularly Okimoto and Ernst.

[139]See Kroll and Kimball, *Santa Clara Valley R&D Dilemma*.

[140]Peter W. Schulze, *Shifts in the World Economy and the Restructuring of Economic Sectors: Increased Competition and Strategic Alliances in the Microelectronics Industries*, paper prepared for the International Seminar on New Technologies, Rio de Janeiro, 26–8 January 1987 (Berkeley, University of California Institute of International Studies).

[141]Ibid.

[142]Ernst, *U.S.–Japanese Competition*.

[143]Carol A. Parsons, *Flexible Production Technology and Industrial Restructuring: Case Studies of the Metalworking, Semiconductor and Apparel Industries*, PhD dissertation (Berkeley, University of California Department of City Planning, 1987).

[144]M. Castells et al., *El Desafío Tecnologico*, (Madrid, Alianza Editorial, 1986).

[145]M. Castells, "High Technology, World Development and Structural Transformation: The Trends and the Debate," *Alternatives*, XI, 3, July 1986, pp. 297–344.

[146]Research in progress by M. Castells and Peter Hall on Silicon Valley's recent spatial restructuring.

[147]Ernst, *Micro-electronics and Global Restructuring*; Ernst, *U.S.–Japanese Competition*; Carnoy and Castells, *Technology and Economy in the U.S.*; Schulze, *Shifts in the World Economy*.

[148]See, for instance, J. Muntendam, "Philips in the World: A View of a Multinational on Resource Allocation," in Van der Knapp and Wever, *New Technology and Regional Development*, pp. 136–44.

[149]See, for instance, the argument put forward in this respect by K. Ohmae, *Triad Power: The Coming Shape of Global Competition* (New York, Free Press, 1985).

[150]Procedure used to rank selected metropolitan areas of the US according to their R&D potential, circa 1977.

(1) The database used is Edward J. Malecki's elaboration of various sources (see notes 75, 76 to Chapter 2).

(2) The first step of the analysis established four rankings for the main sources of information in industrial R&D: universities, government, large corporations, and technological industrial milieux. The indicators used were, respectively: total R&D performed by universities in top 200 (in dollars), with indication of number of universities in top 200 in the metropolitan area; location of federally employed scientists and engineers, top 20 metropolitan areas; number of industrial research laboratories, top 20 metropolitan areas; and 10 top metropolitan areas in terms of both laboratories and employment. On the basis of these indicators, each metropolitan area received a score between 1 and 20 in terms of its position regarding university R&D, government R&D, or corporate research, with 1 representing the highest level of research and 20 the lowest among the top 20 metropolitan areas. Since some areas were among the top 20 in one of the scales but not present in other(s) (for instance, Madison, Wisconsin was seventh in university research but not present in government or corporate research), an arbitrary but systematic criterion was introduced: any area not present in a ranking was given a score of 25.

Another procedural factor must be noted. The indicator for the generation of an industrial milieu is a dichotomic one: it is a closed list of 10 metropolitan areas whose index of concentration in R&D laboratories and R&D employment has a value of one standard deviation above the rankings for 177 metropolitan areas. In this case, I have simply denoted the presence ($+$) or the absence ($-$) of such a milieu for any given metropolitan area.

(3) The second step was to rank metropolitan areas according to sources of finance. At this stage of the research there is still no reliable systematic indicator of spatial distribution of venture capital, although work in this direction is in progress. So, metropolitan areas are ranked according to two indicators: total DoD and NASA R&D (in millions of dollars); and total private R&D laboratories. Scores between 1 and 25 were given to each metropolitan area following the same procedure as in the series of indicators in (2) above.

(4) Thirdly, the areas were ranked according to the sources of technical research labor, on the basis of two indicators: for the existence of a self-sustaining technical labor market, we used the absolute number of engineers and scientists employed in R&D or administration of R&D; on the basis of this criterion, each area was given a score between 1 and 25. A second indicator was the presence or absence of a major university complex able to provide highly skilled research personnel. In this case presence ($+$) or absence ($-$) was denoted for each area.

(5) Having arrived at eight scores for each area, three synthetic ranking scores were established by combining the four indicators for information, the two indicators for capital, and the two indicators for labor. In the case of capital, it was simple: both scores were added and the total divided by two. In the two other cases (information, labor) it was necessary to combine ordinal scores with nominal scores. Here a systematic criterion was used to project the same influence of the presence of a powerful source of information or of labor in each metropolitan area: in the case of information, the three ordinal scores were added and the total divided by a denominator of four in the case of the presence of an innovative milieu, of three in the case of its absence; for sources of research labor, we divided by two when a major university was present as source of labor, leaving the score unaffected in the case of absence.

(6) Finally, the three synthetic scores were simply added to combine a global score allowing a synthetic overall ranking.

These procedural decisions are admittedly arbitrary, but their systematic use, and their explicit description, provide a basis for evaluating relative rankings of each area within the limits of the *illustrative* purpose of these calculations.

Chapter 3

[1] See Pascal Petit, *Slow Growth and the Service Economy* (London, Pinter, 1986) and the classic work by Victor Fuchs, *The Service Economy* (New York, National Bureau of Economic Research, 1968).

[2] James Brian Quinn, "The Impacts of Technology in the Services Sector," in Bruce

R. Guile and Harvey Brooks (eds), *Technology and Global Industry: Companies and Nations in the World Economy* (Washington DC, National Academy Press, 1987), p. 119.

[3]The notion of a post-industrial society is generally associated in the US with Daniel Bell, *The Coming of Post-industrial Society* (New York, Basic Books, 1973), and in Europe with Alain Touraine, *La Société post-industrielle* (Paris, Denoel, 1969). It is undeniable that both authors have made major contributions to the understanding of fundamental structural change in our societies, regardless of whether and to what extent one agrees with their interpretation of such changes. Here I am not criticizing their theories (to do so would require a longer and more systematic discussion) but rejecting the notion of post-industrialism which, I believe, actually contradicts the analysis put forward by both Bell and Touraine. A knowledge-based society, or a "société programmée," is not simply post-industrial: it opens up a new historic era, a new "mode of development," as I have argued in chapter 1, that is no more post-industrial than the industrial society was post-agrarian. This is why the concept of an informational society, as a result of an informational "mode of development" seems to be more adequate.

[4]For an analysis of the impact of information-based processes on the economic structure, see Tom Stonier, *The Wealth of Information: A Profile of the Post-industrial Economy* (London, Thames Methuen, 1983).

[5]See Thomas J. Stanback, *Understanding the Service Economy* (Baltimore, John Hopkins University Press, 1979).

[6]See the pathbreaking study by Joachim Singelmann, *The Transformation of Industry: From Agriculture to Service Employment* (Beverly Hills, Ca, Sage, 1977).

[7]James P. Smith and Michael P. Ward, *Women's Wages and Work in the 20th Century* (Santa Monica, Ca, Rand Corporation, 1984).

[8]Stephen Cohen and John Zysman, *Manufacturing Matters* (New York, Basic Books, 1987).

[9]Singelmann, *The Transformation of Industry*.

[10]Peter Hall, *Regions in the Transition to the Information Economy*, paper delivered at the Rutgers University Conference on America's New Economic Geography, Washington DC, 29-30 April 1987.

[11]Thomas J. Stanback et al., *Services, The New Economy* (Montclair, NJ, Allanheld, Osman, 1982).

[12]Manuel Castells, "The Service Economy and Postindustrial Society: A Sociological Critique," in *International Journal of Health Services*, 6,4 (1979).

[13]Stanback, *Understanding the Service Economy*, p. 29.

[14]Edward D. Dennison, *Accounting for Slower Economic Growth in the U. S.* (Washington DC, Brookings Institution, 1979).

[15]Stanback, *Understanding the Service Economy*; Petit, *Slow Growth and the Service Economy*.

[16]Jerome A. Mark and William H. Waldorf, "Multifactor Productivity: A New BLS Measure," *Monthly Labor Review*, 106, 12 (December 1983), pp. 3–15.

[17]David Collier, "The Services Sector Revolution: The Automation of Services," in *Long Range Planning*, 16 (December 1983), pp.10–20.

[18]S. Roach, "The Information Economy Comes of Age," in *Information Management Review*, Summer 1985, pp. 9-18.

[19]Marc Porat, *The Information Economy* (Washington DC, Department of Commerce, Office of Telecommunications, 1977).

[20]Rob Kling and Clark Turner, *The Structure of the Information Labor Force: Good Jobs and Bad Jobs* (Irvine, University of California, Department of Information and Computer Science, Public Policy Research Organization, 1987).

[21]For a discussion of the different definitions of the information work force and information industries see Raul L. Katz, "Measurement and Cross-National Comparisons of the Information Work Force," in *The Information Society*, 4, 4 (1986), pp. 231–77. For each specific definition underlying the data presented here I refer to the corresponding source.

[22]See James B. Quinn, "Technology Adoption: The Services Industries," in Ralph Landau and Nathan Rosenberg (eds), *The Positive Sum Strategy: Harnessing Technology for Economic Growth* (Washington DC, National Academy Press, 1986), pp. 357–72.

[23]For the role of information in economic growth, see Nathan Rosenberg and L.E. Birdzell, *How the West Grew Rich: The Economic Transformation of the Industrial World* (New York, Basic Books, 1986).

[24]J. de Bandt (ed.), *Les Services dans les sociétés industrielles avancées*, (Paris, Economica, 1985).

[25]See Micheal L. Dertouzos and Joel Moses, *The Computer Age: A Twenty Year View* (Cambridge, Mass., MIT Press, 1981).

[26]See Quinn, "Impacts of Technology."

[27]Micheal Laub and Charles R. Hoffman, "The Structure of the Financial Services Industry," in *Contemporary Policy Issues*, 2, January 1983; Wallace O. Sellers, "Technology and the Future of the Financial Services Industry,"in *Technology in Society*, 7 (1985), pp. 1–9.

[28]Lionel Nicol, *Information Technology, Information Networks, and On-Line Information Services: Technology, Industrial Structure, Markets, and Potential for Economic Growth*, working paper, Institute of Urban and Regional Development (Berkeley, University of California, 1983).

[29]Theodore J. Gordon, "Computers and Business," in Bruce R. Guile (ed.), *Information Technologies and Social Transformation* (Washington DC, National Academy Press, 1985).

[30]See Alfred D. Chandler, *The Visible Hand: The Managerial Revolution in American Business* (Cambridge, Mass., Harvard University Press, 1977).

[31]See David Birch, *The Job Generation Process* (Cambridge, Mass., MIT Press, 1979).

[32]See Ann Markusen and Michael Teitz, *The World of Small Business: Turbulence and Survival*, working paper no. 408, Institute of Urban and Regional Development (Berkeley, University of California, 1983).

[33]US Congress, Office of Technology Assessment (henceforth OTA), *Automation of America's Offices* OTA-CIT-287 (Washington DC, US Government Printing Office, 1985).

[34]Quinn, "Impacts of Technology," p. 125.

[35]OTA, *Automation*, p. 6.

[36]OTA, *Automation*, p. 7.

[37]Lionel Nicol, "Communications Technology: Economic and Spatial Impacts," in Manuel Castells (ed.), *High Technology, Space, and Society* (Beverly Hills, Ca, Sage, 1985).

[38]See a detailed report of the technological foundations of office automation in OTA, *Automation*, 1985, Appendix A.

[39]Harry Braverman, *Labor and Monopoly Capital* (New York, Monthly Review Press, 1974).

[40]See Larry Hirschhorn, *Beyond Mechanization* (Cambridge, Mass., MIT Press, 1984); International Labour Organization, *The Effects of Technological and Structural Changes on the Employment and Working Conditions of Non-Manual Workers*, 8th Session, Report II (Geneva, ILO, 1981).

[41]Paul A. Strassman, *Information Payoff: The Transformation of Work in the Electronic Age* (New York, Free Press, 1985).

[42]Tora Bikson, Don Manken, and Cathleen Statz, *Individual and Organizational Impacts of Computer Mediated Work: A Case Study*, study prepared for the office of Technology Assessment (Santa Monica, Ca, Rand Corporation, 1985).

[43]Mitchell L. Moss (ed.), *Telecommunications and Productivity* (Reading, Mass., Addison-Wesley, 1981).

[44]On the constitution of information systems, see Nicol, *Information Technology* and "Communications Technology"; also Tom Forester, *High Tech Society* (Oxford, Blackwell, 1987).

[45]See OTA, *Automation*, Appendix.

[46]See Michael Hammer and Michael Zisman, *Design and Implementation of Office Information Systems* (MIT, Laboratory of Computer Science, 1979); Kelly Services Inc., *The Kelly Report on People in the Electronic Office* (Research and Forecasts Inc., 1984); Matthew P. Drennan, *Implications of Computer and Communications Technology for Less Skilled Service Employment Opportunities*, Final Report to the US Department of Labor (New York, Columbia University, 1983).

[47]Barbara Baran, *Technological Innovation and Deregulation: The Transformation of the Labor Process in the Insurance Industry*, PhD dissertation (Berkeley: University of California, 1986).

[48]Barbara Baran, "Office Automation and Women's Work: The Technological Transformation of the Insurance Industry," in Castells, *High Technology, Space, and Society*, pp. 143–71.

[49]Barbara Baran, *The Transformation of the Office Industry*, master's thesis (Berkeley, University of California, 1982); Baran, *Technological Innovation and Deregulation*; Barbara Baran and Suzanne Teegarden, *Women's Labor in the Office of the Future*, Berkeley Roundtable on the International Economy (Berkeley, University of California, 1983).

[50]Baran and Teegarden, *Women's Labor*, p. 13.

[51]Larry Hirschhorn, "Information Technology and the New Services Game," in Castells, *High Technology, Space, and Society*, pp. 172–90.

[52]Paul Adler, *Rethinking the Skill Requirements of New Technologies*, working paper, Graduate School of Business Administration (Cambridge, Mass., Harvard University, 1983).

[53]OTA, *Automation*, p. 104.

[54]*New York Times*, 9 January 1988, p. 1.

[55]Quinn, "Impacts of Technology."

[56]Sellers, "Financial Services Industry."

[57]Thierry Noyelle and Thomas J. Stanback, *The Economic Transformation of American Cities* (Totowa, NJ, Rowman and Allanheld, 1984); Thomas J. Stanback and

Thierry Noyelle, *Cities in Transition* (Totowa, NJ, Allanheld, Osman and Gee, 1982).

[58]Matthew P. Drennan, *Information Intensive Industries: A Metropolitan Perspective* (New York, New York University Graduate School of Public Administration, 1986).

[59]Kling and Turner, *Structure of the Information Labor Force*, 1987.

[60]Robert Cohen, *The Corporation and the City*, Conservation of Human Resources Project (New York, Columbia University, 1979); Noyelle and Stanback, *Economic Transformation of American Cities*.

[61]Mitchell L. Moss., "Telecommunications and the Future of Cities," in *Land Development Studies*, 3 (1986), pp. 33–44; *Telecommunications Policy and World Urban Development*, paper delivered at the Annual Meeting of the International Institute of Communications, Edinburgh, September 1986; *Telecommunications, World Cities, and Urban Policy*, Graduate School of Public Administration (New York, New York University, 1987); "A New Agenda for Telecommunications Policy," in *New York Affairs*, Spring 1986.

[62]Mitchell Moss, *Telecommunications: Shaping the Future*, paper presented at the Rutgers University Conference on America's New Economic Geography, Washington DC, 29–30 April 1987.

[63]Mitchell Moss, *Information Cities: The Example of New York City*, paper presented at the Critical Issues on National Computerization Policy Conference, Honolulu, 31 July 1983; and "New York isn't just New York any more" in *Intermedia*, 12, 4/5 (July–September 1984).

[64]Corporate Design, "OlympiaNet's Gamble on Telecommunications," *Corporate Design*, May/June 1984; Ronald Derven, "Smart Buildings Features Save a Tenant Cash Despite Expensive Buyout of Bell Phone Contract," *Facilities Design and Management*, February/March 1984.

[65]C. Jonscher, *The Impact of Information Technology on the Economy*, paper prepared for the Conference on the Impact of Information Technology on the Service Sector, Philadelphia, University of Pennsylvania, February 1985.

[66]Moss, *Telecommunications: Shaping the Future*.

[67]See Moss, "Telecommunications and the Future of Cities," p. 38.

[68]See Matthew P. Drennan, *Economy of New York State and New York City*, Graduate School of Public Administration (New York, New York University, 1986).

[69]See David Vogel, *The Future of New York City as a Financial Center: An International Perspective*, paper prepared for the Workshops on Metropolitan Dominance, Committee on New York City (New York, Social Science Research Council, 1986).

[70]Peter W. Daniels (ed.), *Spatial Patterns of Office Growth and Location* (New York, Wiley, 1979).

[71]Moss, *Information Cities*.

[72]Raymond Vernon, *New York: Anatomy of a Metropolis* (Cambridge, Mass., Harvard University Press, 1959).

[73]See John D. Kasarda, "Urban Change and Minority Opportunities," in Paul Peterson (ed.), *The New Urban Reality* (Washington DC, Brookings Institution, 1985), pp. 33–67.

[74]Hall, *Regions in the Transition to the Information Economy*.

[75]Noyelle and Stanback, *Economic Transformation of American Cities*.

[76]Edwin S. Mills, *Service Sector Suburbanization*, paper delivered at the Rutgers

University Conference on America's New Economic Geography, Washington DC, 29–30 April 1987.

[77]Christopher B. Leinberger and Charles Lockwood, "How Business Is Reshaping America," in *The Atlantic*, October 1986, pp. 43–63.

[78]Ibid.

[79]David Dowall and Marcia Salkin, *Office Automation and the Implications for Office Development*, IURD Working Paper No. 447 (Berkeley, University of California, 1986).

[80]Peter Daniels, *Service Industries: Growth and Location* (Cambridge, Cambridge University Press, 1982).

[81]Leinberger and Lockwood, "How Business Is Reshaping America."

[82]W. Randy Smith and David Selwood, "Office Location and the Density–Distance Relationship," *Urban Geography*, 4, 4 (1983), pp. 302–16.

[83]Stanback, *Understanding the Service Economy*.

[84]Kristin Nelson, *Back Office and Female Labor Markets: Office Suburbanization in the San Francisco Bay Area*, unpublished PhD dissertation (Berkeley, University of California, 1984).

[85]Cited by Dowall and Salkin, *Office Automation*, p. 113.

[86]Alain Touraine, *Sociologie de l'Action* (Paris, Seuil, 1965).

[87]See Nelson, *Back Office and Female Labor Markets*.

[88]See Daniels, *Service Industries*.

[89]Wolfgang Quante, *The Exodus of Corporate Headquarters from New York City* (New York, Praeger, 1976).

[90]Regina Armstrong, "National Trends in Office Construction, Employment and Headquarters Location in U.S. Metropolitan Areas," in Daniels, *Spatial Patterns*, pp. 61–93.

[91]Cynthia Kroll, *Employment Growth and Office Space Along the 680 Corridor: Booming Supply and Potential Demand in a Suburban Area*, Center for Real Estate and Urban Economics, Working Paper 84–75 (Berkeley, University of California, 1984).

[92]Dowall and Salkin, *Office Automation*.

[93]Baran, *Technological Innovation and Deregulation*.

[94]Jean Marion Ross, *Technology and the Relocation of Employment in the Insurance Industry*, Berkeley Roundtable on the International Economy (Berkeley, University of California, 1985).

[95]Nelson, *Back Office and Female Labor Markets*.

[96]Dowall and Salkin, *Office Automation*.

[97]OTA, *Automation*, pp. 211–30.

[98]OTA, *Automation*, pp. 189–208.

[99]Alvin Toffler, *The Third Wave* (New York, William Morrow, 1980).

[100]OTA, *Automation*, pp. 189–208.

[101]Margrethe H. Olson, *Overview of Work-at-Home Trends in the United States* (New York, New York University Graduate School of Business Administration, Center for Research on Information Systems, 1983).

[102]Paul G. Gretsos, *A Critical Analysis of Telecommuting: The Political Economy of Work at Home*, Graduate Seminar Paper for CP 284, Department of City and Regional Planning (Berkeley, University of California, 1987).

[103]Penny Gurstein, *A Research Proposal on the Implications of the Electronic Home on*

Socio-Spatial Patterns, Graduate Seminar Paper for CP 284, Department of City and Regional Planning (Berkeley, University of California, 1987).
[104]OTA, *Automation*, pp. 283–93.
[105]Allan Pred, "On the Spatial Structure of Organizations and the Complexity of Metropolitan Interdependence," in *Papers of the Regional Science Association*, 35 (1974), pp. 115–43.

Chapter 4

[1]See Nathan Rosenberg, *Perspectives on Technology* (New York, Cambridge University Press, 1976).
[2]See US Congress, Office of Technology Assessment, *Computerized Manufacturing Automation: Employment, Education, and the Workplace* (Washington DC, Government Printing Office, 1984).
[3]See Eli Ginzberg, Thierry J. Noyelle, and Thomas M. Stanback Jr, *Technology and Employment: Concepts and Clarifications* (Boulder, Col., Westview, 1986).
[4]Harry Braverman, *Labor and Monopoly Capital: The Degradation of Work in the Twentieth Century* (New York, Monthly Review Press, 1974).
[5]Larry Hirschhorn, *Beyond Mechanization* (Cambridge, Mass., MIT Press, 1985).
[6]Richard M. Cyert and David C. Mowery (eds), *Technology and Employment: Innovation and Growth in the U.S. Economy*, Report of the Panel on Technology and Employment, National Academy of Sciences, National Academy of Engineering, Institute of Medicine (Washington DC, National Academy Press, 1987).
[7]H. A. Hunt and T. L. Hunt, *Human Resource Implications of Robotics* (Kalamazoo, Mi., W. E. Upjohn Institute for Employment Research, 1983); N. Maeda, "A Fact-finding Study on the Impacts of Microelectronics on Employment," in *Microelectronics, Productivity and Employment* (Paris, OECD, 1980) pp. 155–80; D. Cockroft, "New Office Technology and Employment," *International Law Review*, 119, 6, November–December 1980; M. P. Drennan, *Implications of Computer and Telecommunications Technology for Less Skilled Service Employment Opportunities*, New York, Columbia University, Research Report to the US Department of Labor (New York, Columbia University, 1983); J. D. Roessner et al., *The Impact of Office Automation on Clerical Employment, 1985–2000* (Westport, Conn., Quorum, 1985).
[8]Nathan Rosenberg and L. E. Birdzell, *How the West Grew Rich: The Economic Transformation of the Industrial World* (New York, Basic Books, 1986).
[9]Raphael Kaplinsky, *Microelectronics and Employment Revisited: A Review*, a report prepared for the International Labour Office, World Employment Program (Brighton, University of Sussex, Institute of Development Studies, 1986).
[10]Ibid., p. 153.
[11]P. M. Flynn, *The Impact of Technological Change on Jobs and Workers*, paper prepared for the US Department of Labor, Employment Training Administration, 1985.
[12]R. A. Levy, M. Bowes, and J. M. Jondrow, "Technical Advance and Other Sources of Employment Change in Basic Industry," in E. L. Collins and L. D. Tanner (eds), *American Jobs and the Changing Industrial Base* (Cambridge, Mass., Ballinger, 1984), pp. 77–95.

[13]D. R. Howell, "The Future Employment Impacts of Industrial Robots: An Input-Output Approach," in *Technological Forecasting and Social Change*, 28 (1985), 297–310.

[14]W. Leontieff and F. Duchin, *The Future Impact of Automation on Workers* (New York, Oxford University Press, 1985).

[15]See Cyert and Mowery, *Technology and Employment*, p. 95.

[16]R. Gordon and L. M. Kimball, *High Technology, Employment, and the Challenges to Education*, Silicon Valley Research Group Monograph (Santa Cruz, University of California, 1985).

[17]Ibid., p. 23.

[18]Robert Z. Lawrence, *The Employment Effects of Information Technologies: An Optimistic View*, paper delivered at the OECD Conference on the Social Challenge of Information Technologies, Berlin, 28–30 November 1984.

[19]Ibid., p. 31.

[20]See Ralph Landau and Nathan Rosenberg (eds), *The Positive Sum Strategy: Harnessing Technology for Economic Growth* (Washington DC, National Academy Press, 1986).

[21]K. Young and C. Lawson, *What Fuels U.S. Job Growth? Changes in Technology and Demand on Employment Growth Across Industries, 1972–84*, paper prepared for the Panel on Technology and Employment of the National Academy of Sciences, 1984, as cited by Cyert and Mowery, *Technology and Employment*.

[22]US Bureau of Labor Statistics, *Employment Projections for 1995: Data and Methods* (Washington DC, Government Printing Office, 1986).

[23]See Martin Carnoy, *The Labor Market in Silicon Valley and its Implications for Education*, research report (Stanford, Stanford University, School of Education, 1985).

[24]G. T. Sylvestri, J. M. Lukasiewicz, and M. A. Einstein, "Occupational Employment Projections Through 1995," in *Monthly Labor Review*, November 1983, pp. 37–49.

[25]R. W. Rumberger and H. M. Levin, *Forecasting the Impact of New Technologies on the Future Job Market*, research report (Stanford, Stanford University School of Education, 1984).

[26]Bluestone and Harrison, 1982.

[27]Gordon and Kimball, *Challenges to Education*.

[28]Carnoy, *Labor Market in Silicon Valley*; Allen Scott, *New Industrial Spaces* (London, Pion, 1988); Gordon and Kimball, "Industrial Structure."

[29]Michael Teitz, "The California Economy: Changing Structure and Policy Responses," in John J. Kirlin and Donald R. Winkler (eds), *California Policy Choices* (Los Angeles, University of Southern California, School of Public Administration, 1984), p. 53.

[30]R. W. Riche, D. H. Hecker, and J. D. Burgan, "High Technology Today and Tomorrow: A Small Slice of the Employment Pie," in *Monthly Labor Review*, November 1983, pp. 50–8.

[31]See Myra H. Strober and Carolyn L. Arnold, "Integrated Circuits/Segregated Labor: Women in Computer-Related Occupations and High-Tech Industries," in Heidi I. Hartmann (ed.), *Computer Chips and Paper Clips* (Washington DC, National Academy Press, 1987), 2, pp. 136–84.

[32]Russell W. Rumberger, "High Technology and Job Loss," in *Technology in Society*, 6 (1984), pp. 263–84.

[33]Silvestri, Lukasiewiez, and Einstein, "Occupational Employment Projections."

[34]R. E. Kutscher, *Factors Influencing the Changing Employment Structure of the U.S.*, paper delivered at the Second International Conference of Progetto Milano, Milan, 25 January 1985.

[35]Michael Piore and Charles Sabel, *The Second Industrial Divide* (New York, Basic Books, 1984).

[36]N. Belussi, *Innovation in Production: The Benetton Case*, BRIE Working Paper (Berkeley, University of California, 1986).

[37]Susumu Watanabe, "Labour-saving versus Work-amplifying Effects of Micro-electronics," in *International Labour Review*, 125, 3, May–June 1986, pp. 243–59.

[38]David F. Noble, *Forces of Production: A Social History of Industrial Automation* (New York, Knopf, 1984).

[39]Harley Shaiken, *Work Transformed: Automation and Labor in the Computer Age* (New York, Holt, Rinehart and Winston, 1985).

[40]Carol A. Parsons, *Flexible Production Technology and Industrial Restructuring: Case Studies of the Metalworking, Semiconductor and Apparel Industries*, PhD dissertation (Berkeley, University of California, 1987).

[41]Donald A. Hicks, *Automation Technology and Industrial Renewal: Adjustment Dynamics in the U.S. Metalworking Sector* (Washington DC, AEI, 1986), as cited by Parsons, *Flexible Production Technology*, p. 159.

[42]Parsons, *Flexible Production Technology*, p. 163.

[43]Ibid., p. 324.

[44]Eileen Appelbaum, *Technology and the Redesign of Work in the Insurance Industry*, project report (Stanford, Stanford University, Institute of Research on Educational Finance and Governance, 1984).

[45]Roessner et al., *Impact of Office Automation*.

[46]Appelbaum, *Insurance Industry*, pp. 12–14.

[47]Barry Bluestone and Bennett Harrison, *The Great American Job Machine: The Proliferation of Low Wage Employment in the U.S. Economy*, study prepared for the Joint Economic Committee of the US Congress, December 1986.

[48]Bob Kuttner, "The Declining Middle," in *The Atlantic Monthly*, July 1983, pp. 60–72.

[49]Lester C. Thurow, "The Disappearance of the Middle Class," *New York Times*, 5 February 1984.

[50]Steven Rose, *Social Stratification in the United States* (Baltimore, Social Graphics, 1983).

[51]See, for instance, Fabian Linden, "Myth of the Disappearing Middle Class," *Wall Street Journal*, 23 January 1984.

[52]For a discussion of the relevant research on the "declining middle," and an assessment of the continuing debate, see Nancy Leigh-Preston, National and Regional Change in the Middle of the Earnings and Households Income Distributions, PhD dissertation (in progress) (Berkeley, University of California).

[53]Bennett Harrison, Chris Tilly, and Barry Bluestone, *The Great U-Turn: Increasing Inequality in Wage and Salary Income in the U.S.*, paper presented at the Symposium of the US Congress Joint Economic Committee on "The American Economy in Transition," Washington DC, 16–17 January 1986.

[54]Barry Bluestone, Bennett Harrison, and Alan Matthews, "Structure Vs. Cycle in the Development of American Manufacturing Employment Since the Late 1960s," *Industrial Relations*, 25, 2, Spring 1986.

[55]Thurow, "Disappearance of the Middle Class."

[56]Larry Sawers and William K. Tabb (eds), *Sunbelt/Snowbelt: Urban Development and Regional Restructuring* (New York, Oxford University Press, 1984).

[57]Joe Feagin and Michael Smith (eds), *The Capitalist City* (Oxford, Blackwell, 1986).

[58]Diana Dillaway, *The Politics of Restructuring in a Declining City: Buffalo, NY*, master's thesis (Berkeley, University of California, 1987).

[59]William Wilson, "The Urban Underclass in Advanced Industrial Society," in Paul E. Peterson (ed.), *The New Urban Reality* (Washington DC, Brookings Institution, 1985).

[60]Thierry Noyelle and Thomas J. Stanback, *The Economic Transformation of American Cities* (Totowa, NJ, Rowman and Allanheld, 1984).

[61]B. Bluestone and B. Harrison, *The Deindustrialization of America* (New York, Basic Books, 1982).

[62]John D. Kasarda, "Urban Change and Minority Opportunities," in Paul Peterson (ed.), *The New Urban Reality* (Washington DC, Brookings Institution, 1985).

[63]Ibid., p. 57.

[64]Norman Fainstein, "The Underclass/Mismatch Hypothesis as an Explanation for Black Economic Deprivation," in *Politics and Society*, 15, 4 (1986-7), pp. 403-51.

[65]Saskia Sassen, "Issues of Core and Periphery: Labour Migration and Global Restructuring," in Jeff Henderson and Manuel Castells (eds), *Global Restructuring and Territorial Development* (London, Sage, 1987); and Sassen, The Mobility of Labor and Capital (New York, Cambridge University Press, 1988).

[66]John Mollenkopf, "Economic Development," in C. Brecher and R. Horton (eds), *Setting Municipal Priorities: American Cities and the New York Experience* (New York, New York University Press, 1984).

[67]I have benefited greatly from the perceptive, well documented analysis by Samuel M. Ehrenhalt, *New York City in the New Economic Environment: New Risks and a Changing Outlook* (New York, Regional Commissioner, US Bureau of Labor Statistics, 1988) (paper communicated by the author).

[68]Ehrenhalt, *New York City*, p. 12.

[69]Thomas Bailey and Roger Waldinger, *Economic Change and the Ethnic Division of Labor in New York City*, paper prepared for the Social Science Research Council Committee on New York City, February 1988.

[70]See the studies presented in John H. Mollenkopf and Manuel Castells (eds), *Restructuring New York: Dual City* (forthcoming); see also Gus Tyler, "A Tale of Three Cities – Upper Economy, Lower – and Under," in *Dissent*, special issue: "In Search of New York," Fall 1987, pp. 463-71; Emanuel Tobier, "Population" in Brecher and Horton, *Setting Municipal Priorities*; Roger Waldinger, *Changing Ladders and Musical Chairs: Ethnicity and Opportunity in Post-industrial New York*, paper delivered at the International Conference on Ethnic Minorities, University of Warwick, UK, September 1985.

[71]Saskia Sassen, "The Informal Economy in New York City," in Alejandro Portes, Manuel Castells, and Lauren Benton (eds), *The Informal Economy* (Baltimore: Johns Hopkins University Press, 1989).

[72]Saskia Sassen, "New York City's Informal Economy," paper prepared for the Social Science Research Council Committee on New York City, February 1988.

[73]Saskia Sassen and C. Benamou, *Hispanic Women in the Garment and Electronics Industries in New York Metropolitan Area*, research report to the Revson Foundation, New York, 1985.

[74]For the whole of the US, estimates of cash flow generated by drug traffic oscillate between $60 billion and $120 billion. This capital has to be recycled in the formal economy through laundering. See Jeff Gerth, "Vast Flow of Cash Threatens Currency, Banks and Economies," *New York Times*, 11 April 1988, p. A8.

[75]See Nancy Foner (ed.) *New Immigrants in New York* (New York, Columbia University Press, 1987); Philip Kasinitz "The City's New Immigrants," in *Dissent*, Fall 1987, pp. 497–506.

[76]Roger Waldinger, *Through the Eye of the Needle: Immigrants and Enterprise in New York's Garment Trades* (New York, New York University Press, 1986).

[77]Bailey and Waldinger, *Economic Change and the Ethnic Division of Labor*.

[78]Portes and Bach, *Latin Journey*; Foner, *New Immigrants in New York*; Sassen, "Issues of Core and Periphery."

[79]Sassen *New York City's Informal Economy*, p. 1.

[80]Richard Harris, *Home and Work in New York Since 1950*, paper prepared for the Social Science Research Council Committee on New York City, February 1988.

[81]William Kornblum, *The White Ethnic Neighborhoods in New York City*, paper prepared for the Social Science Research Council on New York City, 1988.

[82]Harris, *Home and Work in New York*, p. 34.

[83]Edward W. Soja, "Taking Los Angeles Apart: Some Fragments of a Critical Human Geography," in *Environment and Planning: D. Space and Society*, special issue on Los Angeles, 4, 3 (September 1986) pp. 255–73.

[84]Edward W. Soja, "Economic Restructuring and the Internationalization of the Los Angeles Region," in Feagin and Smith, *The Capitalist City*.

[85]Edward Soja, Rebecca Morales, and Goetz Wolff, "Urban Restructuring: An Analysis of Social and Spatial Change in Los Angeles," in *Economic Geography*, 59, 2 (April 1983), pp. 195–230.

[86]On suburban office development in Los Angeles, as linked to the process of spatial restructuring, see Tamara Phibbs, *Linkages, Labor, and Localities in the Location of Suburban Office Centers: A Case Study of Office Establishments in Orange County, California*, Master's thesis in Urban Planning (Los Angeles, University of California, 1989).

[87]*Los Angeles Times*, 9 April 1988.

[88]It is, of course a classic theme of the Chicago School of urban sociology. See, for instance Harvey Zorbaugh, *The Gold Coast and the Slum* (Chicago, University of Chicago Press, 1927).

[89]A theme that I have developed in *The City and the Grassroots* (Berkeley, University of California Press, 1983).

Chapter 5

[1]Ian Gough, *The Political Economy of the Welfare State* (London, Macmillan, 1979); Harold L. Wilensky, *The Welfare State and Equality* (Berkeley, University of California Press, 1975); OECD, *The Welfare State in Crisis* (Paris, OECD, 1981); Charles W. Taylor (ed.), *Why Governments Grow* (Beverly Hills, Sage, 1983).

[2]Morris Janowitz, *Social Control of the Welfare State* (Chicago, University of Chicago Press, 1976), p. 3.

[3]Although it has been attempted by some authors; see Gough, *Political Economy of the Welfare State*; Jim O'Connor, *The Fiscal Crisis of the State* (New York, St Martin's, 1973); Vicente Navarro, *The Welfare State and its Distributive Effects: Part of the Problem or Part of the Solution?*, paper delivered at the International Conference on the Economic Crisis and the Welfare State, International University Menendez y Pelayo, Barcelona, Spain, 8–11 April 1987.

[4]For a thorough analysis of the political process surrounding the growth and decline of the welfare state in the US, see Vicente Navarro, "The 1980 and 1984 US Elections and the New Deal: An Alternative Interpretation," in R. Miliband, J. Saville, and M. Liebman (eds), *The Socialist Register 1985* (London, 1985).

[5]Samuel Bowles and Herbert Gintis, "The Crisis of Liberal Democratic Capitalism: The Case of the United States," *Politics and Society*, II, 1 (1982).

[6]For a theoretical analysis of current trends of transformation of the state in advanced capitalism, see Gordon L. Clark and Michael Dear, *State Apparatus* (Boston, Allen & Unwin, 1984); Colin Crouch (ed.), *State and Economy in Contemporary Capitalism* (London, Croom Helm, 1979); Martin Carnoy, *State and Political Theory* (Princeton, NJ: Princeton University Press, 1984).

[7]Martin Carnoy, Derek Shearer, and Russell Rumberger, *A New Social Contract* (New York, Harper and Row, 1983), p. 120.

[8]Allan Wolfe, *Limits of Legitimacy* (New York, Basic Books, 1976); Carnoy, *State and Political Theory*.

[9]Jim O'Connor, *Accumulation Crisis* (Oxford, Blackwell, 1984).

[10]Navarro, "The 1980 and 1984 US Elections."

[11]Peter Marris and Martin Rein, *Dilemmas of Social Reform* (London, Routledge & Kegan Paul, 1972); Frances Piven and Richard Cloward, *Regulating the Poor* (New York, Random House, 1971); Frank Gould, "The Growth of Public Expenditures," in Taylor, *Why Governments Grow*, note 1.

[12]J. David Greenstone, *Labor in American Politics* (Chicago: University of Chicago Press, 1977); Irving Bernstein, *The Lean Years* (Boston, Houghton Mifflin, 1972).

[13]Carnoy, Shearer, and Rumberger, *A New Social Contract*.

[14]See Roderick Aya and Norman Miller (eds), *The New American Revolution* (New York, Free Press, 1971).

[15]John Mollenkopf, *The Contested City* (Princeton, NJ, Princeton University Press, 1983).

[16]Terry N. Clark and Lorna C. Ferguson, *City Money: Political Processes, Fiscal Strain and Retrenchment* (New York; Columbia University Press, 1983).

[17]Douglas Yates, *The Ungovernable City* (New Haven, Yale University Press, 1977).

[18]Manuel Castells, *The City and the Grassroots* (Berkeley, University of California Press, 1983), pp. 49–66.

[19]Mollenkopf, *Contested City*.

[20]Mollenkopf, *Contested City*, p. 20.

[21]Herbert Marcuse, *The One-Dimensional Man* "After the Crisis?".

[22]Martin Carnoy and Manuel Castells, "After the Crisis?," *World Policy Journal*, Spring 1984.

[23]Hugh C. Mosley, *The Arms Race: Economic and Social Consequences* (Lexington, Mass., Lexington, 1985).

[24]Carnoy, Shearer, and Rumberger, *A New Social Contract*, p. 150.

[25]Joel Krieger, *Reagan, Thatcher, and the Politics of Decline* (New York, Oxford University Press, 1986).

[26]J. Coates and M. Killian, *Heavy Losses: The Dangerous Decline of American Defense* (New York, Viking, 1985).

[27]John Tirman (ed.), *The Militarization of High Technology* (Cambridge, Mass., Ballinger, 1984).

[28]David Stockman, *The Triumph of Politics* (New York, Harper and Row, 1986).

[29]I am relying here on current research on "Yuppies as a Social Phenomenon" conducted by Arlene Stein, a sociology graduate at the University of California at Berkeley.

[30]See Joe Feagin, *Houston Boomtown* (New Brunswick, NJ, Rutgers University Press, 1988).

[31]See US Congress, Office of Technology Assessment, *Automation of America's Offices* (Washington DC, Government Printing Office, 1985).

[32]Douglas E. Ashford (ed.), *Financing Urban Government in the Welfare State* (London, Croom Helm, 1980).

[33]Piven and Cloward, *Regulating the Poor*.

[34]Mollenkopf, *Contested City*.

[35]Castells, *City and Grassroots*.

[36]Larry Hirschhorn et al., *Cutting Back: Retrenchment and Redevelopment in Human and Community Services* (San Francisco, Jossey-Bass, 1983).

[37]Mark I. Gelfand, "How Cities Arrived in the National Agenda in the US," in Ashford, *Financing Urban Government*, pp. 28–49.

[38]David H. McKay, "The Rise of the Topocratic State: US Intergovernmental Relations in the 1970s," in Ashford, *Financing Urban Government*, pp. 50–70.

[39]McKay, "The Rise of the Topocratic State."

[40]Gelfand, "How Cities Arrived in the National Agenda."

[41]Douglas E. Ashford, "Political Choice and Local Finance," in Ashford, *Financing Urban Government*, pp. 9–27.

[42]Gelfand, "How Cities Arrived in the National Agenda."

[43]Daniel P. Moynihan, *Maximum Feasible Misunderstanding* (Glencoe, Ill., Free Press, 1969).

[44]Harry C. Boyte, *The Backyard Revolution* (Philadelphia, Temple University Press, 1980).

[45]Robert Leckachmann, *Greed is not Enough: Reaganomics* (New York, Pantheon, 1981).

[46]Marris and Rein, *Dilemmas of Social Reform*; Ralph M. Kramer, *Voluntary Agencies in the Welfare State* (Berkeley, University of California Press, 1981).

[47]Matthew A. Crenson, *Neighbourhood Politics* (Cambridge, Mass., Harvard University Press, 1983).

[48]George Vernez, "Overview of the Spatial Dimensions of the Federal Budget," in Norman Glickman (ed.), *The Urban Impacts of Federal Policies* (Baltimore, Johns Hopkins University Press, 1980), pp. 67–102.

[49]Robert W. Burchell and David Listokin (eds), *Cities Under Stress: The Fiscal Crisis of Urban America* (Piscataway, NJ, Center for Urban Policy Research, 1981); Clark and Ferguson, *City Money*; Hirschhorn et al., *Cutting Back*.

[50]Burchell and Listokin, *Cities Under Stress*.

[51]Peter Marcuse, "The Targeted Crisis: On the Ideology of the Urban Fiscal Crisis and its Uses," *International Journal of Urban and Regional Research*, 5, 3, 330–55.

[52]Roy Bahl (ed.), *Urban Government Finances in the 1980s* (Beverly Hills, Sage, 1981).

[53]Burchell and Listokin, *Cities Under Stress*.

[54]John L. Mikesell, "The Season of Tax Revolt," in John P. Blair and David Nacmias (eds), *Fiscal Retrenchment and Urban Policy* (Beverly Hills, Sage, 1979).

[55]Lawrence Susskind (director), *Proposition 2 1/2: Its Impact on Massachusetts* (Cambridge, Mass., OGH, 1983).

[56]Donald Tomaskovic-Devey and S. M. Miller, "Recapitalization: The Basic US Urban Policy of the 1980s," in Norman I. Fainstein and Susan Fainstein (eds), *Urban Policy Under Capitalism* (Beverly Hills, Sage, 1982), p. 25.

[57]Ibid.

[58]William K. Tabb, *The Long Default: New York City and the Urban Fiscal Crisis* (New York: Monthly Review Press, 1982). For dissenting views of the process, see Daniel P. Moynihan, "On the Origins of New York's Crisis," *The Public Interest*, Spring 1978, and Charles R. Morris, *The Cost of Good Intentions: New York City and the Liberal Experiment* (New York, Norton, 1980).

[59]Of course, Tabb does not consider that the situation in New York was so bright, except for a minority of its residents.

[60]Roger Starr, "Stagnant Metropolis," *Society*, May/June 1976.

[61]For comprehensive analysis of the transformation of New York City, see John Mollenkopf (ed.), *Power, Culture, and Place: Essays on New York City* (New York, Russell Sage Foundation, 1988).

[62]See Charles Brecher and Raymond D. Horton, *Politics in the Postindustrial City*, paper prepared for the Social Science Research Council Committee on New York City, February 1988; and Charles Brecher and Raymond D. Horton (eds), *Setting Municipal Priorities 1988* (New York, New York University Press, 1988).

[63]See John Mollenkopf, *Political Inequality in New York City*, paper prepared for the Social Science Research Council Committee on New York City, February 1988.

[64]See special issue of *Dissent*, "In Search of New York," Fall 1987.

[65]For a socio-political analysis of the evolution of the local state in New York, see Norman I. Fainstein and Susan S. Fainstein, "Stages in the Politics of Urban Development: New York since 1945," in Mollenkopf, *Power, Culture, Place*.

[66]For a political analysis of the fiscal crisis in Cleveland, see Todd Swanstrom, *The Crisis of Growth Politics: Cleveland, Kucinick and the Limits of Local Democracy*, PhD dissertation, Princeton University, 1981); for a comprehensive analysis of urban decline and urban revival see Louise Jezierski, *Urban Politics and Urban Crises: A Comparative Analysis of Pittsburgh and Cleveland*, PhD dissertation (Berkeley, University of California, 1987); for a broader perspective see Paul Kantor, *The Dependent City: The Changing Political Economy and Urban Economic Development in the US*, paper presented at the 1985 annual meeting of the American Political Science Association, 29 August 1985, New Orleans.

[67]Norman J. Glickman, *Economic Policy and the Cities: In Search of Reagan's Real Urban Policy*, paper presented at the North American meetings of the Regional Science Association, Chicago, 11–13 November 1983; published in summarized form in *Journal of American Planning Association*, Autumn 1984, pp. 471–84.

[68]*New York Times*, 16 February 1988.

[69]Glickman, *Economic Policy and the Cities*.

[70]See John L. Palmer and Isabel Sawhill (eds), *The Reagan Experiment* (Washington DC, Urban Institute Press, 1982).

[71]See special issue of *Business Week*, "After Reagan," 1 February 1988.

[72]Frank Barnaby, "Microelectronics and War," in Tirman, *Militarization of High Technology*, pp. 45–62.

[73]Richard R. Nelson, *High Technology Policies: A Five-Nation Comparison* (Washington DC, American Enterprise Institute, 1984).

[74]Seymour Melman (ed.), *The War Economy of the United States* (New York, St Martin's, 1971).

[75]Daniel Bell, *The Coming of Post-industrial Society* (New York, Basic Books, 1973), p. 355.

[76]Bell, *Post-industrial Society*, p. 356.

[77]Fred Hiatt and Rick Atkinson, "Arms and America's Fortunes," *Washington Post*, 12 January 1985, p. A-1.

[78]See the major documented work on the matter: Hugh C. Mosely, *The Arms Race: Economic and Social Consequences* (Lexington, Mass., Lexington, 1985).

[79]Karen Pennar, "Pentagon Spending is the Economy's Biggest Gun," *Business Week*, 21 October 1985, pp. 60–4.

[80]Pennar, "Pentagon Spending."

[81]Ann Markusen, *Defense Spending: A Successful Industrial Policy?* IURD Working Paper 424 (Berkeley, June 1984).

[82]US Congress, Office of Technology Assessment, *Information Technology R&D: Critical Trends and Issues* (Washington DC, Government Printing Office, 1985), pp. 45–6.

[83]Manuel Castells and Rebecca Skinner, *The State and Technological Policy in the U.S.: the Strategic Defense Initiative* (Berkeley, University of California, Institute of International Studies, 1988).

[84]This is particularly the argument forcefully put forward by Seymour Melman in *The Permanent War Economy: American Capitalism in Decline* (New York, Simon and Schuster, 1974).

[85]Wassily Leontieff and Faye Duchin, *Military Spending: Facts and Figures, Worldwide Implications, and Future Outlook* (New York, Oxford University Press, 1983).

[86]David Gold, Christopher Paine, and Gail Shields, *Misguided Expenditure: An Analysis of the Proposed MX Missile System* (New York, Council on Economic Priorities, 1981).

[87]Robert B. Reich, "High Technology, Defense, and International Trade" in Tirman, *Militarization of High Technology*, pp. 33–43.

[88]Markusen, *Defense Spending*; and Ann R. Markusen, *The Economic and Regional Consequences of Military Innovation*, IURD, Working Paper 442 (Berkeley, May 1985).

[89]Lloyd J. Dumas, "University Research, Industrial Innovation, and the Pentagon" in Tirman, *Militarization of High Technology*, pp. 123–57.

[90]David F. Noble, *Forces of Production: A Social History of Industrial Automation* (New York, Knopf, 1984).

[91]Mary Kaldor, *The Baroque Arsenal* (New York, Hill and Wang, 1981).

[92]Jay Stowsky, *Beating Our Plowshares into Double-Edged Swords: The Impact of Pentagon Policies on the Commercialization of Advanced Technologies*, BRIE Working Paper (Berkeley, April 1986), pp. 61–2.

[93]Jacques S. Gansler, *The Defense Economy* (Cambridge, Mass., MIT, 1984); Richard R. Nelson, *High Technology Policies: A Five-Nation Comparison* (Washington DC, American Enterprise Institute, 1984).

[94]Such is the main theme of the major recent book on the subject: Tirman, *Militarization of High Technology*. See particularly the excellent analysis by John Tirman, "The Defense-Economy Debate," pp. 1–32.

[95]Eisenhower, speaking in 1961, as quoted by Dumas, "University Research," p. 149.

[96]Gordon Adams, *The Iron Triangle: The Politics of Defense Contracting* (New Brunswick, NJ, Transaction Books, 1982).

[97]Caspar Weinberger, speech before the Miami Chamber of Commerce, 15 September 1982. Quoted by Tirman, *Militarization of High Technology*, p. 4.

[98]Markusen, *Defense Spending*; Tirman, *Militarization of High Technology*.

[99]Robert DeGrasse, "The Military and Semiconductors," in Tirman, *Militarization of High Technology*, pp. 77–104.

[100]R. Carlson and T. Lyman, *U.S. Government Programs and their Influence on Silicon Valley*, research report (Menlo Park, SRI International, 1984).

[101]Markusen, *Defense Spending*, p. 12.

[102]See a non-partisan description of the structure and activity of DARPA in J. Botkin, D. Dimancescu, and R. Stata, *The Innovators* (New York, Harper and Row, 1984).

[103]Ken Julian, "Defense Program Pushes Microchip Frontiers," *High Technology*, May 1985, pp. 49–57.

[104]Leslie Brueckner and Michael Borrus, *Assessing the Commercial Impact of the VHSIC Program*, BRIE Working Paper, (Berkeley, University of California, November 1984).

[105]Dwight B. Davis, "Assessing the Strategic Computing Initiative," *High Technology*, April 1985, pp. 41–9.

[106]Stowsky, *Beating our Plowshares*.

[107]On the strategic importance of semiconductors production equipment, see Jay Stowsky, *The Weakest Link: Semiconductor Production Equipment, Linkages, and the Limits to International Trade*, BRIE Working Paper (Berkeley, August 1987).

[108]This section summarizes analysis and information presented in our research monograph: Manuel Castells and Rebecca Skinner, *The State and Technological Policy in the U.S.: the SDI Program*, research report (Berkeley, University of California, Berkeley Roundtable on the International Economy, 1989). I refer the reader to this monograph for detailed information and references about SDI as technological policy and as industrial policy.

[109]William J. Broad, "Reagan's Star Wars Bid: Many Ideas Converging," *New York Times*, 4 March 1985, p. 1.

[110]Georges Skelton, "U.S. Fears Soviet Leap in A-Arms," *Los Angeles Times*, 15 February 1985, p. 1; Philip M. Boffrey, "Many Questions Remain as Star Wars Advances," *International Herald Tribune*, 12 March 1985, p. 1.

[111]For a presentation of a reassessment of the American strategic doctrine in the last decade, see the fundamental Pentagon-solicited Report: Fred C. Ikle amd Albert Wohlsletter (co-chairmen), *Discriminate Deferrence: Report of the Commission on Integrated Long-Term Strategy to the Secretary of Defense* (Washington DC, Government Printing Office, January 1988).

[112]E. P. Thompson (ed.), *Star Wars: Science-fiction Fantasy or Serious Probability?* (New York, Pantheon, 1985).

[113]Peter Grier, "U.S. Public Opinion Generally Favors 'Star Wars'," *Christian Science Monitor*, 21 November 1985, p. 3; Kevin Phillips, "Defense Beyond Thin Air: Space Holds the Audience," *Los Angeles Times*, 10 March 1985.

[114]See Thompson, *Star Wars*, pp. 131ff; Ernest Conine, "Star Wars and Economic Power," *Los Angeles Times*, 19 August 1985, p. 115.

[115]Cited by Fred Hiatt and Rich Atkinson, "Arms and America's Fortunes," *Washington Post*, 1 December 1985, p. A1.

[116]David E. Sanger, "But Company Worries Grow," *The New York Times*, 19 November 1985, p. 25.

[117]Council on Economic Priorities, *Star Wars: The Economic Fallout* (Cambridge, Mass., Ballinger, 1988).

[118]G. Adams, *The Iron Triangle: The Politics of Defense Contracting* (New York, Council on Economic Priority, 1981).

[119]William J. Broad, "Scientists Profit from Star Wars," *New York Times*, 5 November 1985, p. 1.

[120]Michael Schrage, "Transporting the Pentagon Into the Future," *Washington Post*, 24 July 1983, p. F6.

[121]See the well documented analysis on the question by Stowsky, *Beating Our Plowshares*; also David Warsh, "Star Wars: Boon or Bane for Economy?" *Boston Globe*, 21 November 1985, p. 57.

[122]See Broad, "Reagan's Star Wars Bid," p. 1.

[123]Robert Scheer, "Star Wars: All-out Publicity Push," *Los Angeles Times*, 29 December 1985, p. 1.

[124]Aaron Wildowsky, "Reagan the Strategist," *Wall Street Journal*, 3 January 1986, p. 10.

[125]As an illustration of the development of the SDI concept in the scientific military establishment prior to the Reagan administration, I can refer to the findings of an investigative report by a journalist, Françoise Sabbah, on the Livermore National Laboratory. She visited Livermore in February 1980 and interviewed a representative of the Laboratory on the research programs under way in that institution. She was told that the priority of the Laboratory had shifted to space-based warfare, with particular emphasis on protecting/destroying the satellite-based communications systems. Most of the concepts that gave birth to the SDI strategy were already at the center of Livermore Laboratory research programs one year before Ronald Reagan's inauguration as President of the United States (personal account from Françoise Sabbah, correspondant for several Spanish newspapers and magazines).

[126]See a good, though partisan, synthesis of the debate in Thompson, *Star Wars*.

[127]David Ignatius, "Analyzing Risks," *Wall Street Journal*, 15 October 1985, p. 1; Bon Oberdofer, "Ex-Defense Chief Calls 'Star Wars' Unrealistic," *Washington Post*, 15 December 1985; Philip M. Boffey, "Dark Side of Star Wars: System Could Also Attack," *New York Times*, 7 March 1985, p. 1; David Perlman, "The Star Wars Scientists Who Doubt It Will Work," *San Francisco Chronicle*, 14 April 1986, p. 8.

[128]Judith Miller, "Allies in West Lend Support to Star Wars," *New York Times*, 30 December 1985, p. 1.

[129]Stowsky, *Beating our Plowshares*.

[130]Stewart Nozette, "A Giant Step Forward in Technology," *New York Times*, 8 December 1985, p. F2.

[131]Ben Thompson, "What is Star Wars?" in Thompson, *Star Wars*, pp. 28–49.

[132]See Walter Zegveld and Christien Enzing, *SDI and Industrial Technology Policy: Threat or Opportunity* (New York, St Martin's, 1987); also the excellent analysis by Mario Pianta, *Star War Economics*, paper presented at the conference "The State of Star Wars," Transnational Institute, Amsterdam, 23–5 January 1987.

[133]Sanger, *But Company Worries Grow*.

[134]Fred Hiatt and Rick Atkinson, "Pentagon's 'Paper Warriors' Find Market for SDI Advice," *Washington Post*, 21 October 1985, p. 1.

[135]Reuters, "Small Firms Capitalize on Pentagon Software," *Los Angeles Times*, 25 November 1985, p. IV1.

[136]Tim Carrington, "Scramble in Space: Star Wars Plans Spur Defense Firms to Vie for Billions in Orders," *Wall Street Journal*, 21 May 1985, p. 1.

[137]Rosy Nimroody and William Hartung, "Putting Industry Even Further Behind," *New York Times*, 8 December 1985, p. F2.

[138]Accentuating the previous trend shown by several authors in Tirman, *Militarization of High Technology*.

[139]Nimroody and Hartung, "Putting Industry even Further Behind."

[140]Schrage, "Transporting the Pentagon."

[141]See Wayne Sandholtz, Jay Stowsky, and Steven K. Vogel, *The Dilemmas of Technological Competition in Comparative Perspective: Is It Guns Vs. Butter?*, Research Report for the UC Berkeley MacArthur Interdisciplinary Group for International Security Studies (Berkeley: University of California, Berkeley Roundtable on the International Economy, April 1988).

[142]Jacqueline Mazza and Dale E. Wilkinson, *The Unprotected Flank: Regional and Strategic Imbalances in Defense Spending Patterns* (Washington DC, Northeast-Midwest Institute, 1980); Roger Bezdek, "The 1980 Economic Impact – Regional and Occupational – of Compensated Shifts in Defense Spending," *Journal of Regional Science*, AS:2 (1975), pp. 183–97; Wassily Leontief et al., "The Economic Impact – Industrial and Regional – of an Arms Cut," *Review of Economics and Statistics*, 47, 3 (1965), pp. 217–44; John Rees, "Defense Spending and Regional Industrial Change," *Texas Business Review*, Jan.–Feb. 1982, 40–4.

[143]Edward J. Malecki, "Military Spending and the US Defense Industry: Regional Patterns of Military Contracts and Subcontracts," *Environment and Planning, C: Government and Policy*, 2 (1984) pp. 31–44.

[144]This is a research program, funded by the NSF, and initiated in 1985 in the Institute of Urban and Regional Development, UC Berkeley. Peter Hall and Ann Markusen are principal investigators. Scott Campbell and Sabina Dietrick, doctoral candidates at UC Berkeley, are research assistants.

[145]G. R. Simonson, *The History of the American Aircraft Industry: An Anthology* (Cambridge, Mass., MIT, 1968).

[146]B. F. Cooling, *War, Business and Society: Historical Perspectives on the Military Industrial Complex* (Port Washington, NY, Kennikat, 1977).

[147]W. G. Cunningham, *The Aircraft Industry: A Study in Industrial Location* (Los Angeles, Morrison, 1951).

[148]J. B. Roe, *Climb to Greatness: The American Aircraft Industry, 1920–1960* (Cambridge, Mass., MIT, 1968).

[149]Interestingly enough, the Pacific War, a factor often cited to explain the west's dominance in the defense industry, does not seem to have been directly a cause for the location pattern. In fact, during the war, the defense industry tended to spread and relocate *inland* for obvious strategic reasons, returning to the west coast, for the most part, at the end of the war. Yet, what was really decisive was the location of the navy and air force bases in the west coast, and the huge contracts provided during World War II to the airframe industries in Los Angeles.

[150]See Peter Hall, "The Creation of the American Aero-Space Complex 1955–65: A

Study in Industrial Inertia," in Michael J. Breheny (ed.), *Defence Expenditure and Regional Development* (London, Mansell, 1988).

[151]B. Bluestone, P. Jordan, and M. Sullivan, *Aircraft Industry Dynamics: An Analysis of Competition, Capital and Labor* (Boston, Auburn House, 1981).

[152]Servet Mutlu, *Inter-regional and International Mobility of Industrial Capital: The Case of American Automobile and Electronics Companies*, unpublished PhD dissertation (Berkeley, University of California, 1979).

[153]R. E. Bilstein, *Flight in America 1900–1983: From the Wrights to the Astronauts* (Baltimore, Johns Hopkins University Press, 1984).

[154]R. C. Estall, *New England: A Study in Industrial Adjustment* (London, G. Bell, 1966).

[155]Paul A. Koistinen, *The Military–Industrial Complex: A Historical Perspective* (New York, Praeger, 1980).

[156]C. D. Bright, *The Jet Makers: The Aerospace Industry from 1945 to 1972* (Lawrence, Ks, The Regents Press of Kansas, 1978).

[157]Gansler, *The Defense Economy*, pp. 36–45.

[158]Adams, *The Iron Triangle*.

[159]Coates and Killian, *Heavy Losses*.

[160]R. E. Bolton, *Defense Purchase and Regional Growth* (Washington DC, Brookings Institution, 1966).

[161]Markusen, *Defense Spending*, p. 21.

[162]Arnold Fleischmann and Joe R. Feagin, "The Politics of Growth-Oriented Urban Alliance: Comparing Old Industrial and New Sunbelt Cities," *Urban Affairs Quarterly*, 23, 2 (December 1987), pp. 207–32.

[163]Ann R. Markusen and R. Bloch, "Defensive Cities: Military Spending, High Technology, and Human Settlements," in Manuel Castells (ed.), *High Technology, Space and Society* (Beverly Hills, Sage, 1985).

[164]N. S. Dorfman, *Massachusetts' High Technology Boom in Perspective: An Investigation of its Dimensions, Causes and the Role of New Firms* (Cambridge, Mass., MIT, Center for Policy Alternatives, 1982).

[165]Hall, "Creation of the American Aero-Space Complex."

[166]Ibid.; P. W. Bowers, *Boeing Aircraft Since 1916* (Fullbrook, Cal., Acre, 1966).

[167]J. J. Horgan, *City of Flight: The History of Aviation in St. Louis* (Gerald, Mo., Patrick Press, 1984).

[168]Charles Tiebout, "The Regional Impact of Defense Expenditures: Its Measurement and Problems of Adjustment," in Roger Bolton (ed.), *Defense and Disarmament* (Englewood Cliffs, NJ, Prentice-Hall, 1984).

[169]Sabina Dietrick, *Military Spending and Migration to California*, unpublished seminar paper (Berkeley, UC Department of City and Regional Planning, 1984).

[170]M. Teitz, "Economic Change and California Public Policy," in Ted Bradshaw and Charles Bell, *The Capacity to Respond: California Political Institutions Face Change* (Berkeley, University of California Institute of Government Studies, 1987).

[171]N. S. Dorfman, "Route 128: the Development of a Regional High Technology Economy," *Research Policy*, 12 (1983), pp. 299–316; the estimate of about one-third of the employment in defense-related jobs has been obtained from J. Markoff, information to the author from the Pacific Studies Center, 1985.

[172]Ann. R. Markusen, *The Economic and Regional Consequences of Military Innovation*, IURD Working Paper 442 (Berkeley, May 1985).

[173]Edward Malecki, "Government-funded R&D: Some Regional Economic Implications," *Professional Geographer*, 33, (1981), pp. 72–82.

[174]Office of Technology Assessment, *Technology and Structural Unemployment: Reemploying Displaced Adults* (Washington DC, US Congress, OTA, 1986).

[175]A. Markusen, P. Hall, and A. Glasmeier, *High Tech America: the What, How, Where and Why of the Sunrise Industries* (Boston, London, Allen & Unwin, 1986).

[176]Ibid.

[177]Markusen and Bloch, "Defensive Cities."

[178]Ann Markusen with G. Clark, C. Curtis, S. Dietrick, G. Fields, A. Henry, E. Ingersoll, J. Levin, W. Patton, J. Ross and J. Schneider, *Military Spending and Urban Development in California*, IURD Working Paper 425 (Berkeley, June 1984).

[179]Markusen and Bloch, "Defensive Cities."

[180]Glickman, "Economic Policy and the Cities."

[181]Rebecca Skinner, *The Urban and Regional Impacts of Defense Oriented Technological Policy: the Case of SDI*, research in progress (Berkeley, University of California, Department of City and Regional Planning, 1988).

[182]Stowsky, *Beating Our Plowshares*.

[183]Committee on Science, Engineering, and Public Policy, *Balancing the National Interest: U.S. National Security Export Controls and Global Economic Competition* (Washington DC, National Academy Press, 1987).

[184]David Fishback, "The Star Wars Laboratory," *Financial Times*, 24 April 1985, p. 9; Charles Stein, "MIT's Lincoln Labs: Unobtrusively Excelling in the Technological World," *Boston Globe*, 15 October 1985, p. 41.

Chapter 6

[1]John Agnew, *The United States in the World Economy: A Regional Geography* (Cambridge, Cambridge University Press, 1987), p. 142.

[2]Ray Marshall and Norman Glickman, *Choices for American Industry*, research report (Austin, University of Texas, Lyndon B. Johnson School of Public Affairs, 1986), p. 11.

[3]Henry B. Schechter, *Imbalances in the Global Economy: Impacts on the United States*, paper delivered at the Rutgers University Conference on America's New Economic Geography, Washington DC, 29–30 April 1987.

[4]Norman J. Glickman, *International Trade, Capital Mobility, and Economic Growth*, a report to the President's Commission For a National Agenda for the Eighties, Washington DC, 3–4 June 1980.

[5]Jane S. Little, "Location Decisions of Foreign Investors in the United States," in *New England Economic Review*, July–August 1978, pp. 43–63.

[6]Alejandro Portes and Robert Bach, *Latin Journey* (Berkeley, University of California Press, 1985).

[7]Regional Plan Association of New York, *New York in the Global Economy: Studying the Facts and the Issues*, research document (New York, April 1987).

[8]Lester Thurow and Laura Tyson, *Adjusting the U.S. Trade Balance: A Black Hole in the World Economy*, BRIE Working Paper, (Berkeley, March 1987).

[9]Bruce R. Guile and Harvey Brooks (eds), *Technology and Global Industry: Companies and Nations in the World Economy* (Washington DC, National Academy Press, 1987).

[10]Laura Tyson, *The U.S. and the World Economy in Transition*, BRIE working paper (Berkeley, July 1986); Robert Z. Lawrence, *Can America Compete?* (Washington DC, Brookings Institution, 1984).

[11]Stephen S. Cohen and John Zysman, *Manufacturing Matters* (New York, Basic Books, 1987).

[12]Thurow and Tyson, *Adjusting the US Trade Balance*.

[13]Michael Borrus, *Chips of State: Microelectronics and American Autonomy*, book manuscript (forthcoming).

[14]Martin Carnoy and Manuel Castells, "After the Crisis?", *World Policy Journal*, Spring 1984.

[15]Cohen and Zysman, *Manufacturing Matters*.

[16]Schechter, *Imbalances in the Global Economy*, p. 24.

[17]Charles Stone and Isabel Sawhill, *Labor Market Implications in the Growing Internationalism of the U.S. Economy*, discussion paper (Washington DC, Urban Institute, 1986).

[18]John Lederer, *High Technology Manufacturing Employment: A Report on Recent Decline in California*, seminar paper for CP 284 (Berkeley, University of California, Department of City and Regional Planning, May 1987).

[19]Agnew, *The United States in the World Economy*, p. 143.

[20]Lester C. Thurow, *The Zero-Sum Society* (New York, Basic Books, 1980).

[21]Cited by Marshall and Glickman, *Choices for American Industry*, box number 7.

[22]*Business Week*, as cited by Marshall and Glickman, *Choices for American Industry*, box number 9.

[23]Candee Harris, "The Magnitude of Job Loss from Plant Closings and the Generation of Replacement Jobs: Some Recent Evidence", *The Annals*, September 1984, pp. 15–27.

[24]Agnew, *The United States in the World Economy*, p. 164.

[25]B. Bluestone and B. Harrison, *The Deindustrialization of America* (New York, Basic Books, 1982).

[26]Peter Hall, *Regions in the Transition to the Information Economy*, paper delivered at the Rutgers University Conference on America's New Economic Geography, Washington DC, 29–30 April 1987.

[27]Leslie Wayne, "U.S. Textile Industry's Turnaround," *New York Times*, 15 February 1988, p. 21.

[28]"America's Deflation Belt," *Business Week*, 9 June 1986, pp. 52–60.

[29]Raul A. Hinojosa and Rebecca Morales, *International Restructuring and Labor Market Interdependence: The Automobile Industry in Mexico and the United States*, paper presented at the Conference on Labor Market Interdependence, El Colegio de Mexico, Mexico DF, 25–7 September 1986.

[30]United Nations Industrial Development Organization (UNIDO), *International Industrial Restructuring and the International Division of Labour in the Automotive Industry* (Vienna, UNIDO, Division for Industrial Studies, 1984).

[31]Alan Altshuler, Martin Anderson, Daniel Jones, Daniel Roos, and James Womak, *The Future of the Automobile: The Report of MIT's International Automobile Program* (Cambridge, Mass., MIT, 1984).

[32]Dennis P. Quinn, *Dynamic Markets and Mutating Firms: The Changing Organization of Production in Automotive Firms*, BRIE working paper (Berkeley, July 1987).

[33]UNIDO, *International Restructuring*.

[34]Ibid., p. 4.

[35]Hinojosa and Morales, *International Restructuring and Labor Market Interdependence*, p. 35.

[36]UNIDO, *International Restructuring*, p. 91.

[37]UNIDO, *International Restructuring*, pp. 92–3.

[38]Hinojosa and Morales, *International Restructuring and Labor Market Interdependence*.

[39]K. Trachte and R. Ross, "The Crisis of Detroit and the Emergence of Global Capitalism," *International Journal of Urban and Regional Research*, 9 (1985), pp. 216–17.

[40]Harley Shaiken, *Work Transformed: Automation and Labor in the Computer Age* (New York, Holt, Rinehart and Winston, 1984).

[41]UNIDO, *International Restructuring*, p. 101.

[42]Trachte and Ross, "The Crisis of Detroit."

[43]Richard C. Hill, *The Auto Industry in Global Transition*, paper presented at the meeting of the American Sociological Association, Detroit, Michigan, 1983.

[44]Agnew, *The United States in the World Economy*, p. 190.

[45]Philip Shapira, *The Crumbling of Smokestack California: A Case Study in Industrial Restructuring and the Reorganization of Work*, IURD working paper (Berkeley, November 1984).

[46]Altshuler et al., *The Future of the Automobile*.

[47]James P. Womack, "Prospects for the U.S. Mexican Relationship in the Motor Vehicle Sector," in Cathryn L. Thorup (ed.), *The U.S. and Mexico: Face to Face with New Technology* (Washington DC, Overseas Development Council, 1987).

[48]"GM: What Went Wrong," *Business Week*, 16 March 1987.

[49]Richard C. Hill, *A Global Marriage of Convenience: General Motors and Toyota at Fremont*, paper presented at the meeting of the society for the Study Social Problems, Detroit, 1983.

[50]Erica Schoenberger, *Technological and Organizational Change in Automobile Production: Spatial Implications*, paper presented at the National Science Foundation/Hungarian Academy of Sciences Conference on Regional Development, Budapest, 1–7 September 1985.

[51]Richard C. Hill, "Global Factory and Company Town: The Changing Division of Labour in the International Automobile Industry," in Jeff Henderson and Manuel Castells (eds), *Global Restructuring and Territorial Development* (London, Sage, 1987), pp. 18–37.

[52]G. Maxcy, *The Multinational Automobile Industry* (New York, St Martin's, 1981).

[53]Servet Mutlu, *Inter-regional and International Mobility of Industrial Capital: The Case of American Automobile and Electronics Companies*, unpublished PhD dissertation (Berkeley, University of California, 1979).

[54]*Business Week*, 16 March 1987.

[55]UNIDO, *International Restructuring*, p. 23.

[56]Hinojosa and Morales, *International Restructuring and Labor Market Interdependence*, p. 35.

[57]Ibid., p. 36.

[58]Harley Shaiken and Stephen Herzenberg, *Automation and Global Production: Automobile Engine Production in Mexico, the United States, and Canada* (San Diego, University of California, Center for US–Mexican Studies, 1987).

[59]UNIDO, *International Restructuring*.

[60]Shaiken and Herzenberg, *Automation and Global Production*.

[61]Hill, "Global Factory and Company Town," p. 35.

[62]Michael A. Shea, "U.S. Affiliates of Foreign Companies: Operations in 1984," *Survey of Current Business*, 66, 10 (1986), pp. 31–46; Jeffrey Arpan, Edward Flowers, and David Ricks, "Foreign Direct Investment in the United States: The State of Knowledge in Research," *Journal of International Business Studies*, Spring/Summer 1981, pp. 137–54.

[63]Erica Schoenberger, "Foreign Manufacturing Investment in the United States: Competitive Strategies and International Location," *Economic Geography*, 61, 3 (July 1985), pp. 241–59.

[64]Schoenberger, *Foreign Manufacturing Investment in the United States*, p. 241.

[65]Ibid., p. 245.

[66]Erica Schoenberger, "Foreign Manufacturing Investment in the United States: Its Causes and Regional Consequences," PhD dissertation (Berkeley, University of California, Department of City and Regional Planning, 1984).

[67]Norman J. Glickman and Douglas P. Woodward, *Regional Patterns of Manufacturing Foreign Direct Investment in the United States*, special project report prepared for the US Department of Commerce (Austin, University of Texas, Lyndon B. Johnson School of Public Affairs, 1987).

[68]Ibid., p. 37.

[69]Saskia Sassen, *The Global City* (Princeton, NJ, Princeton University Press, forthcoming).

[70]John Friedmann and Goetz Wolff, *World City Formation*, (Los Angeles, UCLA, Comparative Urbanization Studies, 1982).

[71]Regional Plan Association of New York, *New York in the Global Economy*.

[72]Sassen, *The Global City*.

[73]Nigel Thrift, "The Fixers: the Urban Geography of International Commercial Capital," in Jeff Henderson and Manuel Castells (eds), *Global Restructuring and Territorial Development* (London, Sage, 1987), pp. 203–33.

[74]Thierry Noyelle, *The Globalization of New York City*, paper prepared for the Social Science Research Council's Committee on New York City, 1988.

[75]Sassen, *The Global City*.

[76]Regional Plan Association of New York, *New York in the Global Economy*.

[77]Ibid.

[78]Ibid., p. 26.

[79]Sassen, *The Global City*, MS p. 154.

[80]Richard Harris, *Home and Work in New York Since 1950*, paper prepared for Social Science Research Council's Committee on New York City, 1988.

[81]John Mollenkopf, "New York: The Great Anomaly," in R. Browning, D. Marshall and D. Tabb (eds), *Race and Politics in American Cities* (New York, Longman, forthcoming).

[82]Robert Goodman, *The Last Entrepreneurs* (New York, Basic Books, 1979).

[83]Michael P. Smith, "Global Capital Restructuring and Local Political Crises in U.S. Cities," in Henderson and Castells, *Global Restructuring*, pp. 234–50.

Index